X/1999 ™

Vol. 15
WALTZ
Shōjo Edition

Story and Art by
CLAMP

X/1999
THE STORY THUS FAR

The End of the World has been prophesied
…and time is running out. Kamui Shiro is a
young man who was born with a special
power—the power to decide the fate of the
Earth itself.

Kamui had grown up in Tokyo, but had
fled with his mother after the suspicious death
of a family friend. Six years later, his mother
too, dies under suspicious circumstances,
engulfed in flames. Her last words to him were
that he should return to Tokyo…that his destiny
awaited him there.

Kamui obeys his mother's words, but
almost immediately upon his arrival, he's chal-
lenged to a psychic duel—a first warning that
others know of his power, and of his return.

Kamui is also reunited with his childhood
friends Fuma and Kotori Monou. Although
Kamui attempts to push his friends away in the
hope of protecting them, they too are soon
drawn into the web of destiny that surrounds
him.

Meanwhile, the two sides to the great con-
flict to come are being drawn. On one side is
the dreamseer Hinoto, a blind princess who
lives beneath Japan's seat of government, the
Diet Building. On the other side is Kanoe,
Hinoto's dark sister with similar powers, but a
different vision of Earth's ultimate future.
Around these two women gather the Dragons of
Heaven and the Dragons of Earth, the forces
that will fight to decide the fate of the planet.
The only variable in the equation is Kamui,
whose fate it will be to choose which side he
will join.

And Kamui finally does make a choice. He
chooses to defend the Earth as it stands now.
But by making this choice, he pays a terrible
price. For fate has chosen his oldest friend to be
his "twin star"—the other "Kamui" who will
fight against him. And in this first battle, the
gentle Kotori is the first casualty.

Now Kamui must face the consequences of
his decision…and try to come to terms with not
only his ultimate fate, but also that of the
Earth…

The Author

Robert J. Baker was born September 9, 1920 in Goshen, Indiana. He is a retired schoolteacher and taught in the public schools of Indiana from 1947 to 1987.

Baker's first published work was in the *Elkhart High School Anthology* while he was a student. He has had published in the religious press numerous poems, articles, and fiction stories. His column for Sunday school teachers titled "If I Were Teaching the Lesson," has appeared in *Builder* since 1965.

A column for the mature reader, "County Road 13," has appeared in *Christian Living* since 1980. He is the author of four published books; *Second Chance, God Healed Me, Insect Parables,* and *I'm Listening Lord, Keep Talking.* He has held numerous seminars for Sunday school teachers throughout the Mennonite church.

He graduated from Goshen College (Indiana) and earned a master of science degree from Indiana University. He also holds a master of arts for teachers from Michigan State University. He received advanced training in both science and teaching pedagogy from the universities of Purdue, Indiana State, Emory, and Ball State. He also studied at Virginia Military Institute and Manchester College. He received local honors for teaching from the Elkhart (Indiana) Community Schools.

Baker was married to Anna Mae Moyer in 1947. They have five children and nine grandchildren. He is an active member of the Belmont Mennonite Church, where he accepted Christ as a young boy during revival meetings.

Since retirement in 1987, Baker spends his time reading, writing, speaking, and doing volunteer work. Each morning you will usually find him striding along the county highways near his home, where he walks from three to five miles for exercise. During that time he picks up aluminum cans which he sells, giving the money to Mennonite Central Committee for relief operations.

Baker is also an amateur beekeeper. He has a small apiary of six hives at the back of the one acre Baker lot in Dunlap, Indiana, a small village near Elkhart.

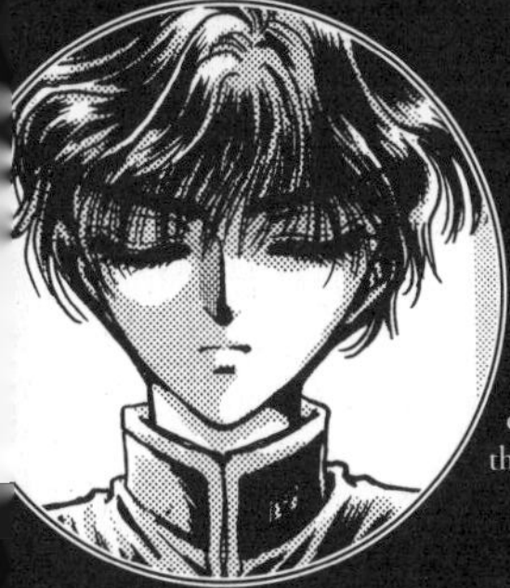

Kamui Shiro
A young man with psychic powers whose choice of destiny will decide the fate of the world.

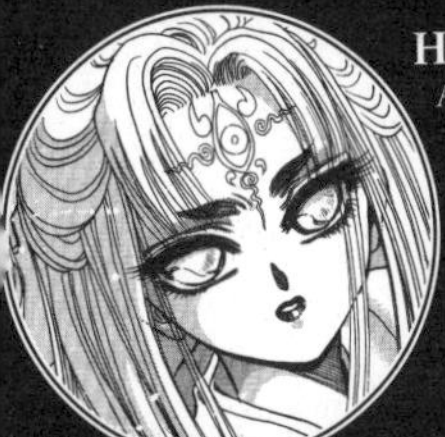

Hinoto
A powerful prophetess who communicates with the power of her mind alone. She lives in a secret shrine located beneath Tokyo's Diet Building.

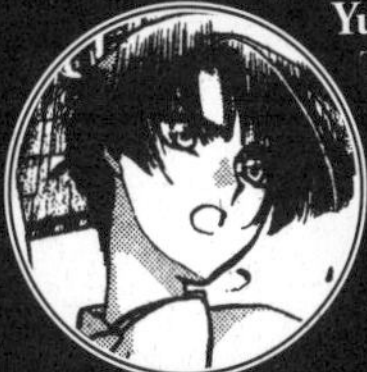

Yuziriha Nekoi
The youngest of the Dragons, she is always accompanied by a spirit dog named Inuki.

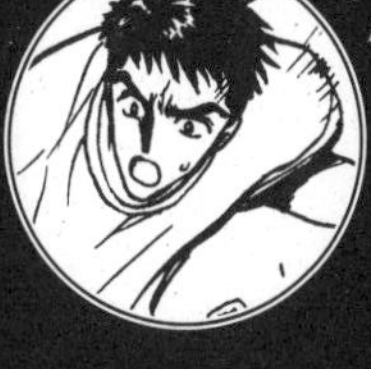

Sorata Arisugawa
A brash, but good-natured priest of the Mt. Koya shrine.

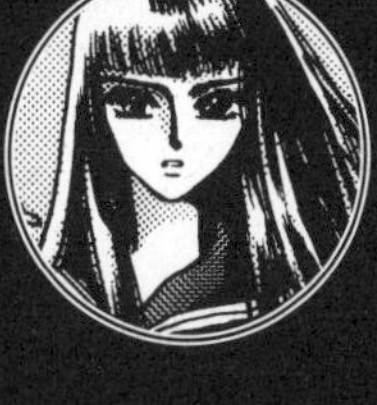

Arashi Kishu
Priestess of the Ise Shrine, Arashi can materialize a sword from the palm of her hand.

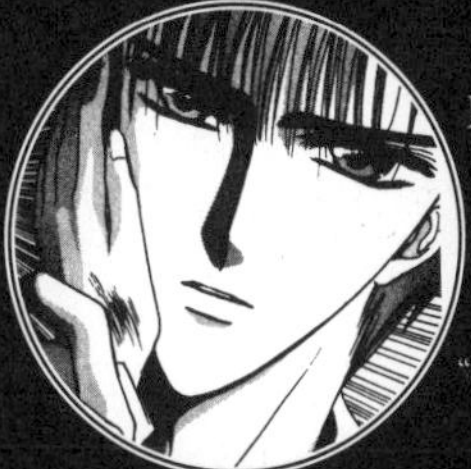

Fuma Monou
Kamui's childhood friend. When Kamui made his choice, Fuma was chosen by fate to become his "Twin Star"—the other "Kamui."

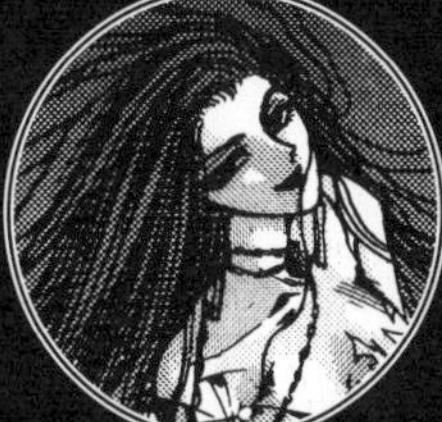

Kanoe
Hinoto's sister shares her ability to see the future… but Kanoe has predicted a different final result.

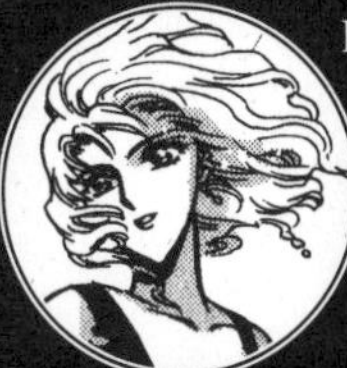

Karen Kasumi
A young woman who works in a Japanese bathhouse (massage parlor). She can control fire.

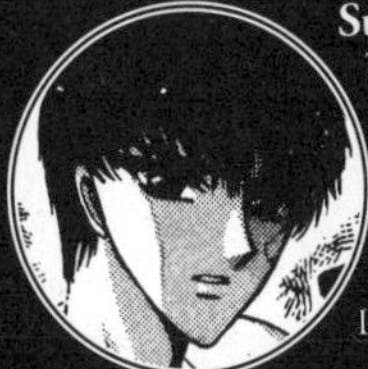

Subaru Sumeragi
The 13th family head of a long line of spiritualists, he is a powerful medium and exorcist. He lost vision in one eye after his encounter with Kamui, Dragon of Earth.

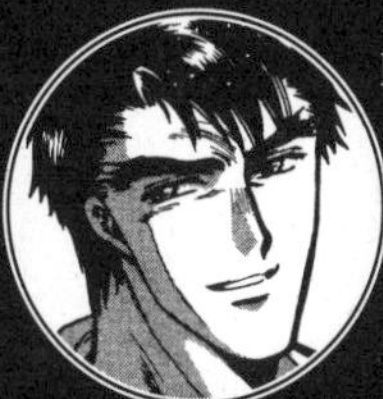

Kusanagi Shiyu
A member of Japan's Self Defense Force, Kusanagi can control earth.

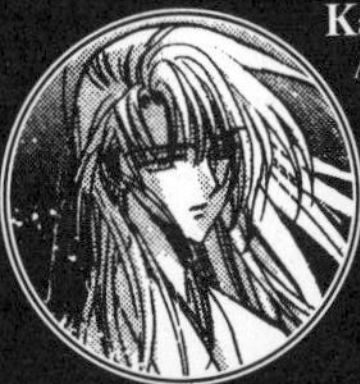

Kakyo Kuzuki
A dreamseer like Hinoto, Kakyo is a hospital-bound invalid kept alive by machines.

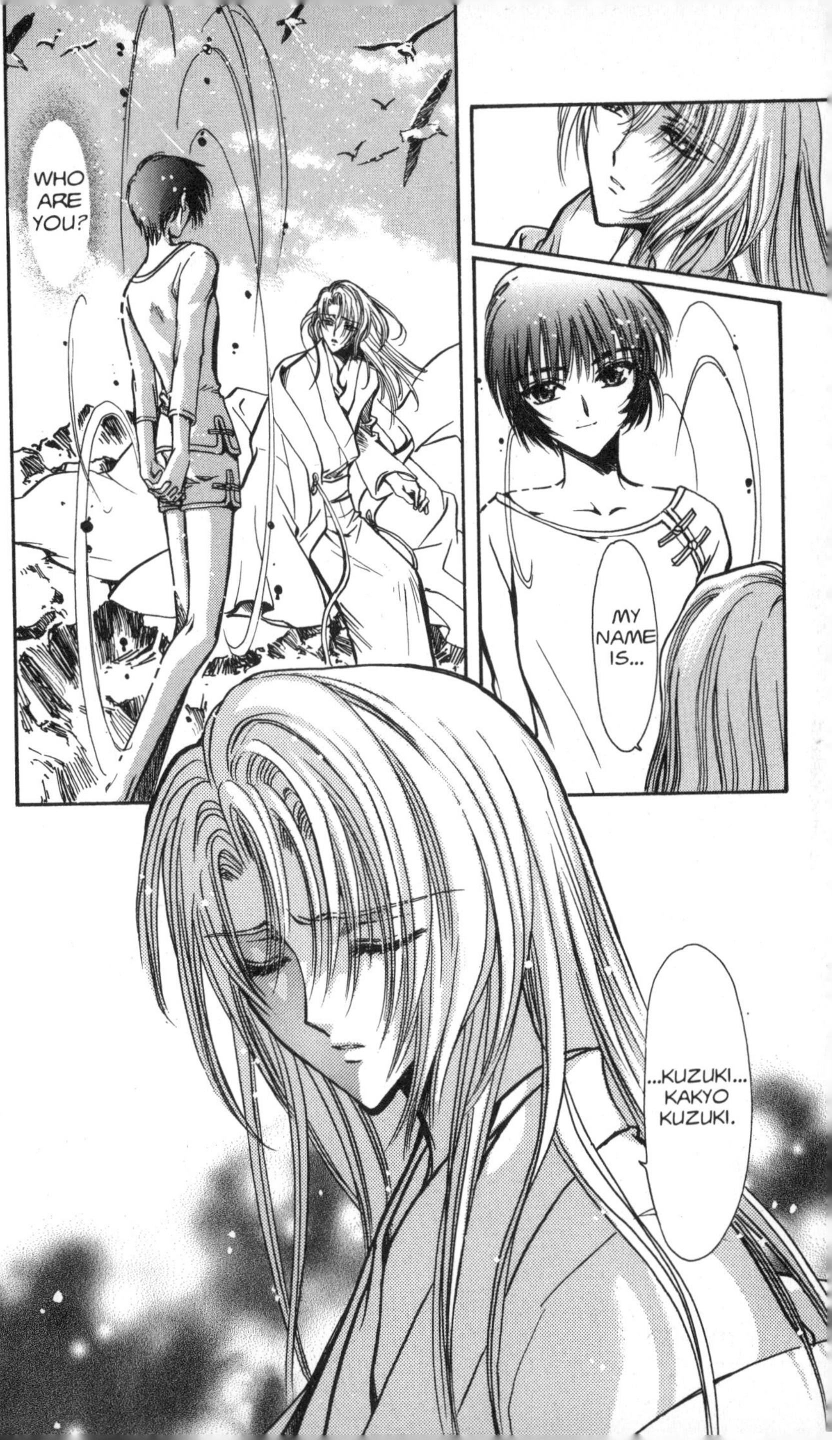
WHO ARE YOU?
MY NAME IS...
...KUZUKI... KAKYO KUZUKI.

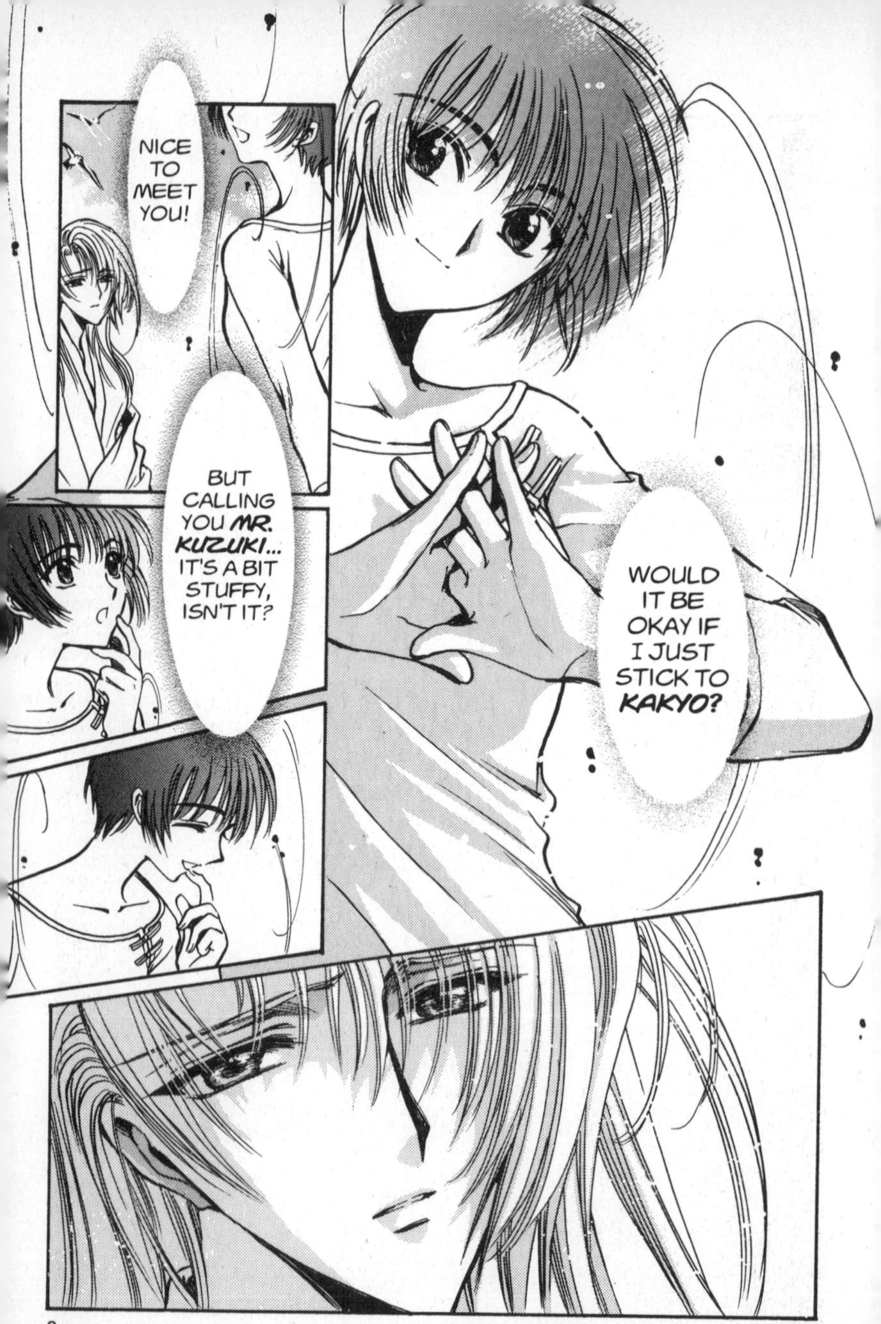
NICE TO MEET YOU!
BUT CALLING YOU MR. KUZUKI... IT'S A BIT STUFFY, ISN'T IT?
WOULD IT BE OKAY IF I JUST STICK TO KAKYO?

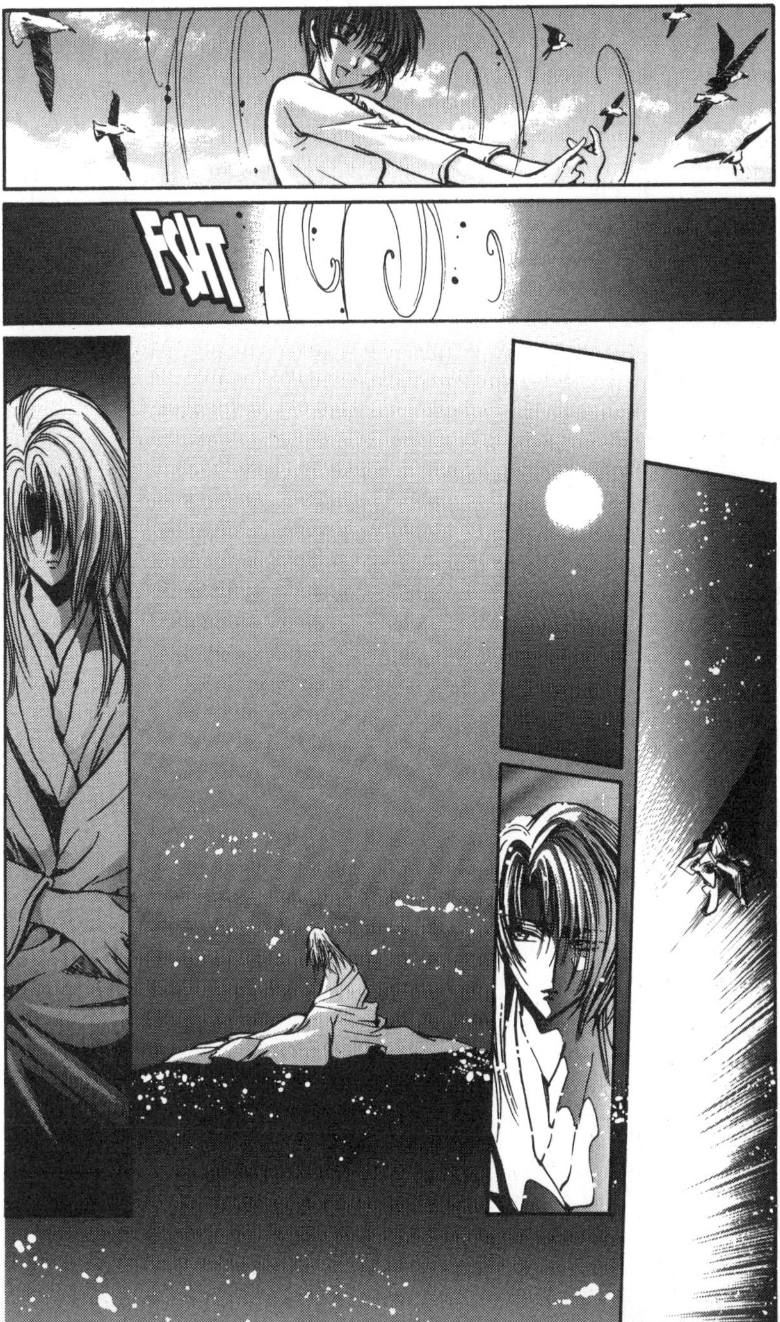
FSHT

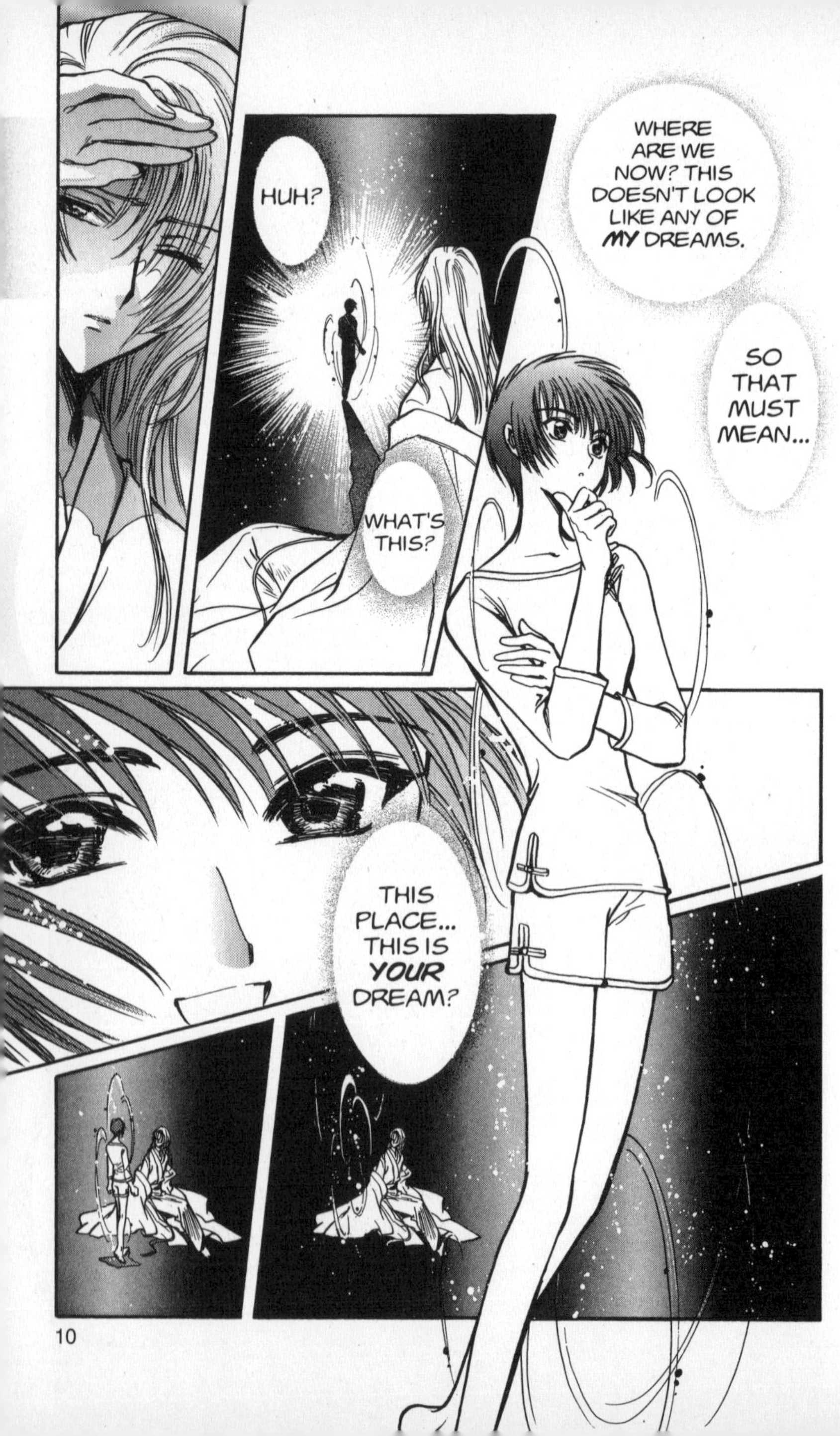
WHERE ARE WE NOW? THIS DOESN'T LOOK LIKE ANY OF *MY* DREAMS.
SO THAT MUST MEAN...
HUH?
WHAT'S THIS?
THIS PLACE... THIS IS ***YOUR*** DREAM?

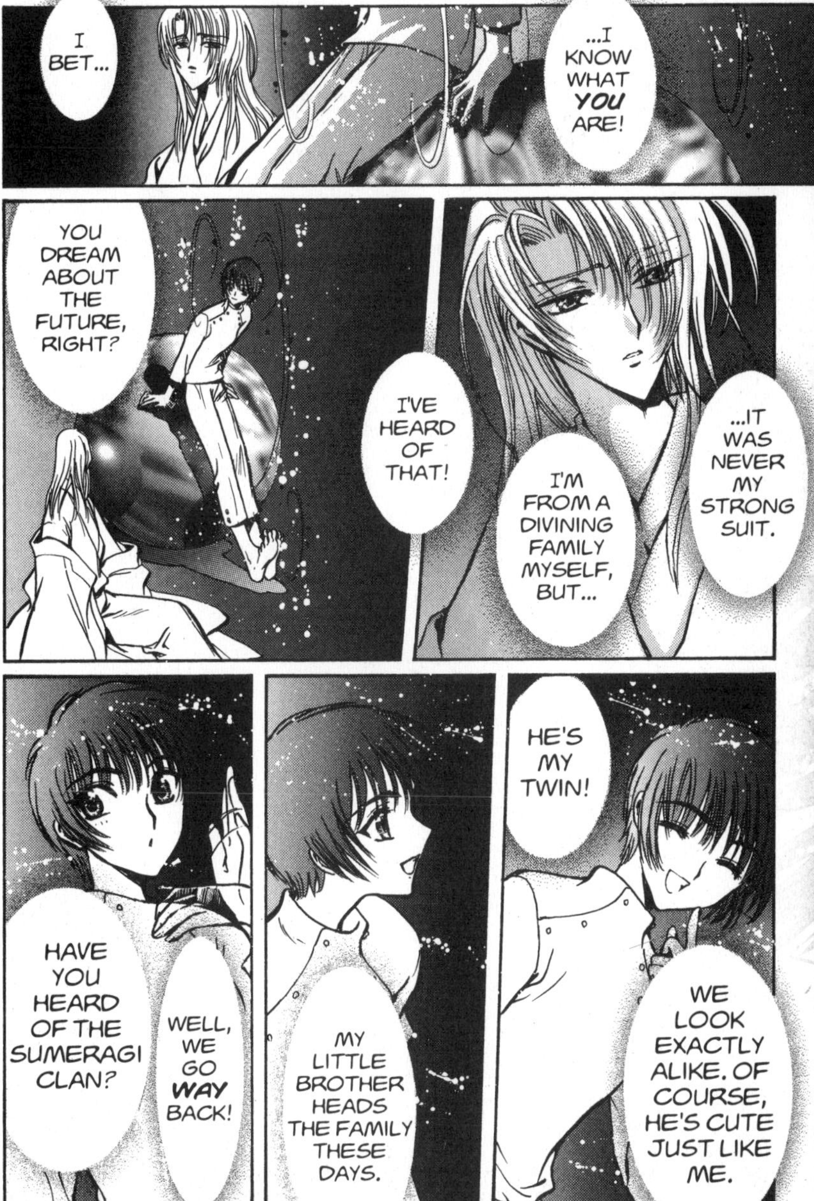
I BET...
...I KNOW WHAT YOU ARE!
YOU DREAM ABOUT THE FUTURE, RIGHT?
I'VE HEARD OF THAT!
I'M FROM A DIVINING FAMILY MYSELF, BUT...
...IT WAS NEVER MY STRONG SUIT.
HAVE YOU HEARD OF THE SUMERAGI CLAN?
WELL, WE GO WAY BACK!
MY LITTLE BROTHER HEADS THE FAMILY THESE DAYS.
HE'S MY TWIN!
WE LOOK EXACTLY ALIKE. OF COURSE, HE'S CUTE JUST LIKE ME.

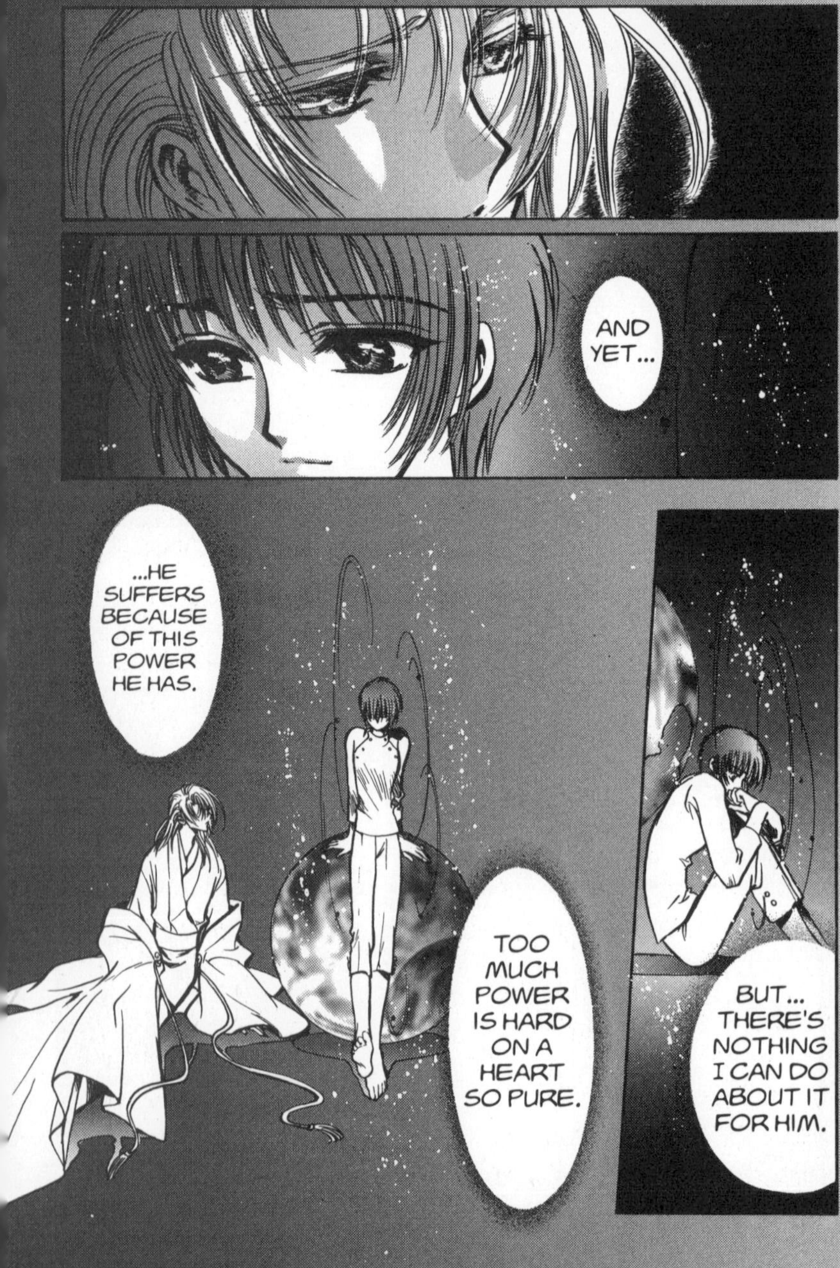
AND YET...
...HE SUFFERS BECAUSE OF THIS POWER HE HAS.
TOO MUCH POWER IS HARD ON A HEART SO PURE.
BUT... THERE'S NOTHING I CAN DO ABOUT IT FOR HIM.

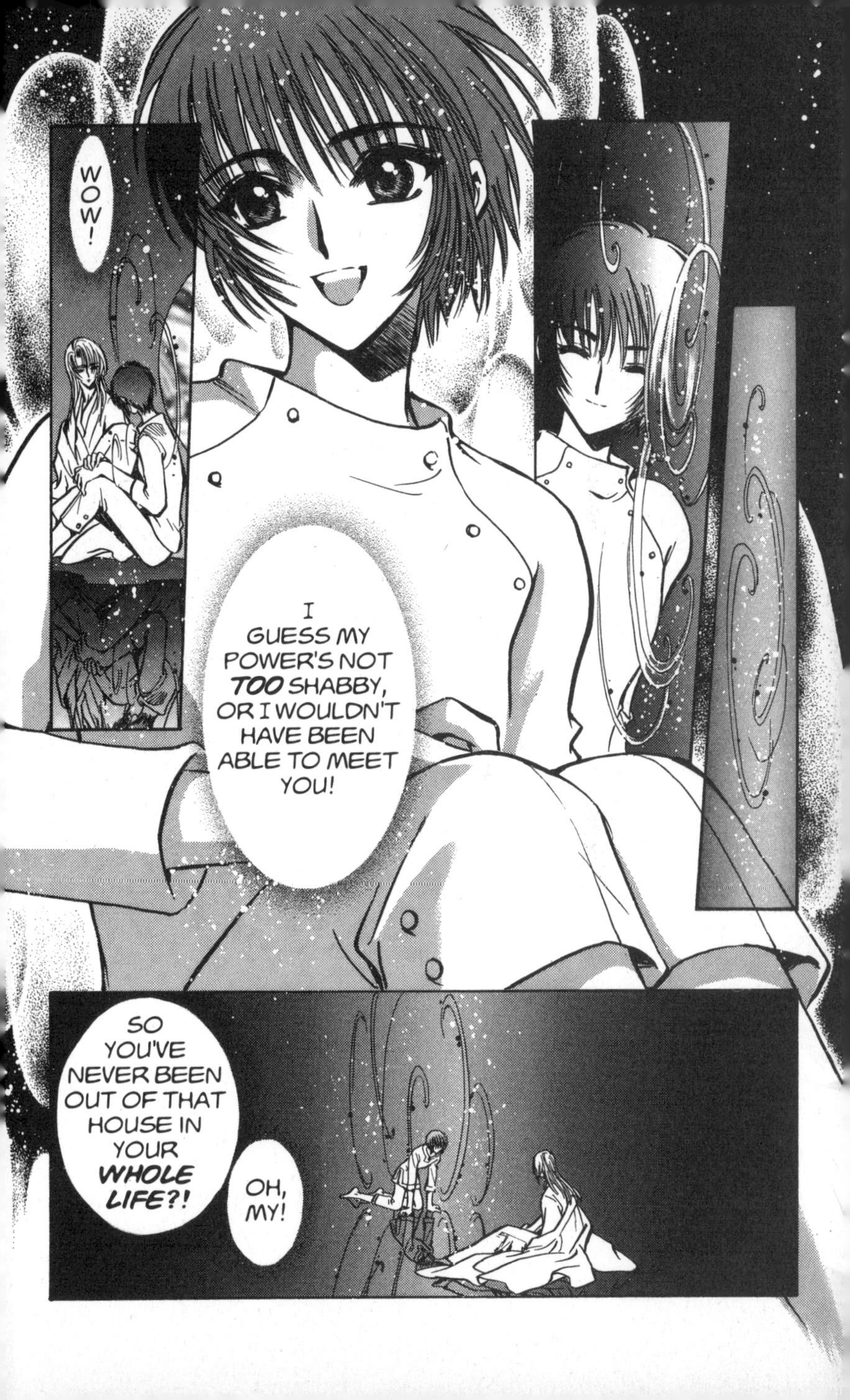
I GUESS MY POWER'S NOT **TOO** SHABBY, OR I WOULDN'T HAVE BEEN ABLE TO MEET YOU!
WOW!
SO YOU'VE NEVER BEEN OUT OF THAT HOUSE IN YOUR **WHOLE LIFE?!**
OH, MY!

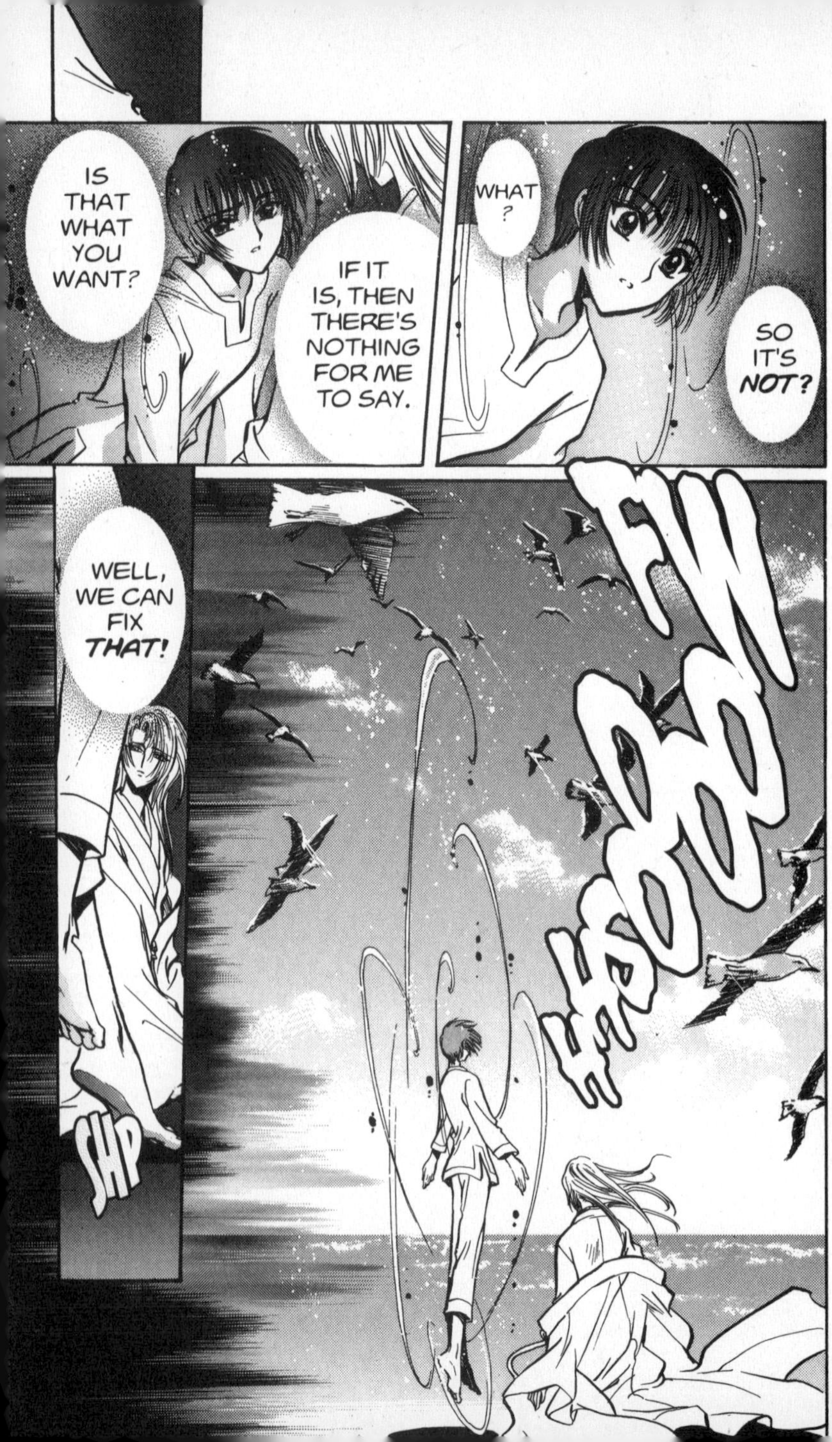
WHAT ?
SO IT'S *NOT?*
IS THAT WHAT YOU WANT?
IF IT IS, THEN THERE'S NOTHING FOR ME TO SAY.
WOOOSH
WELL, WE CAN FIX *THAT!*
SHP

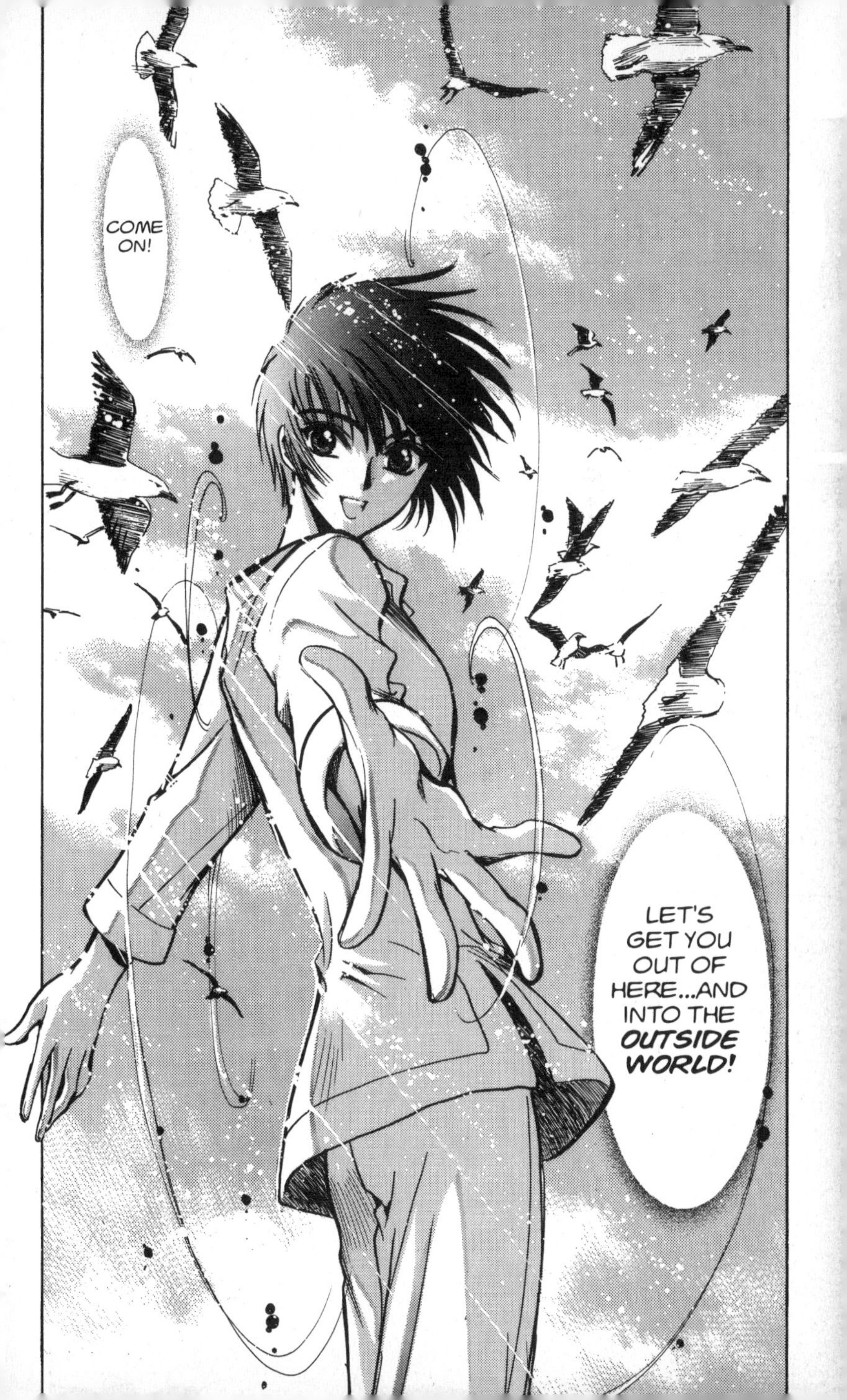

COME ON!
LET'S GET YOU OUT OF HERE...AND INTO THE ***OUTSIDE WORLD!***

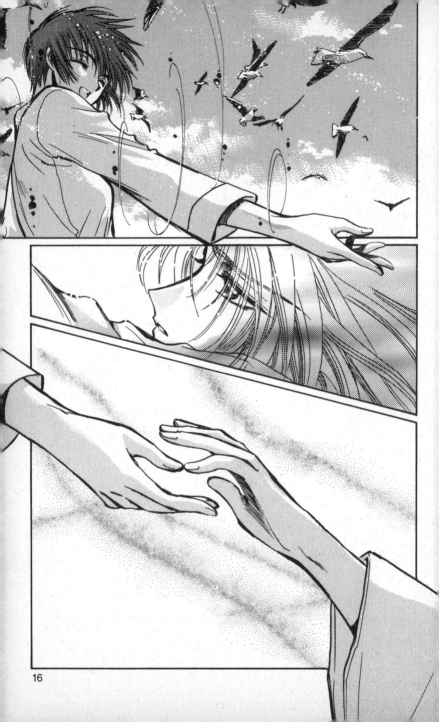

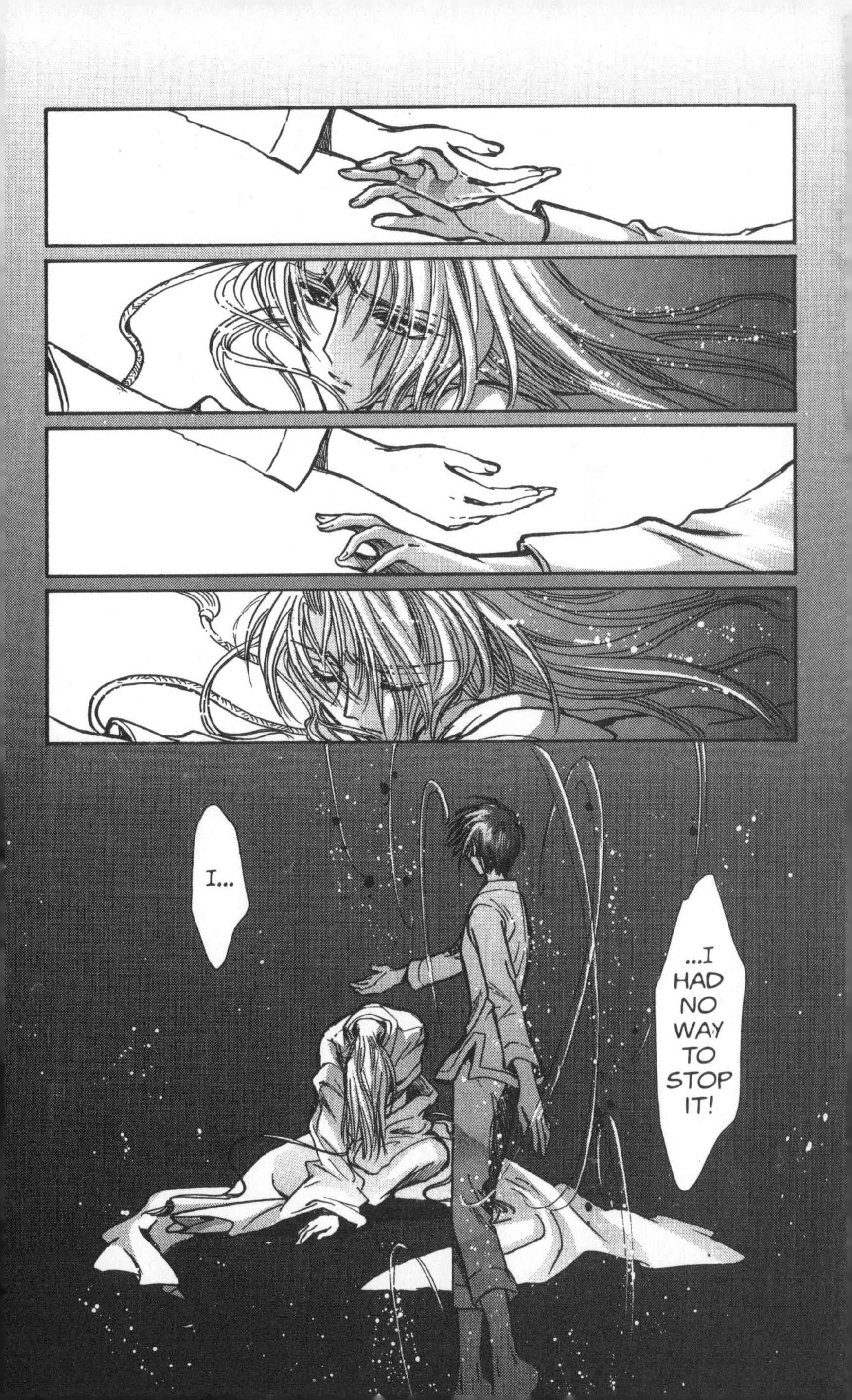
I...
...I HAD NO WAY TO STOP IT!

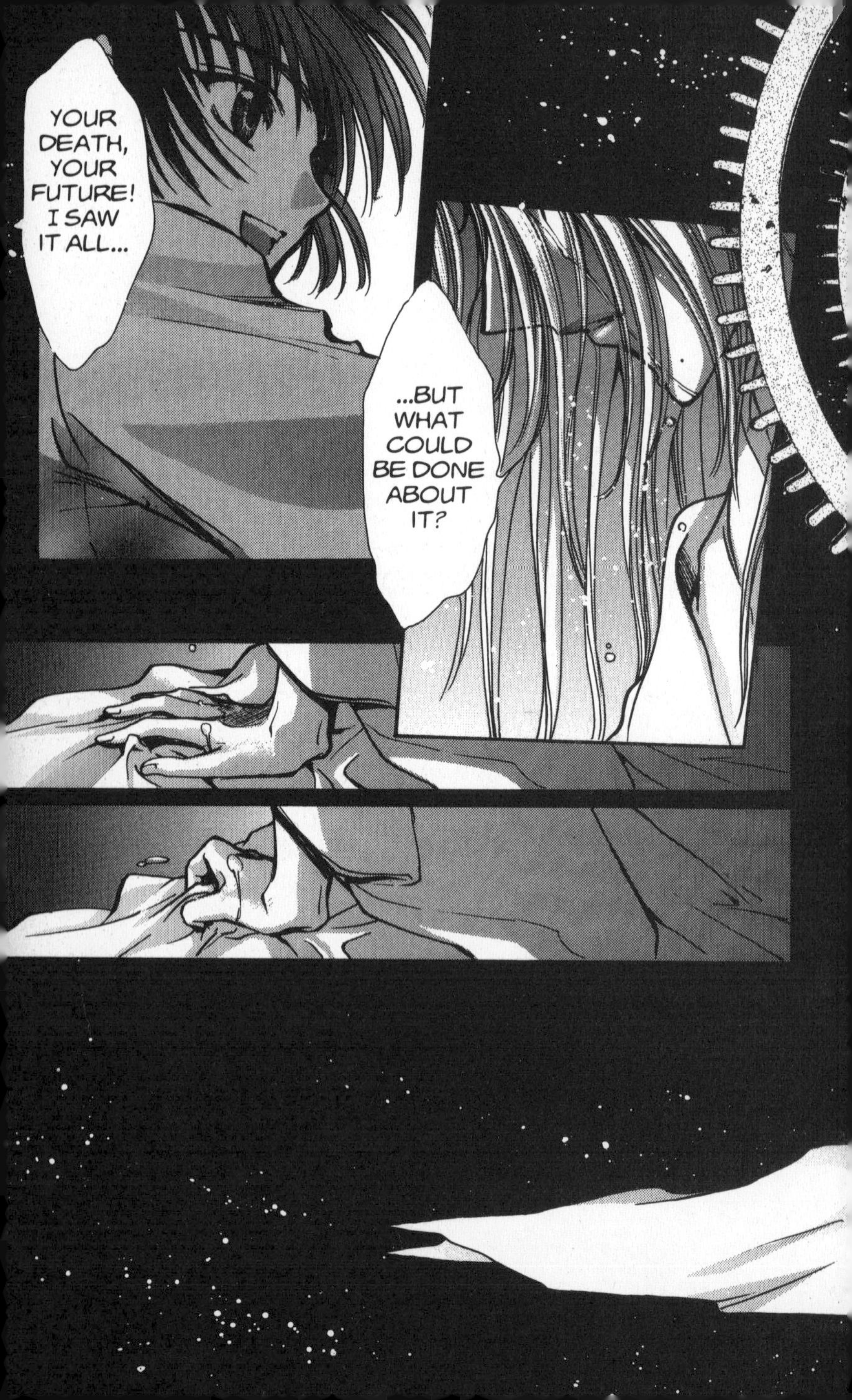
YOUR DEATH, YOUR FUTURE! I SAW IT ALL...
...BUT WHAT COULD BE DONE ABOUT IT?

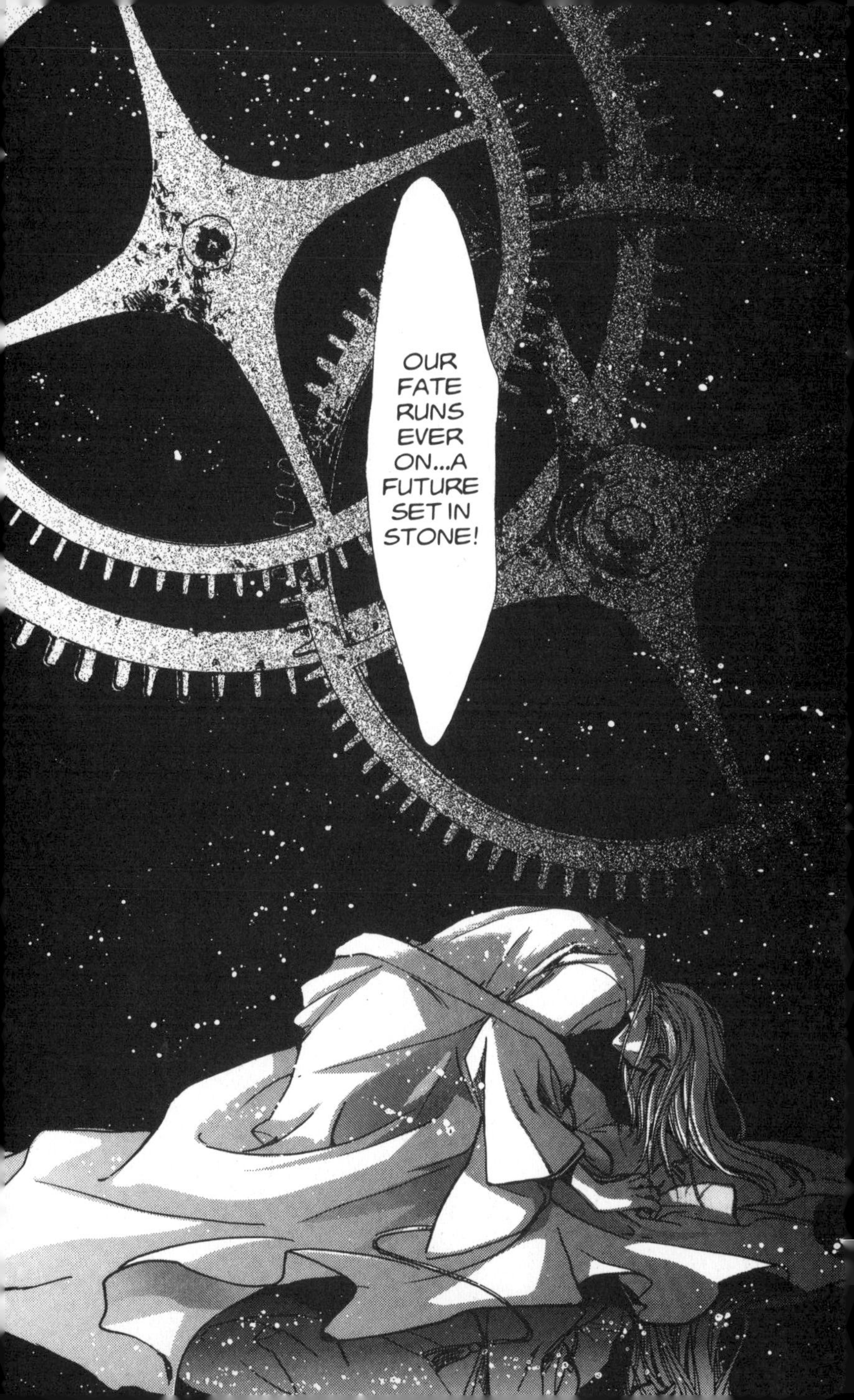
OUR FATE RUNS EVER ON...A FUTURE SET IN STONE!

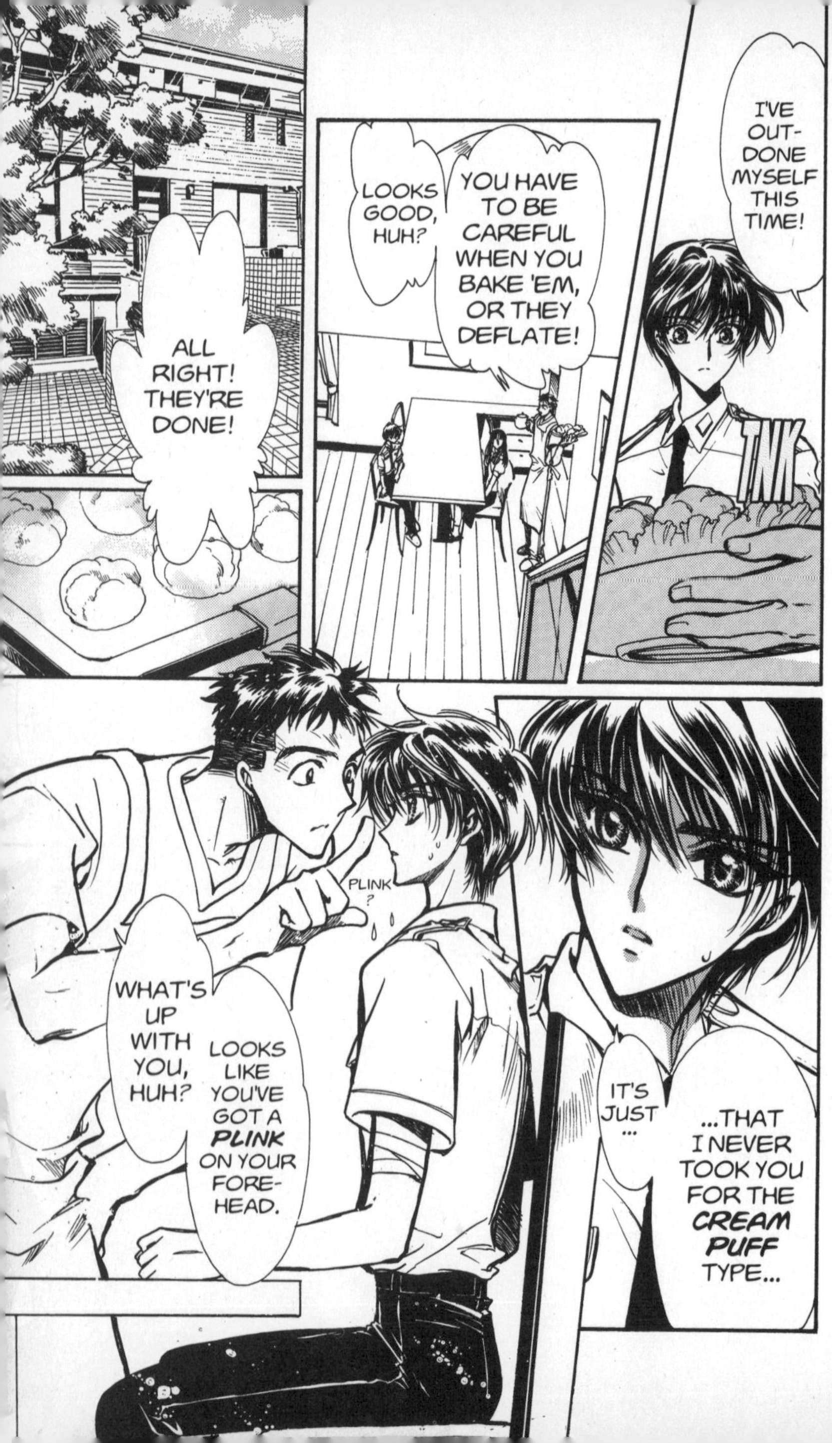
I'VE OUT-DONE MYSELF THIS TIME!
TNK
YOU HAVE TO BE CAREFUL WHEN YOU BAKE 'EM, OR THEY DEFLATE!
LOOKS GOOD, HUH?
ALL RIGHT! THEY'RE DONE!
IT'S JUST ...
...THAT I NEVER TOOK YOU FOR THE CREAM PUFF TYPE...
PLINK ?
LOOKS LIKE YOU'VE GOT A PLINK ON YOUR FORE-HEAD.
WHAT'S UP WITH YOU, HUH?

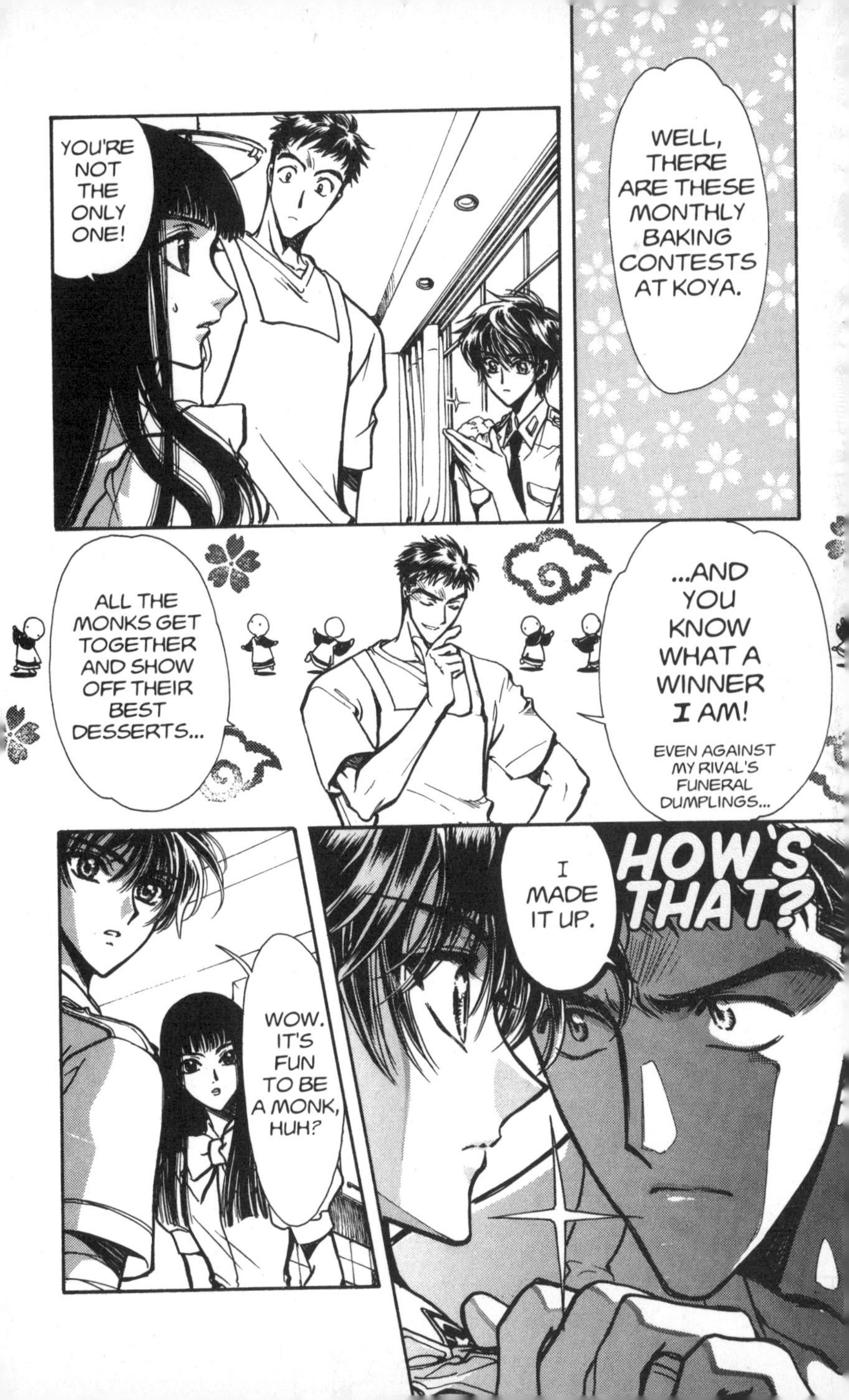
WELL, THERE ARE THESE MONTHLY BAKING CONTESTS AT KOYA.
YOU'RE NOT THE ONLY ONE!
...AND YOU KNOW WHAT A WINNER I AM!
EVEN AGAINST MY RIVAL'S FUNERAL DUMPLINGS...
ALL THE MONKS GET TOGETHER AND SHOW OFF THEIR BEST DESSERTS...
HOW'S THAT?
I MADE IT UP.
WOW. IT'S FUN TO BE A MONK, HUH?

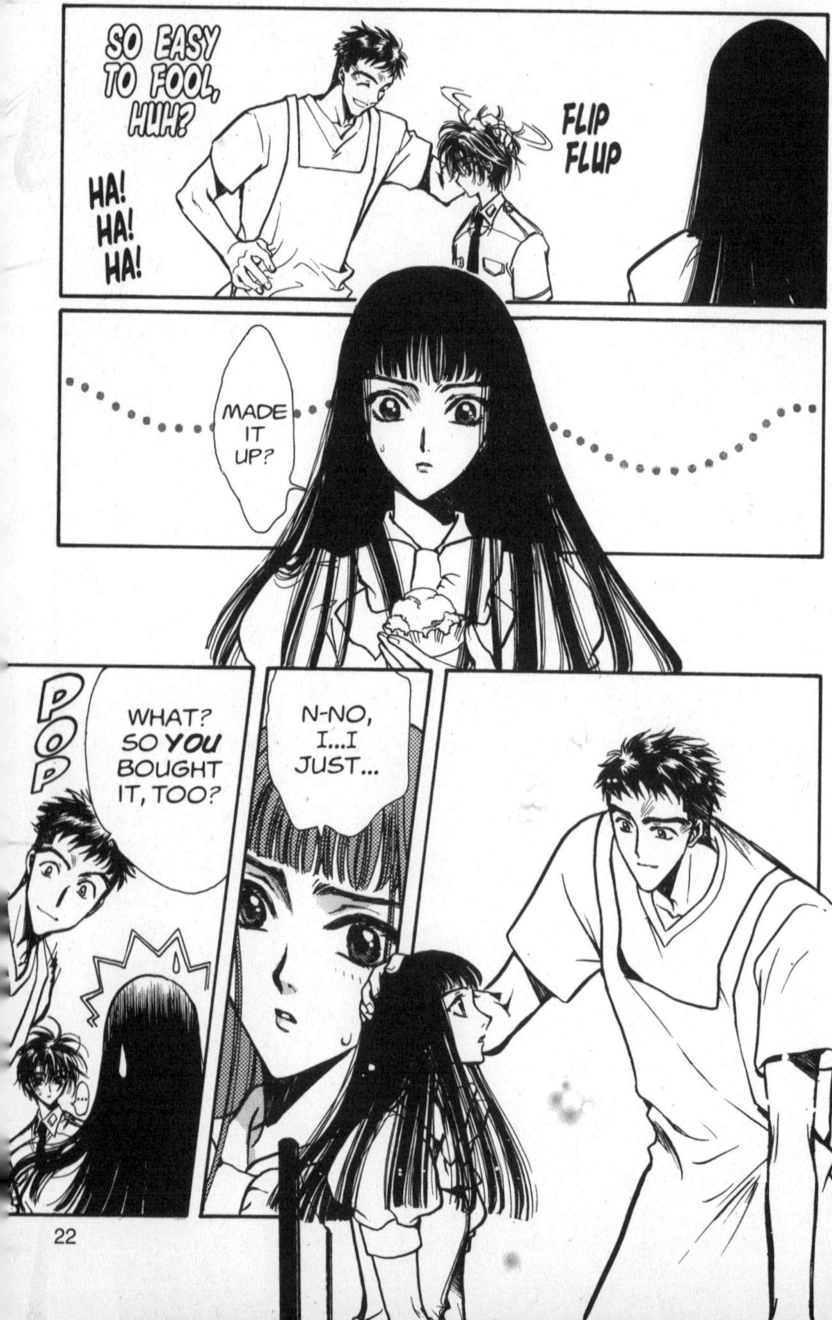
FLIP FLUP
SO EASY TO FOOL, HUH?
HA! HA! HA!
MADE IT UP?
N-NO, I...I JUST...
POP
WHAT? SO YOU BOUGHT IT, TOO?
...

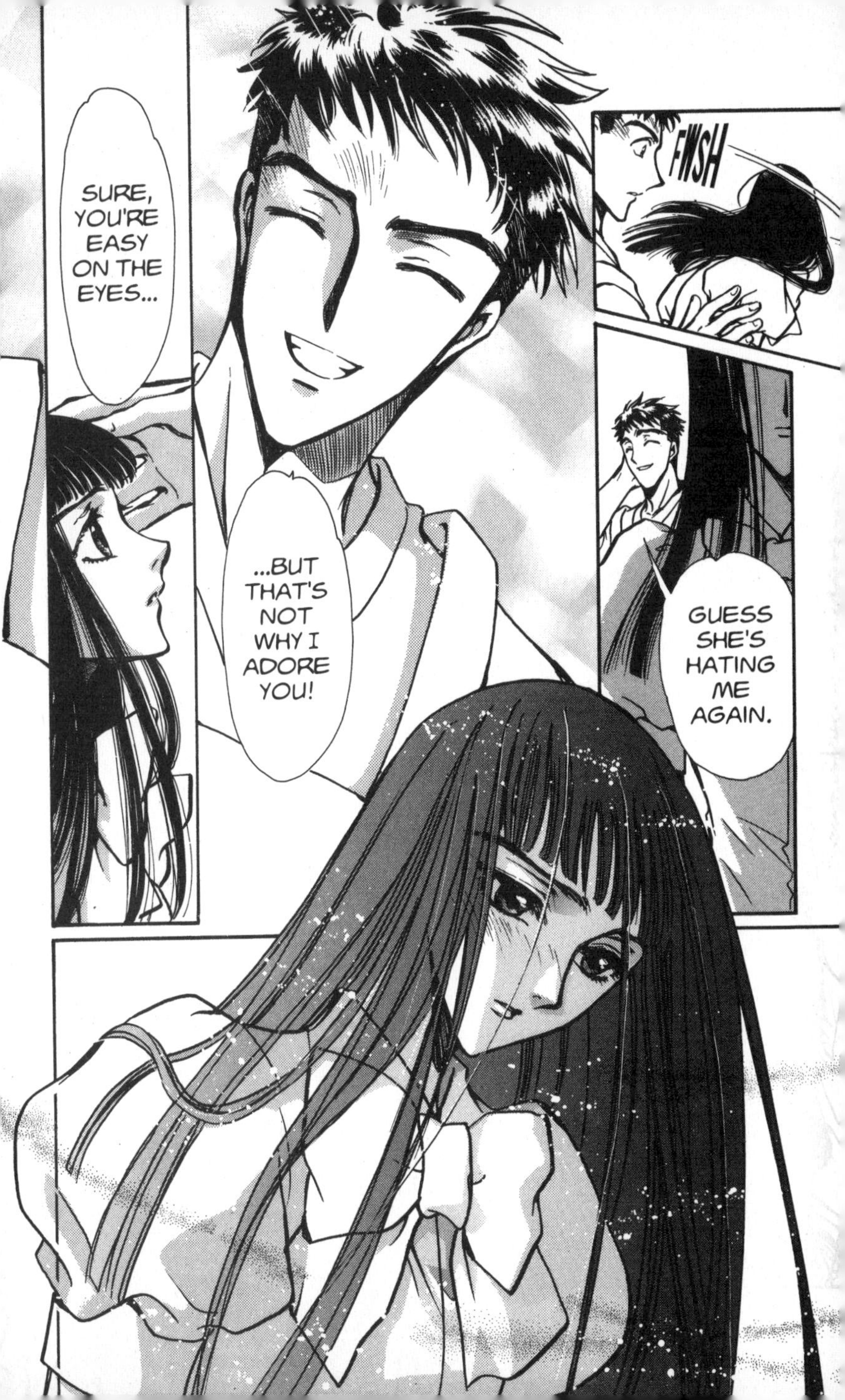
FWSH
GUESS SHE'S HATING ME AGAIN.
SURE, YOU'RE EASY ON THE EYES...
...BUT THAT'S NOT WHY I ADORE YOU!

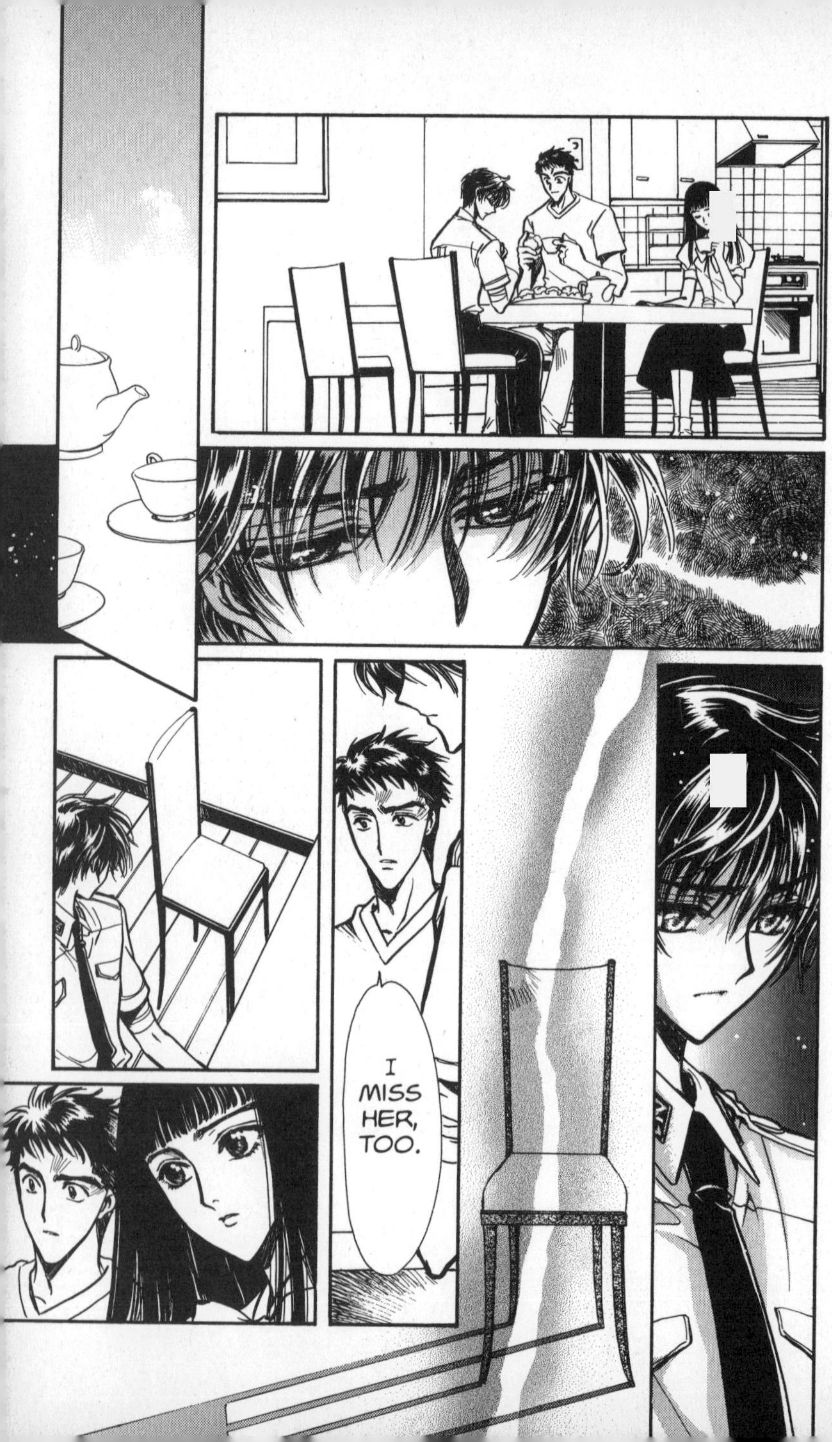
I MISS HER, TOO.

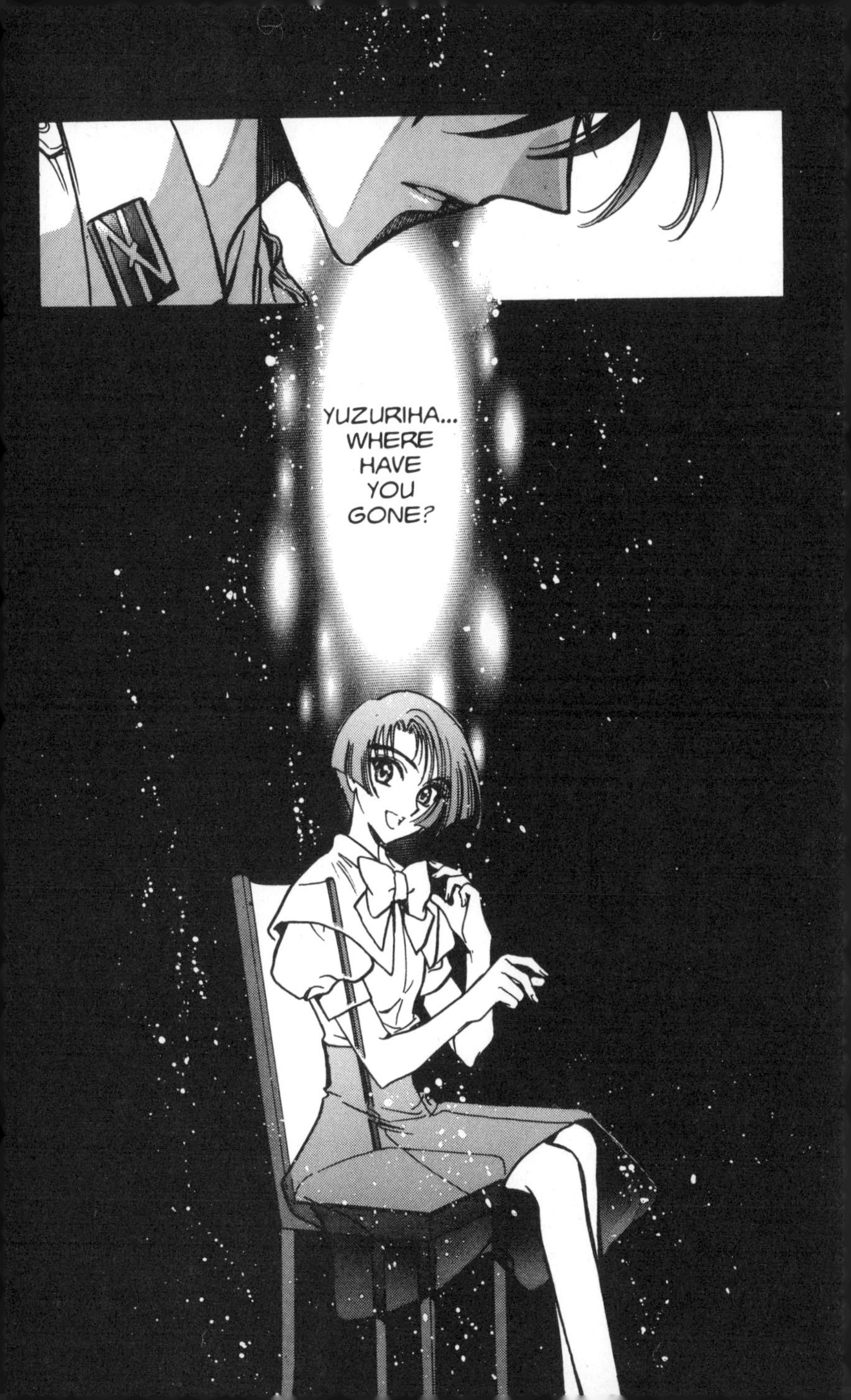
YUZURIHA... WHERE HAVE YOU GONE?

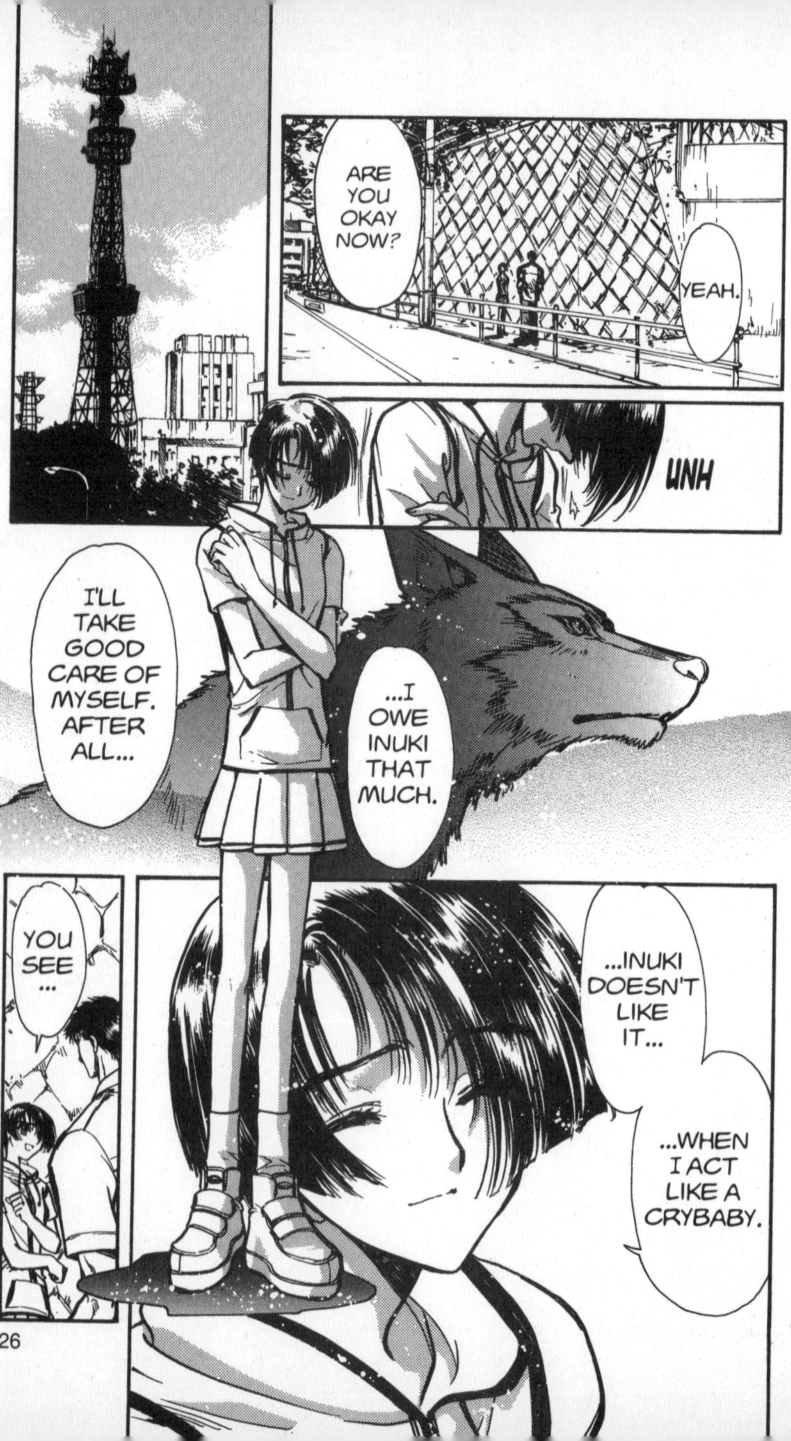
ARE YOU OKAY NOW?
YEAH.
UNH
I'LL TAKE GOOD CARE OF MYSELF. AFTER ALL...
...I OWE INUKI THAT MUCH.
YOU SEE...
...INUKI DOESN'T LIKE IT...
...WHEN I ACT LIKE A CRYBABY.

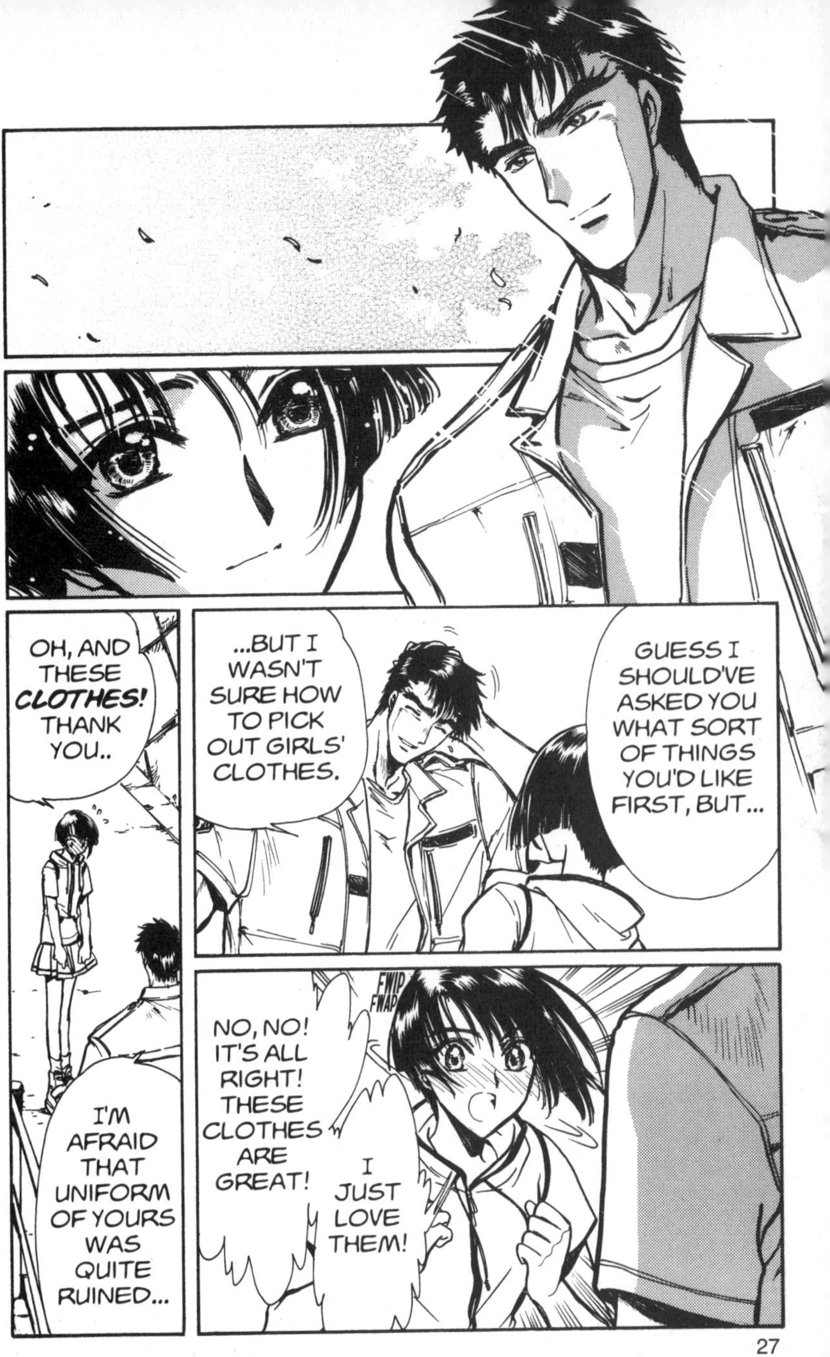
GUESS I SHOULD'VE ASKED YOU WHAT SORT OF THINGS YOU'D LIKE FIRST, BUT...
...BUT I WASN'T SURE HOW TO PICK OUT GIRLS' CLOTHES.
FWIP FWAP
NO, NO! IT'S ALL RIGHT! THESE CLOTHES ARE GREAT!
I JUST LOVE THEM!
OH, AND THESE **CLOTHES!** THANK YOU..
I'M AFRAID THAT UNIFORM OF YOURS WAS QUITE RUINED...

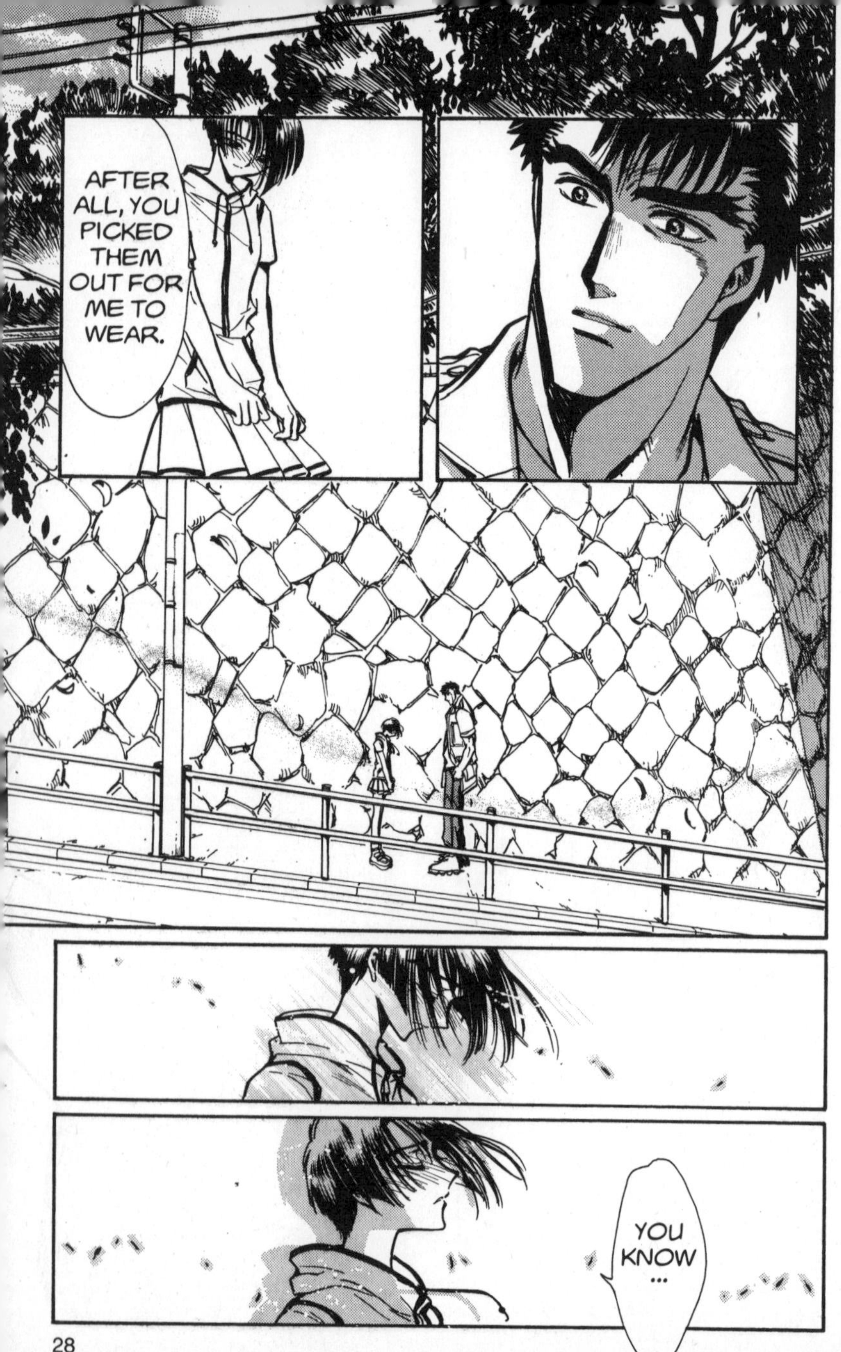
AFTER ALL, YOU PICKED THEM OUT FOR ME TO WEAR.
YOU KNOW ...

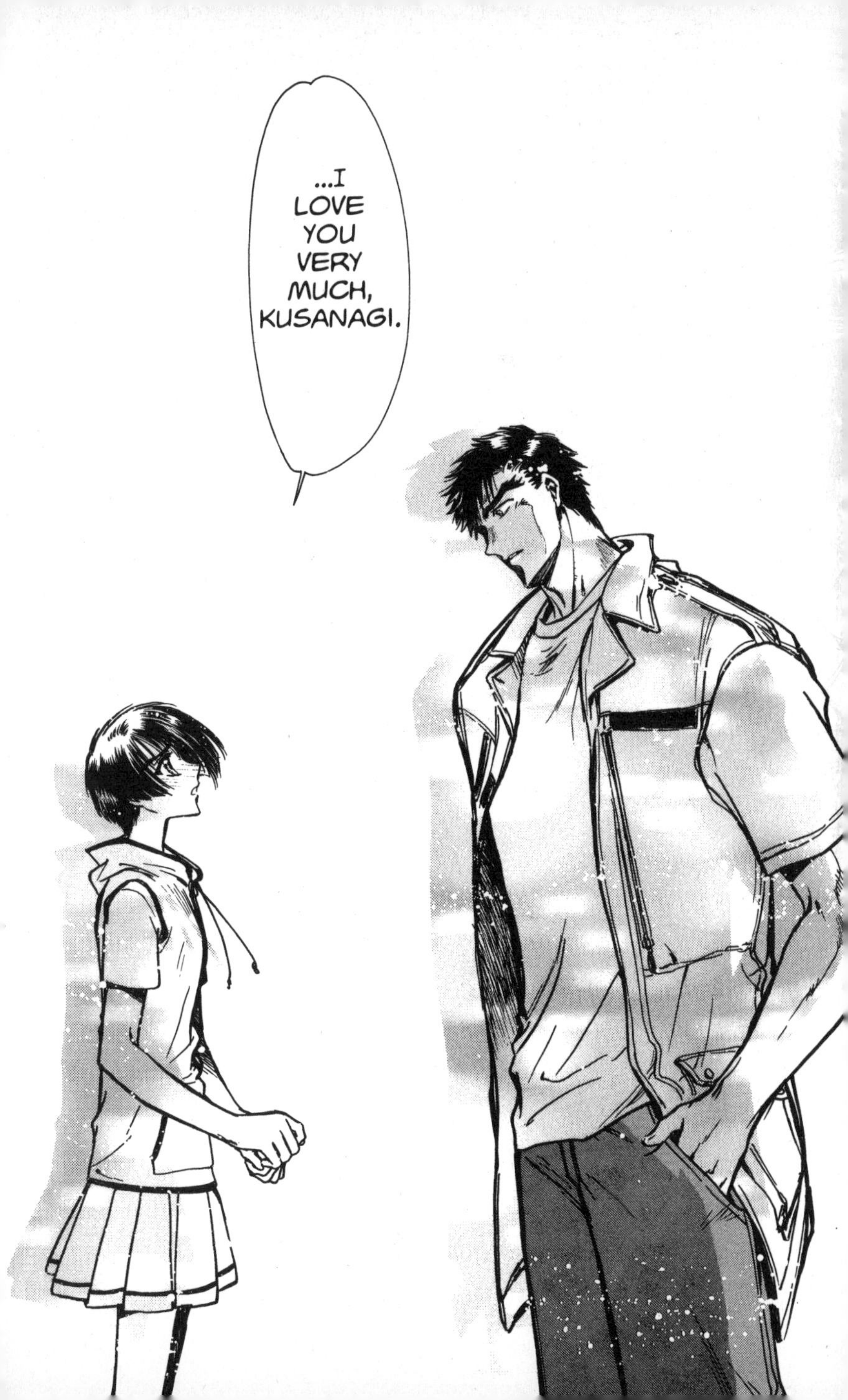
...I LOVE YOU VERY MUCH, KUSANAGI.

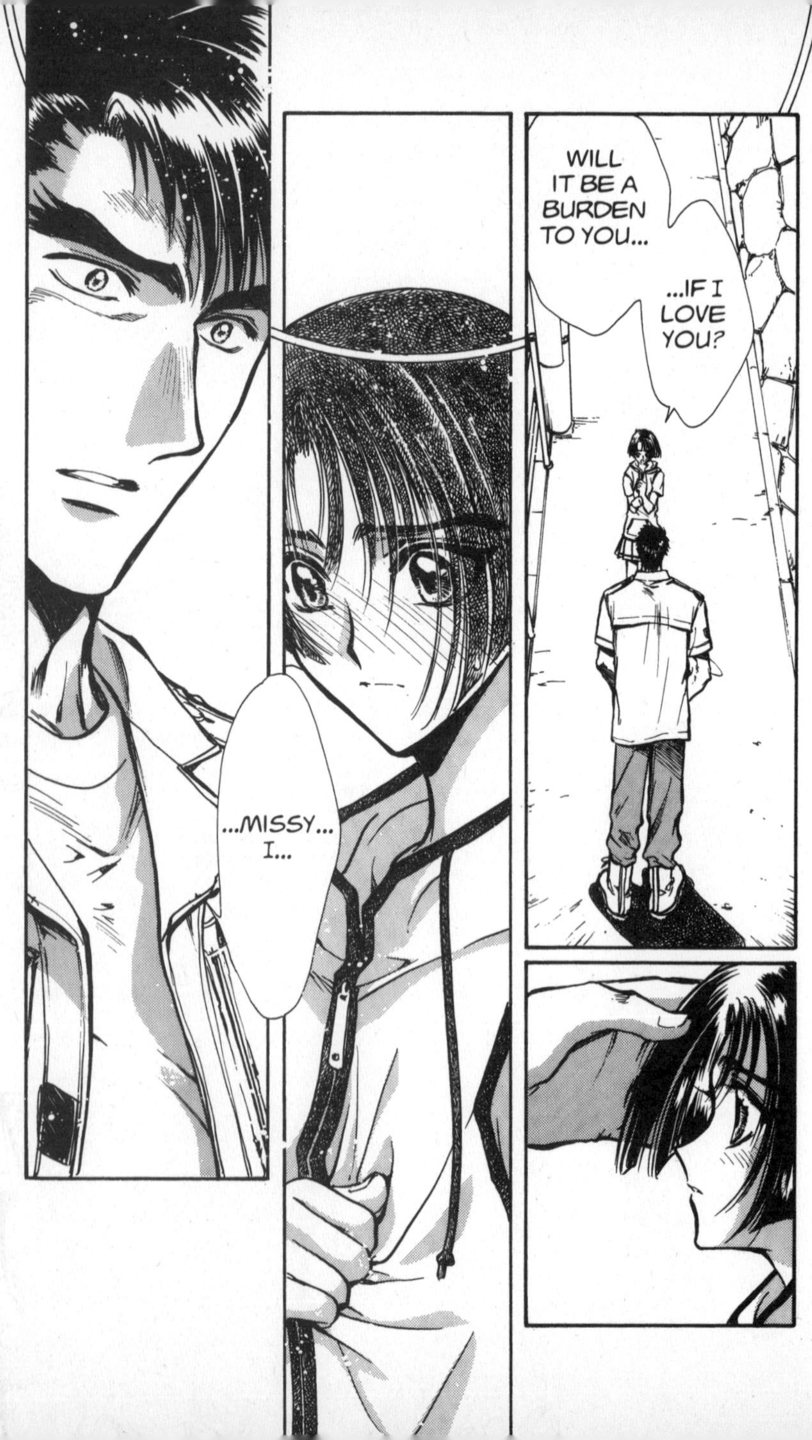
WILL IT BE A BURDEN TO YOU...
...IF I LOVE YOU?
...MISSY... I...

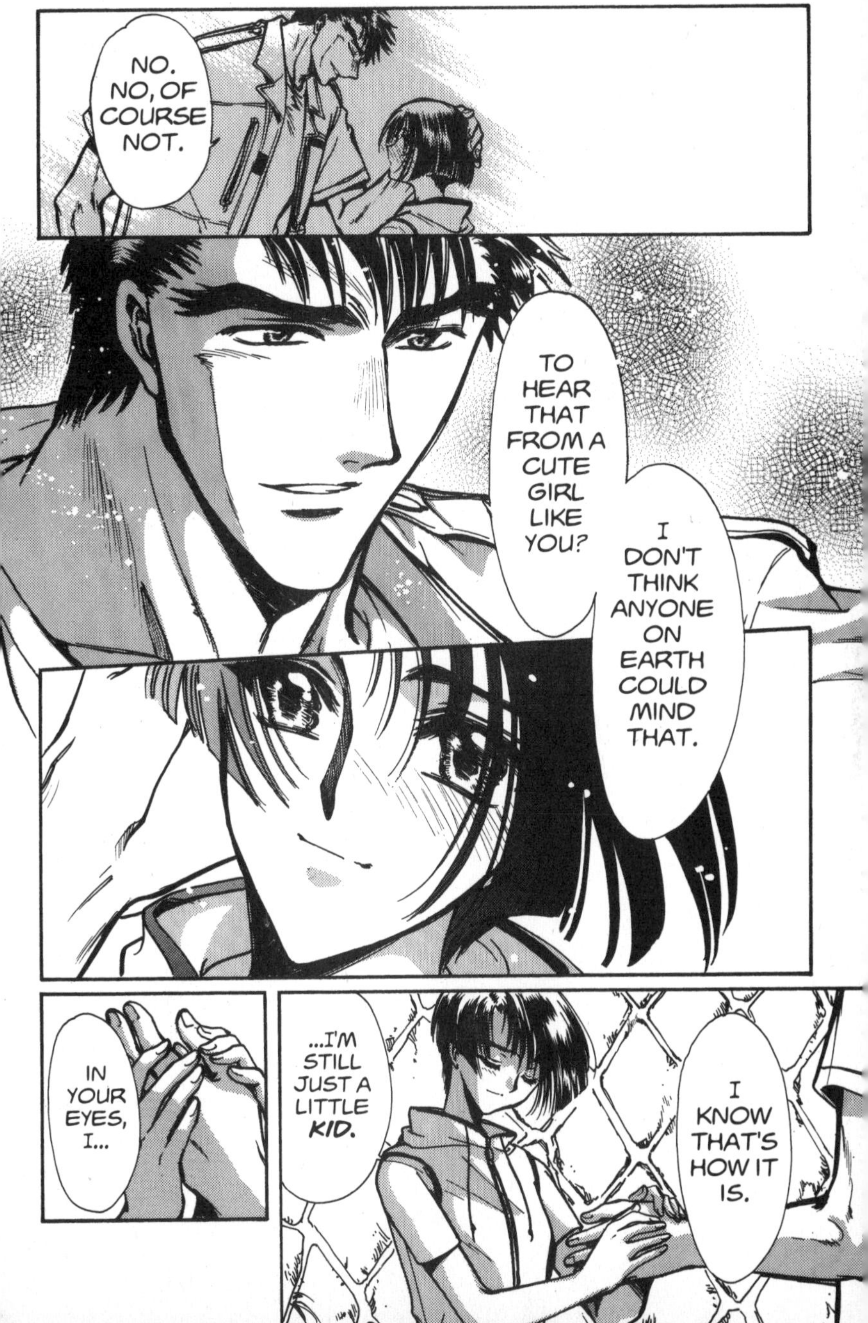
NO. NO, OF COURSE NOT.
TO HEAR THAT FROM A CUTE GIRL LIKE YOU?
I DON'T THINK ANYONE ON EARTH COULD MIND THAT.
IN YOUR EYES, I...
...I'M STILL JUST A LITTLE *KID*.
I KNOW THAT'S HOW IT IS.

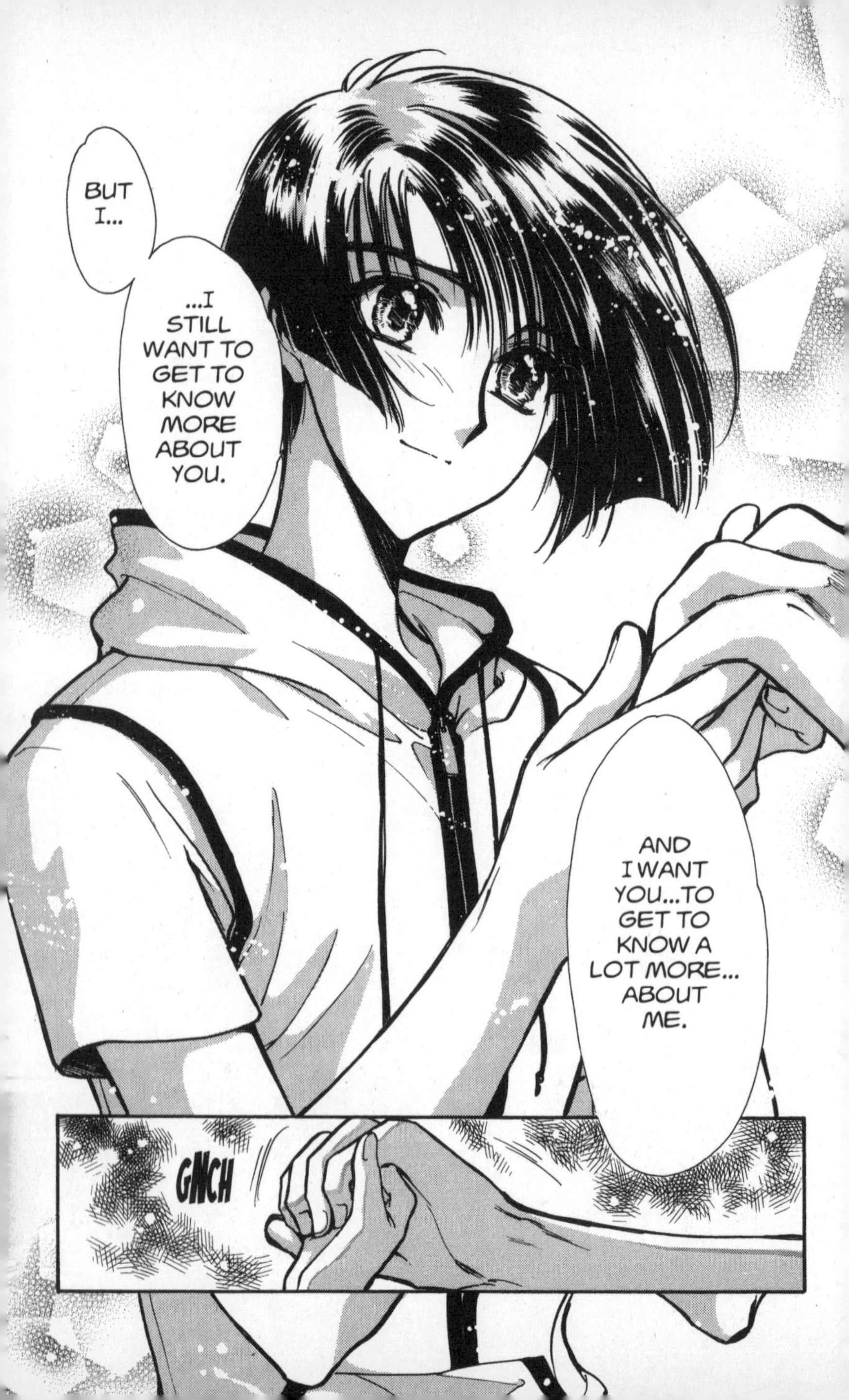
BUT I...
...I STILL WANT TO GET TO KNOW MORE ABOUT YOU.
AND I WANT YOU...TO GET TO KNOW A LOT MORE... ABOUT ME.
GNCH

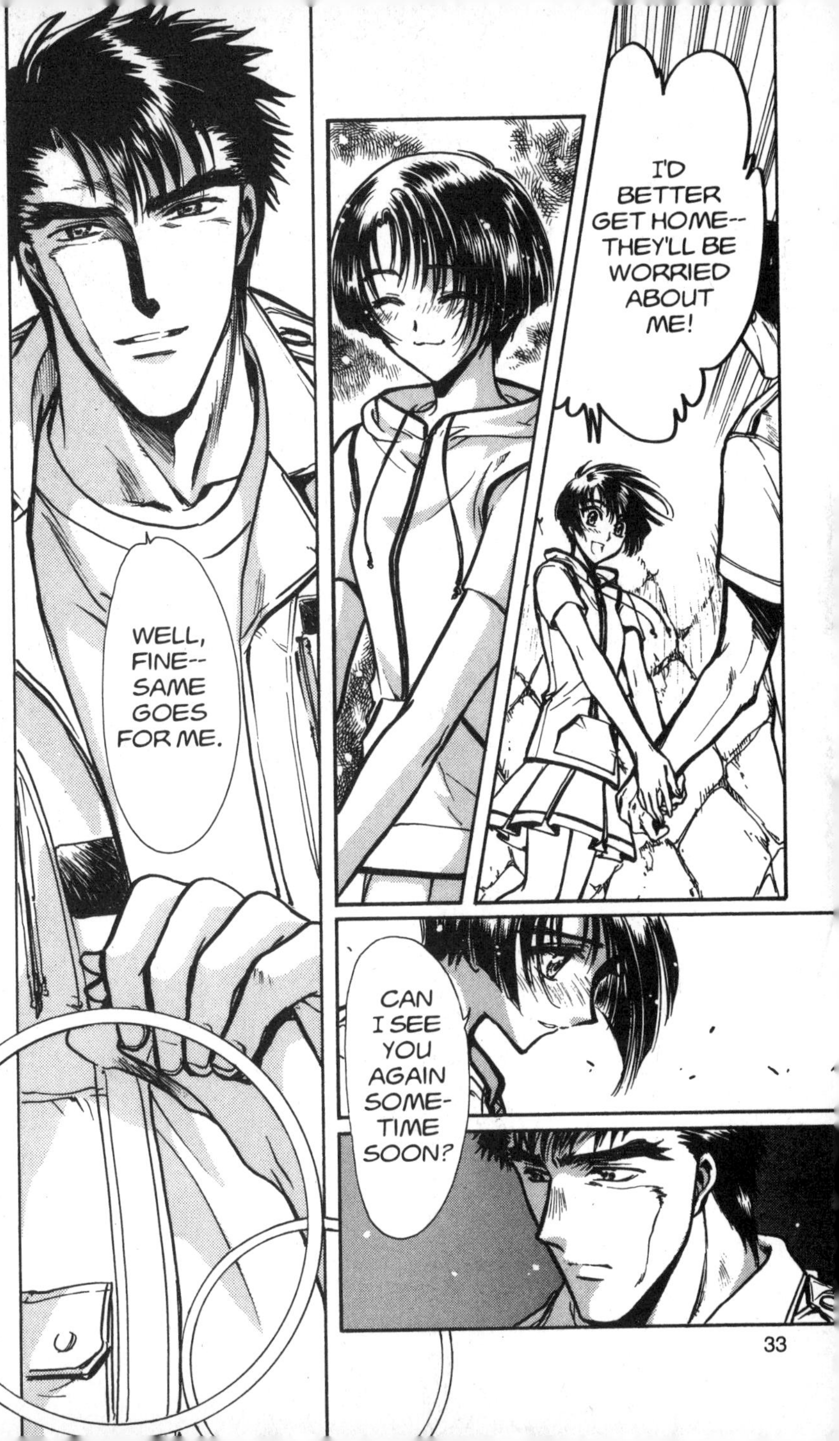
I'D BETTER GET HOME-- THEY'LL BE WORRIED ABOUT ME!
CAN I SEE YOU AGAIN SOME-TIME SOON?
WELL, FINE-- SAME GOES FOR ME.

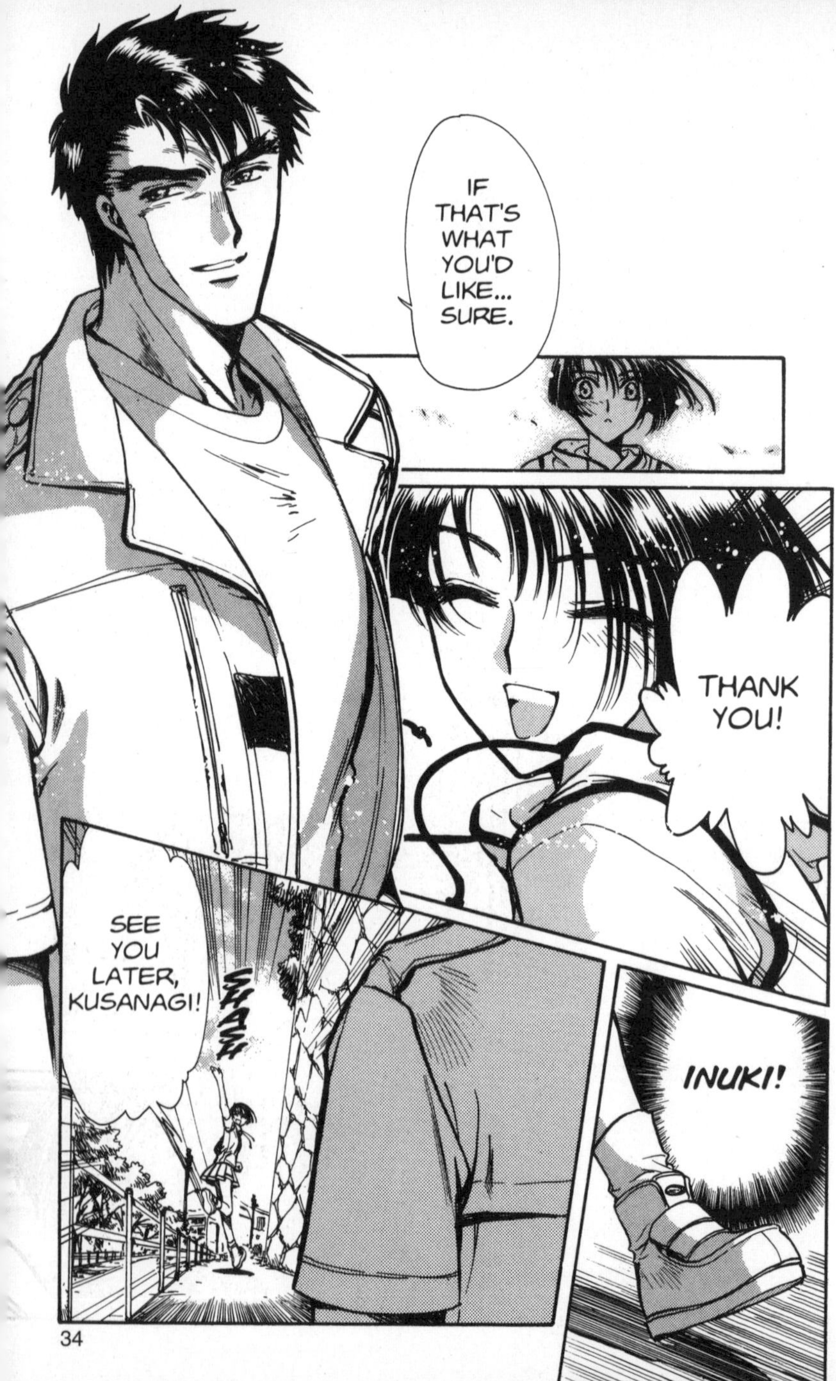
IF THAT'S WHAT YOU'D LIKE... SURE.
THANK YOU!
INUKI!
SEE YOU LATER, KUSANAGI!
SHASH

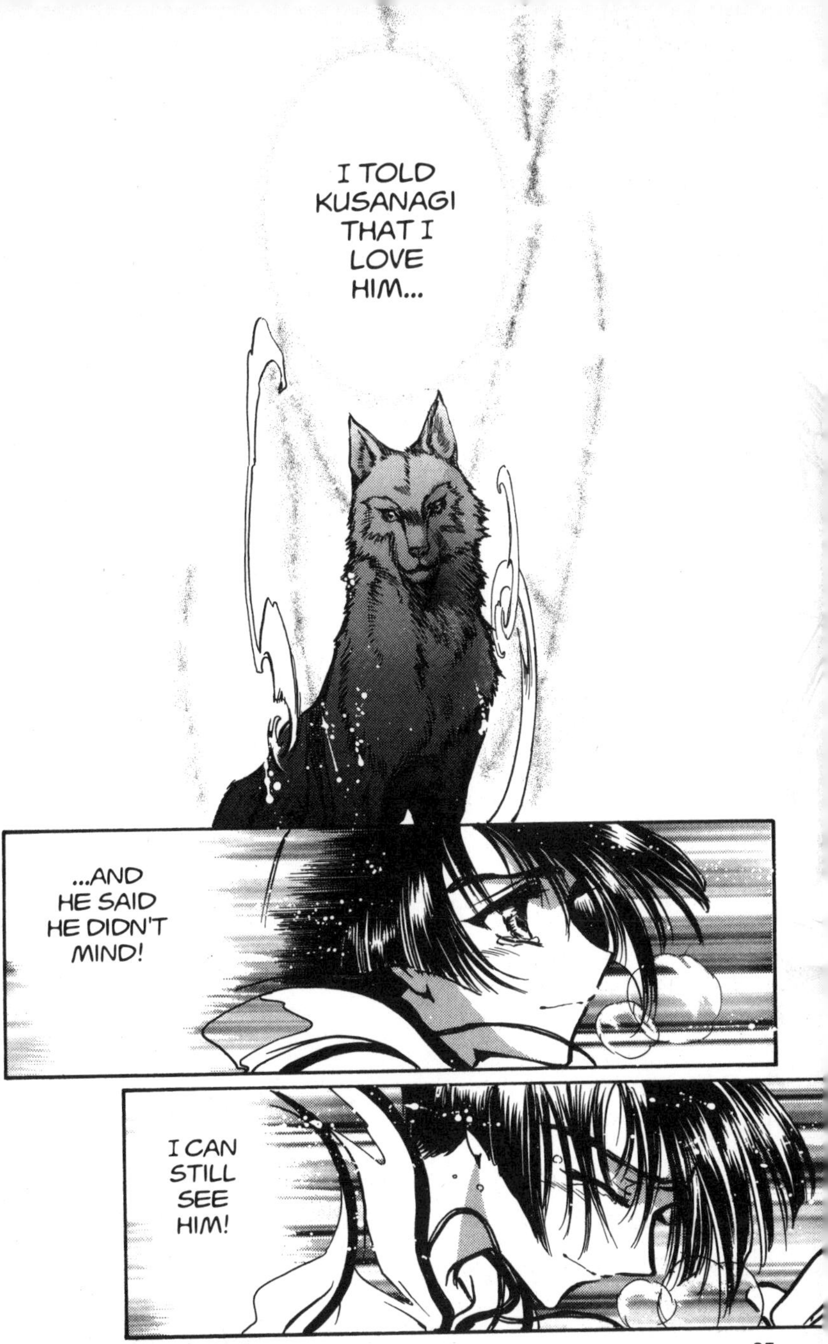
I TOLD KUSANAGI THAT I LOVE HIM...
...AND HE SAID HE DIDN'T MIND!
I CAN STILL SEE HIM!

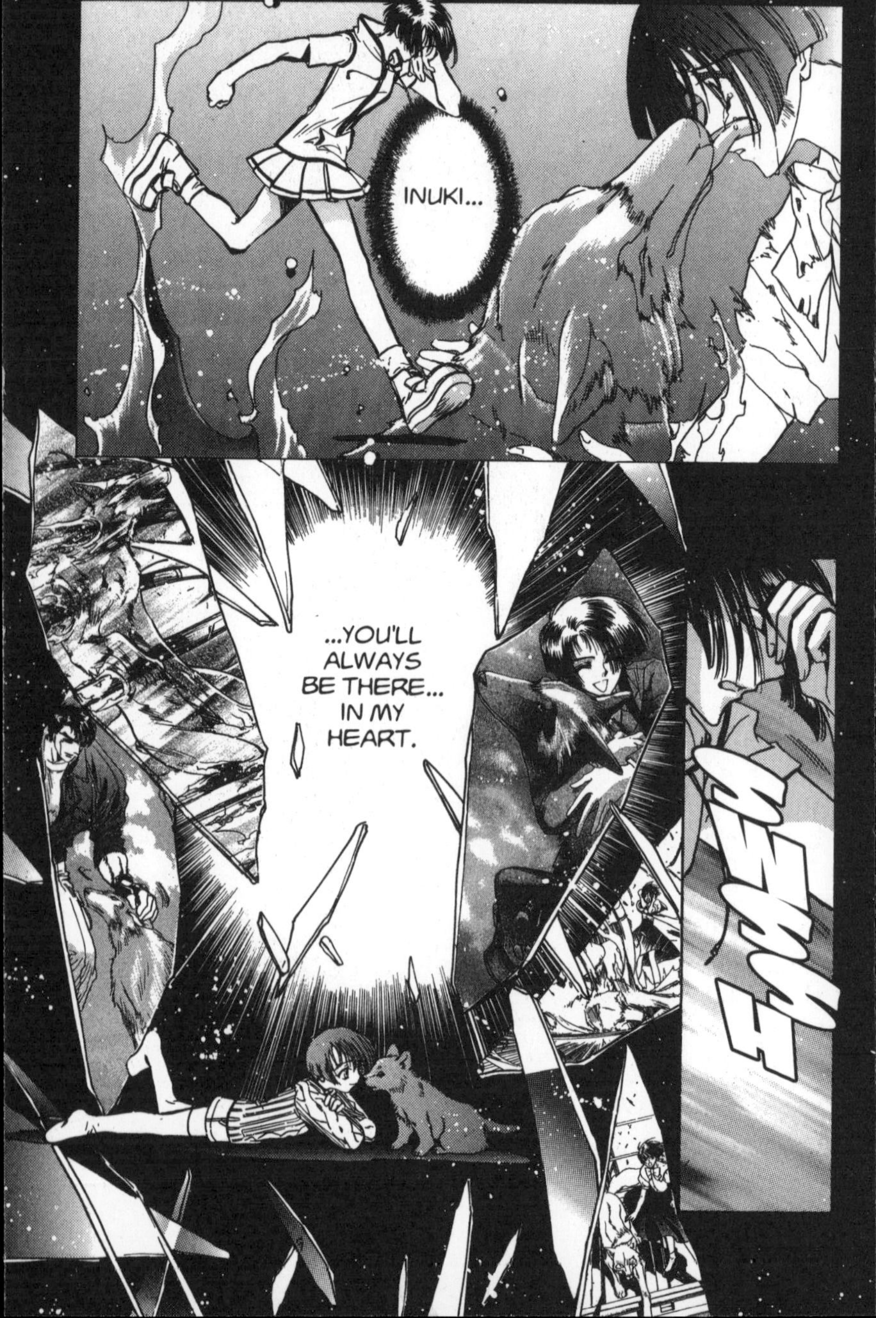
INUKI...
SHASH
...YOU'LL ALWAYS BE THERE... IN MY HEART.

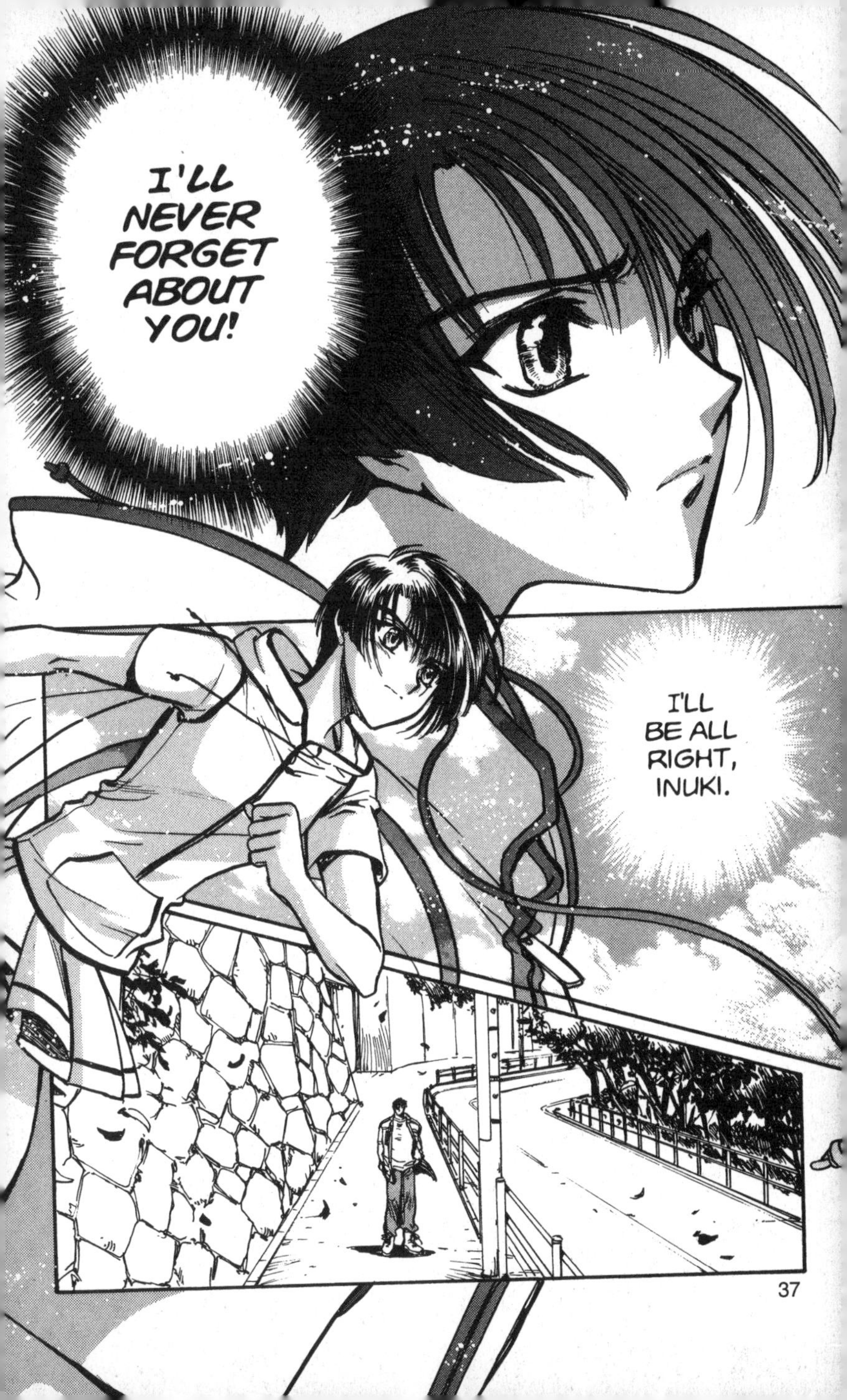
I'LL NEVER FORGET ABOUT YOU!
I'LL BE ALL RIGHT, INUKI.

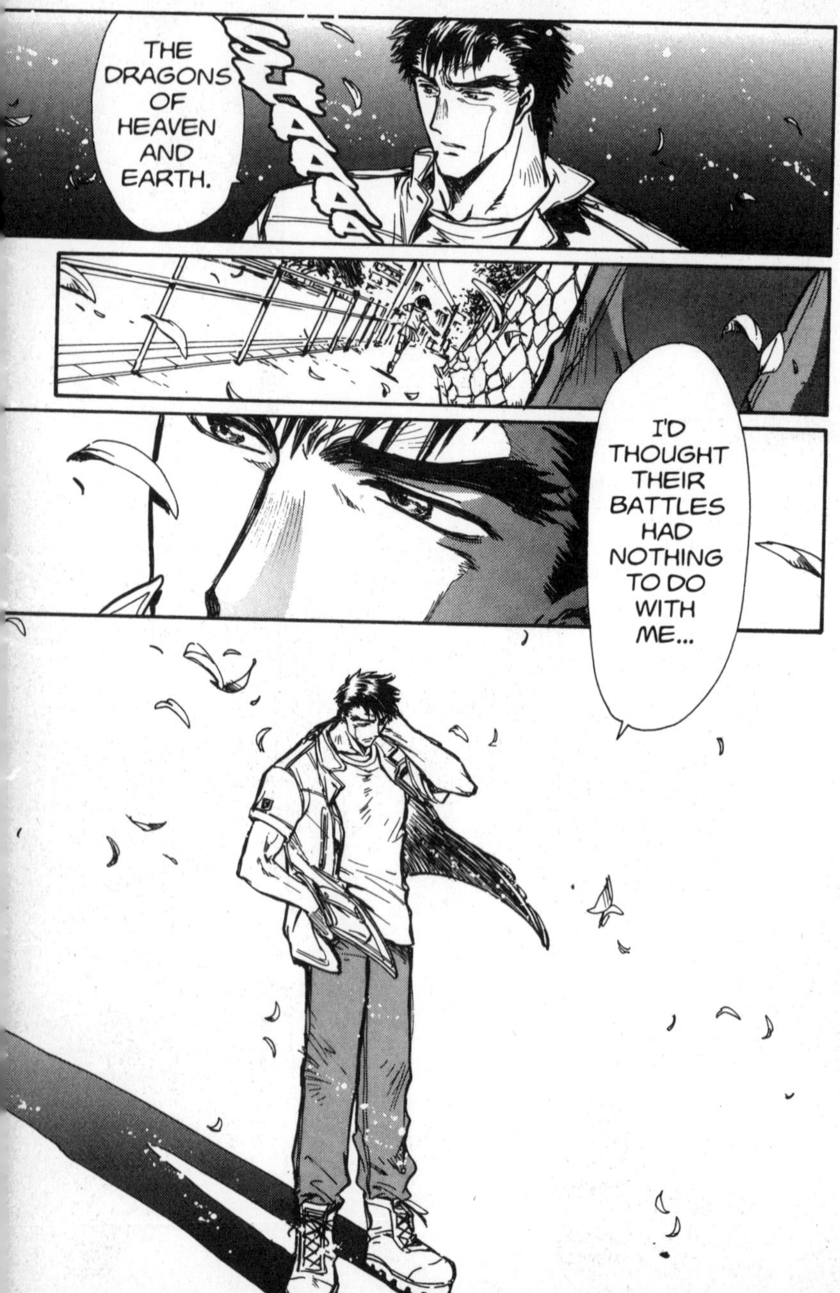
THE DRAGONS OF HEAVEN AND EARTH.
I'D THOUGHT THEIR BATTLES HAD NOTHING TO DO WITH ME...

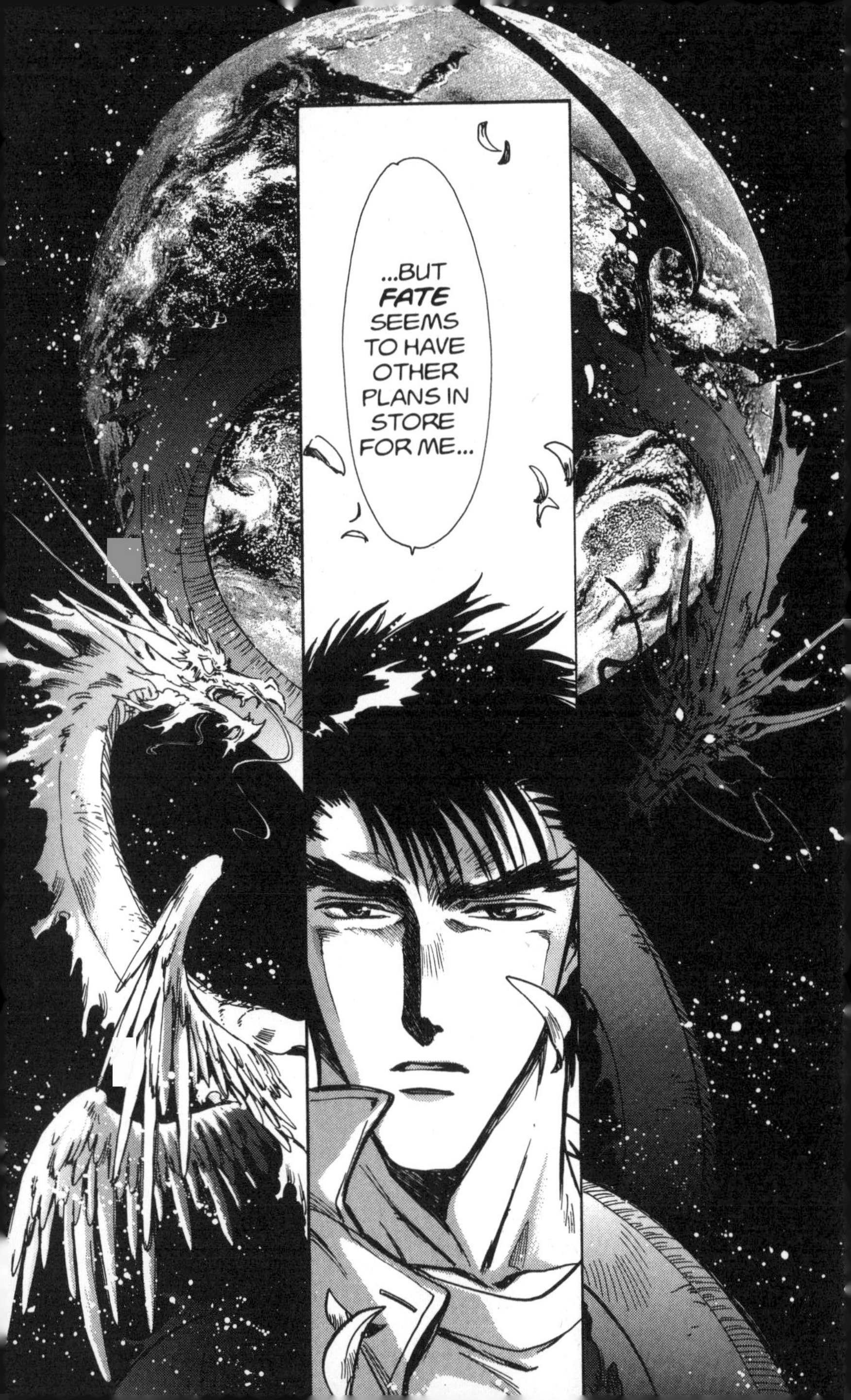
...BUT FATE SEEMS TO HAVE OTHER PLANS IN STORE FOR ME...

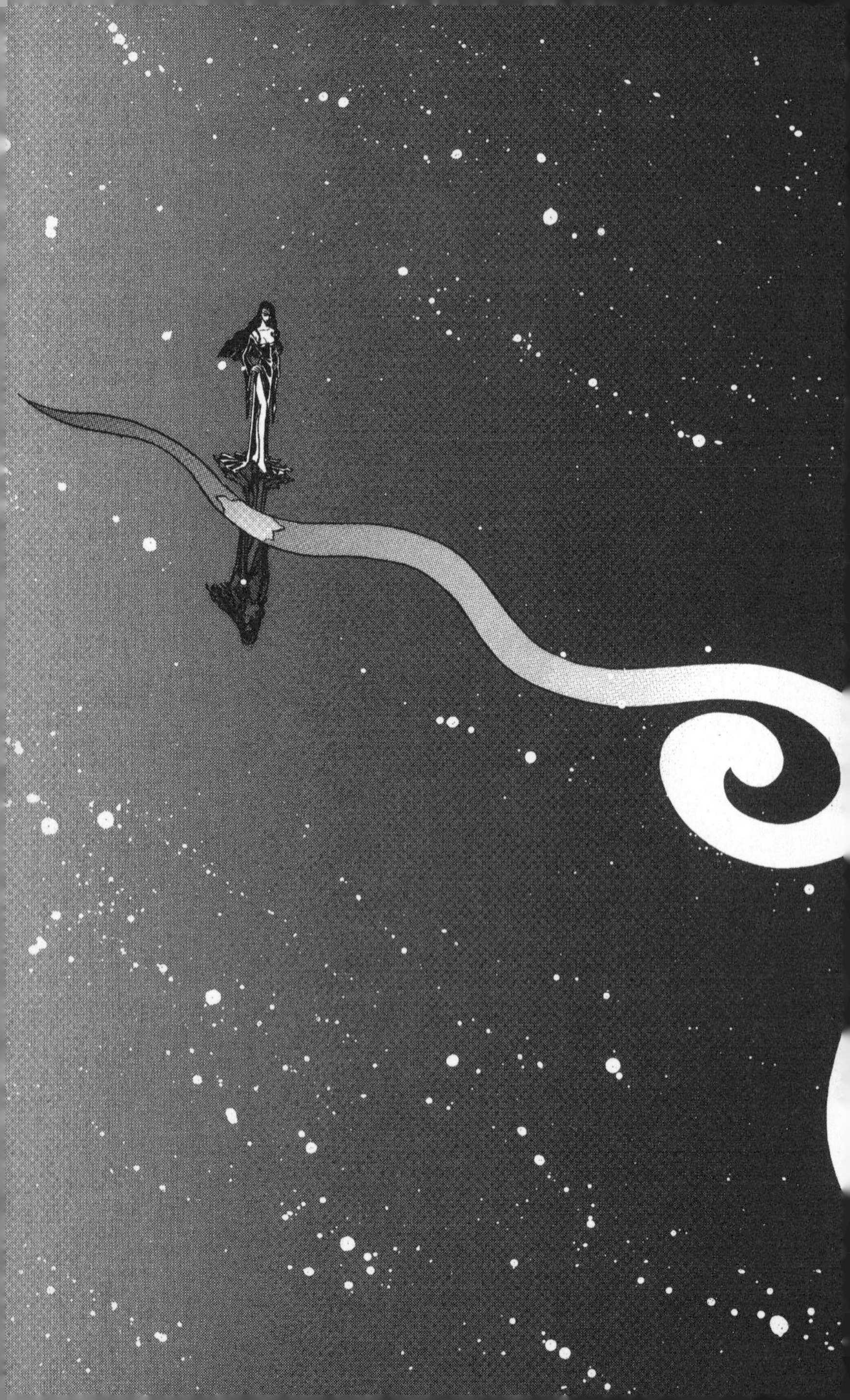

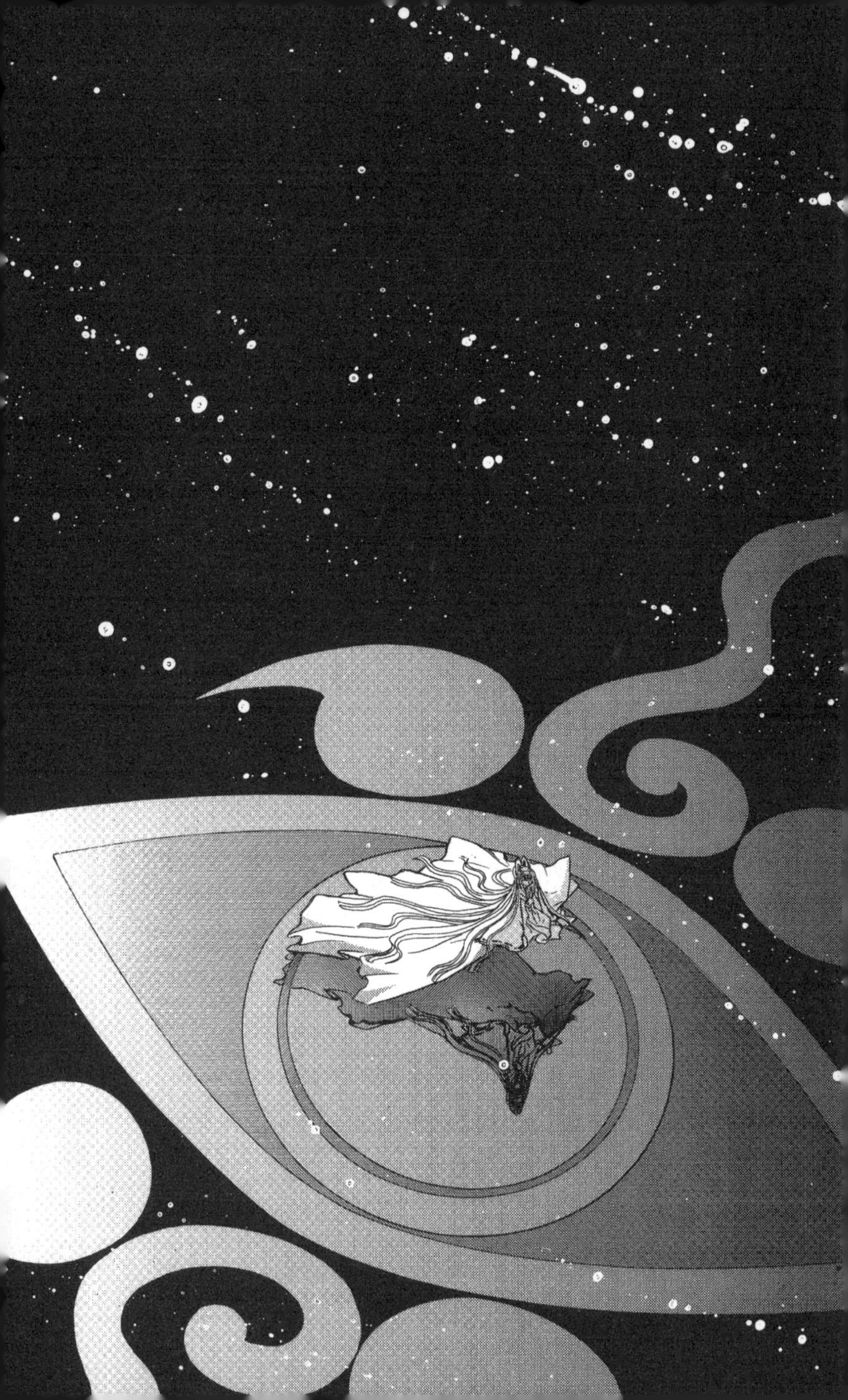

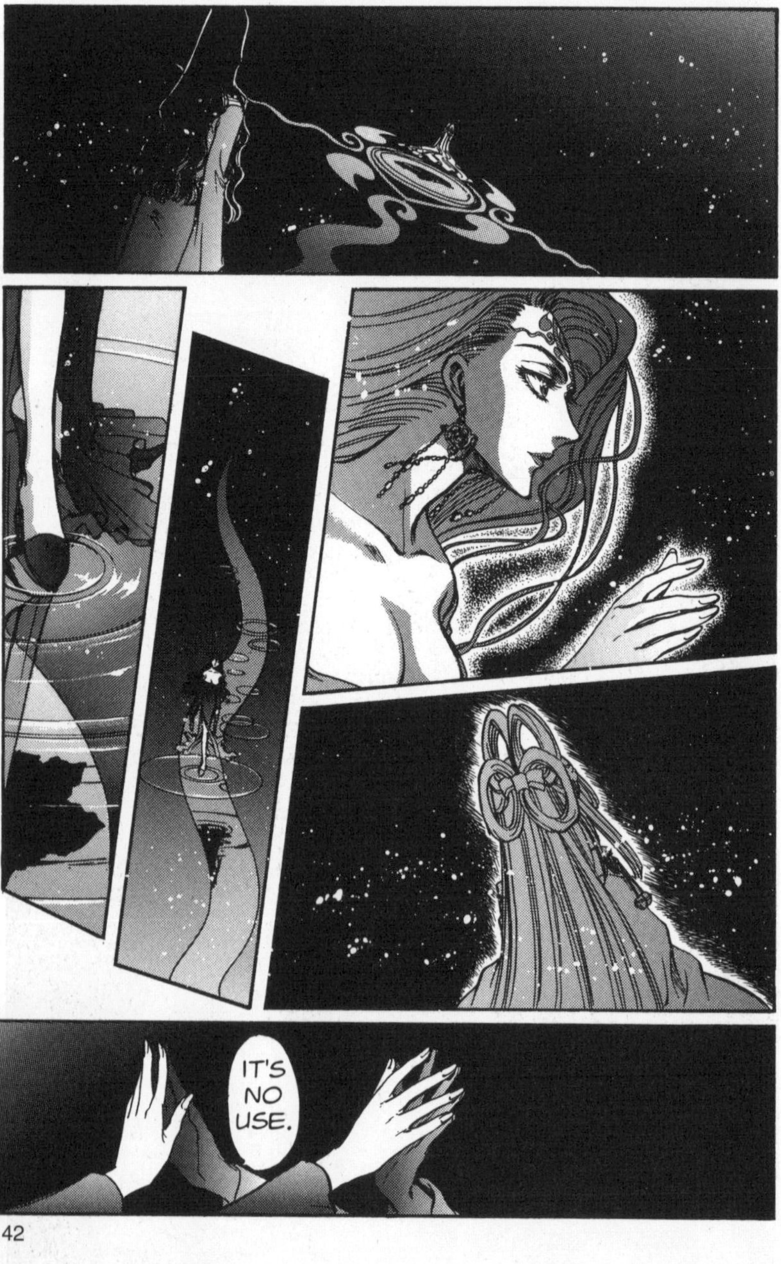
IT'S NO USE.

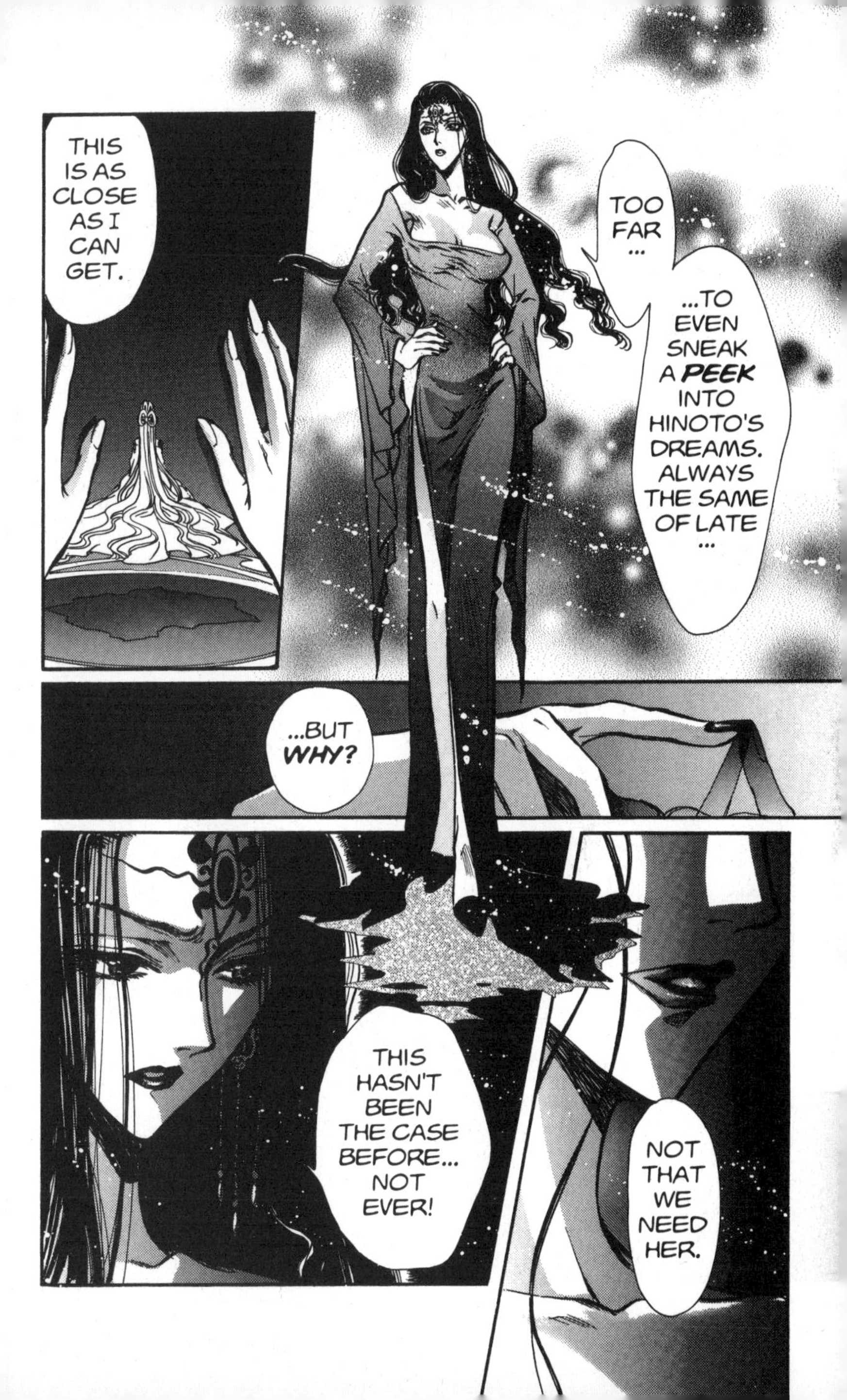
TOO FAR ...
...TO EVEN SNEAK A **PEEK** INTO HINOTO'S DREAMS. ALWAYS THE SAME OF LATE ...
THIS IS AS CLOSE AS I CAN GET.
...BUT **WHY?**
NOT THAT WE NEED HER.
THIS HASN'T BEEN THE CASE BEFORE... NOT EVER!

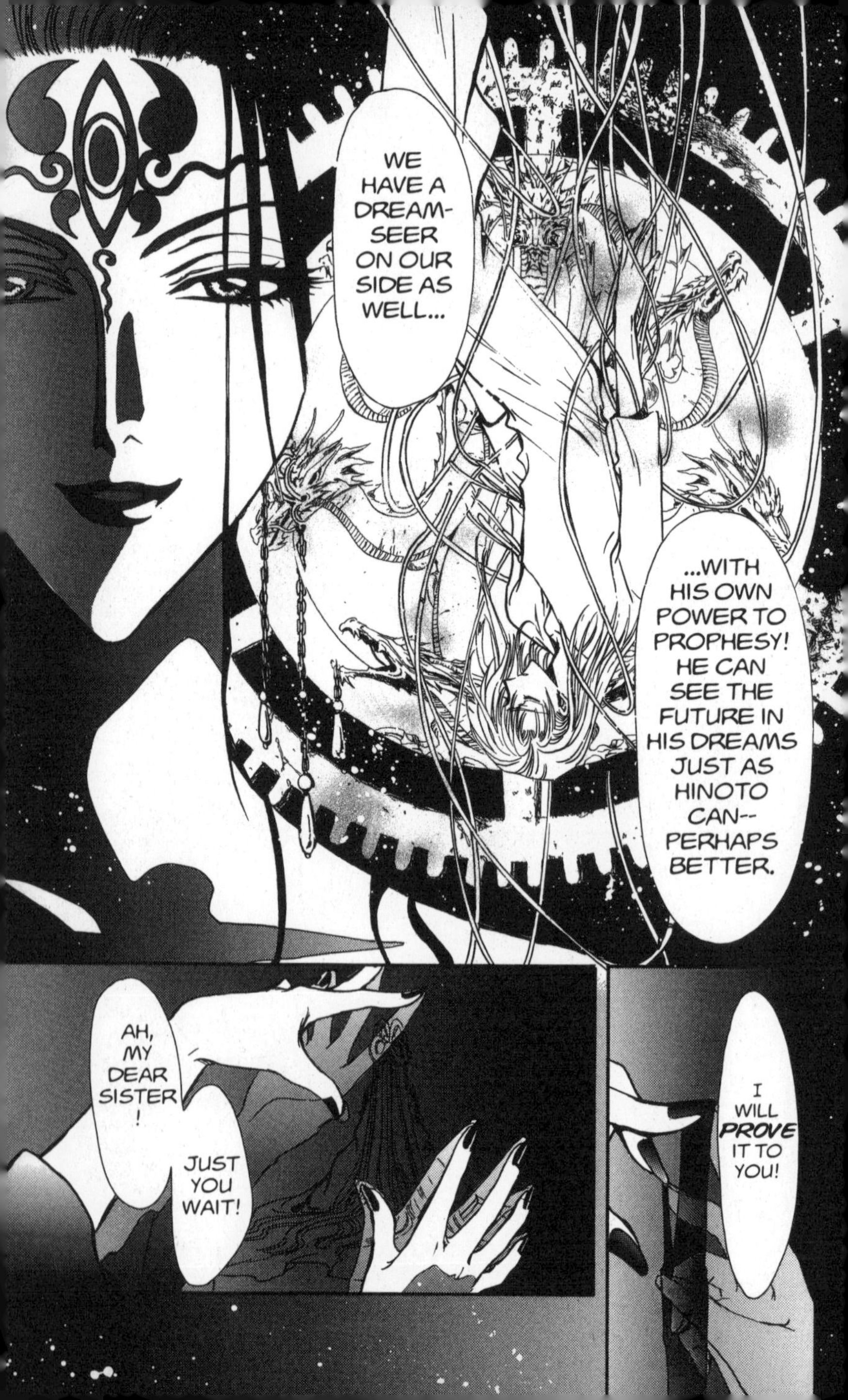

WE HAVE A DREAM-SEER ON OUR SIDE AS WELL...
...WITH HIS OWN POWER TO PROPHESY! HE CAN SEE THE FUTURE IN HIS DREAMS JUST AS HINOTO CAN--PERHAPS BETTER.
I WILL PROVE IT TO YOU!
AH, MY DEAR SISTER!
JUST YOU WAIT!

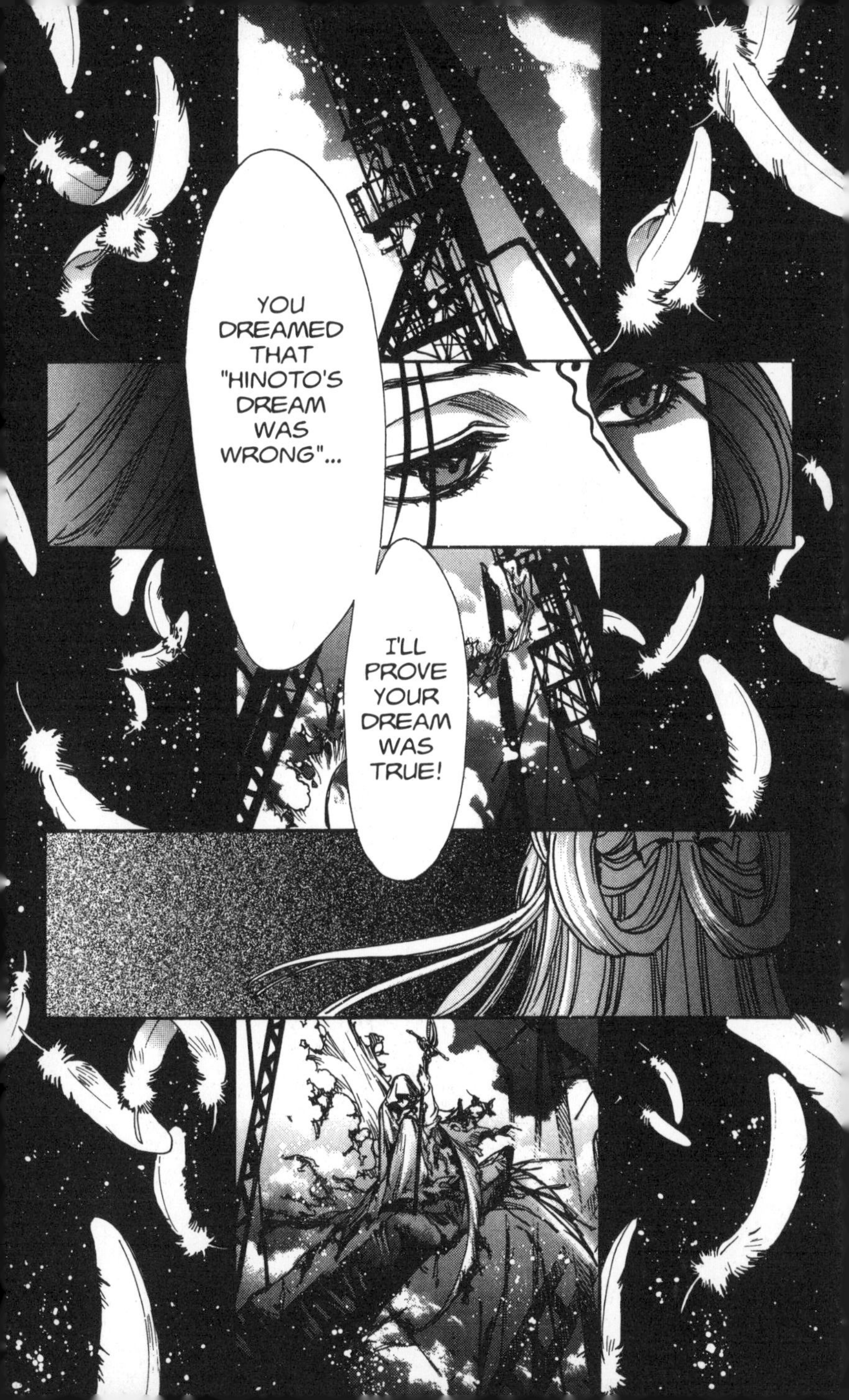
YOU DREAMED THAT "HINOTO'S DREAM WAS WRONG"...
I'LL PROVE YOUR DREAM WAS TRUE!

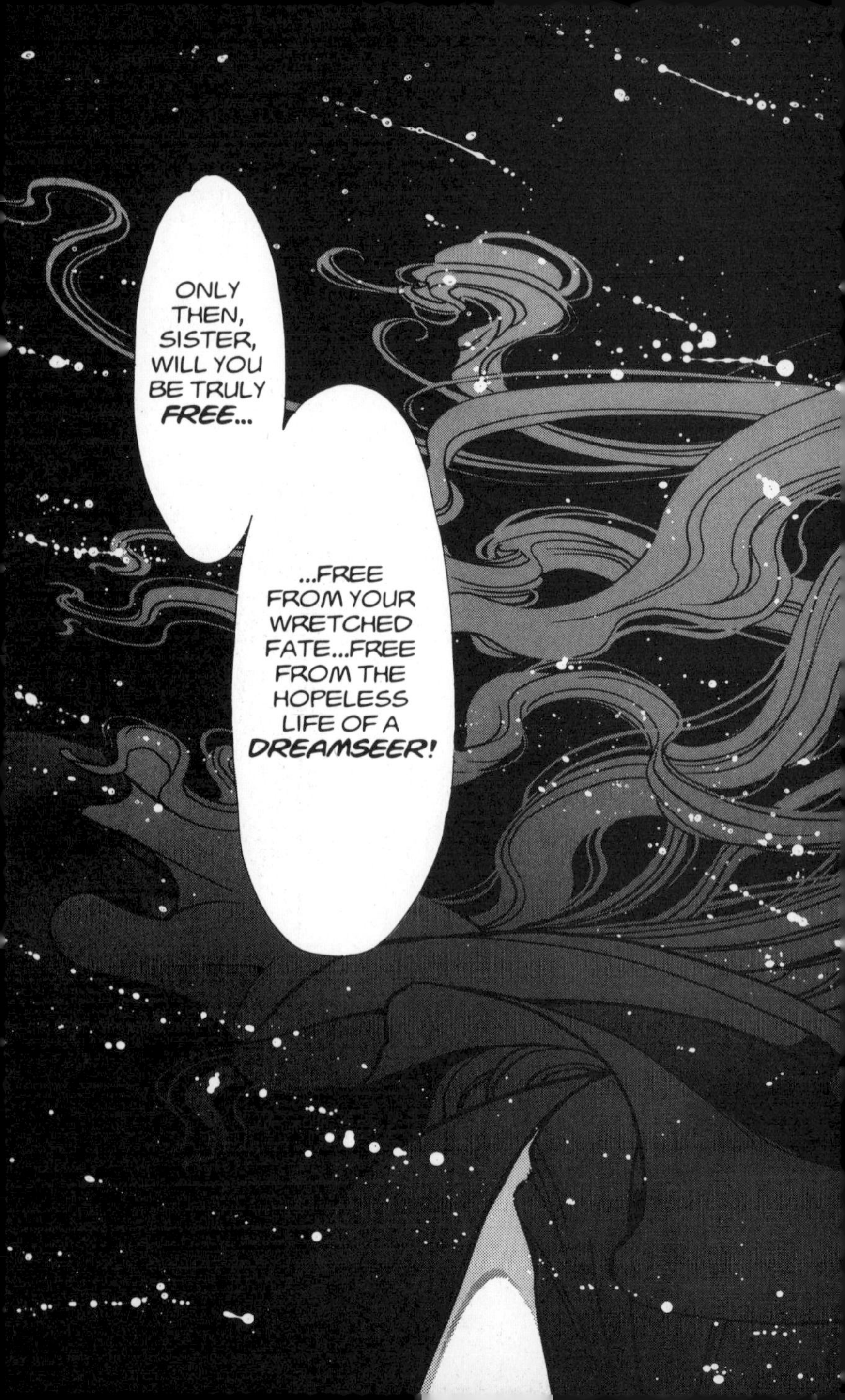
ONLY THEN, SISTER, WILL YOU BE TRULY FREE...
...FREE FROM YOUR WRETCHED FATE...FREE FROM THE HOPELESS LIFE OF A DREAMSEER!

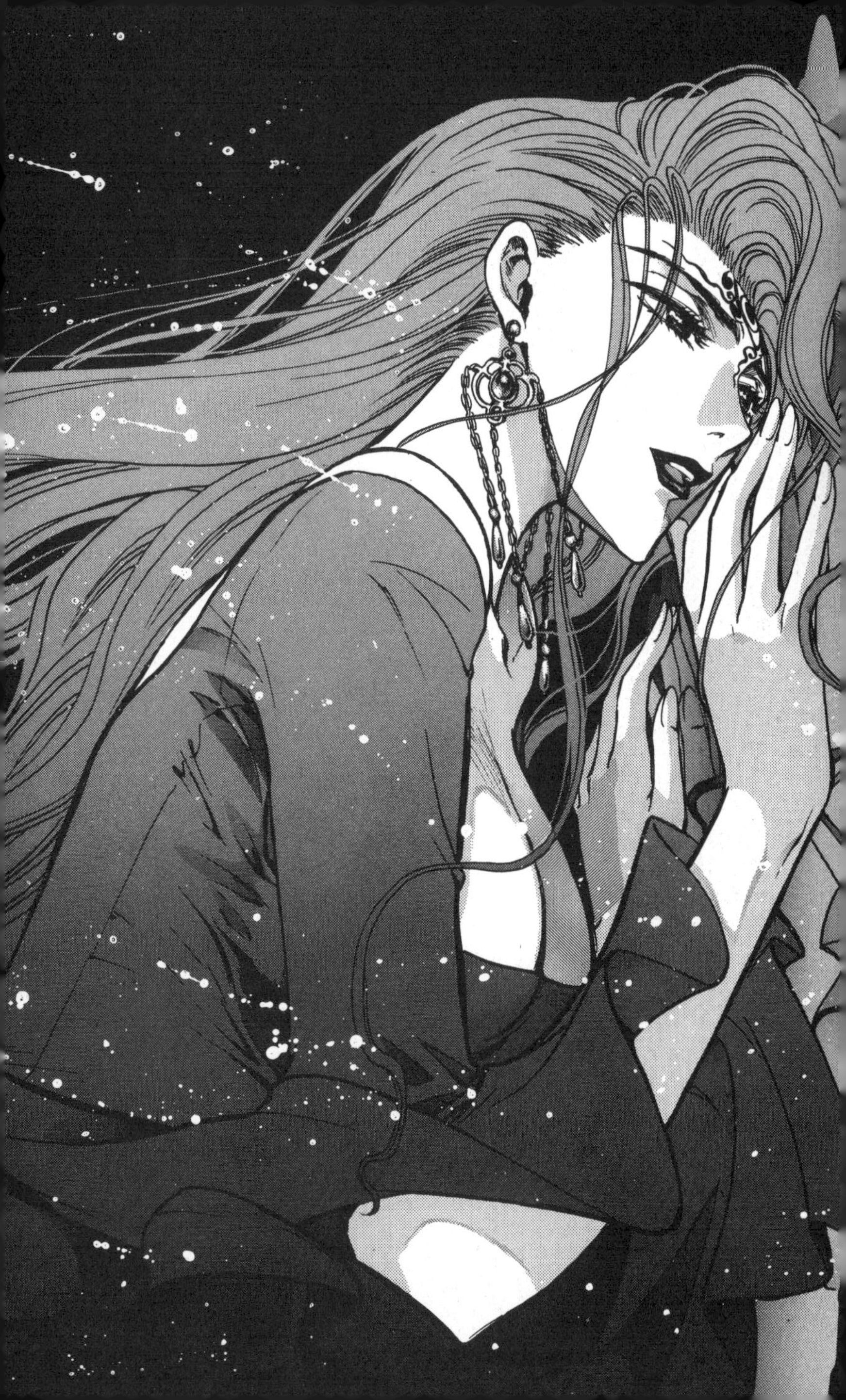

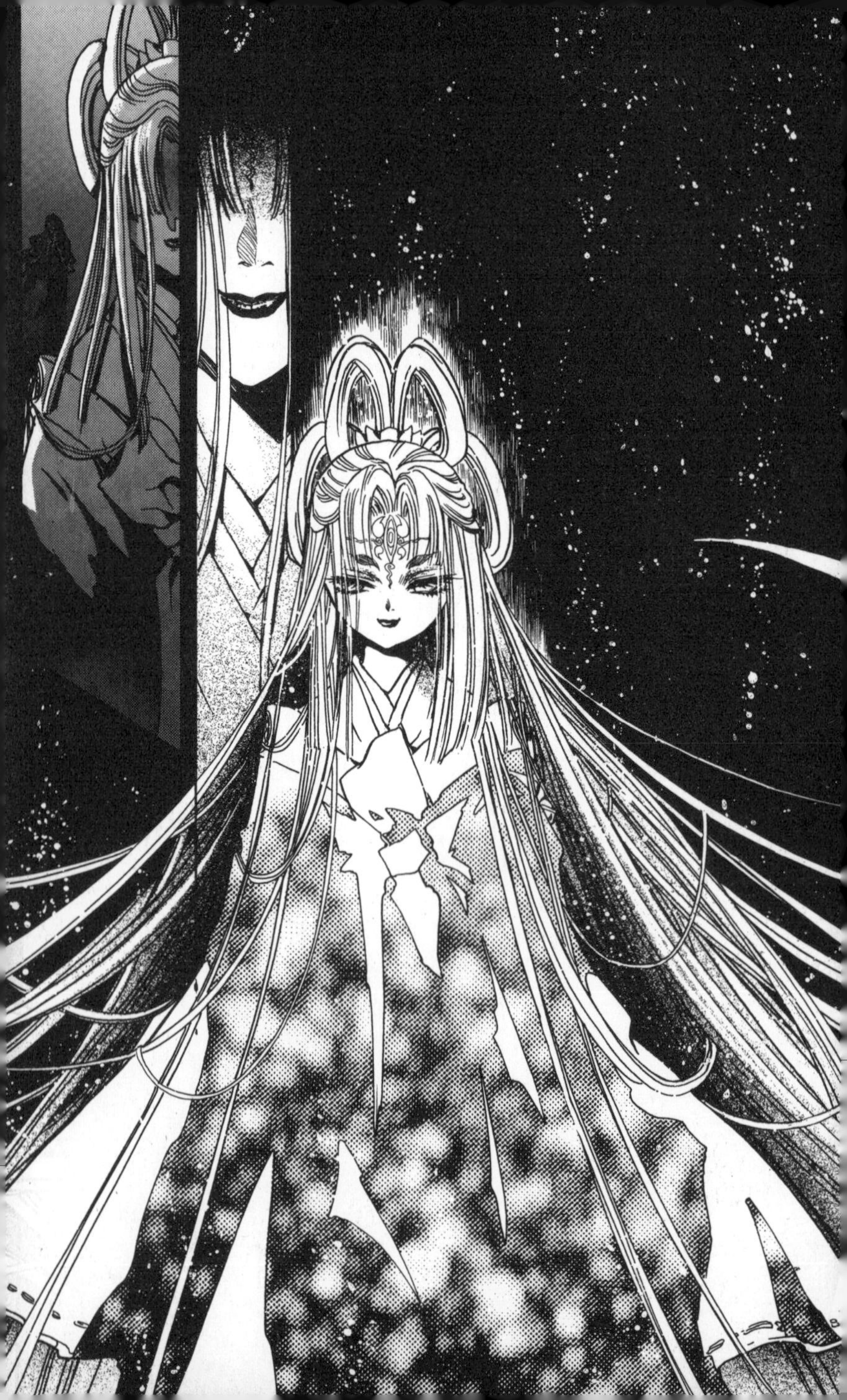

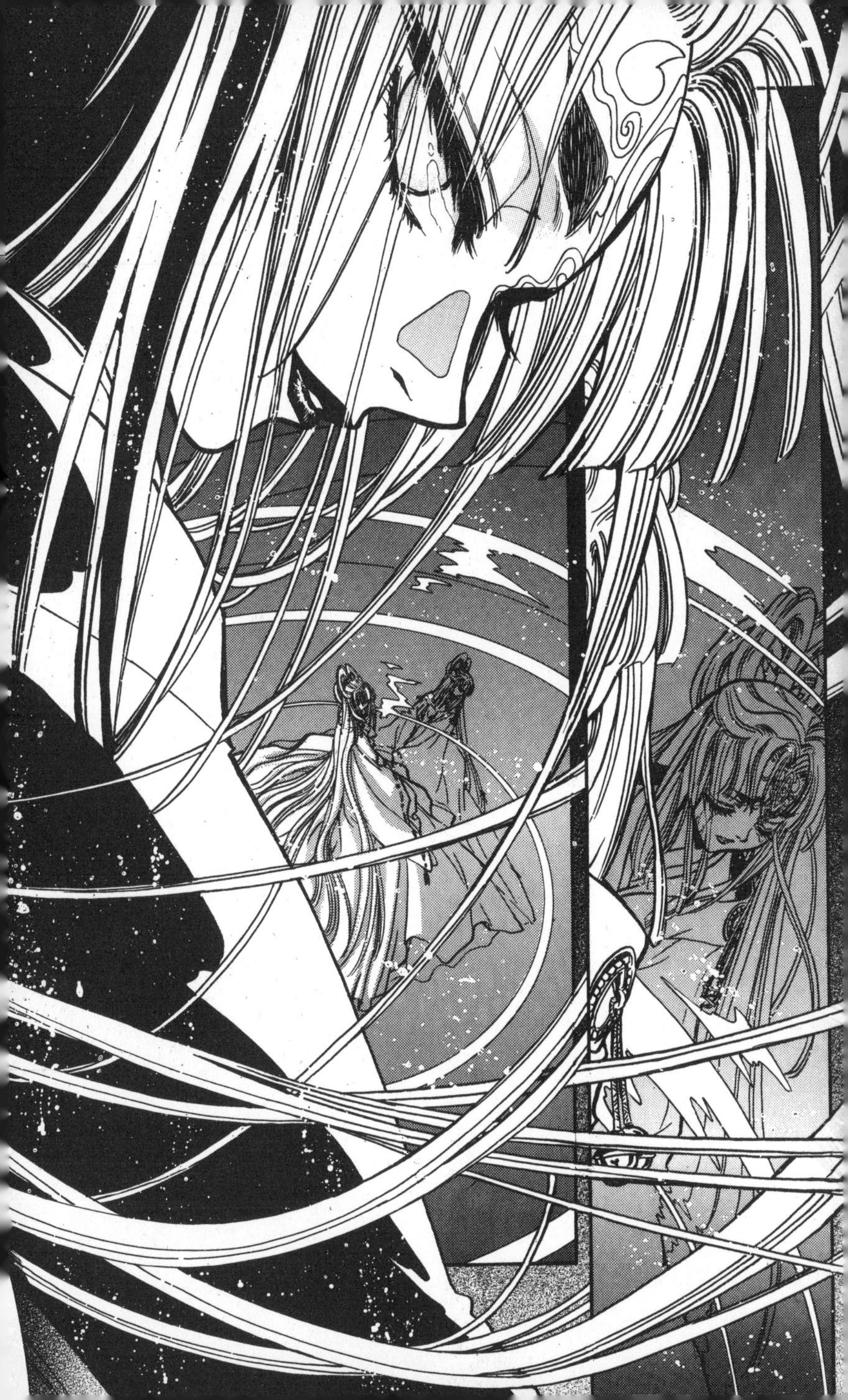

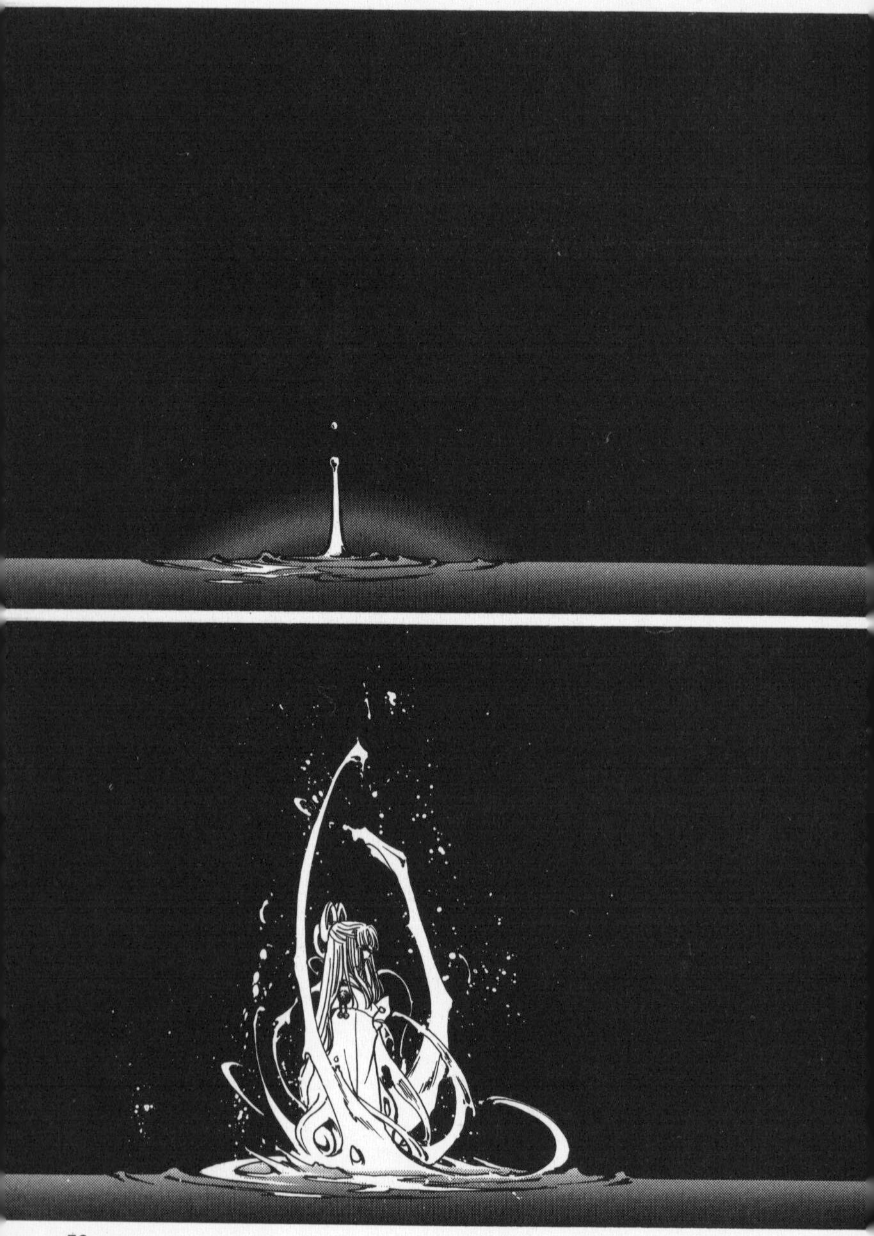

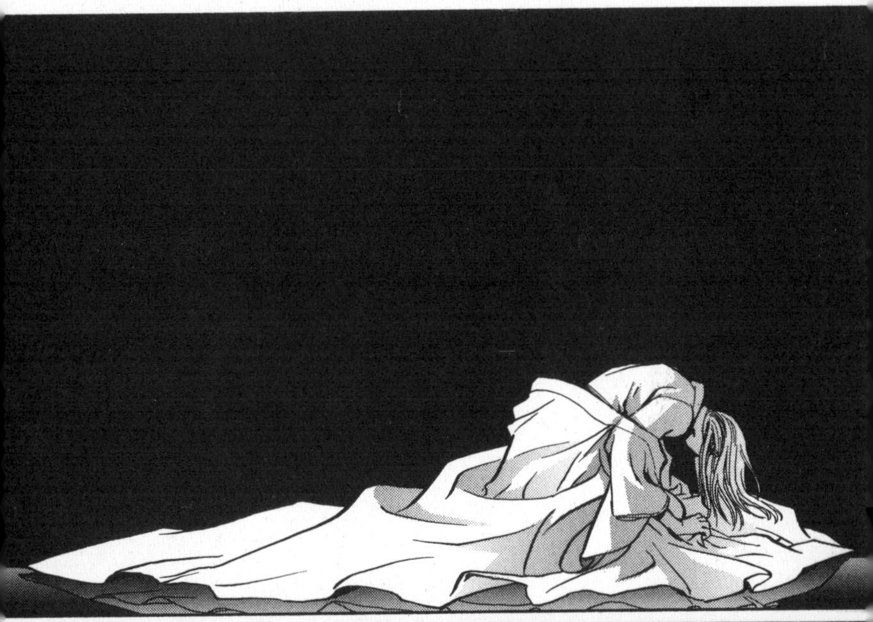
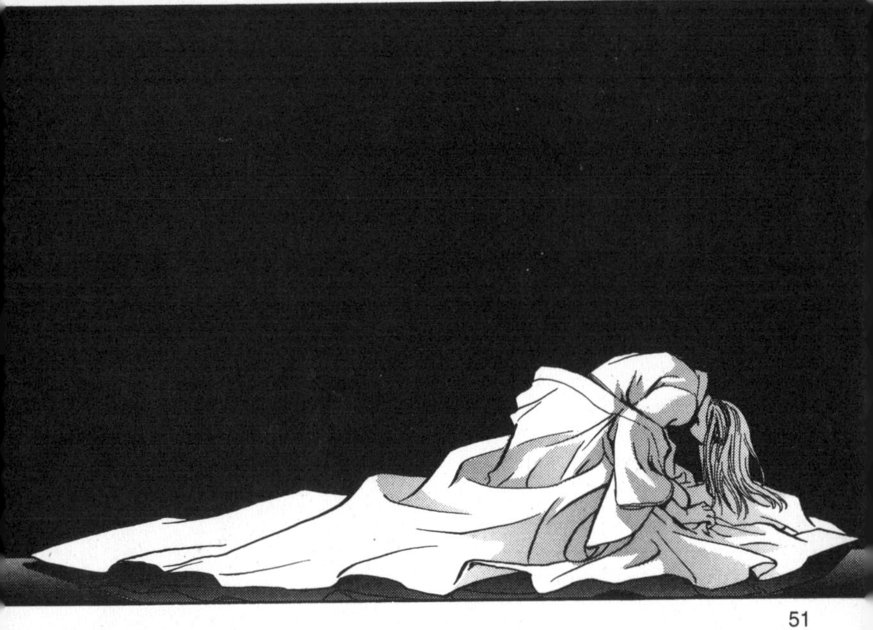

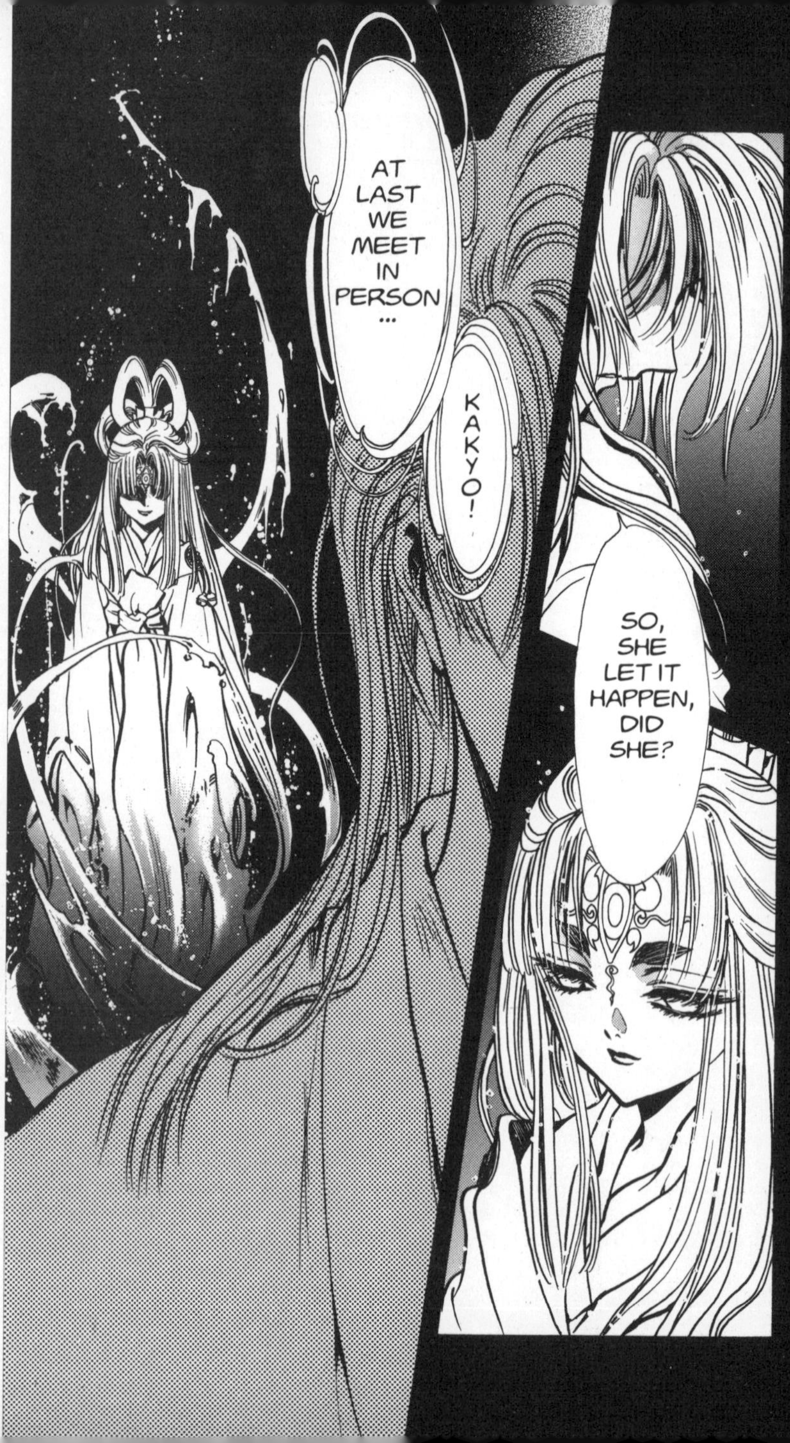
SO, SHE LET IT HAPPEN, DID SHE?
AT LAST WE MEET IN PERSON ...
KAKYO!

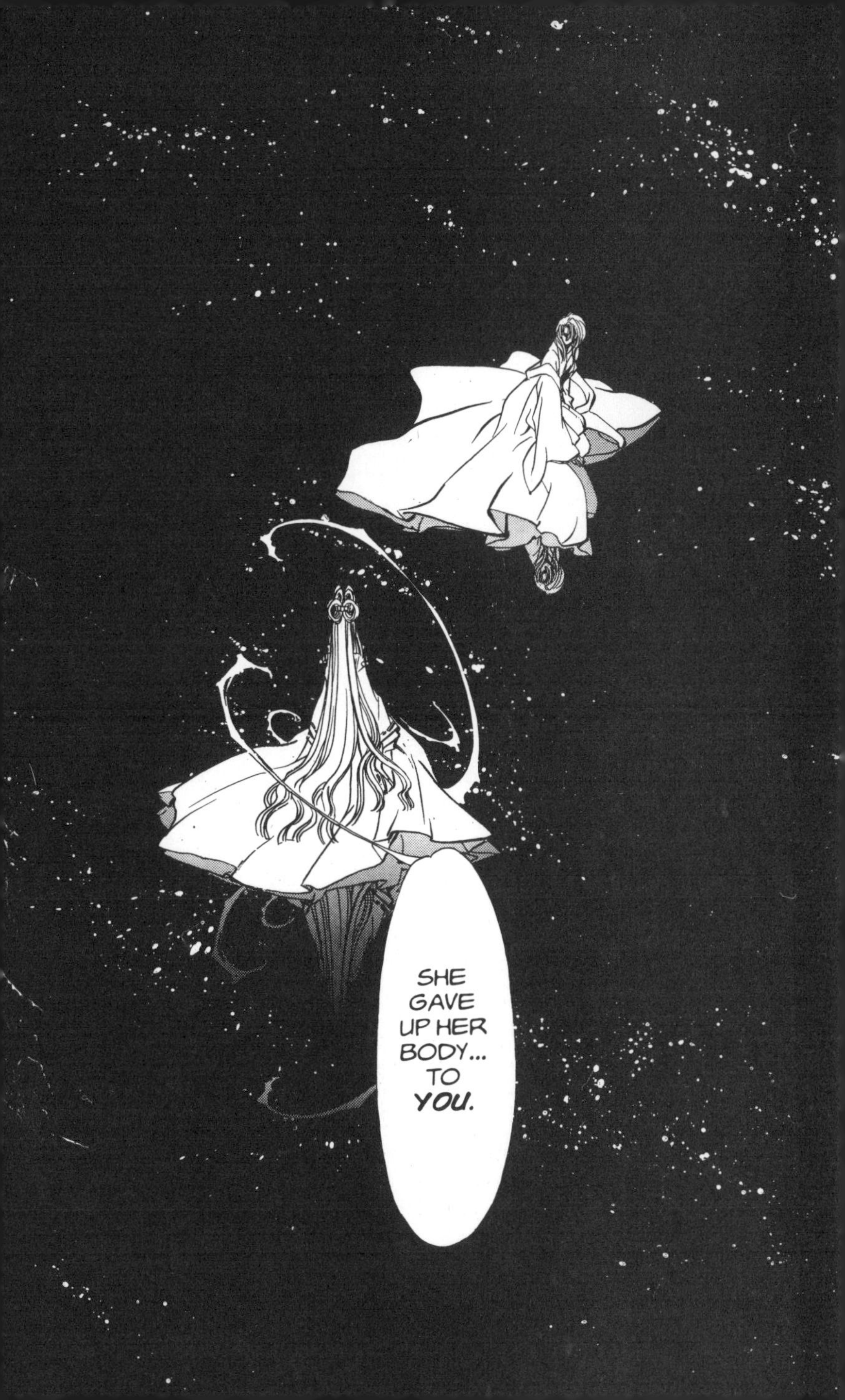
SHE GAVE UP HER BODY... TO *YOU*.

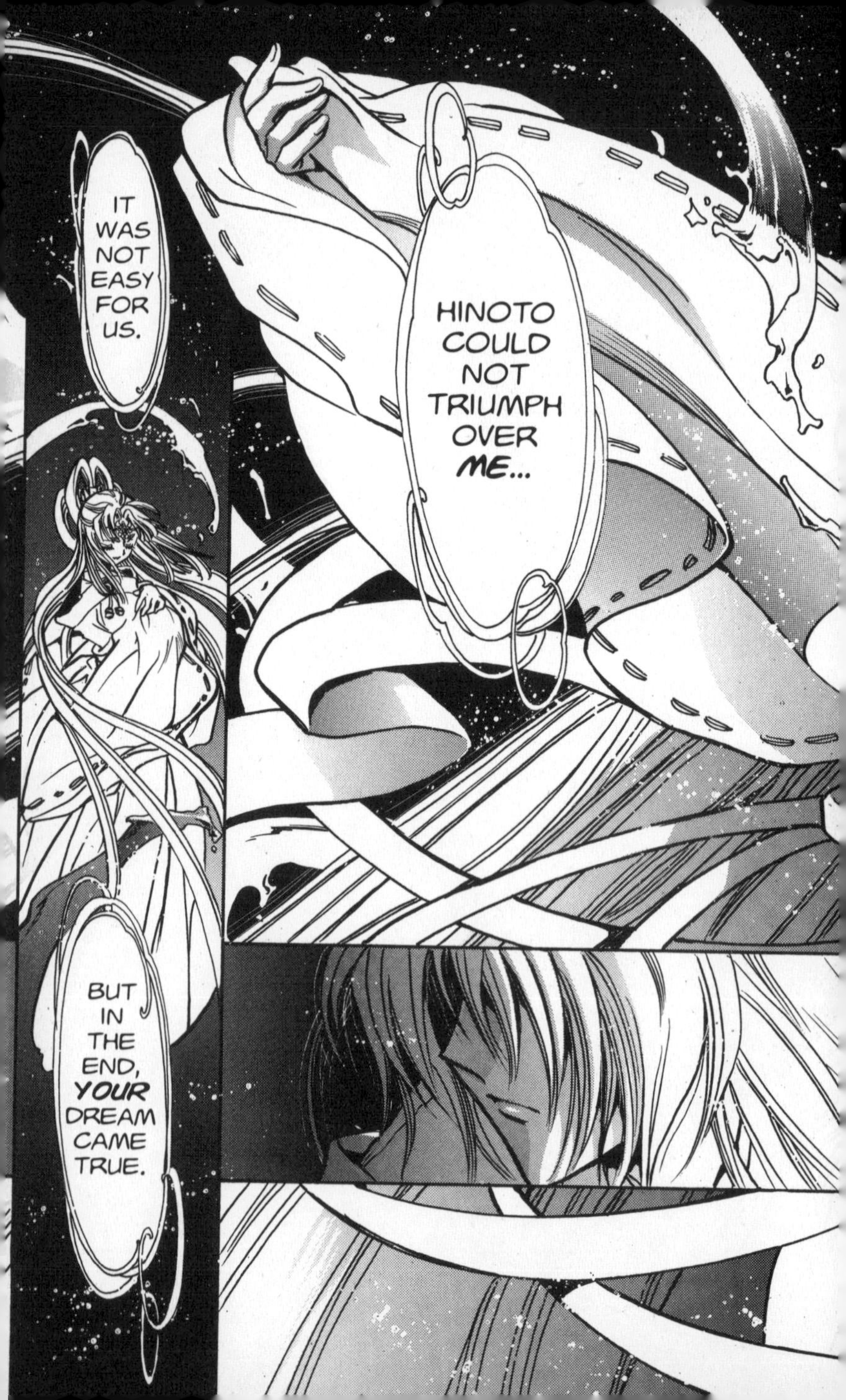
HINOTO COULD NOT TRIUMPH OVER *ME*...
IT WAS NOT EASY FOR US.
BUT IN THE END, ***YOUR*** DREAM CAME TRUE.

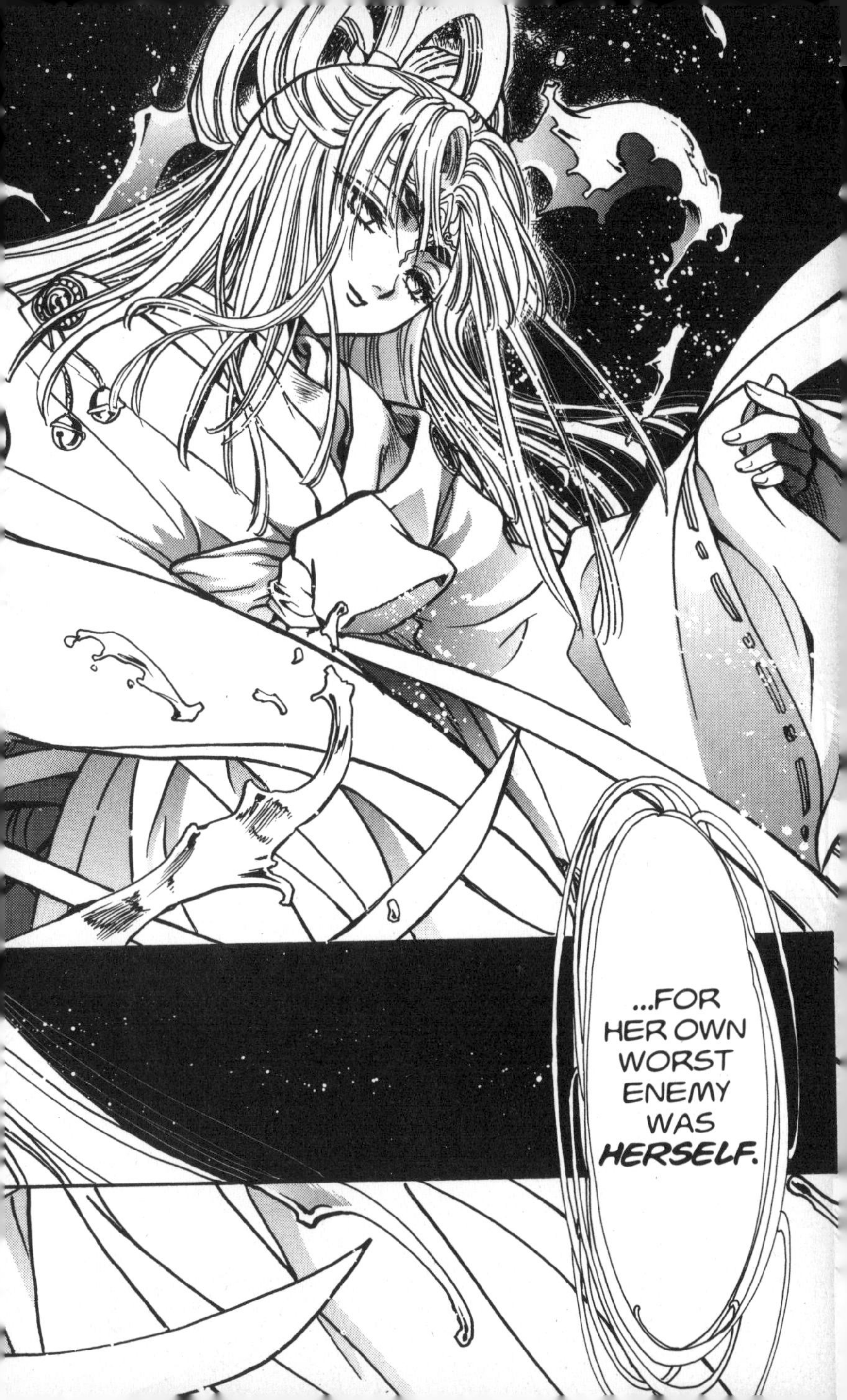
...FOR HER OWN WORST ENEMY WAS HERSELF.

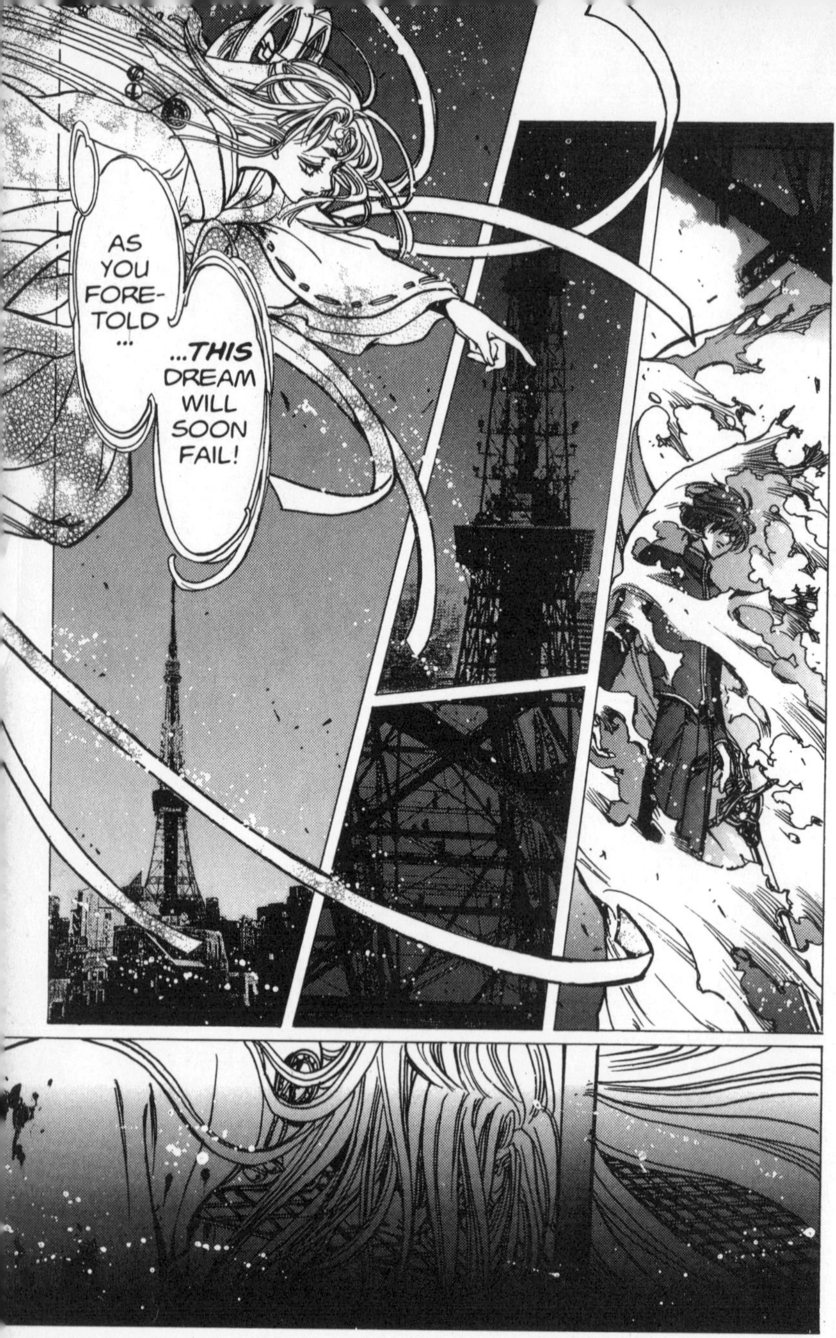
AS YOU FORE- TOLD ...
...THIS DREAM WILL SOON FAIL!

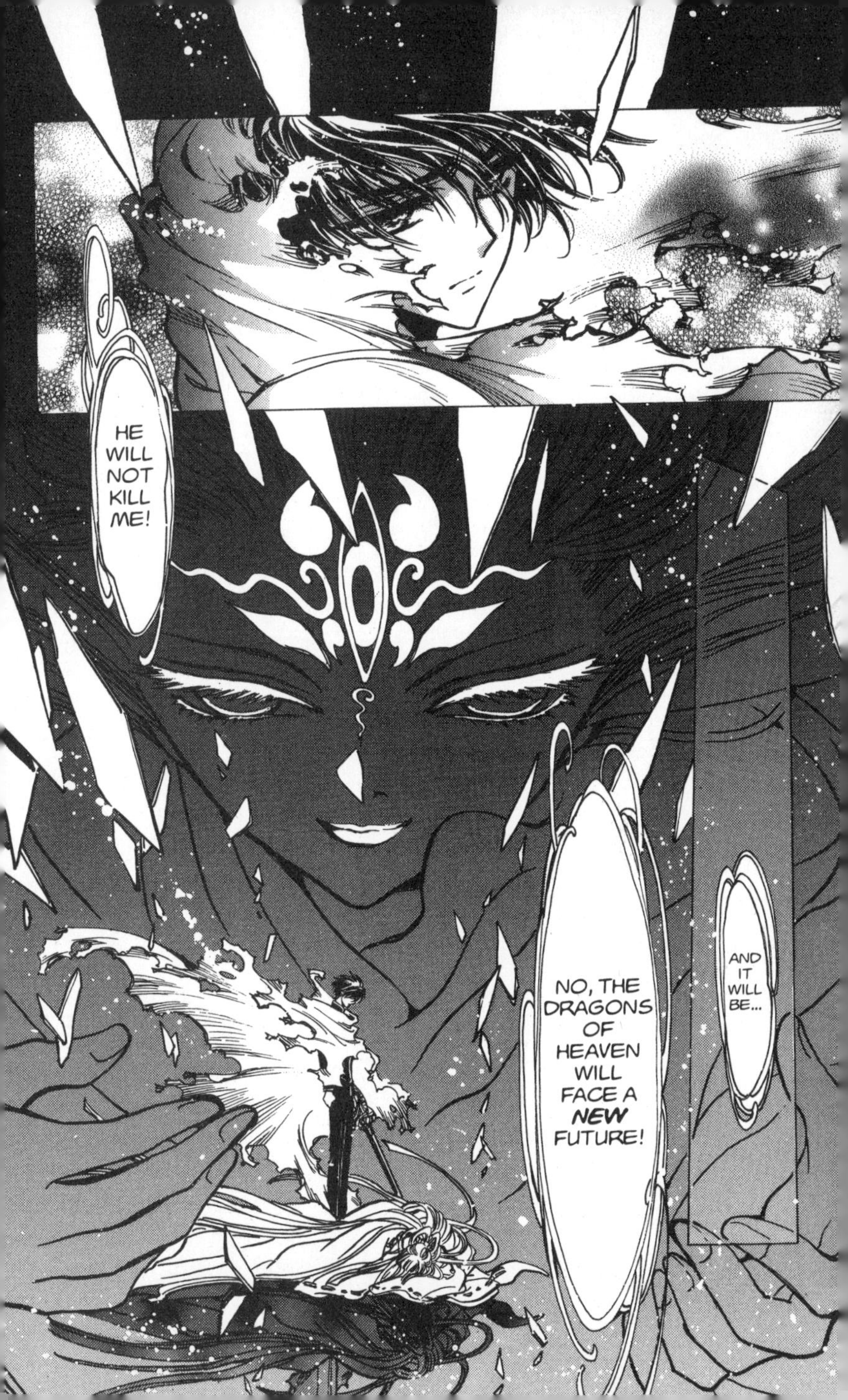
HE WILL NOT KILL ME!
NO, THE DRAGONS OF HEAVEN WILL FACE A **NEW** FUTURE!
AND IT WILL BE...

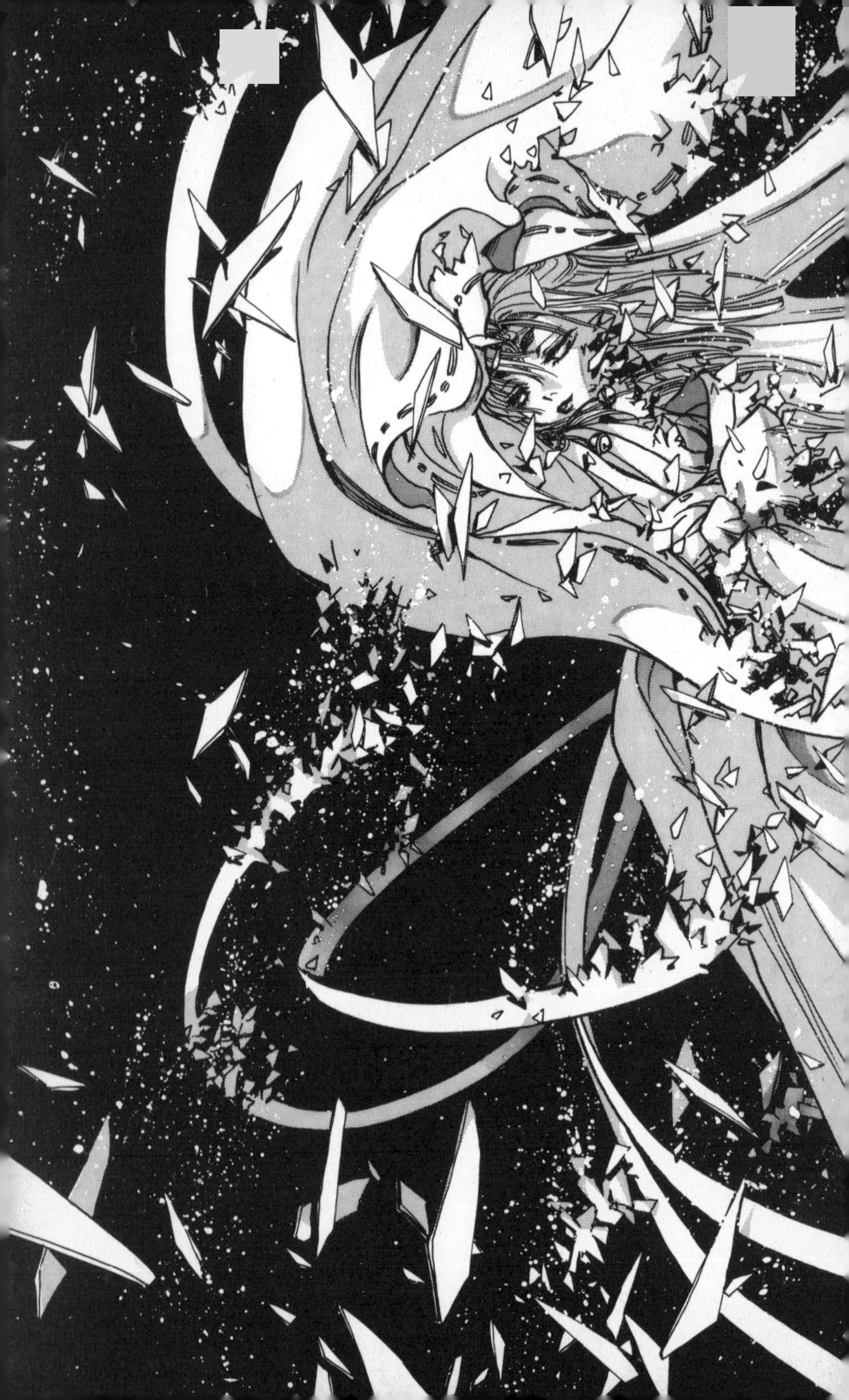

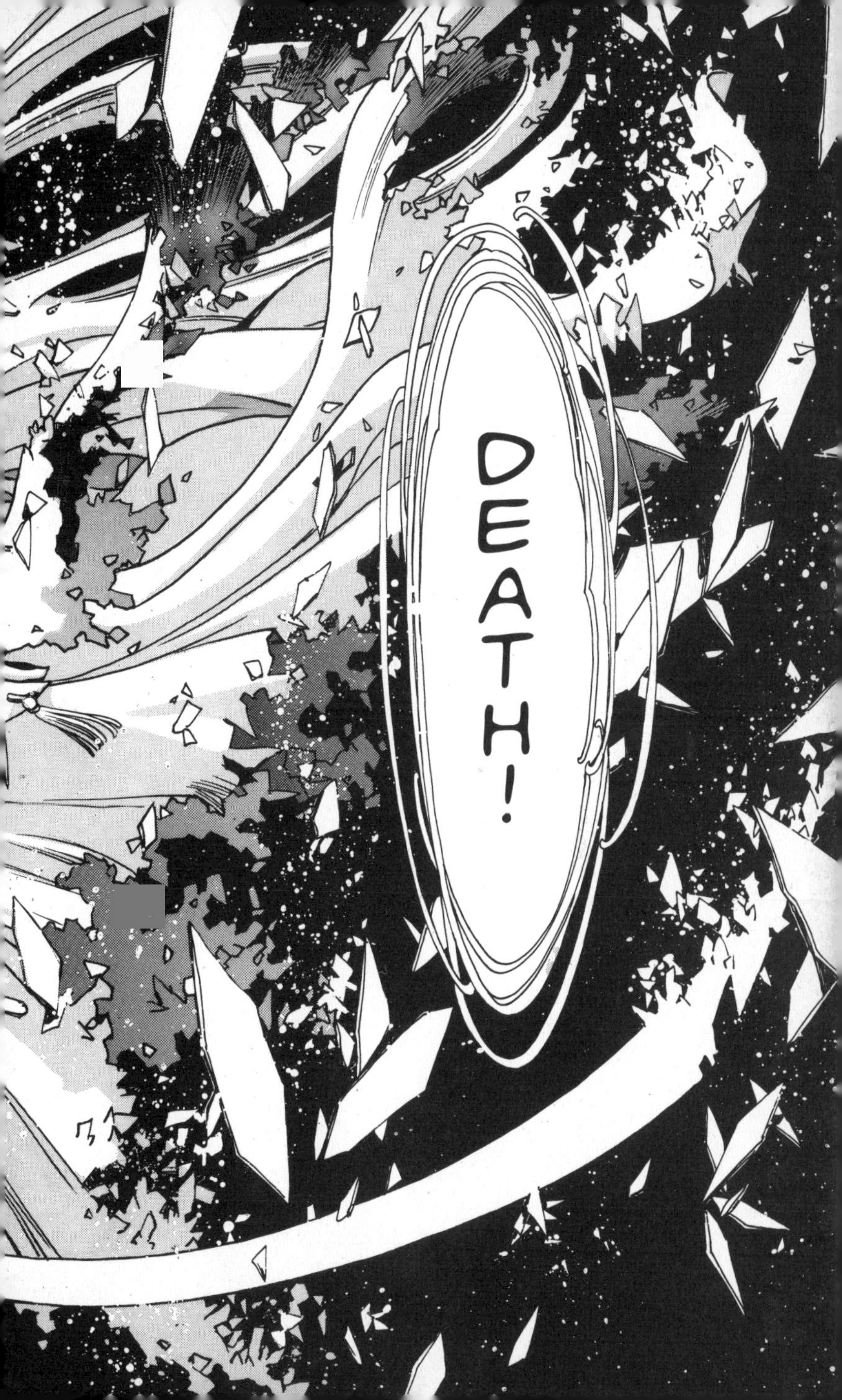
DEATH!

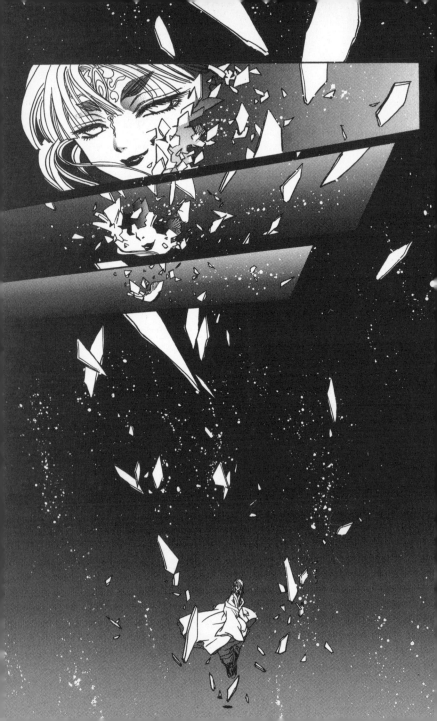

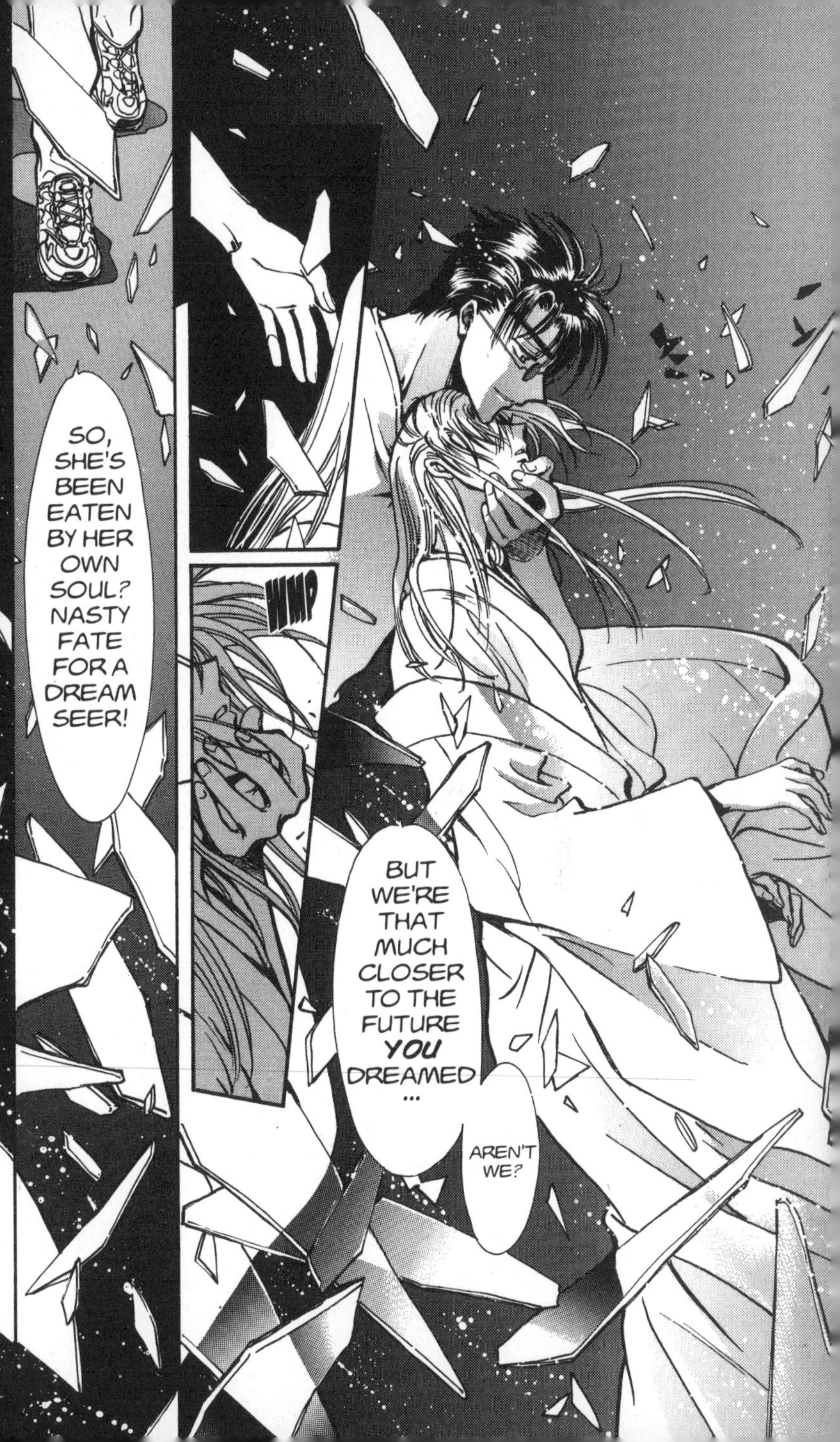
WMP
BUT WE'RE THAT MUCH CLOSER TO THE FUTURE *YOU* DREAMED...
AREN'T WE?
SO, SHE'S BEEN EATEN BY HER OWN SOUL? NASTY FATE FOR A DREAM SEER!

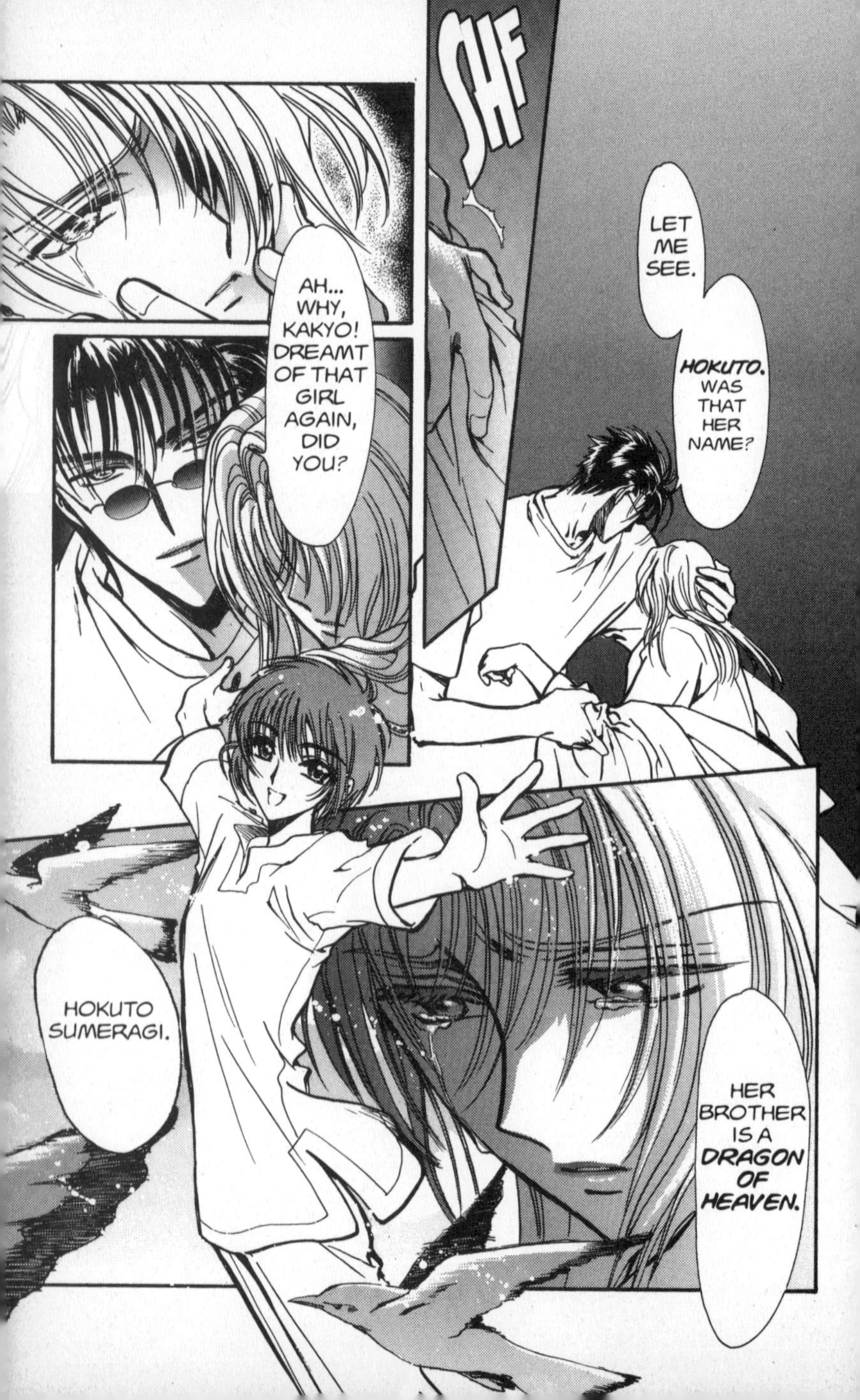
SHF
LET ME SEE.
HOKUTO. WAS THAT HER NAME?
AH... WHY, KAKYO! DREAMT OF THAT GIRL AGAIN, DID YOU?
HOKUTO SUMERAGI.
HER BROTHER IS A DRAGON OF HEAVEN.

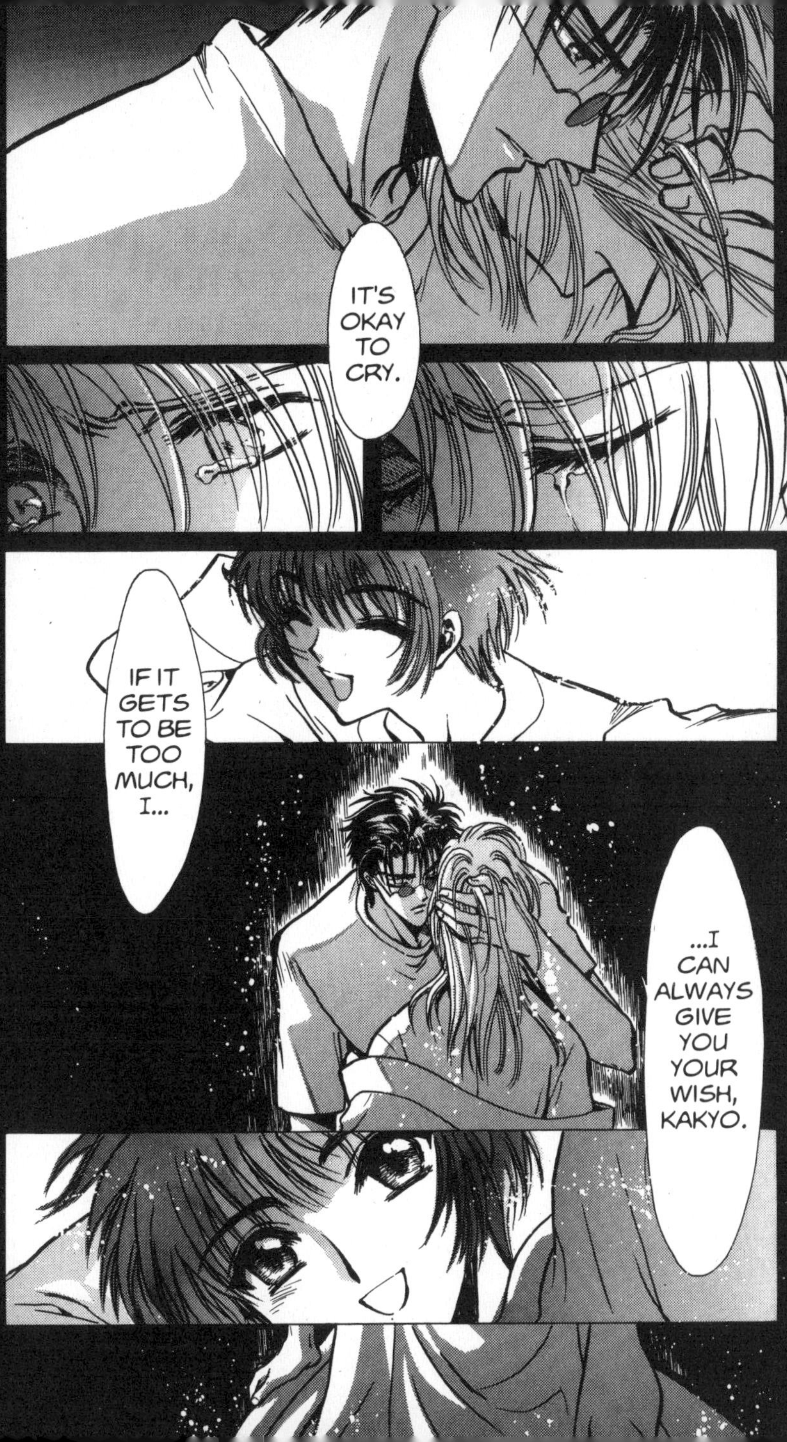
IT'S OKAY TO CRY.
IF IT GETS TO BE TOO MUCH, I...
...I CAN ALWAYS GIVE YOU YOUR WISH, KAKYO.

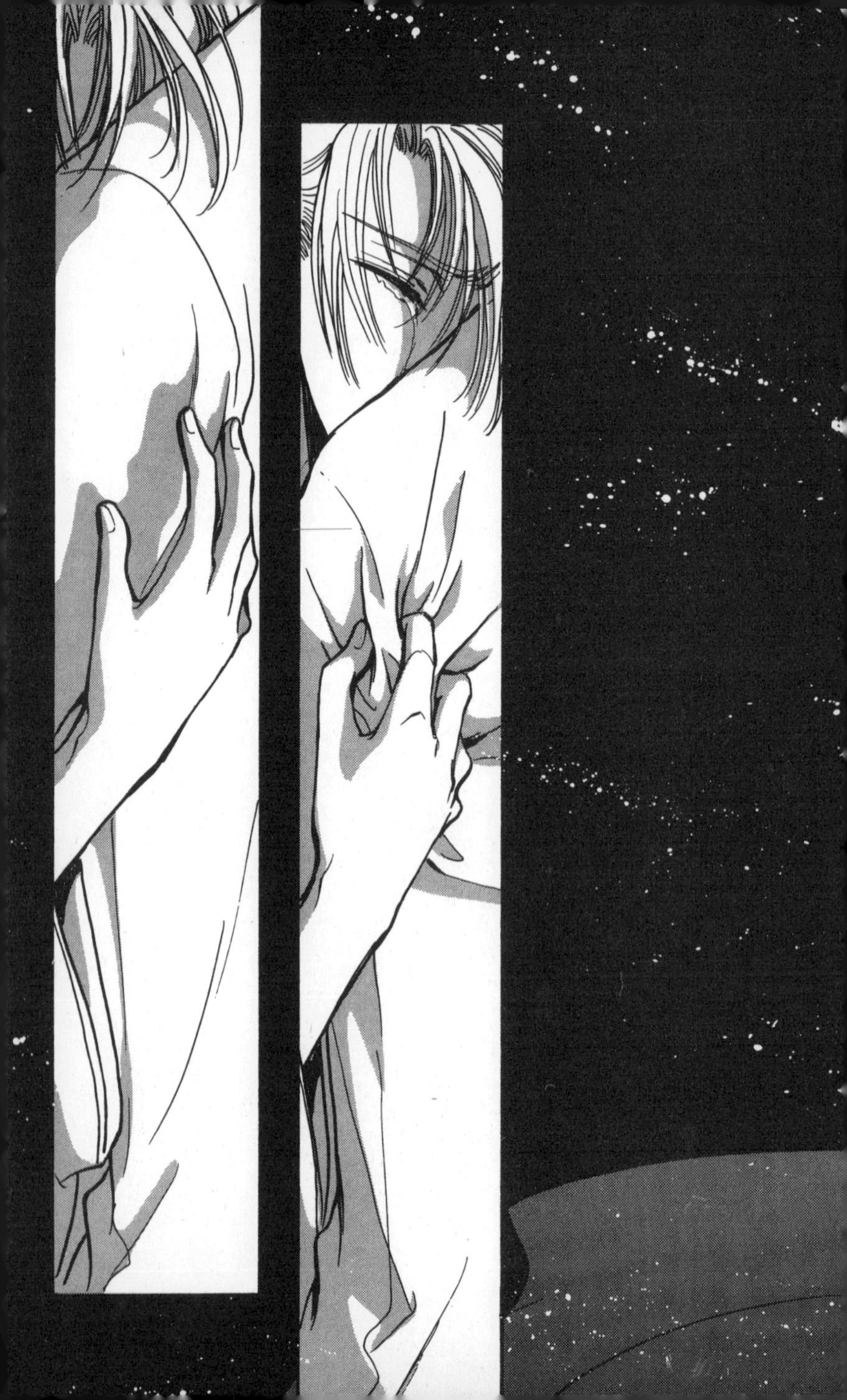

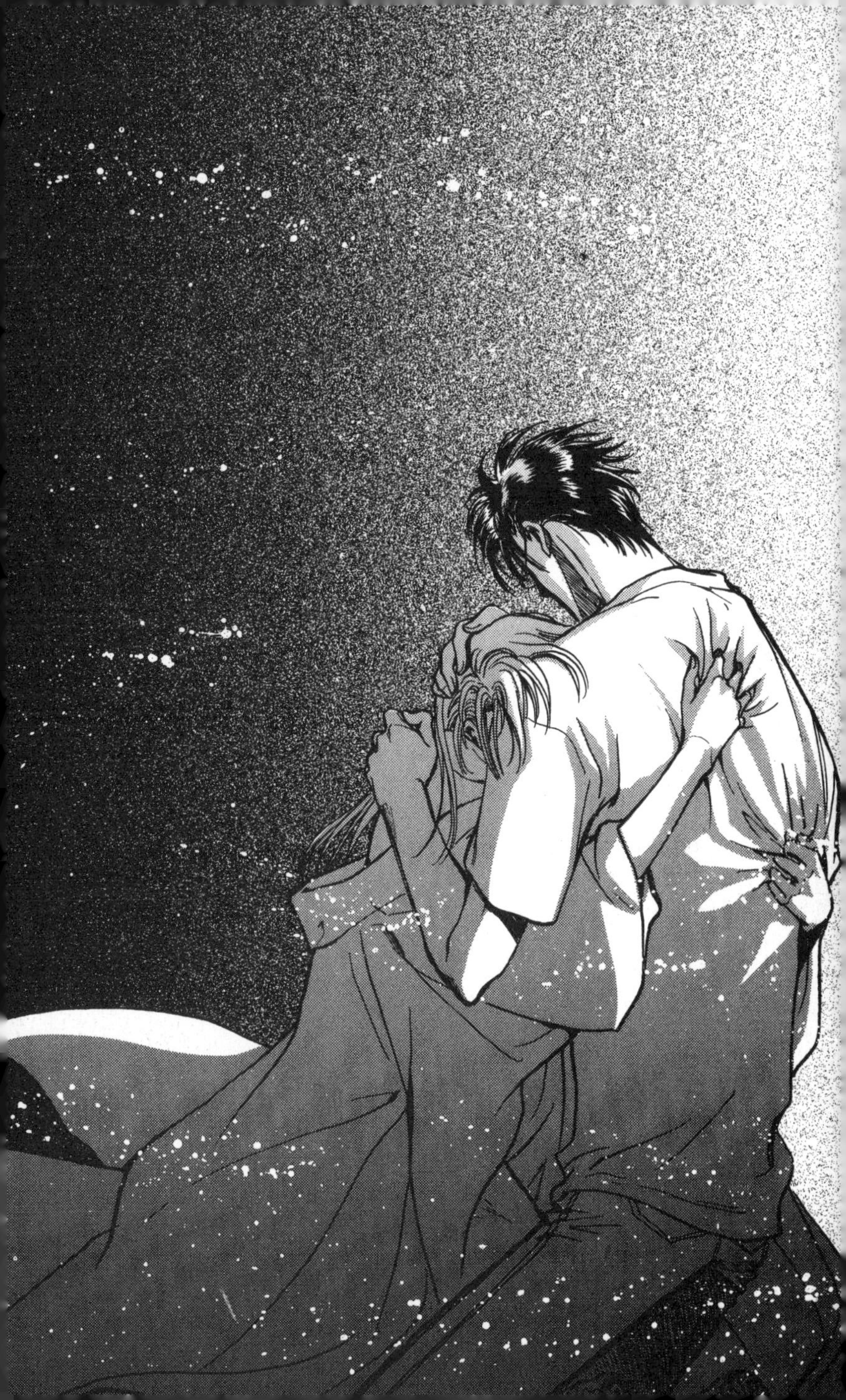

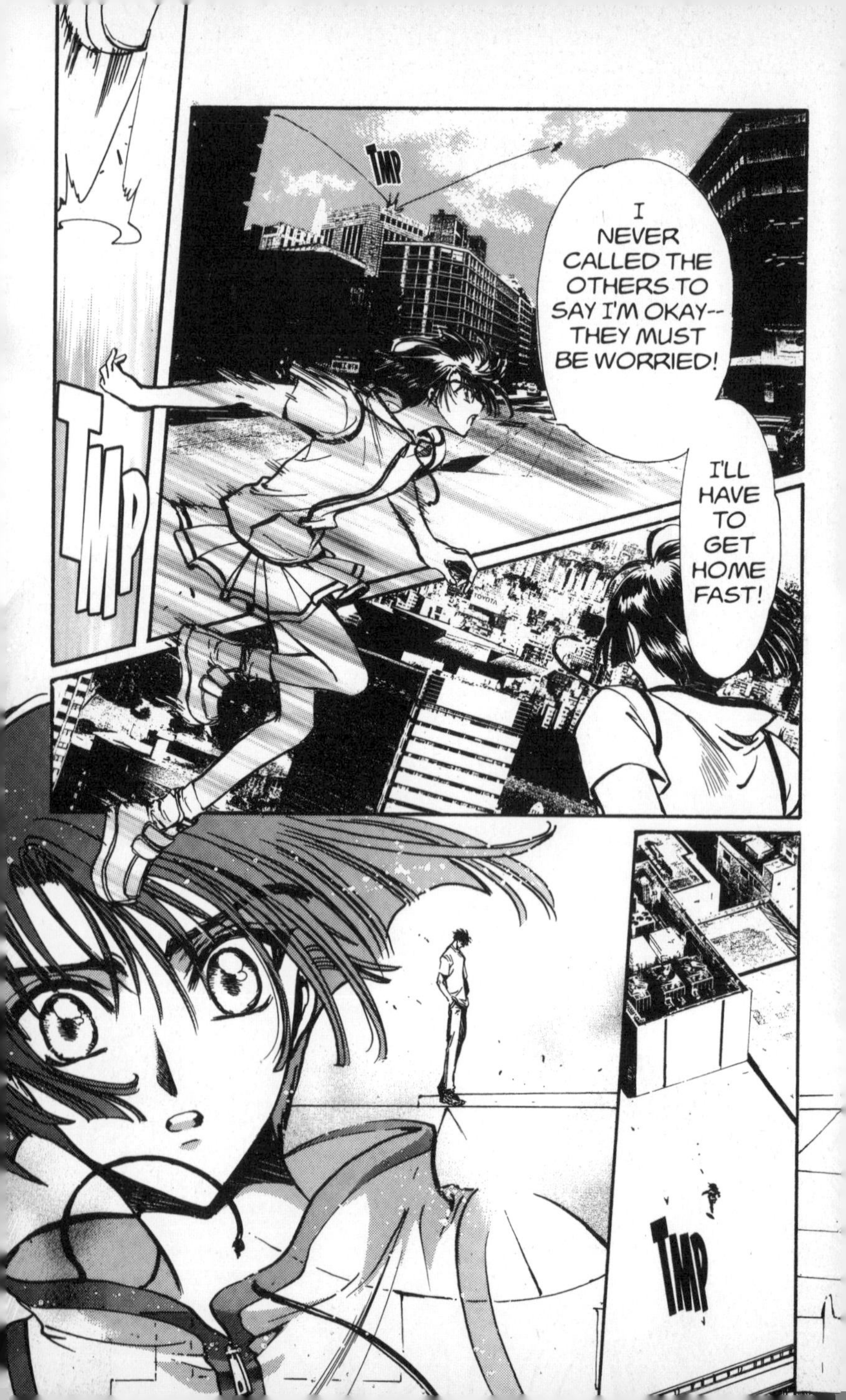
TMP
I NEVER CALLED THE OTHERS TO SAY I'M OKAY-- THEY MUST BE WORRIED!
I'LL HAVE TO GET HOME FAST!
TMP
TMP

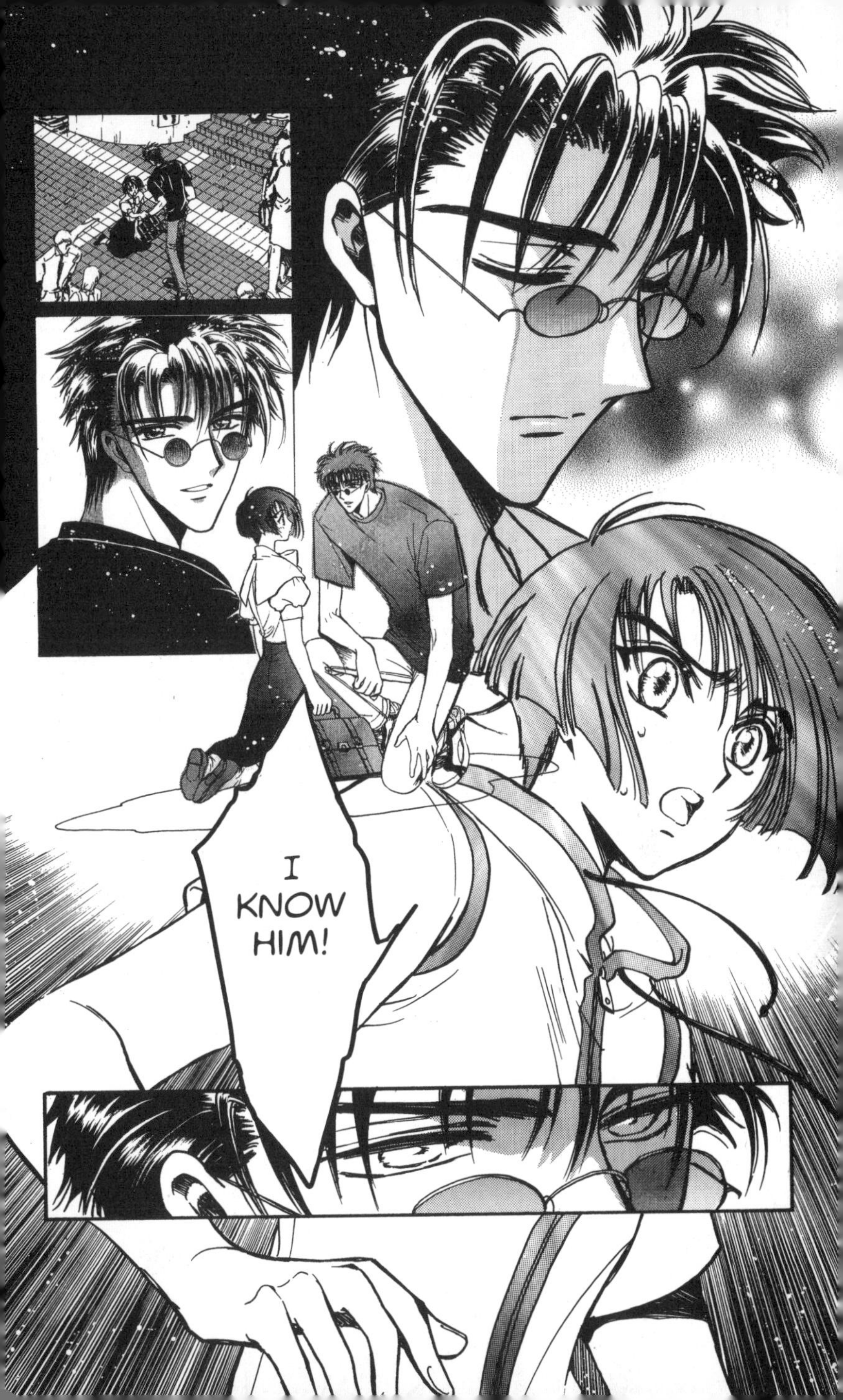
I KNOW HIM!

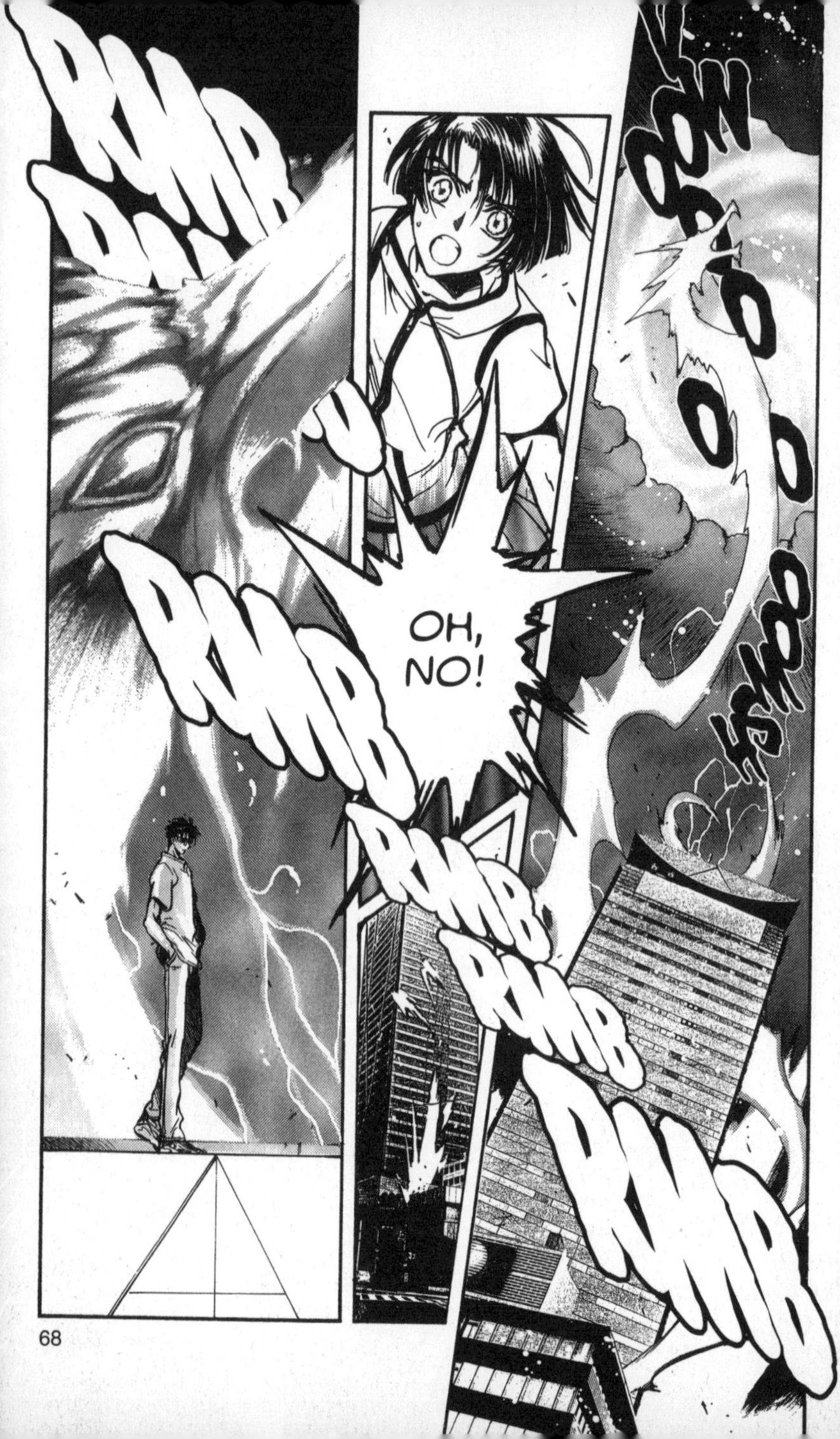
OH, NO!

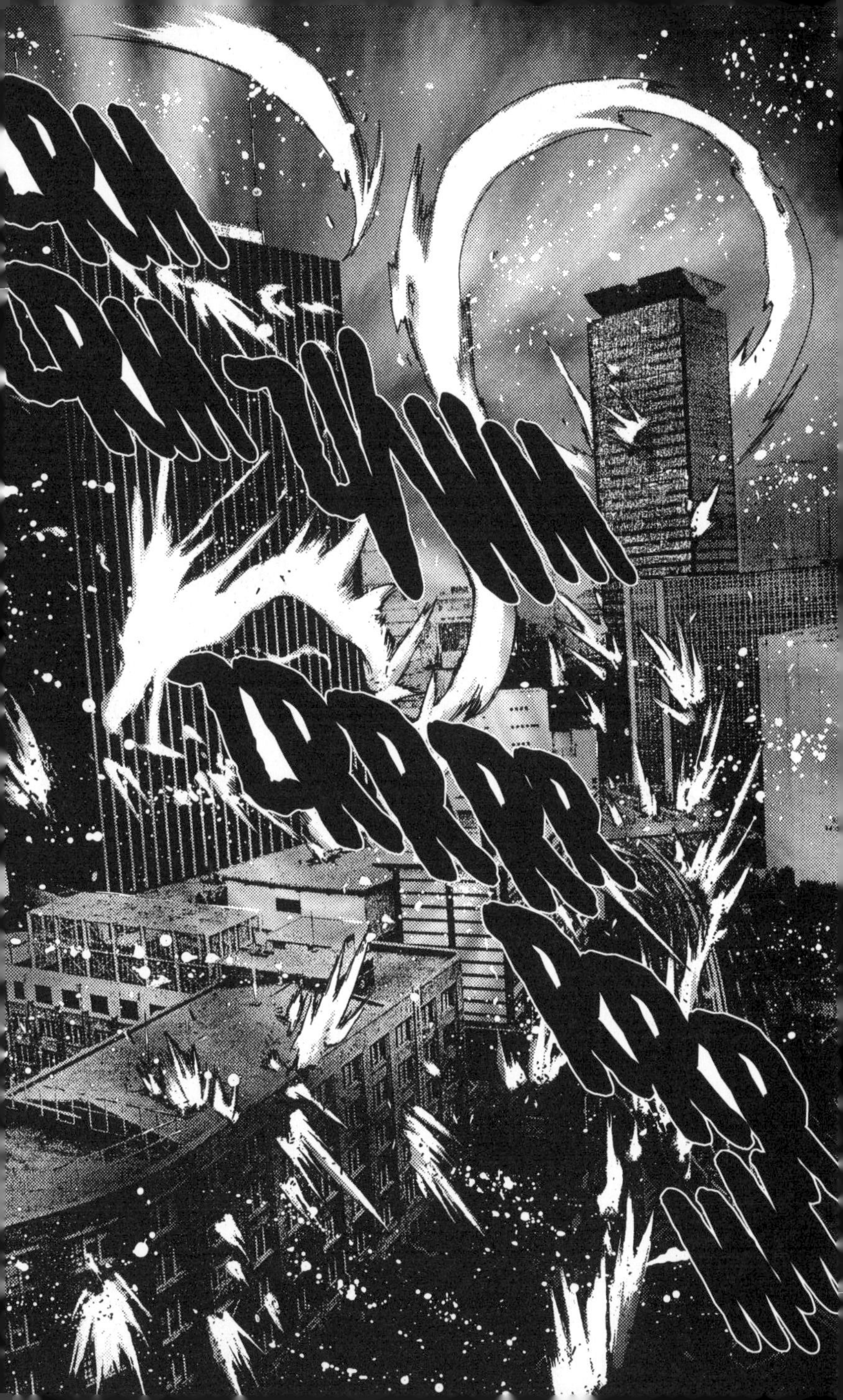

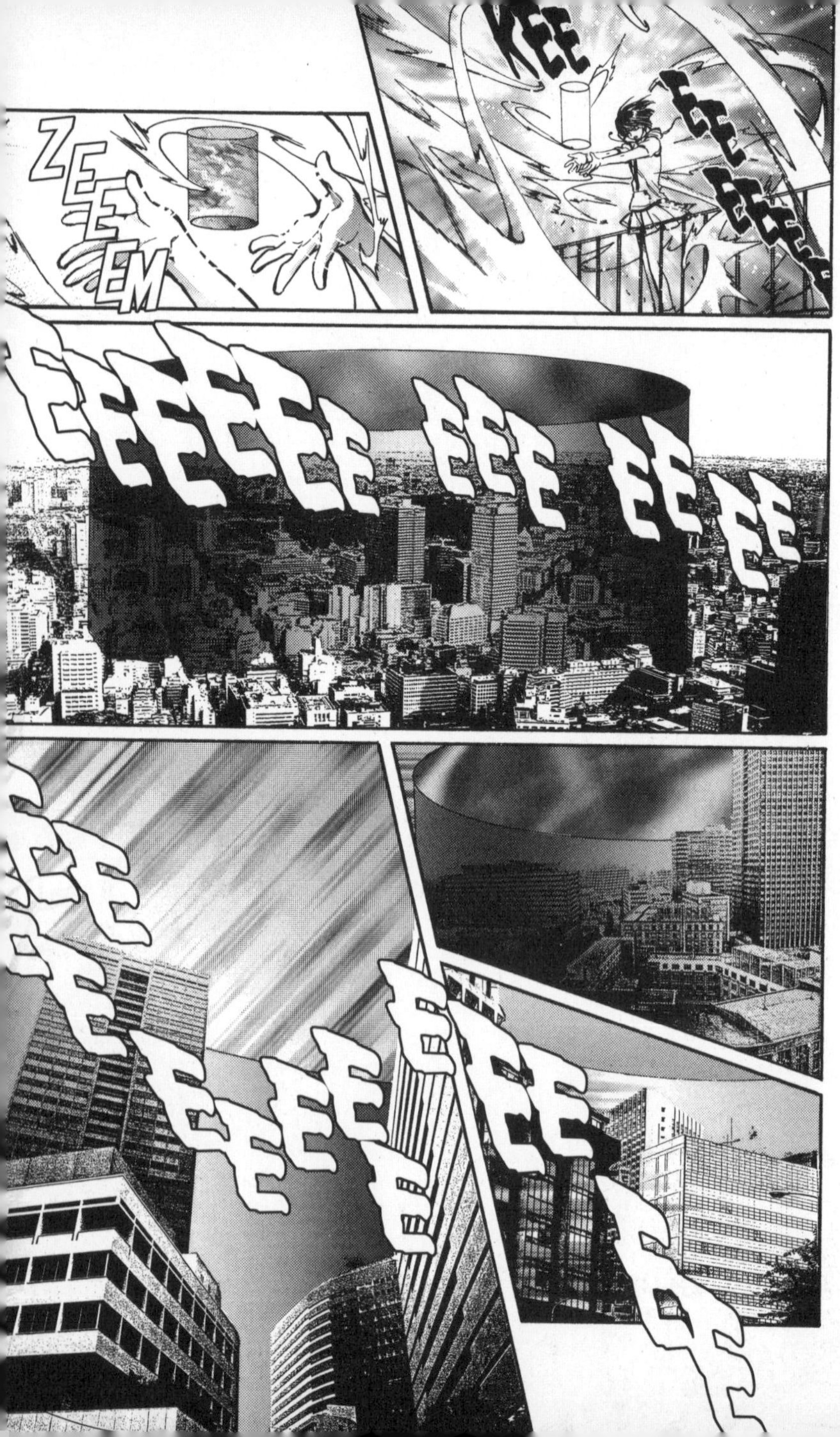
KEE
EEE
EEEE...
ZEEEEM
EEEEEE EEE EE EE

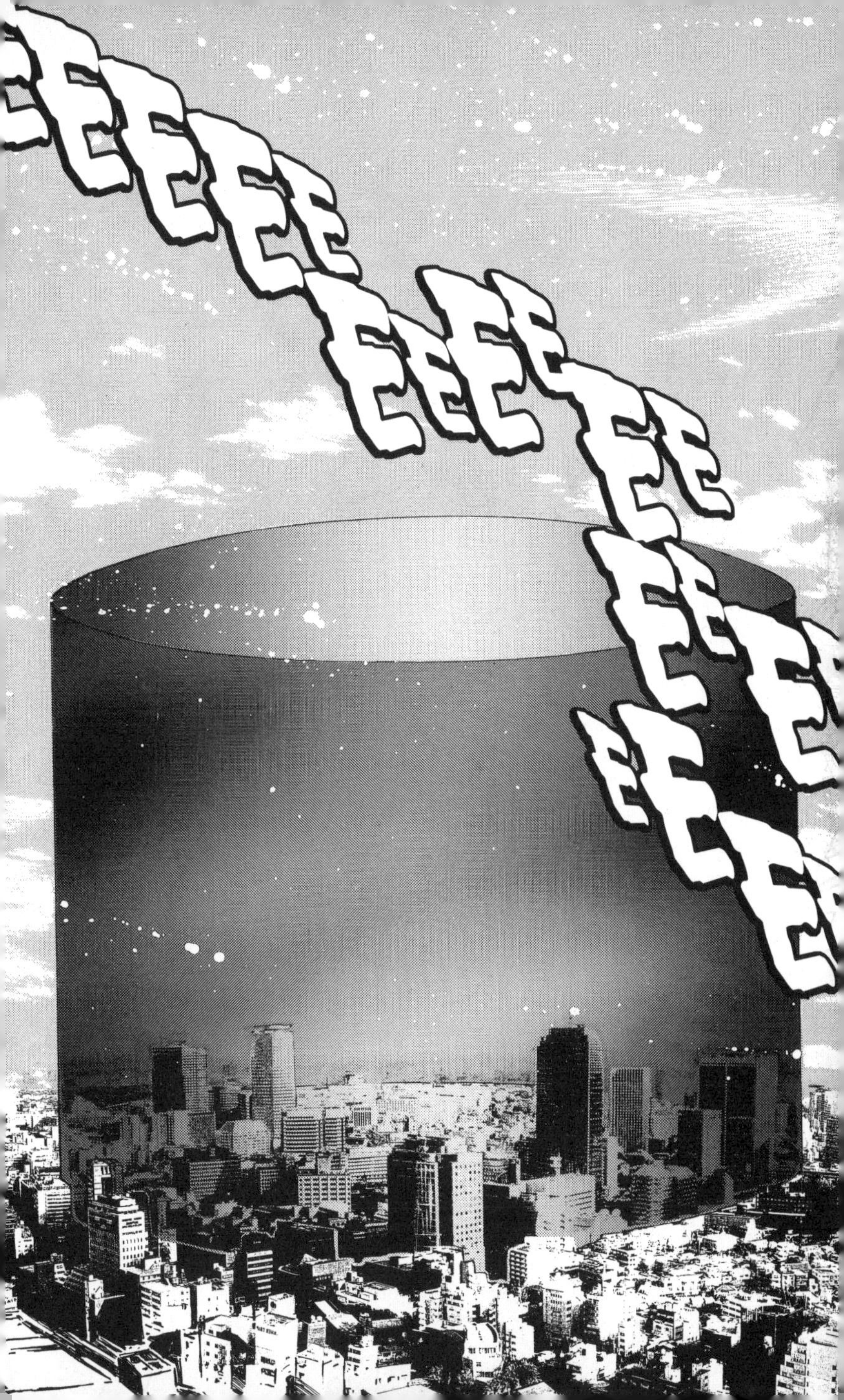
EEEEEEEEEEEEEEEEEEEEEEEE

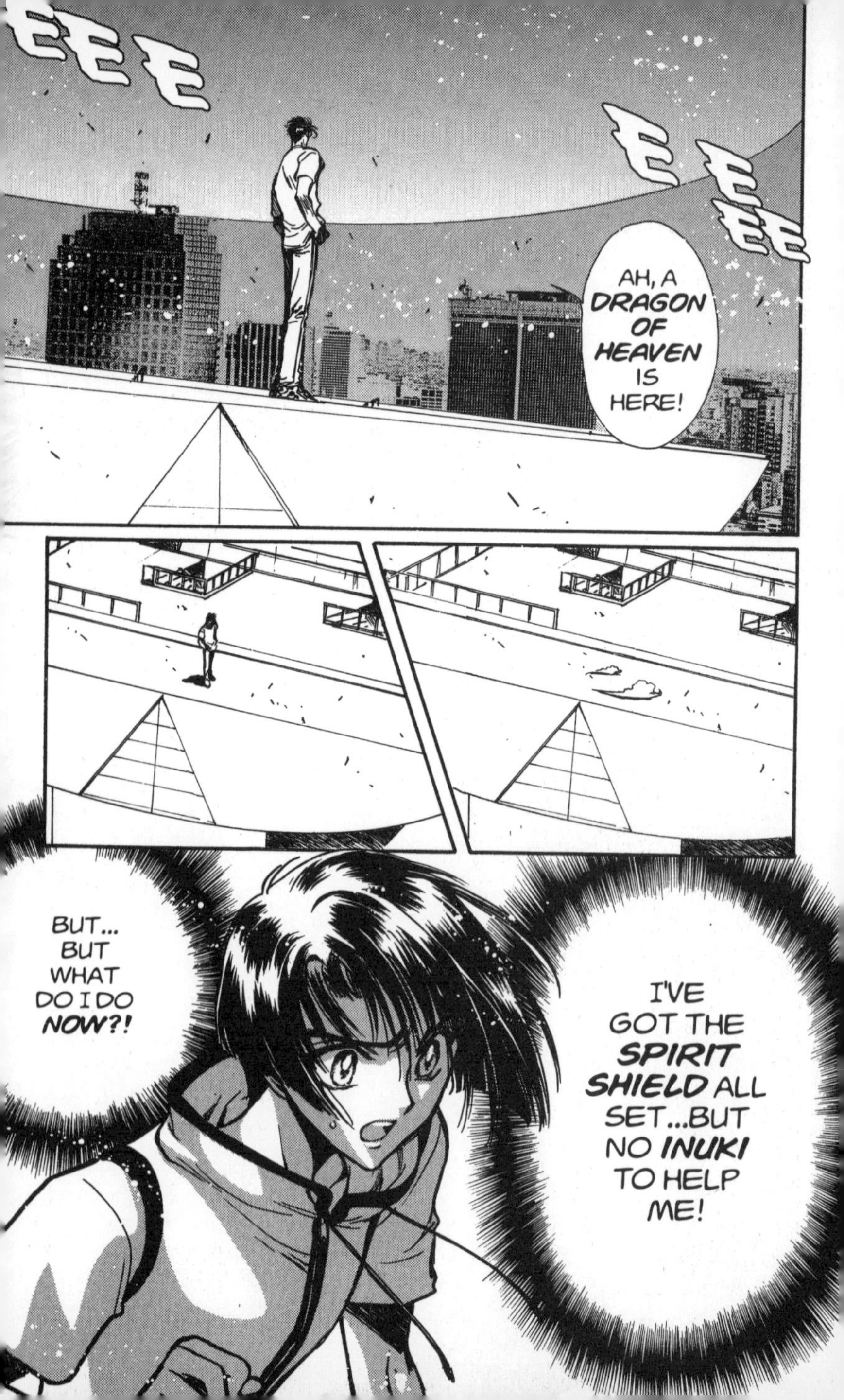

EEEEE
AH, A DRAGON OF HEAVEN IS HERE!
EEEE
I'VE GOT THE SPIRIT SHIELD ALL SET...BUT NO INUKI TO HELP ME!
BUT... BUT WHAT DO I DO NOW?!

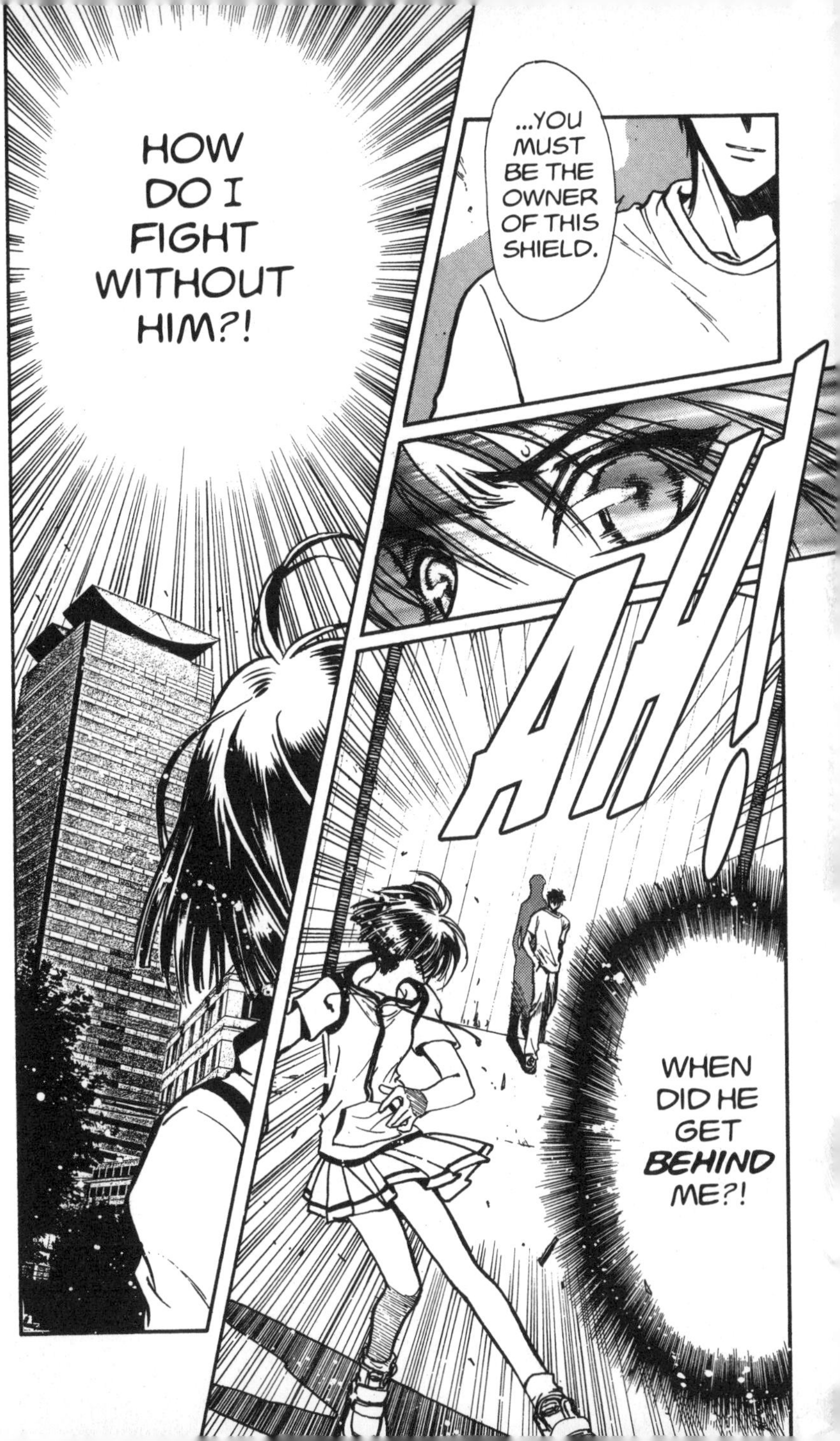
...YOU MUST BE THE OWNER OF THIS SHIELD.
AH!
WHEN DID HE GET **BEHIND** ME?!
HOW DO I FIGHT WITHOUT HIM?!

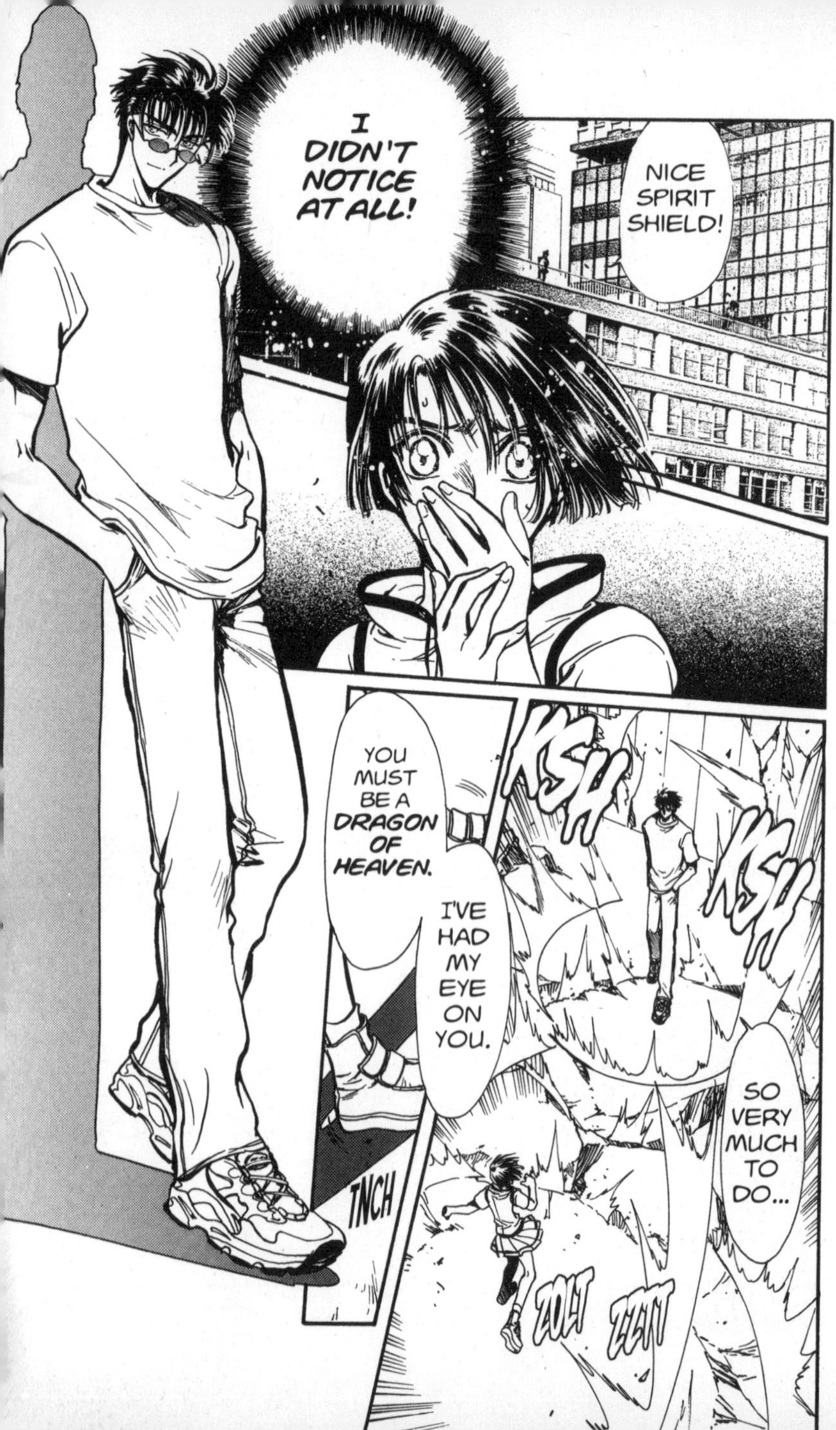
NICE SPIRIT SHIELD!
I DIDN'T NOTICE AT ALL!
KSH
KSH
SO VERY MUCH TO DO...
ZZTT
ZOLT
YOU MUST BE A DRAGON OF HEAVEN.
I'VE HAD MY EYE ON YOU.
TNCH

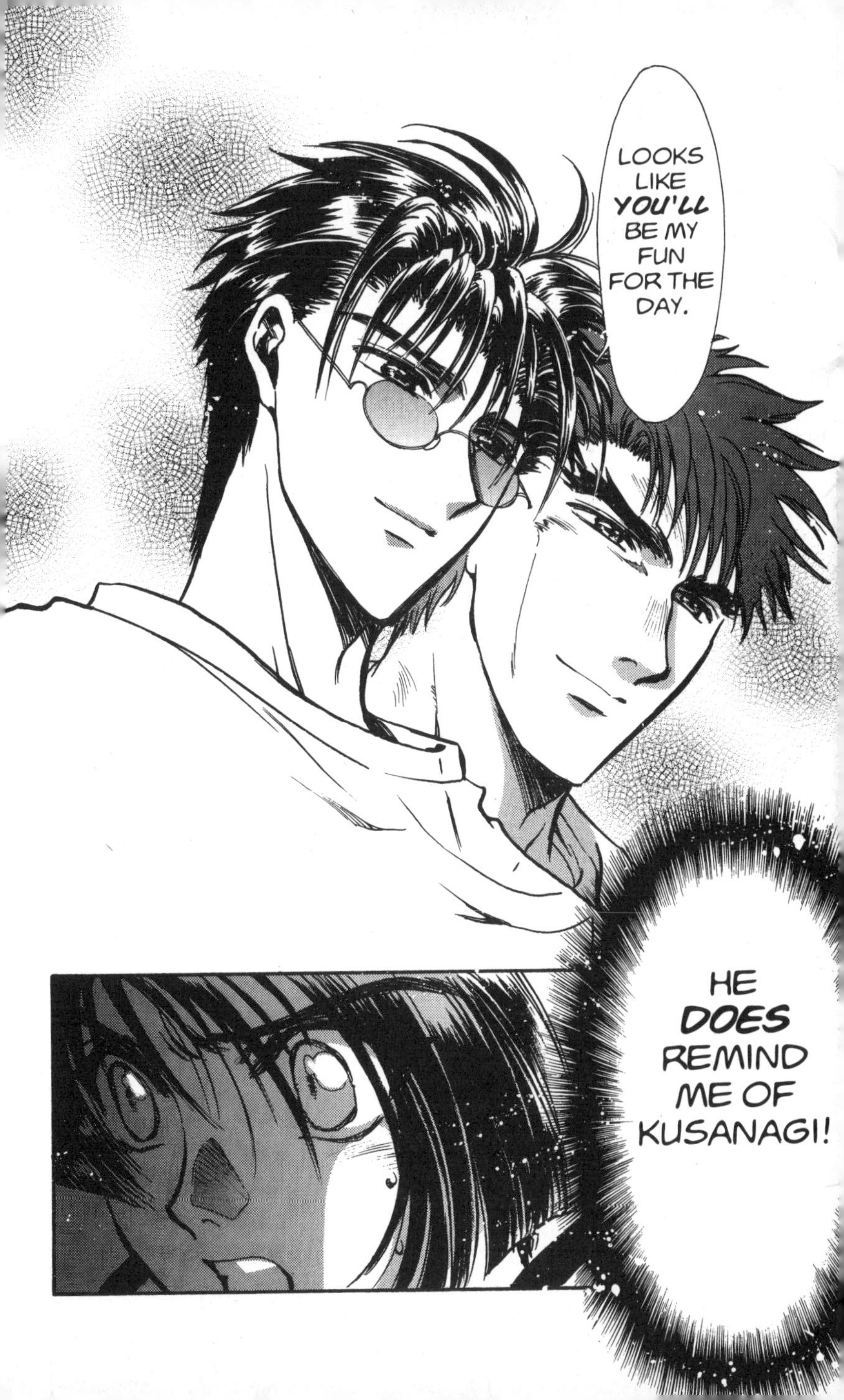
LOOKS LIKE ***YOU'LL*** BE MY FUN FOR THE DAY.
HE ***DOES*** REMIND ME OF KUSANAGI!

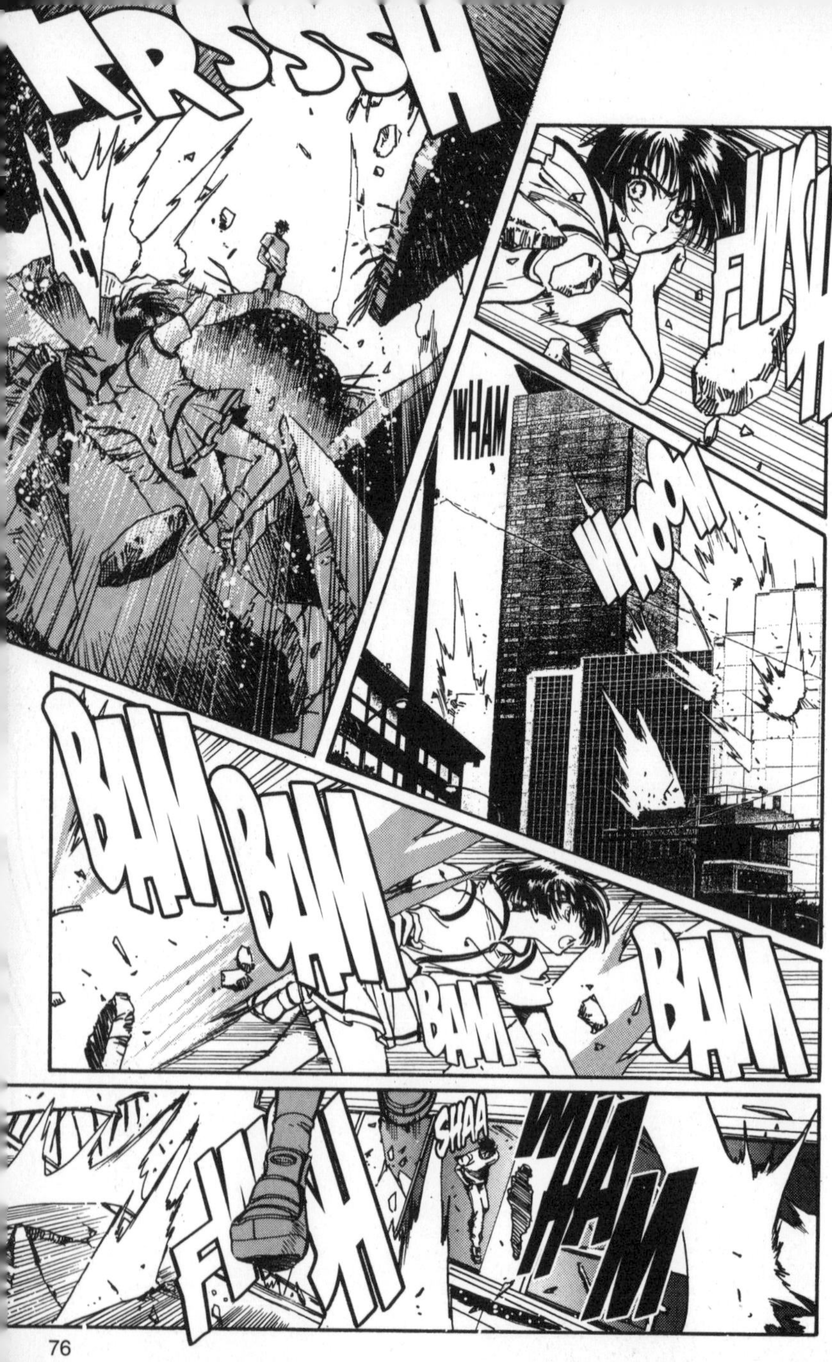
FWISH
WHAM
WHOOM
KRSSSH
BAM
BAM
BAM
BAM
SHAA

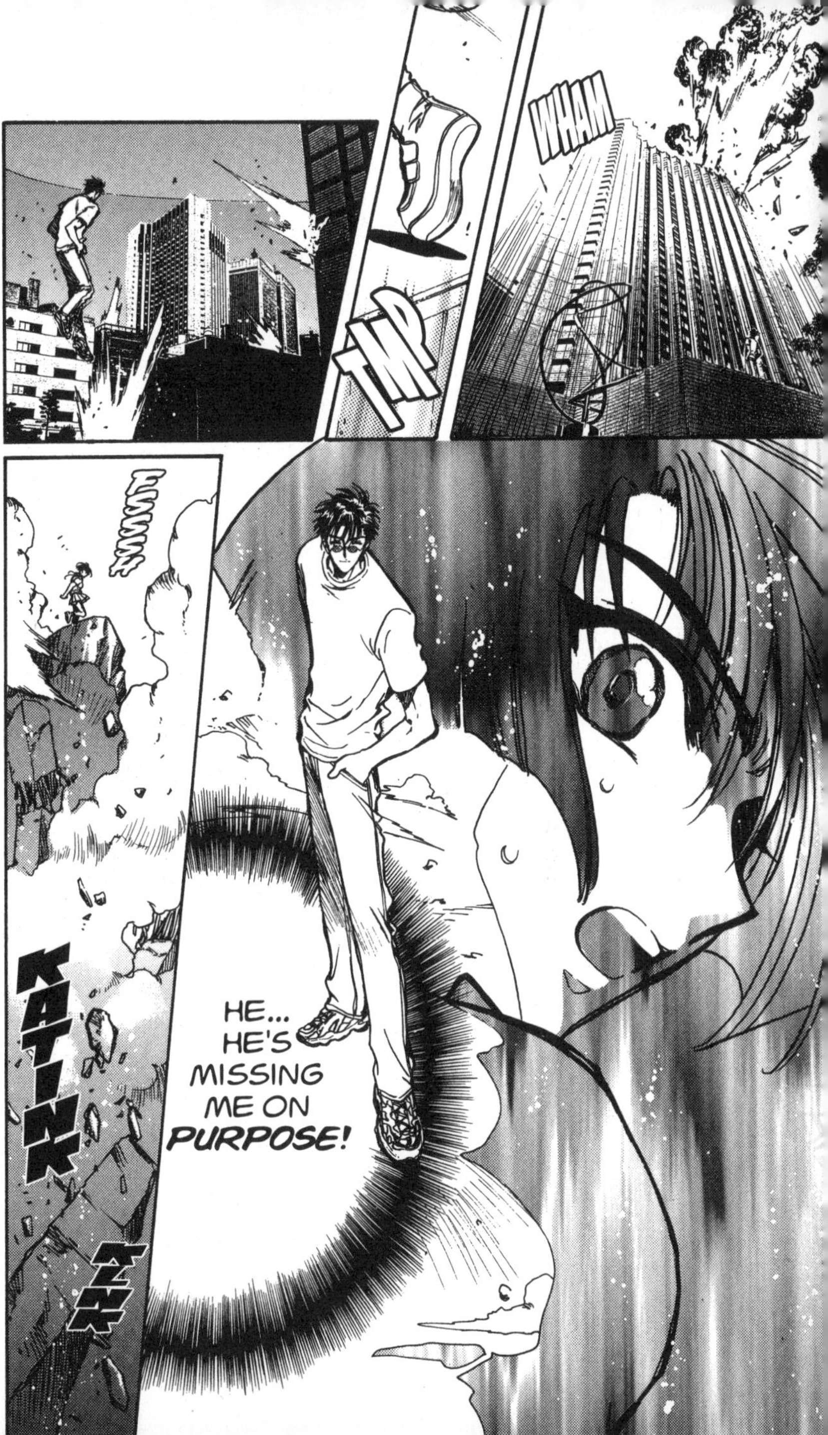
WHAM
TMP
HE... HE'S MISSING ME ON *PURPOSE!*
KATINK
KZNK

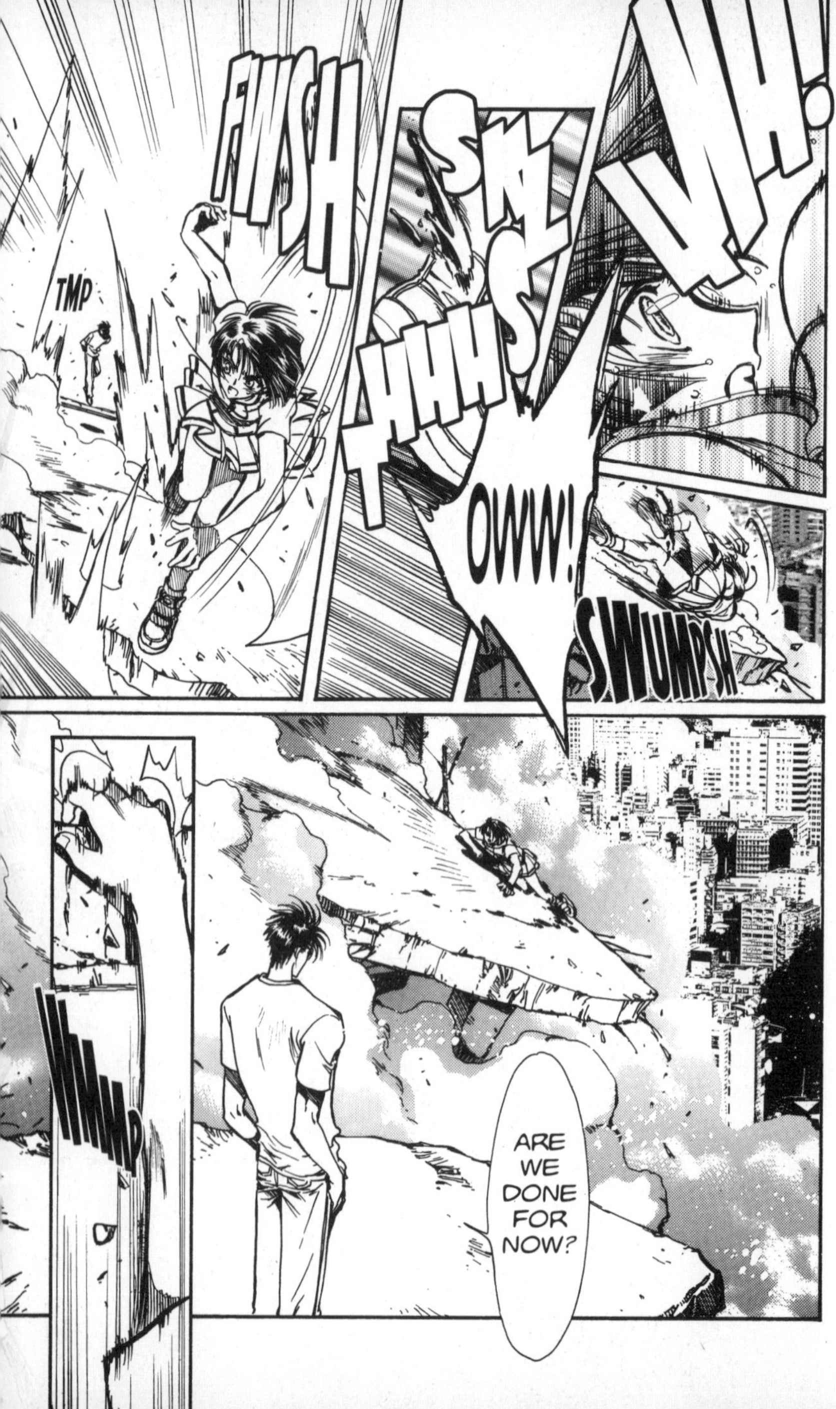
SWUMPSH
OWW!
FWSH
TMP
ARE WE DONE FOR NOW?

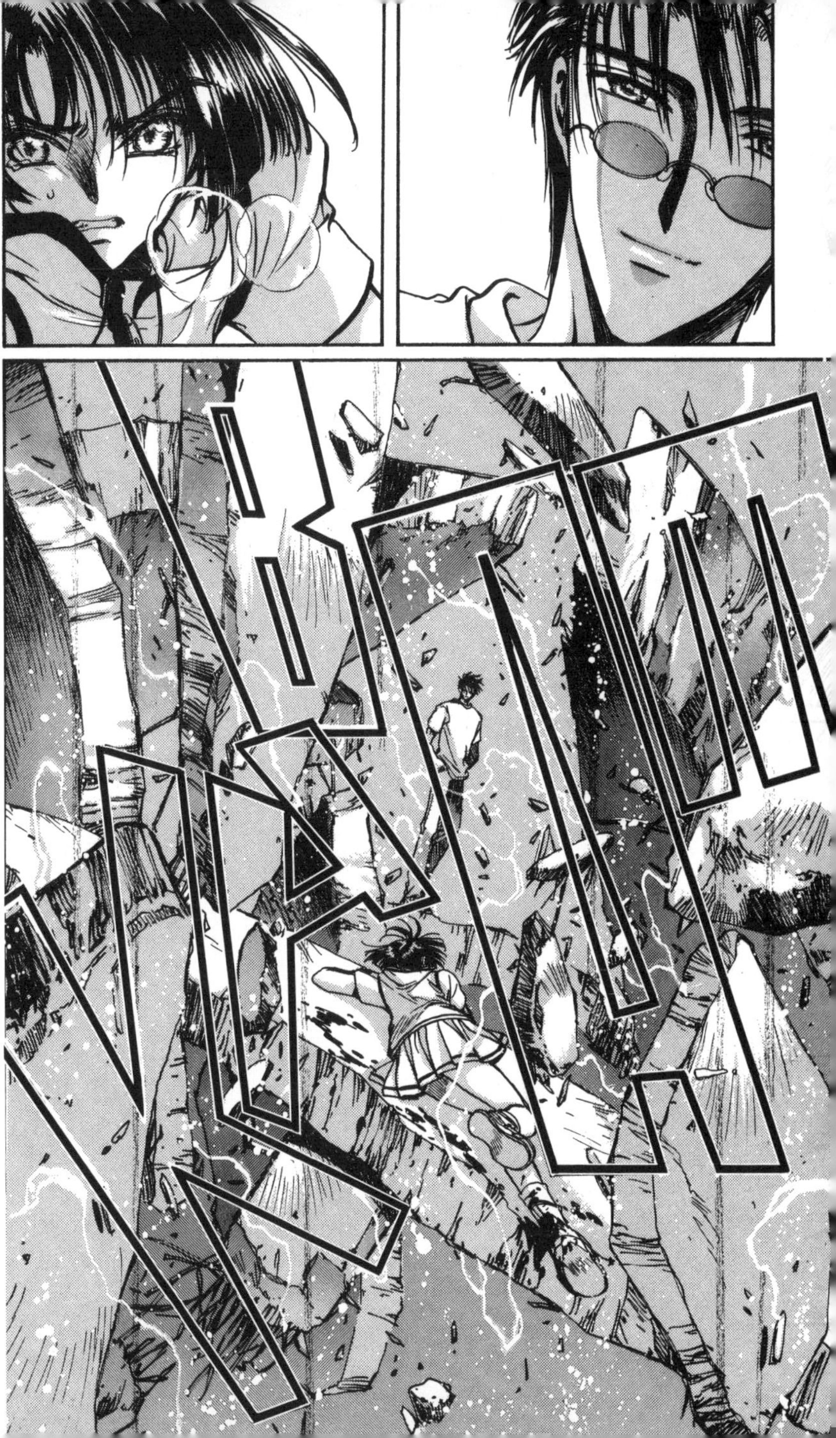

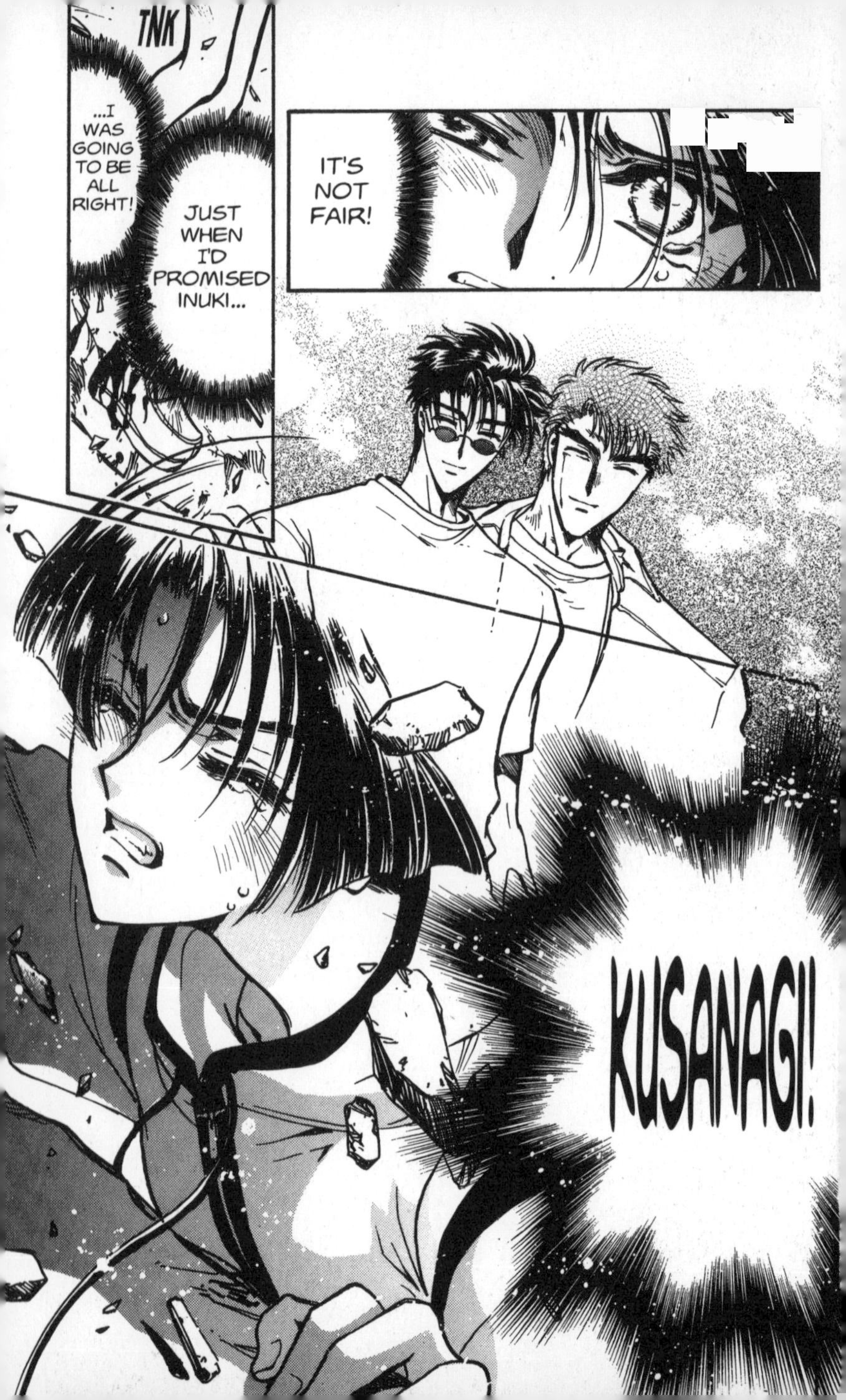
IT'S NOT FAIR!
TNK
JUST WHEN I'D PROMISED INUKI...
...I WAS GOING TO BE ALL RIGHT!
KUSANAGI!

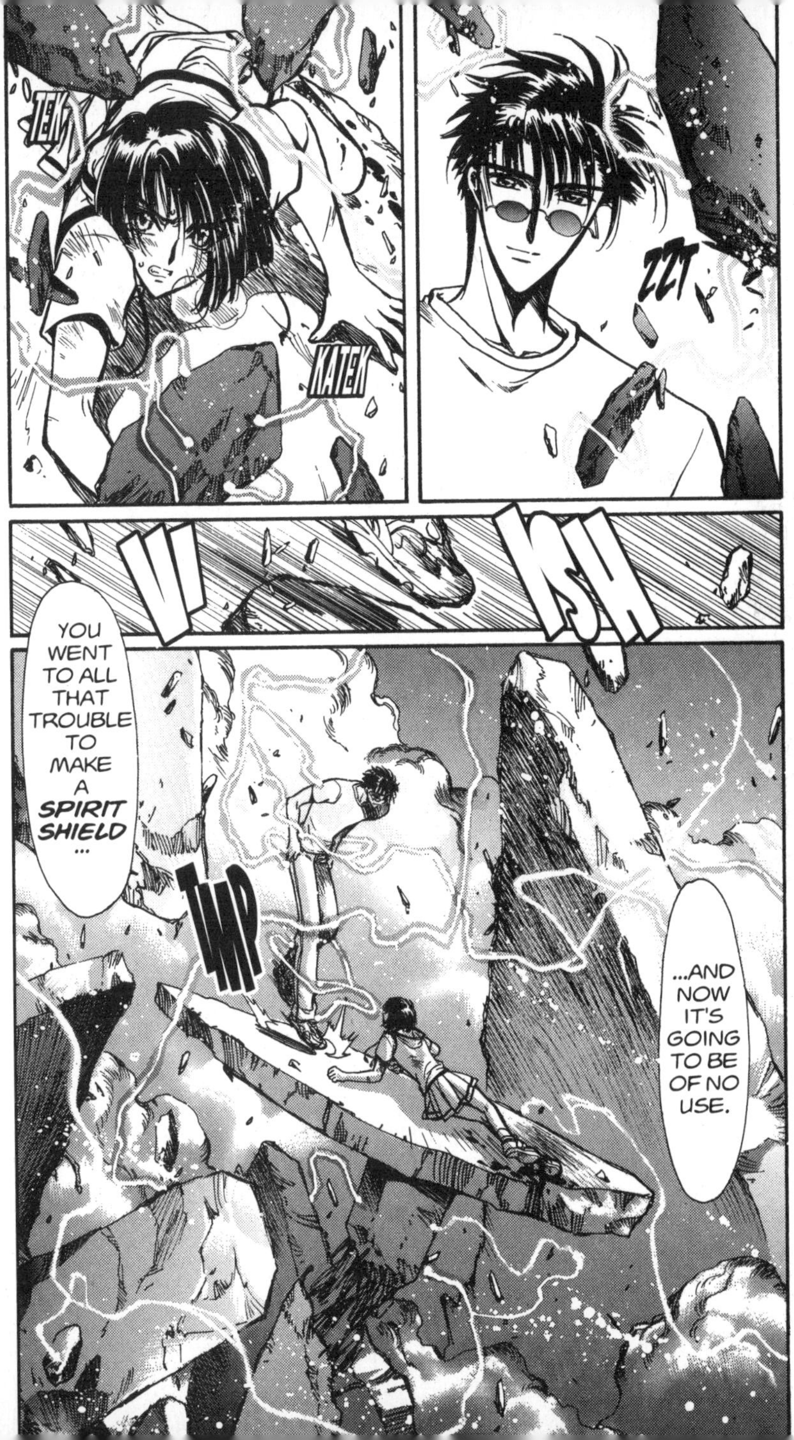
ZZT
TEK
KATEK
VSH
VI
YOU WENT TO ALL THAT TROUBLE TO MAKE A SPIRIT SHIELD...
...AND NOW IT'S GOING TO BE OF NO USE.
TMP

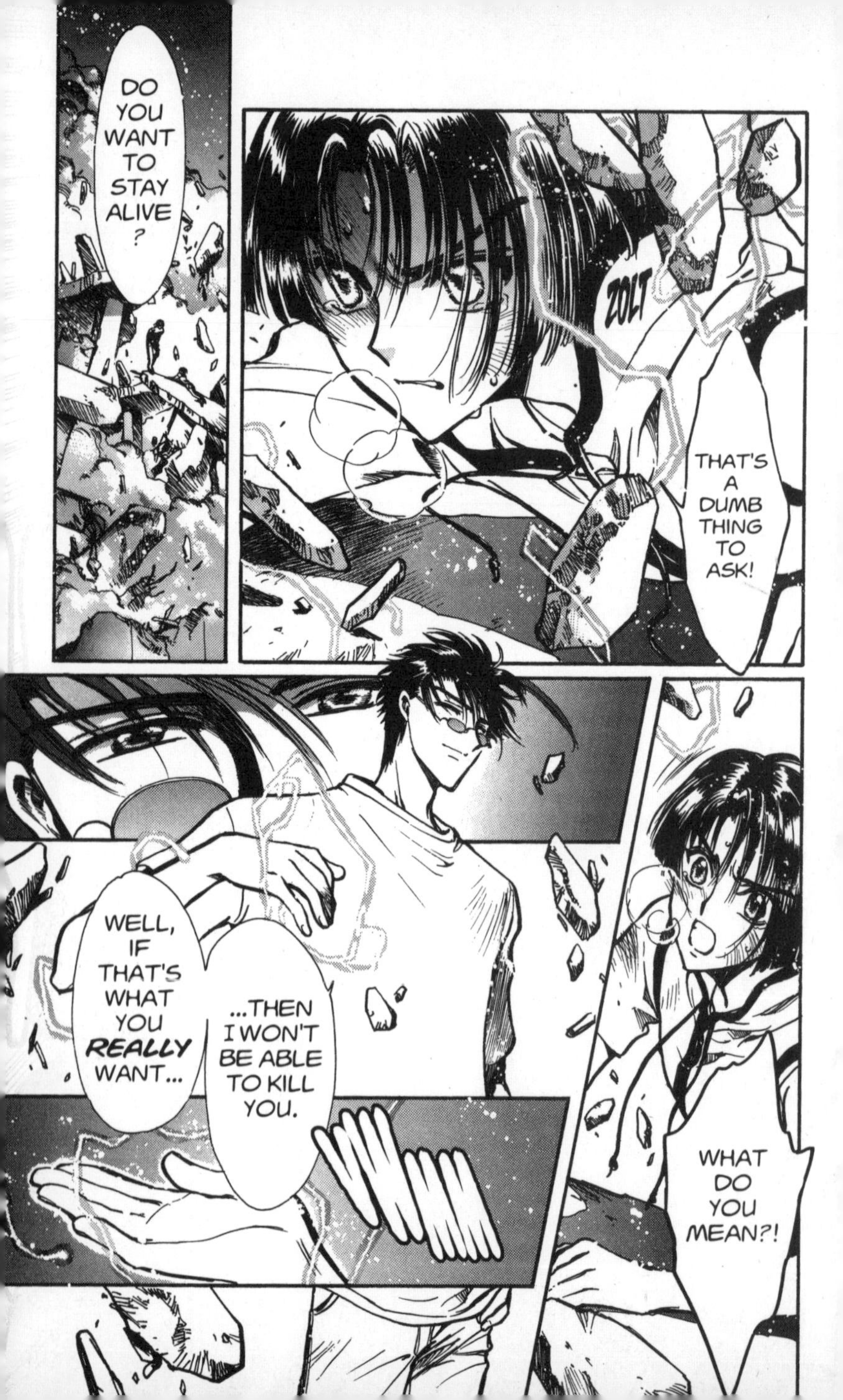
ZOLT
THAT'S A DUMB THING TO ASK!
DO YOU WANT TO STAY ALIVE?
WHAT DO YOU MEAN?!
WELL, IF THAT'S WHAT YOU *REALLY* WANT...
...THEN I WON'T BE ABLE TO KILL YOU.

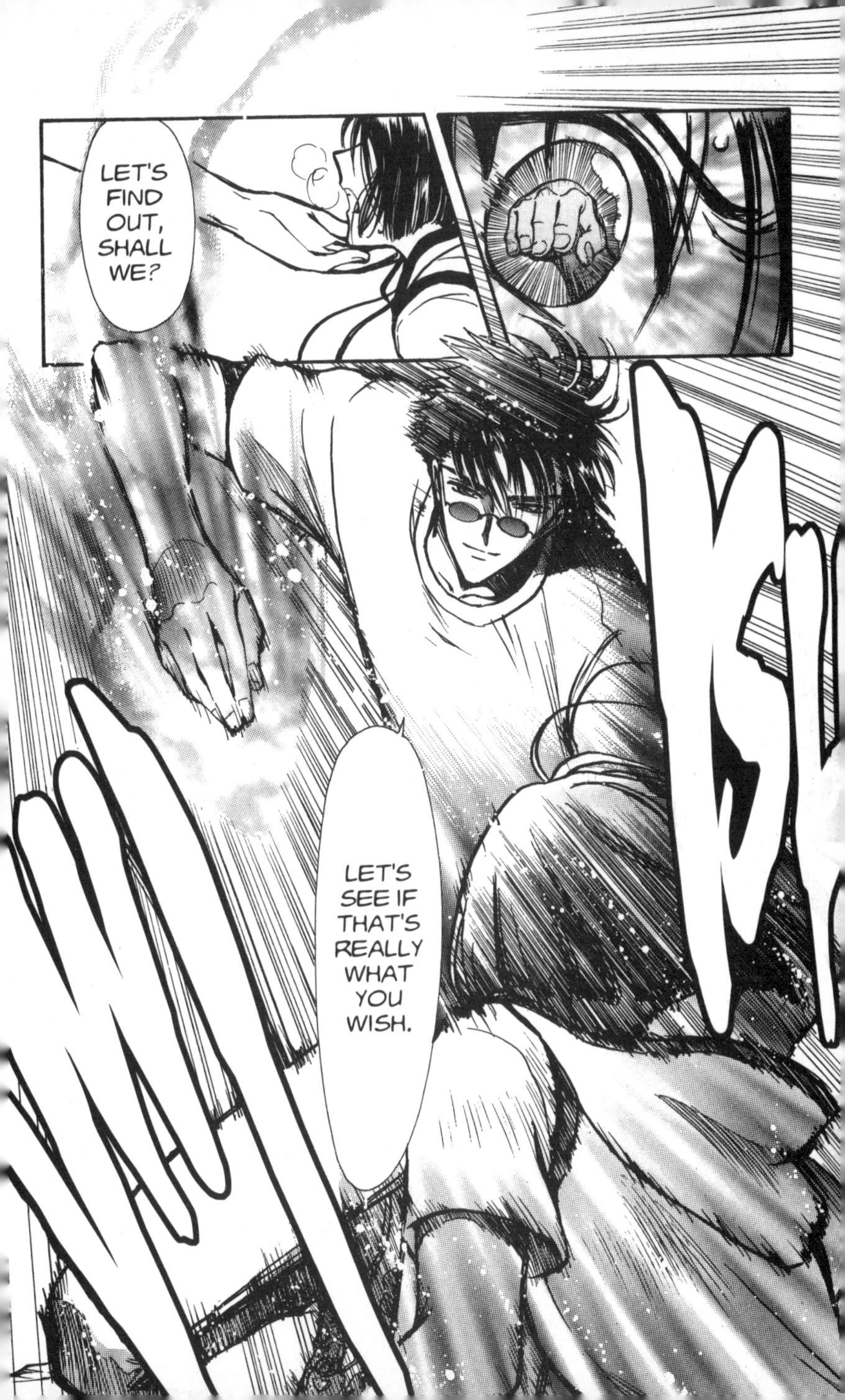
LET'S FIND OUT, SHALL WE?
LET'S SEE IF THAT'S REALLY WHAT YOU WISH.

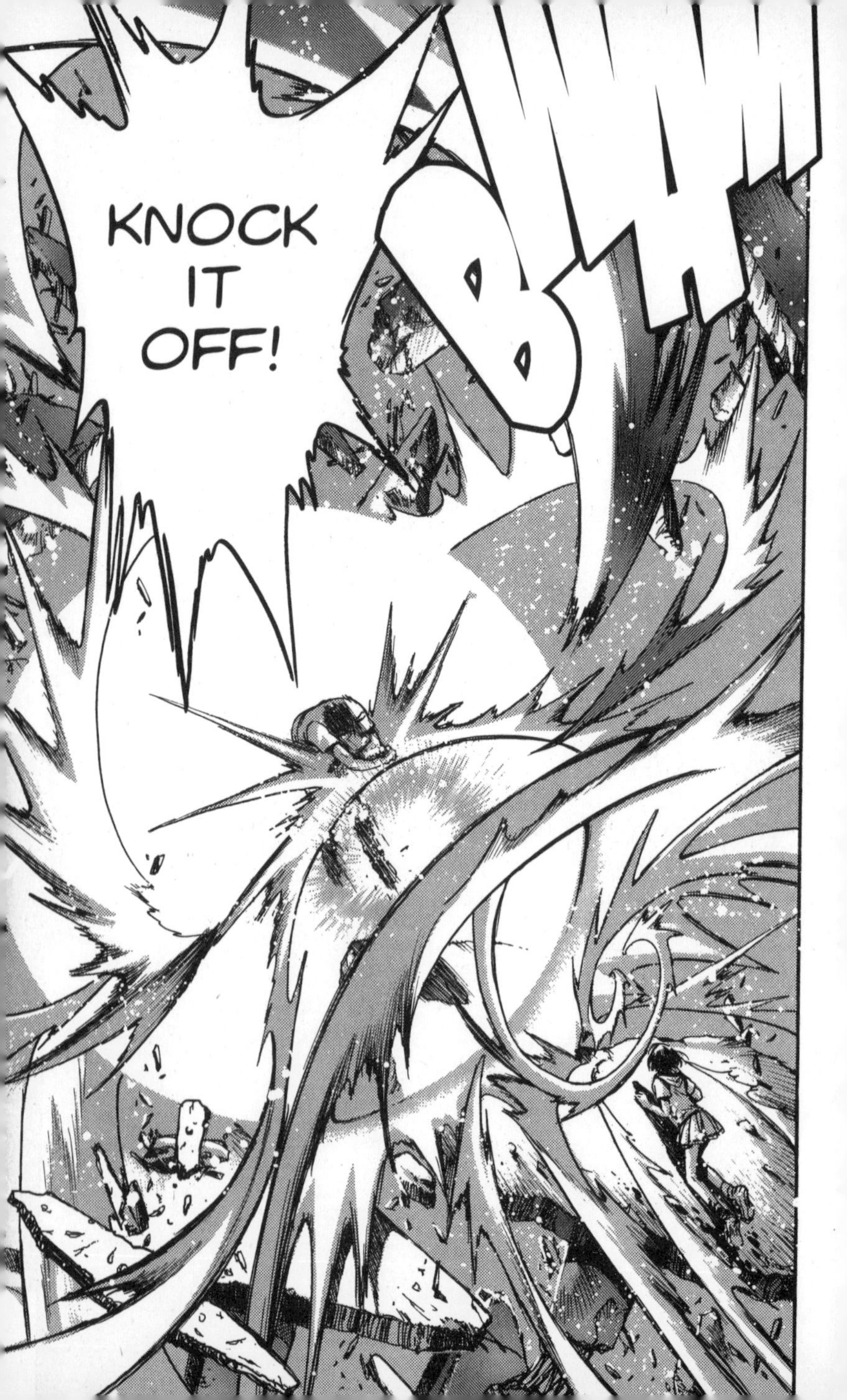
KNOCK IT OFF!

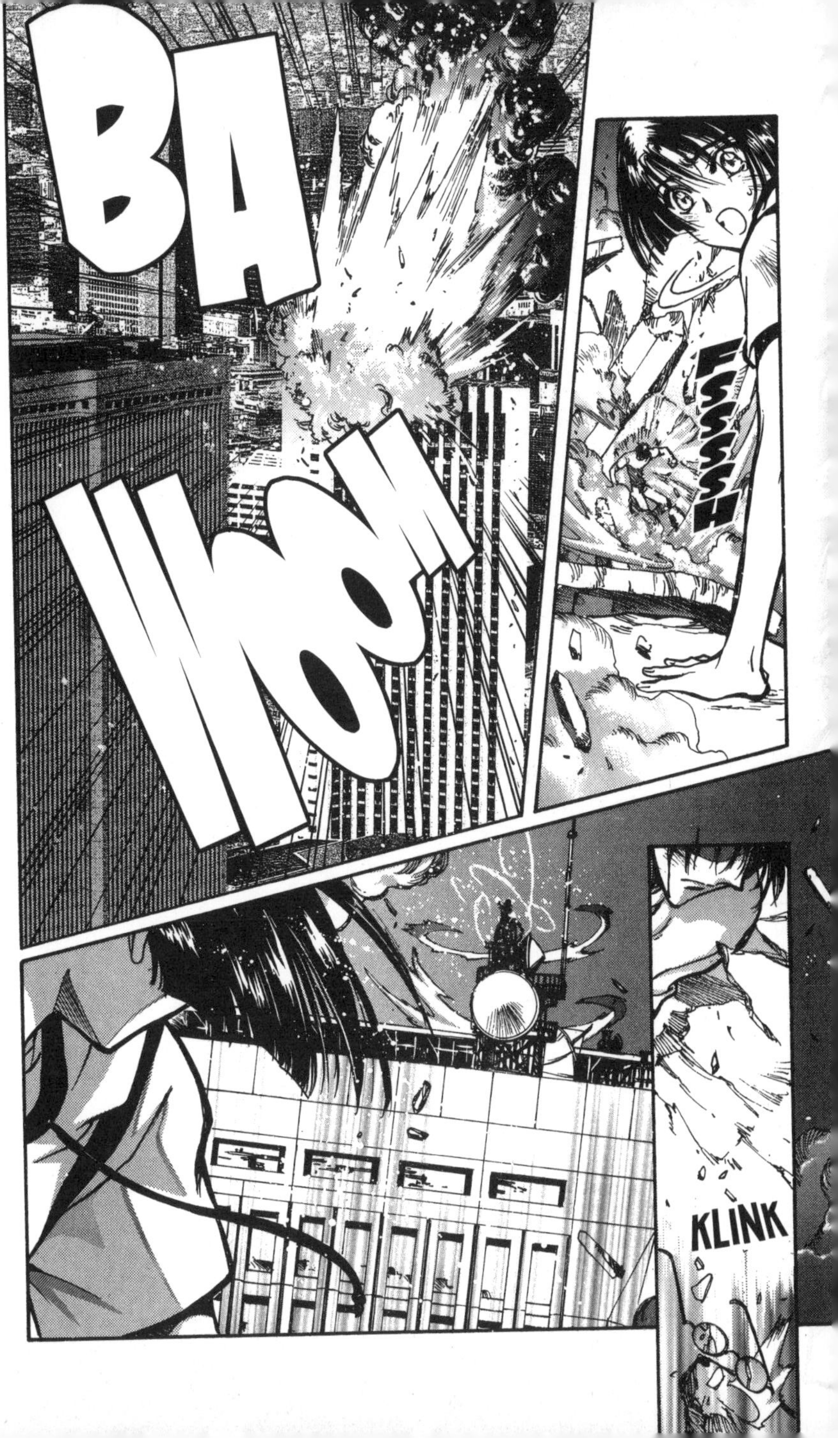
FSSSSH
BA
WOOM
KLINK

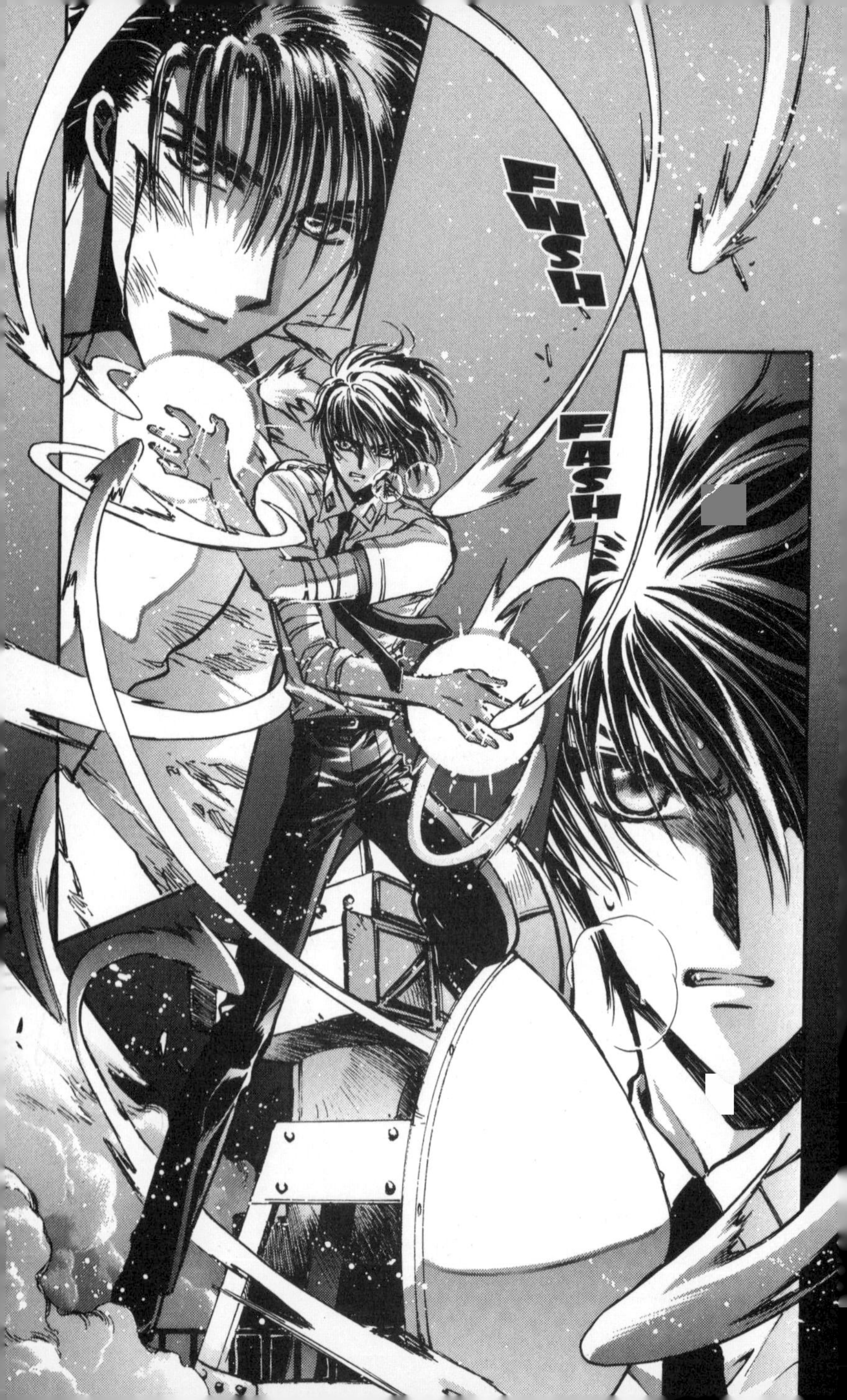
FWSH
FASH

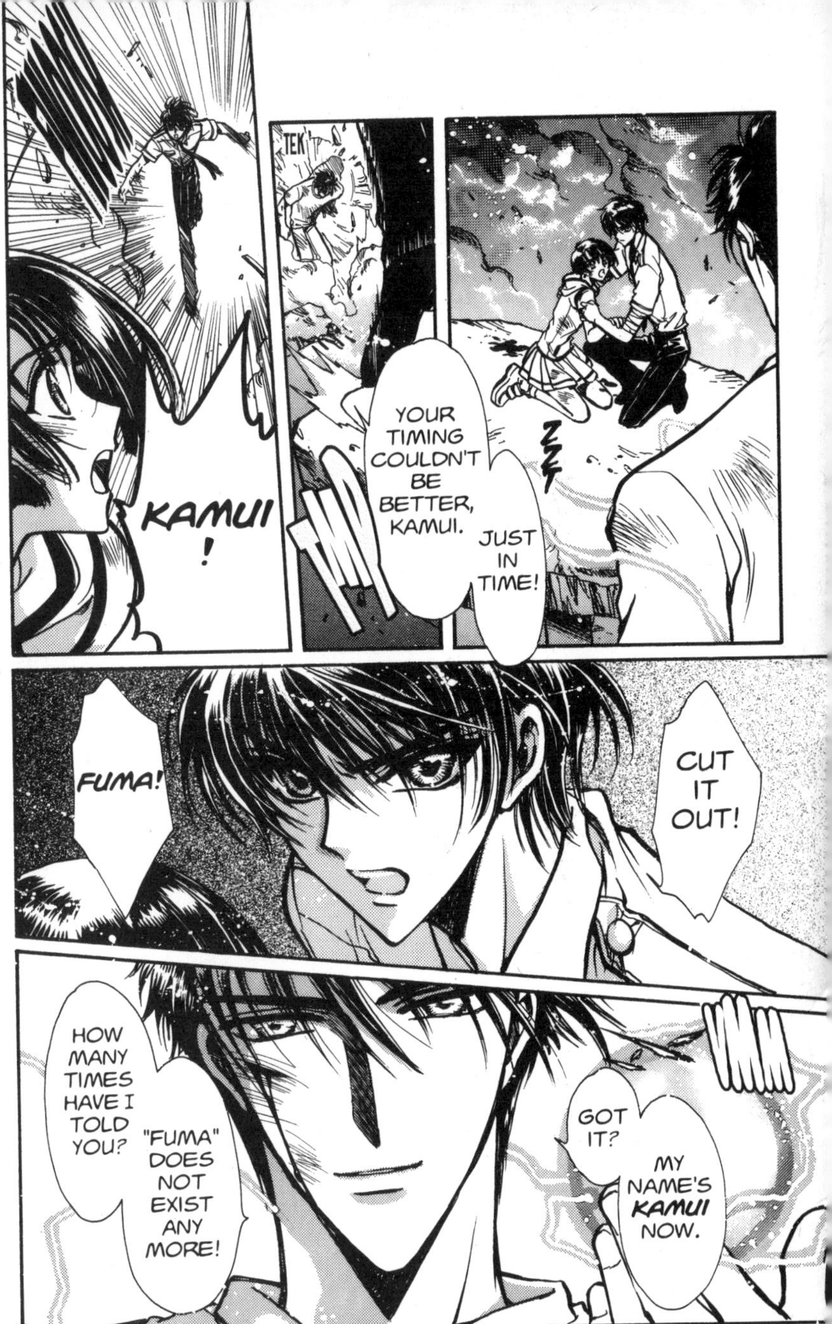
YOUR TIMING COULDN'T BE BETTER, KAMUI.
JUST IN TIME!
TEK
KAMUI!
CUT IT OUT!
FUMA!
HOW MANY TIMES HAVE I TOLD YOU?
"FUMA" DOES NOT EXIST ANY MORE!
MY NAME'S KAMUI NOW.
GOT IT?

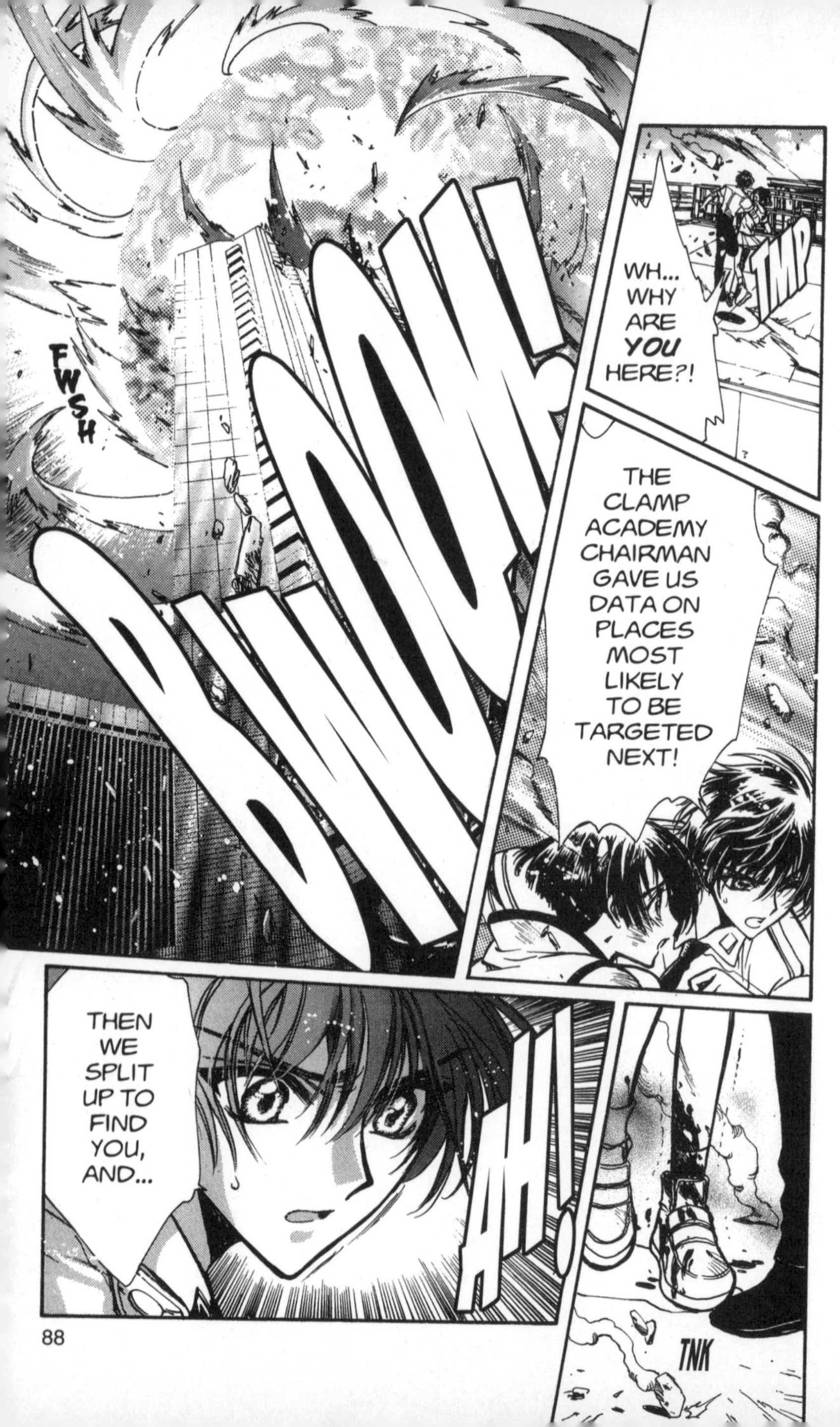
TMP
WH... WHY ARE YOU HERE?!
?
THE CLAMP ACADEMY CHAIRMAN GAVE US DATA ON PLACES MOST LIKELY TO BE TARGETED NEXT!
FWSH
TNK
AH!
THEN WE SPLIT UP TO FIND YOU, AND...

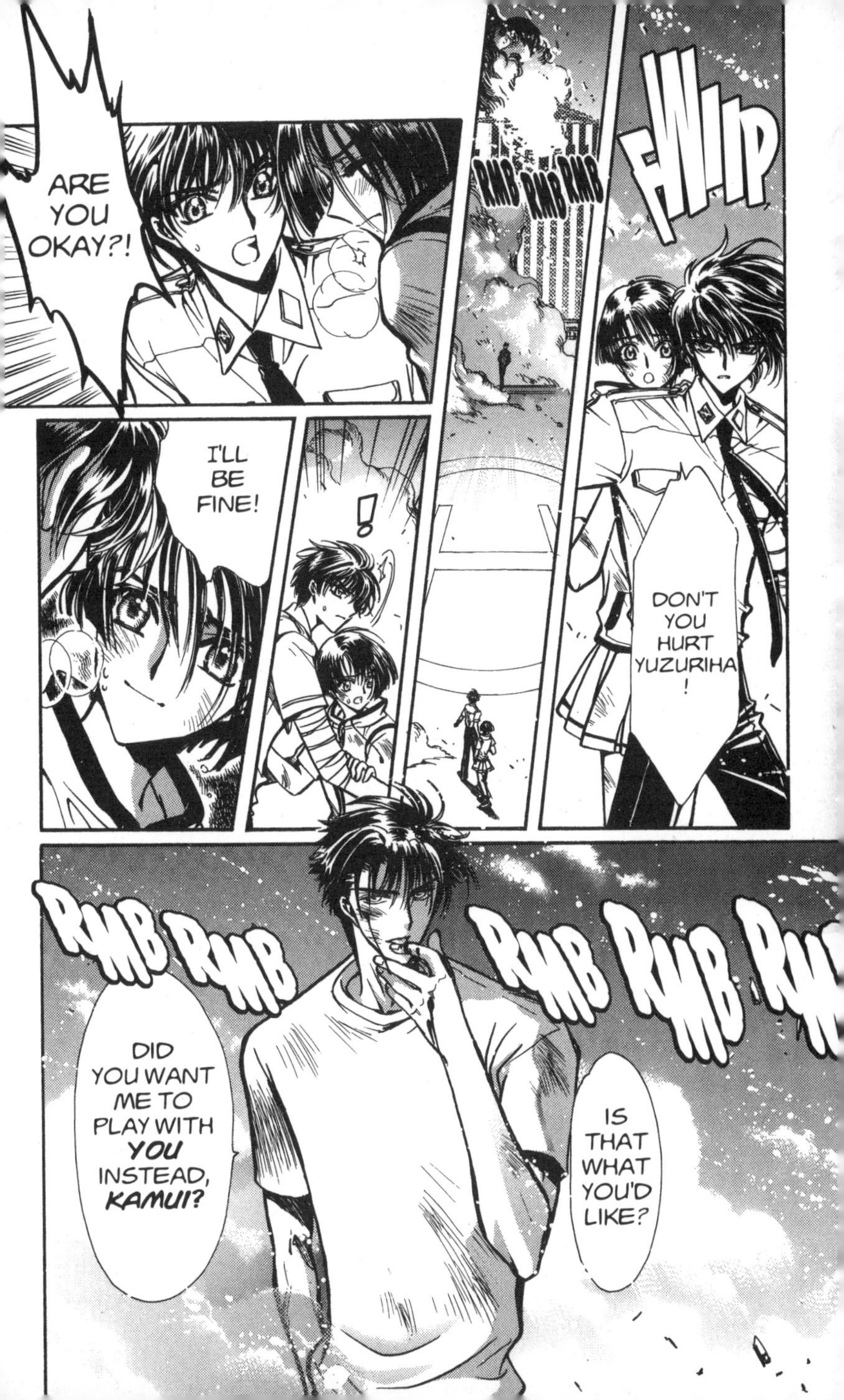
FWHIP
DON'T YOU HURT YUZURIHA!
RMB RMB RMB
ARE YOU OKAY?!
!
I'LL BE FINE!
RMB RMB
RMB RMB
DID YOU WANT ME TO PLAY WITH ***YOU*** INSTEAD, ***KAMUI?***
IS THAT WHAT YOU'D LIKE?

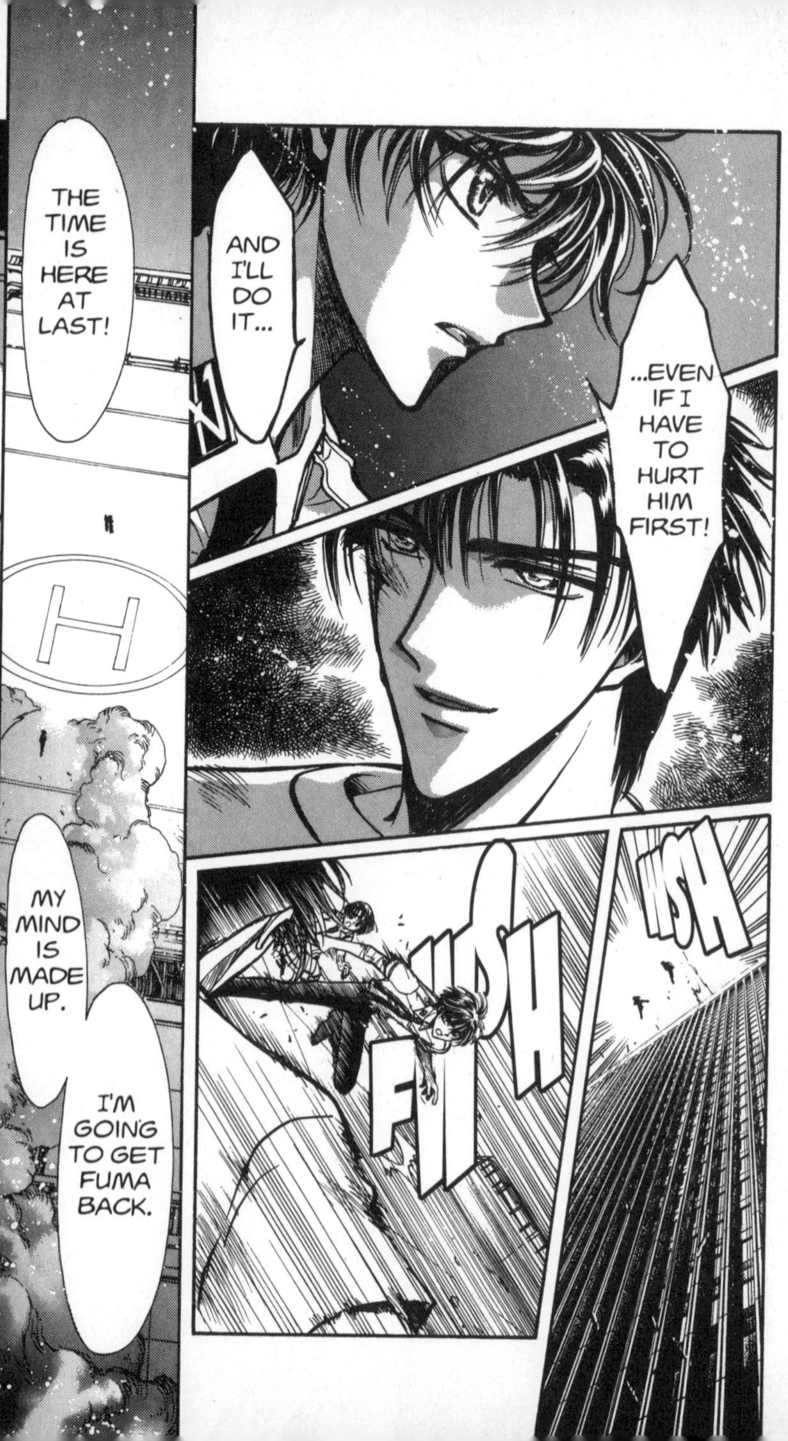
AND I'LL DO IT...
...EVEN IF I HAVE TO HURT HIM FIRST!
WISH
FWISH
THE TIME IS HERE AT LAST!
MY MIND IS MADE UP.
I'M GOING TO GET FUMA BACK.

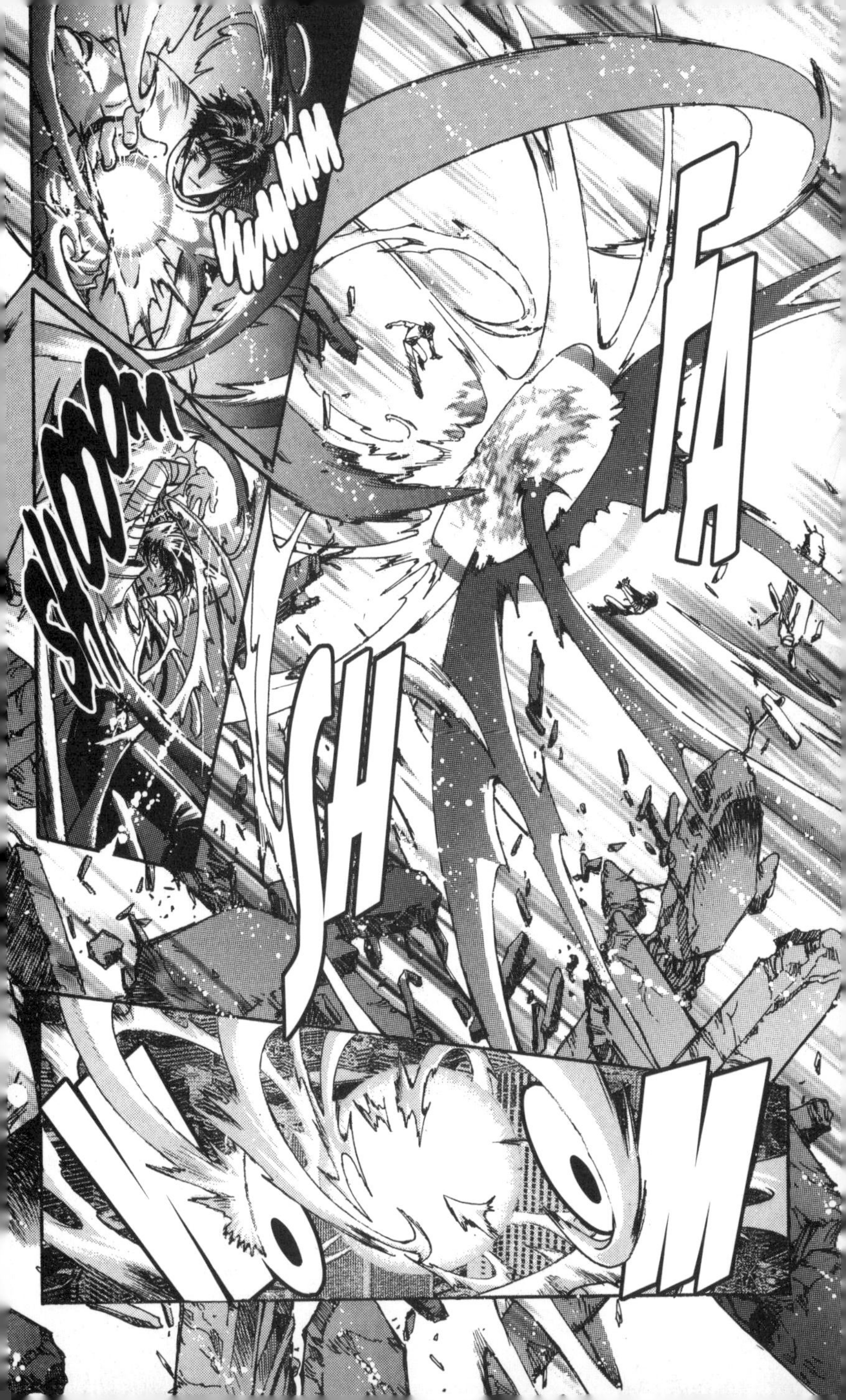
FA
SH
WMMM
SHOOOM
VOOM

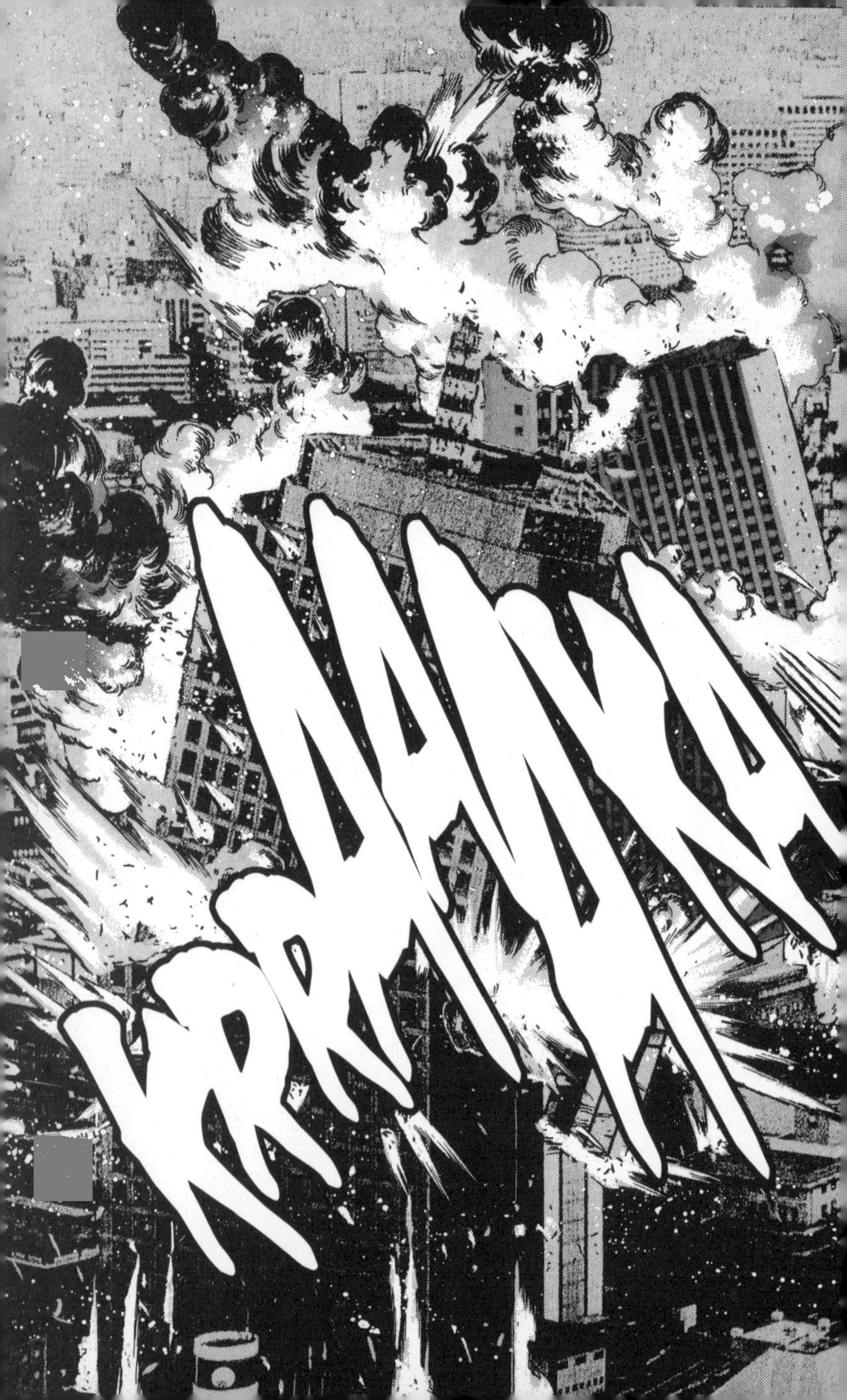

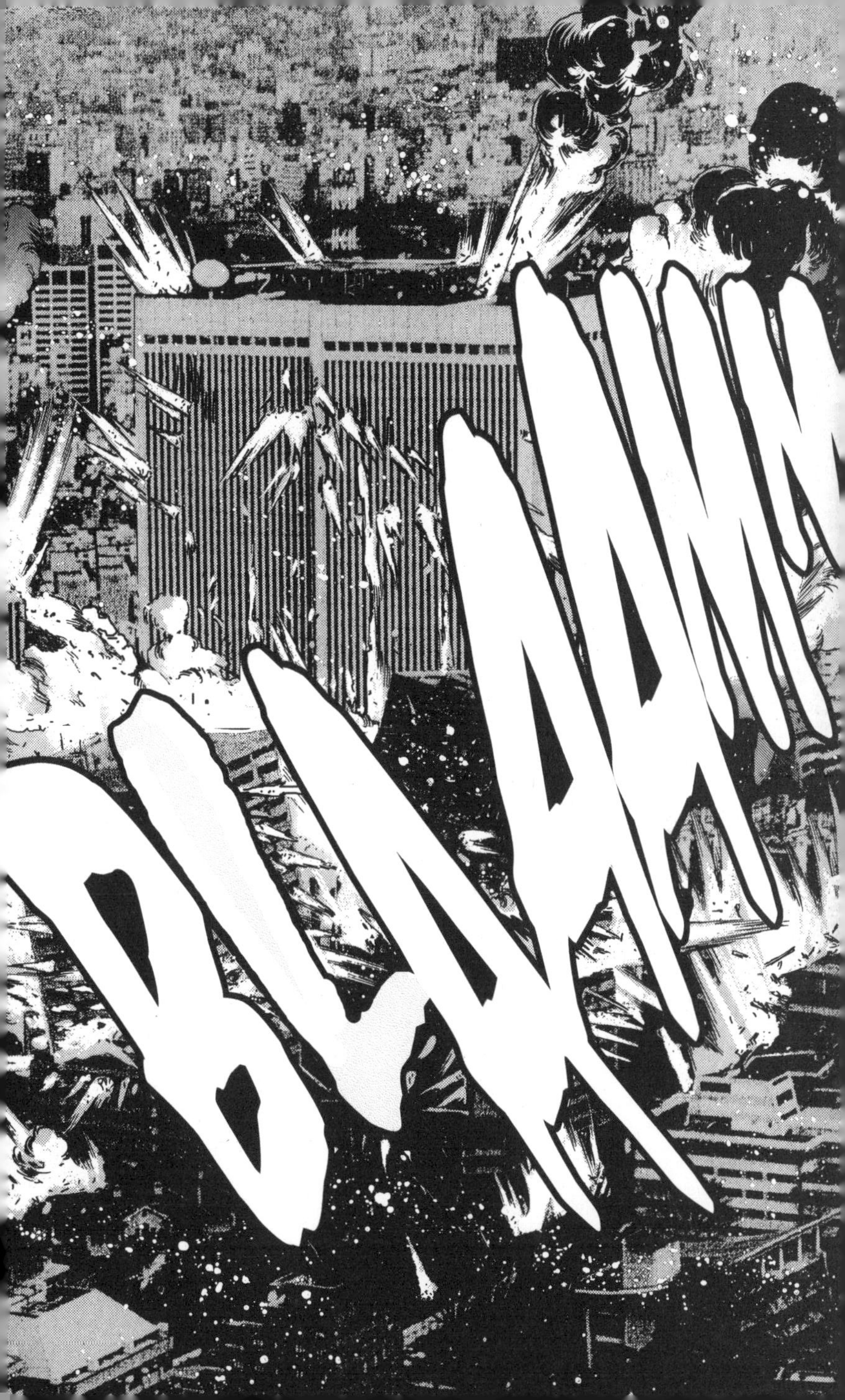
BLAAM

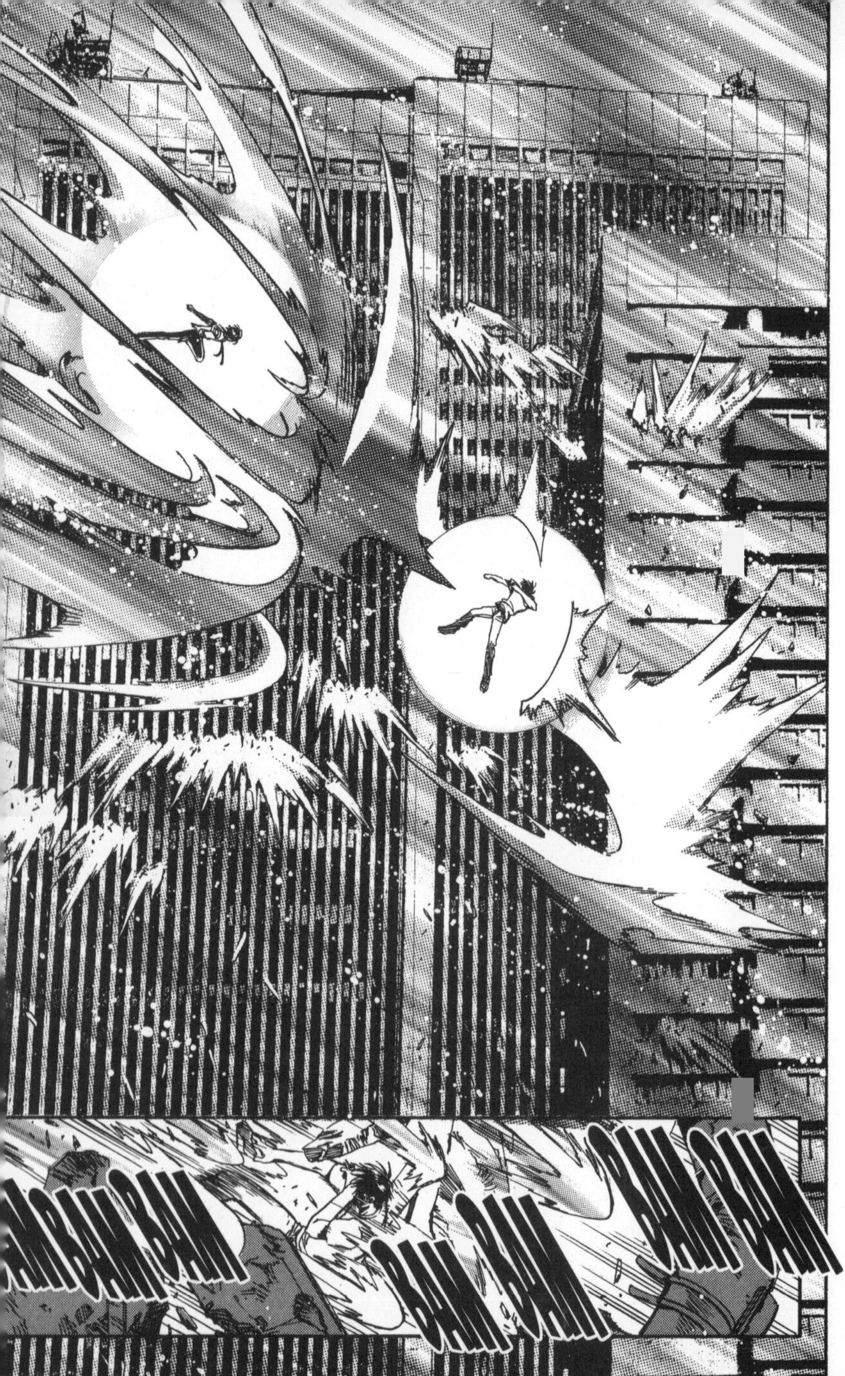
BAM BAM
BAM BAM
BAM BAM

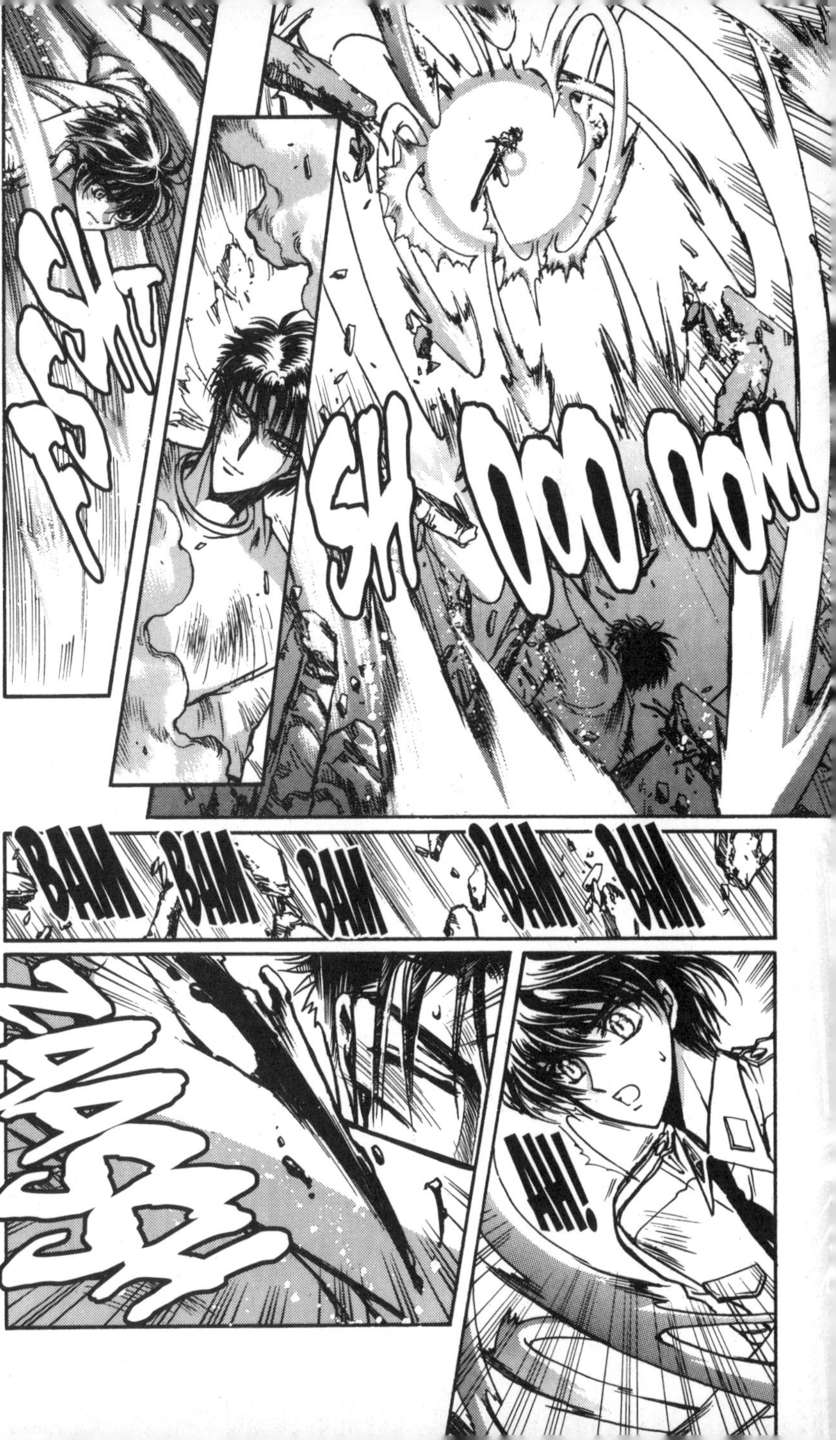

SH OOO OOM
FSSHT
BAM BAM BAM BAM BAM
AHH!
ZAASH

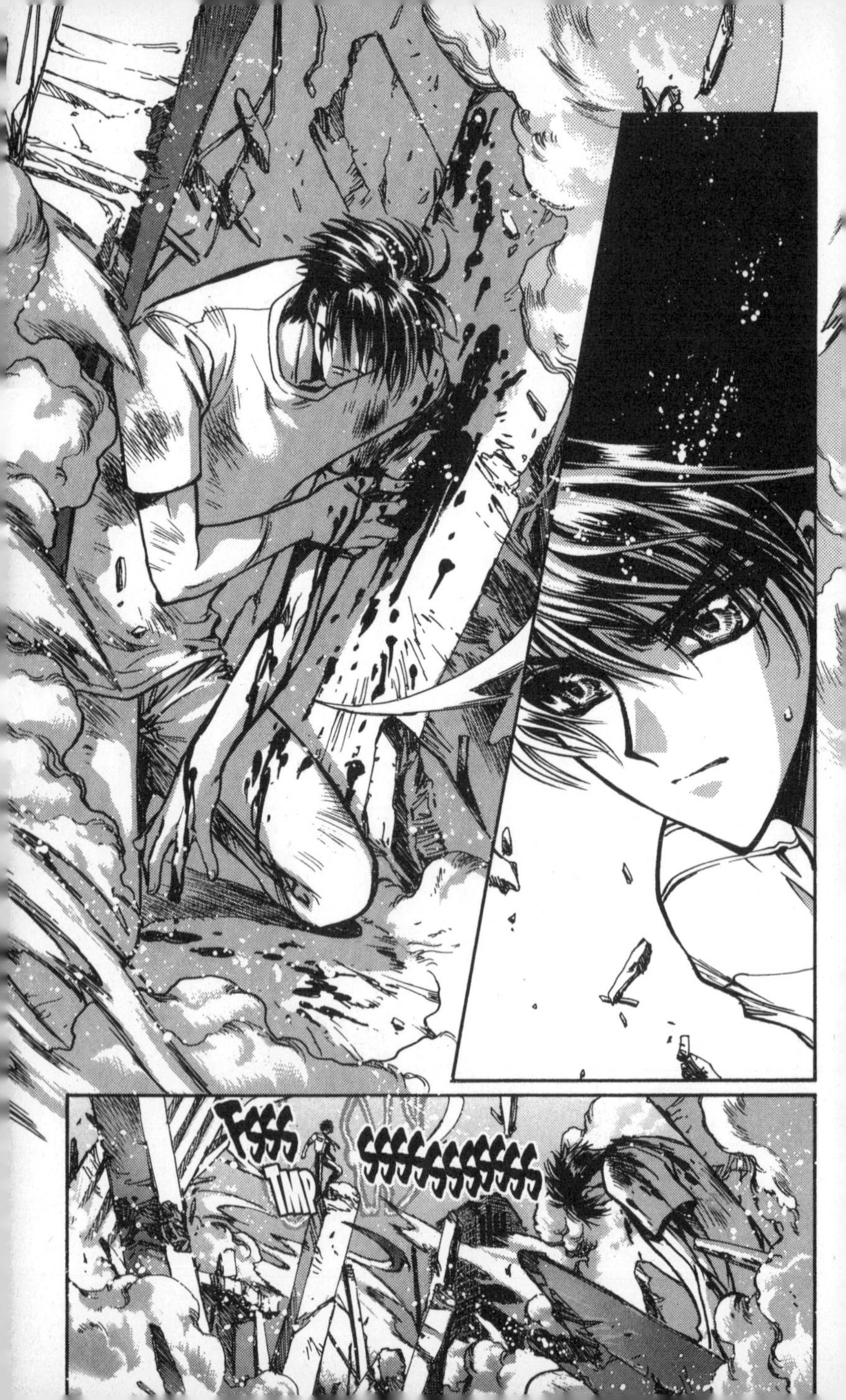
FSSS
SSSSSSSSSSS
TMP

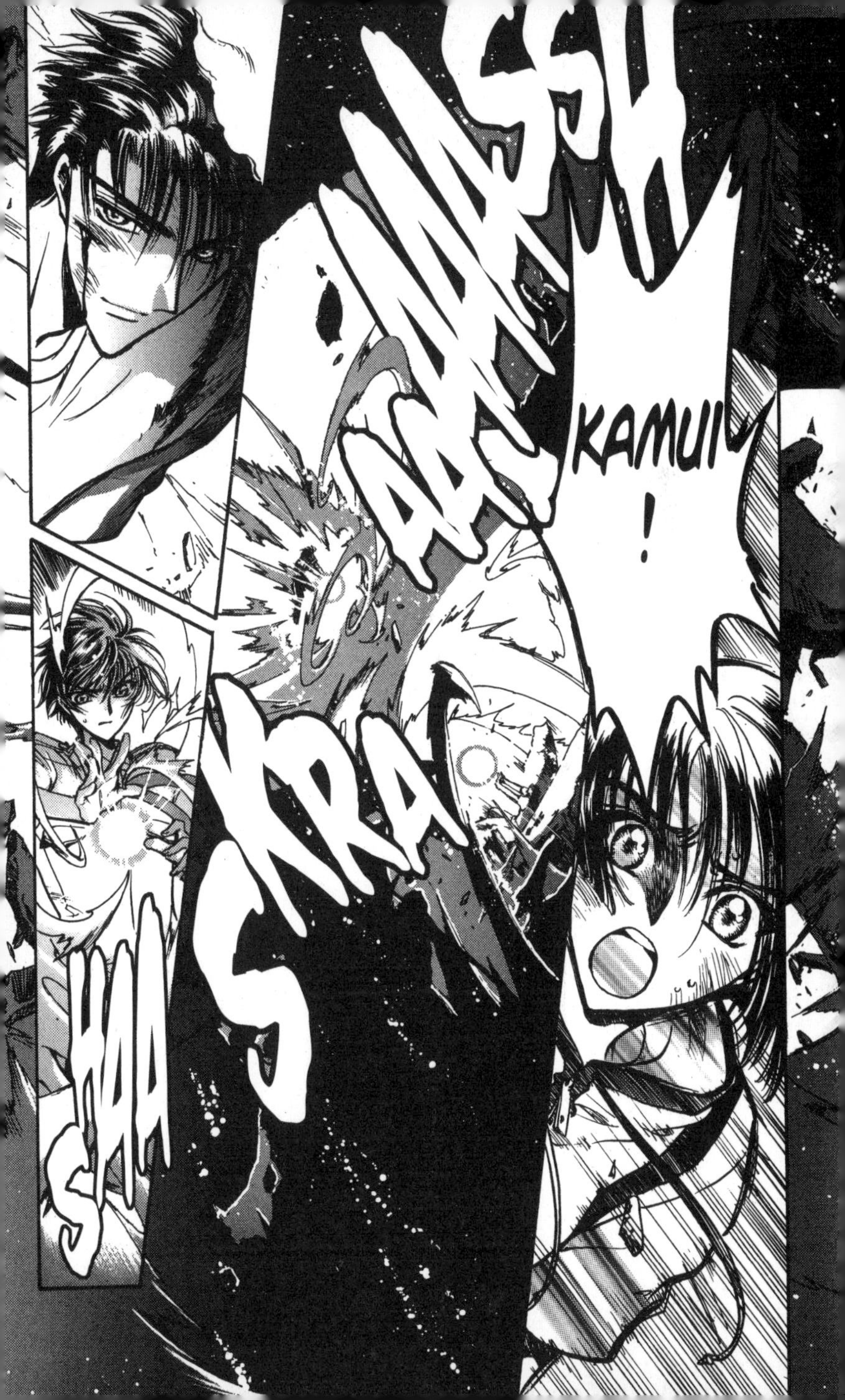

SKRAAAASH
KAMUI!
SHAA

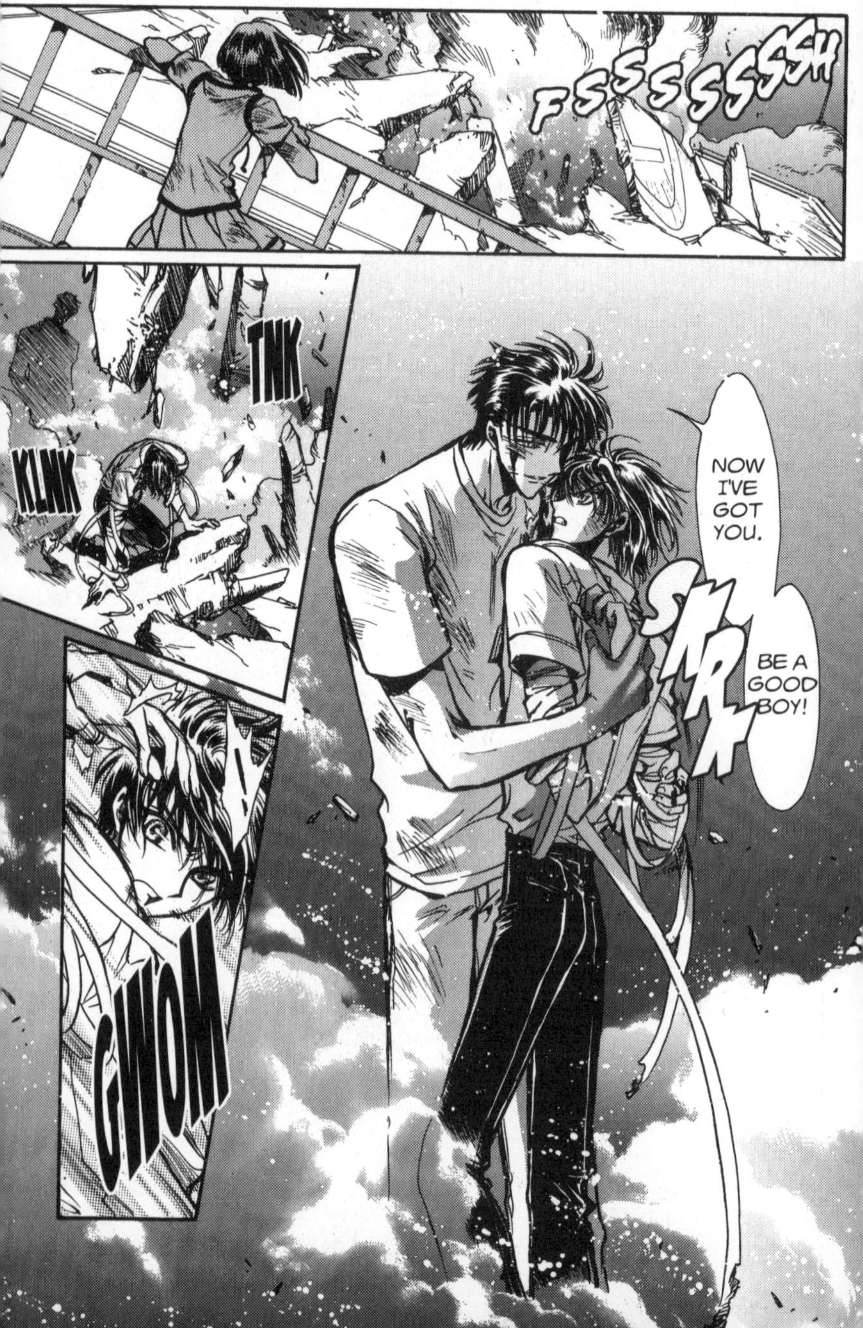
FSSSSSSSH
NOW I'VE GOT YOU.
SKRK
BE A GOOD BOY!
TNK
KLNK
GWOM

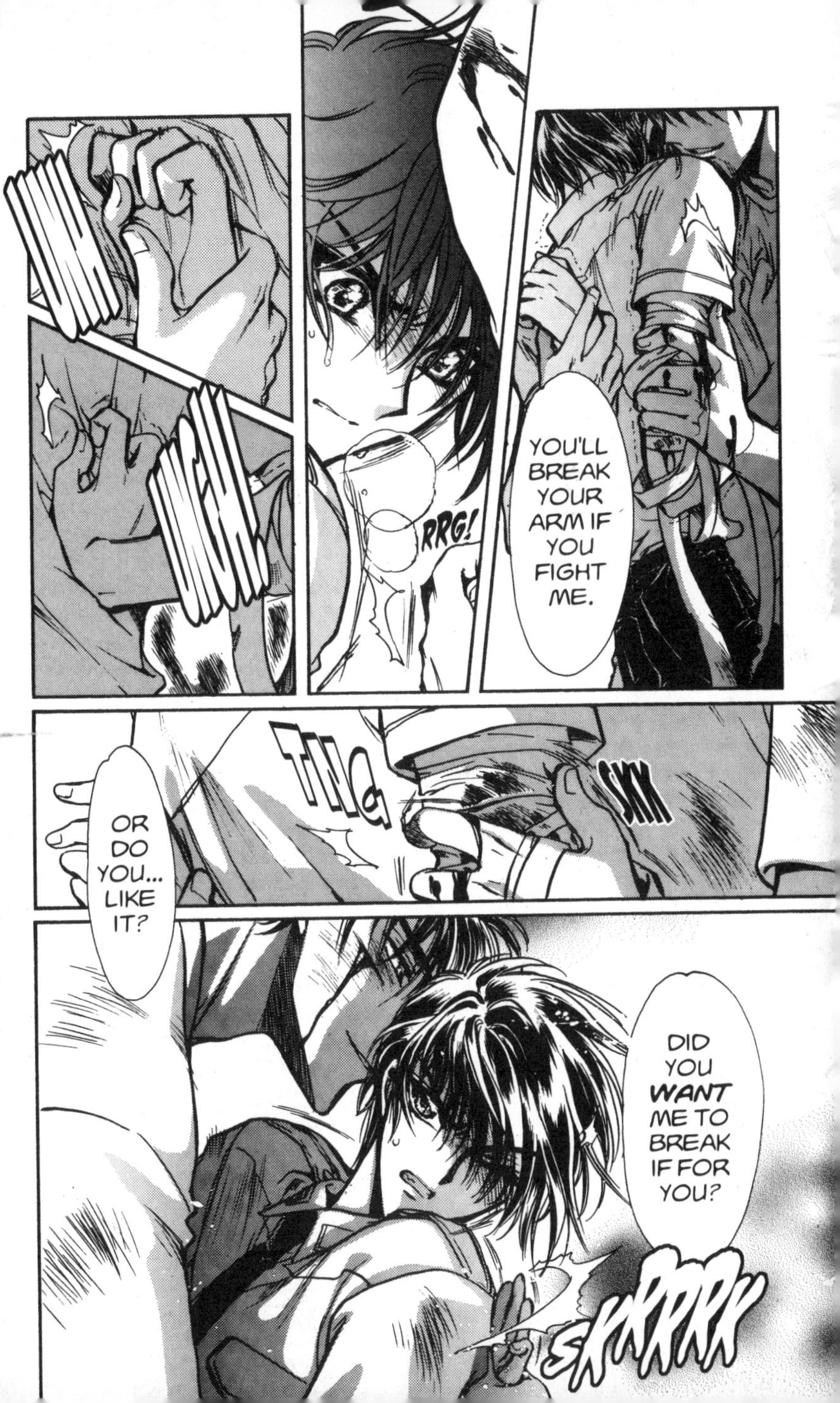
YOU'LL BREAK YOUR ARM IF YOU FIGHT ME.
RRG!
SKK
TING
OR DO YOU... LIKE IT?
DID YOU WANT ME TO BREAK IF FOR YOU?
SKRRRK

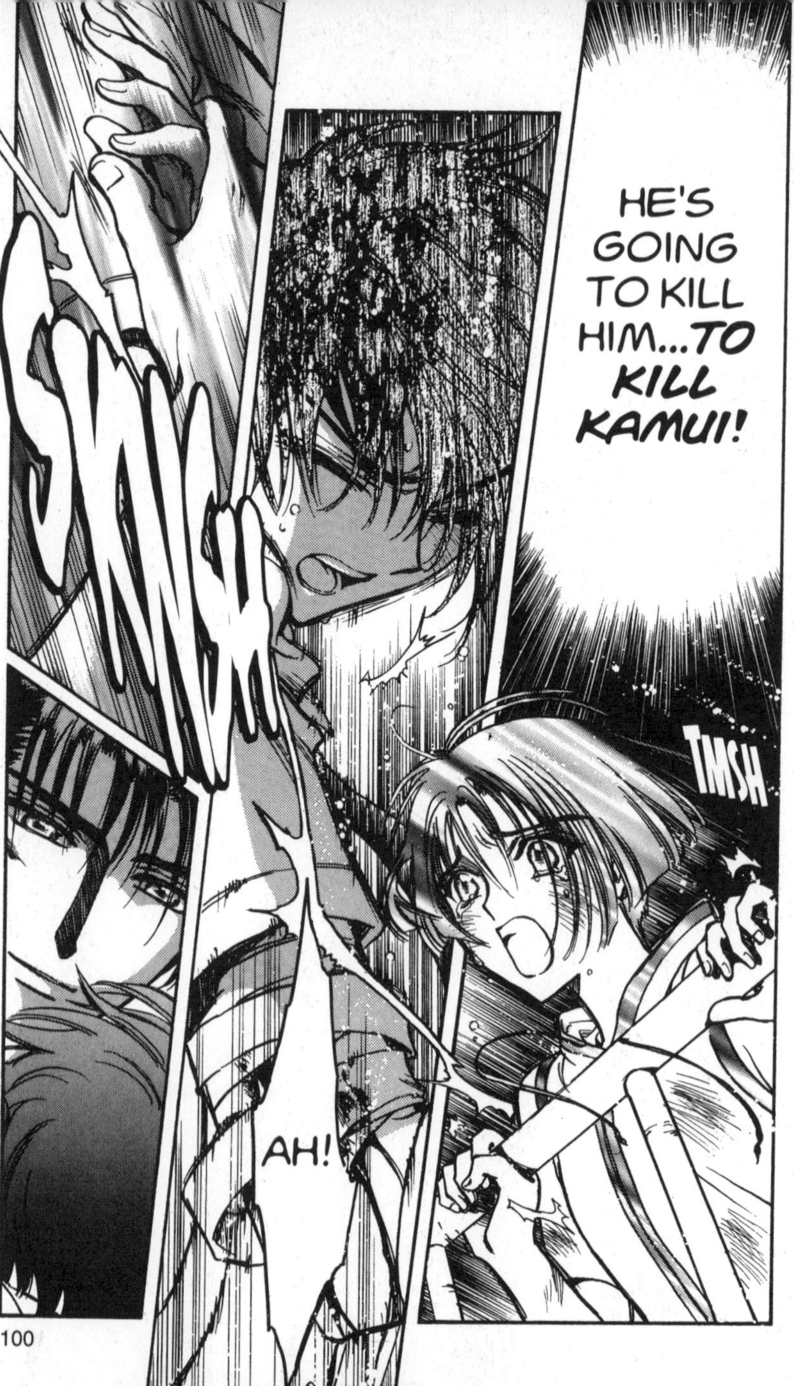
HE'S GOING TO KILL HIM...*TO KILL KAMUI!*
TMSH
AH!

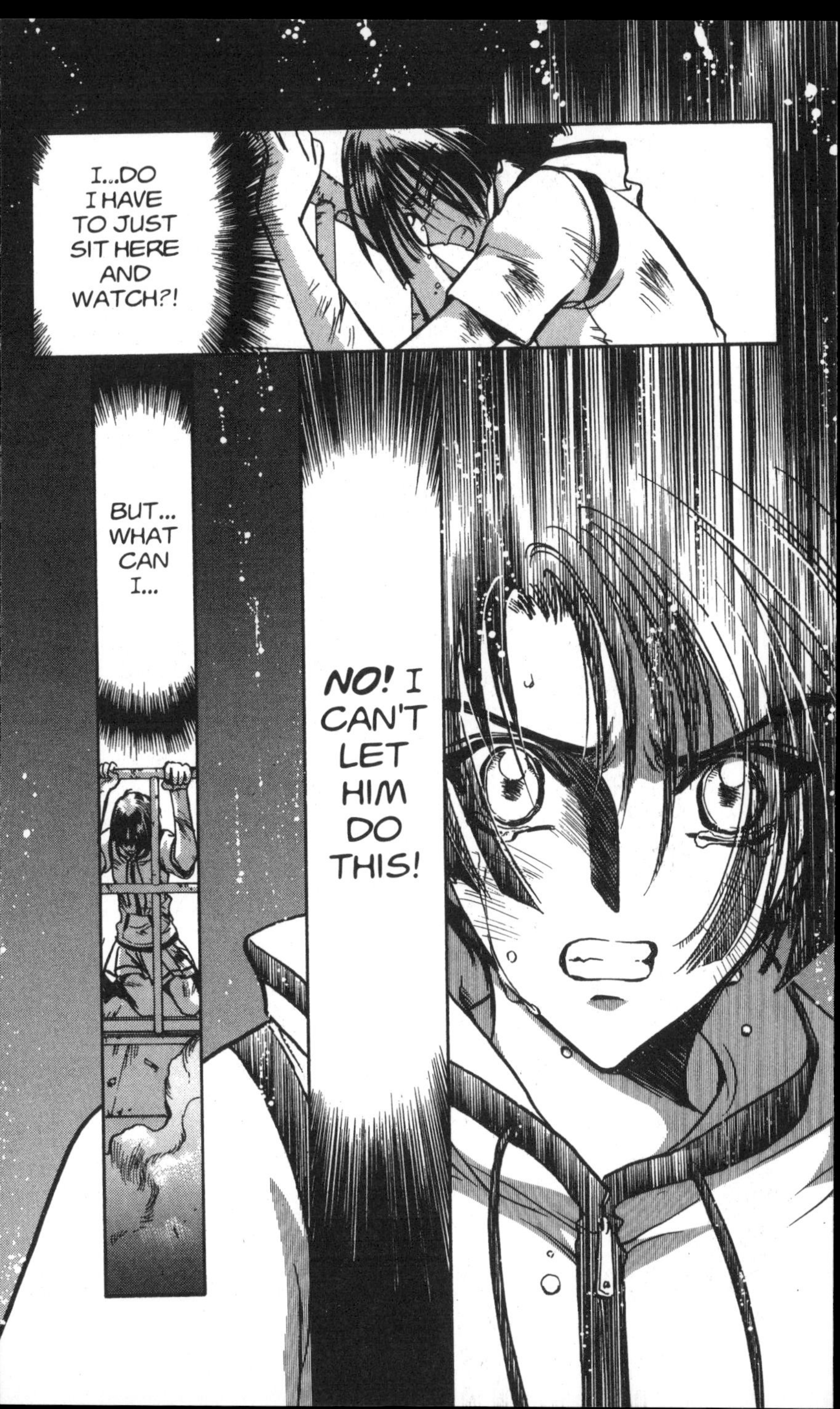
I...DO I HAVE TO JUST SIT HERE AND WATCH?!
BUT... WHAT CAN I...
NO! I CAN'T LET HIM DO THIS!

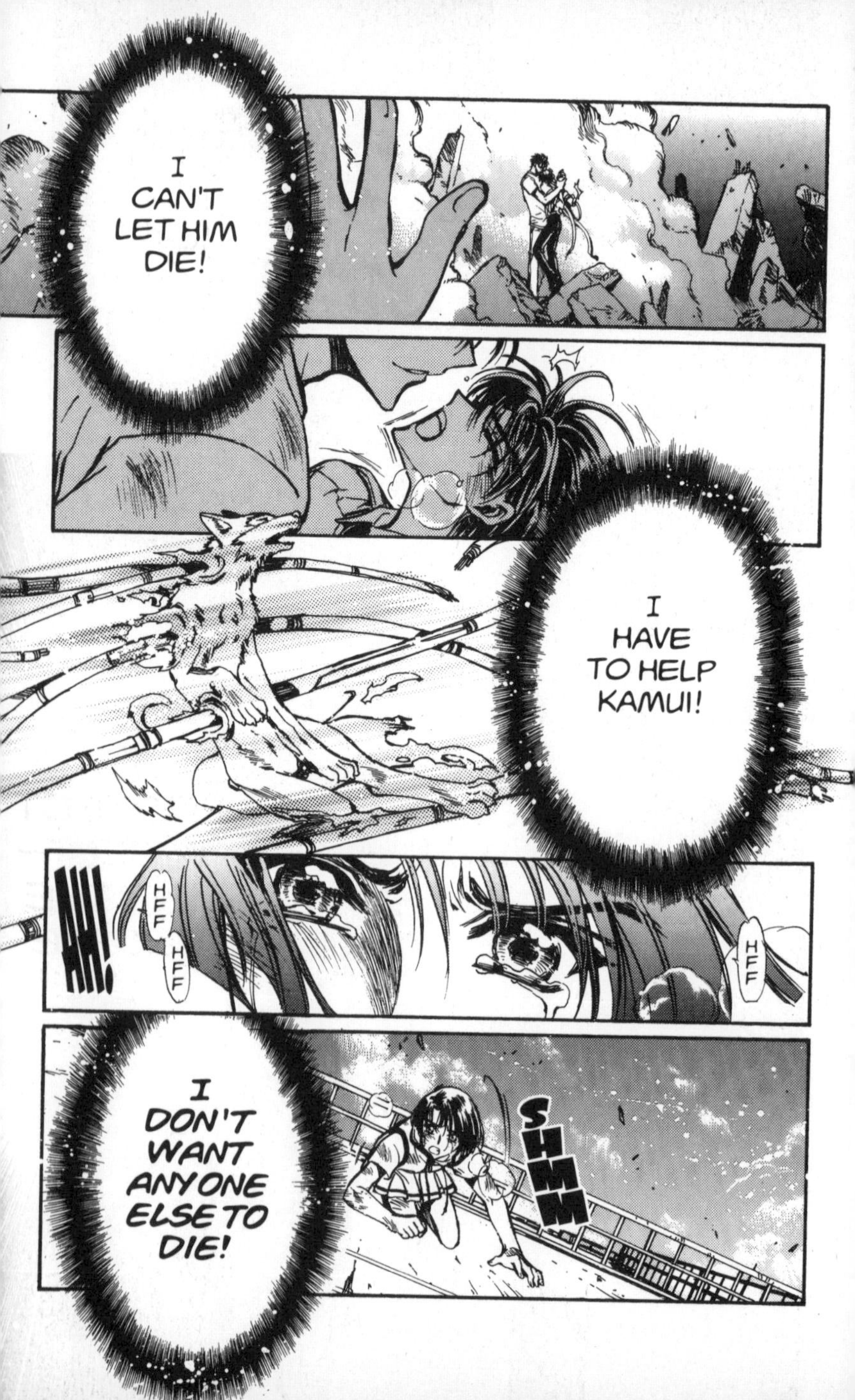
I CAN'T LET HIM DIE!
I HAVE TO HELP KAMUI!
HFF
HFF
HFF
AHH!
SHMM
I DON'T WANT ANYONE ELSE TO DIE!

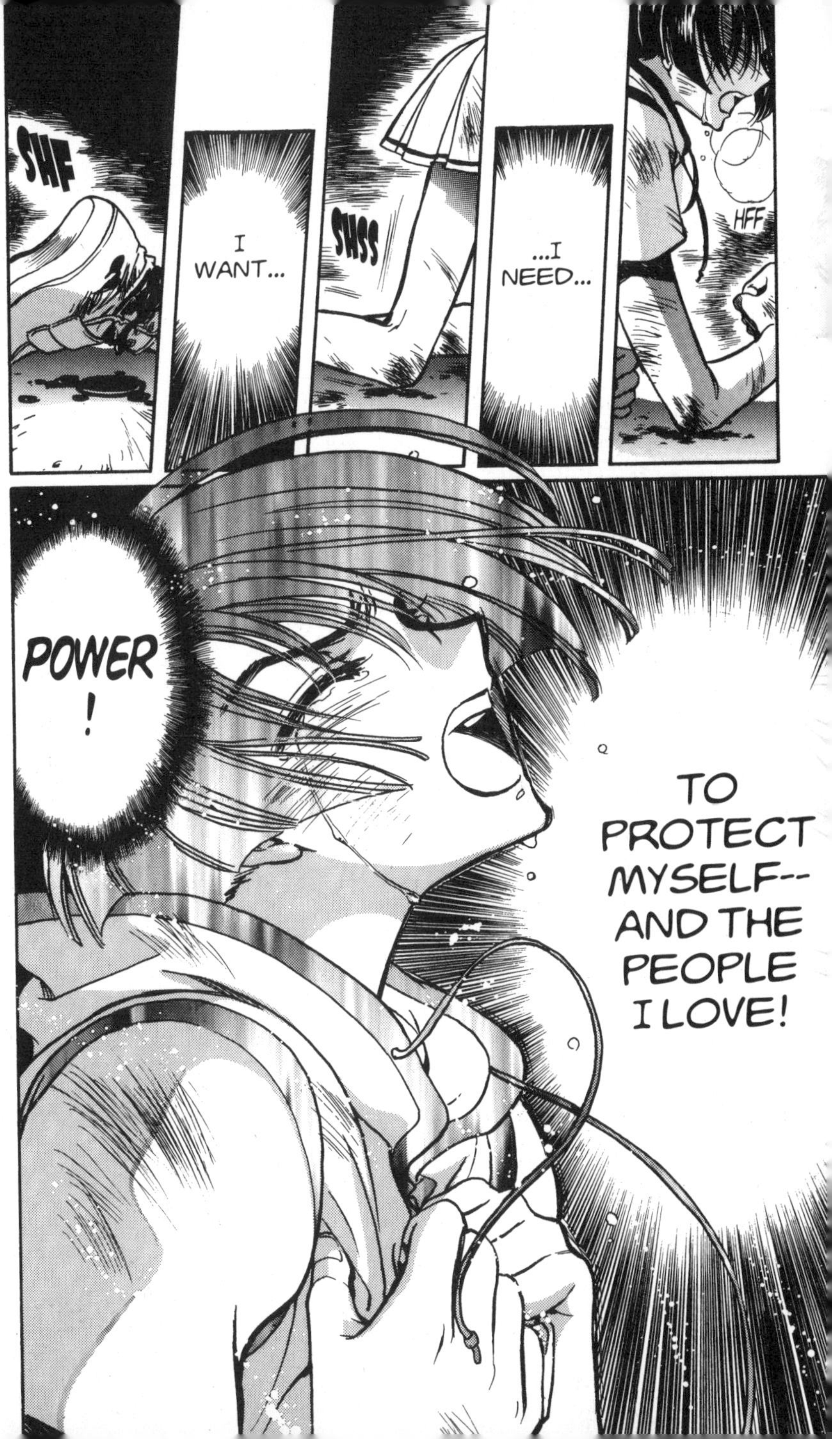
SHF
I WANT...
SHSS
...I NEED...
HFF
POWER!
TO PROTECT MYSELF-- AND THE PEOPLE I LOVE!

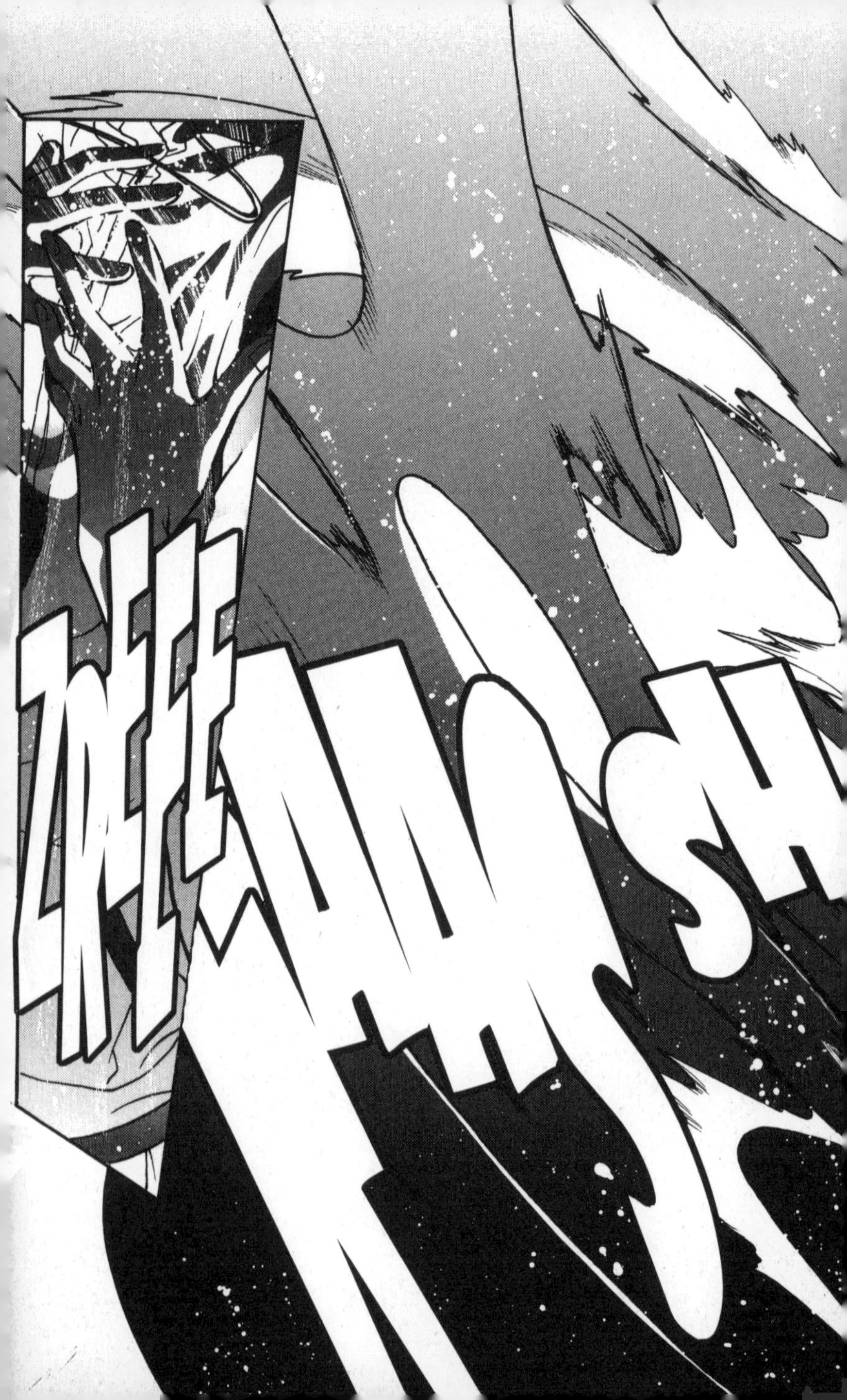

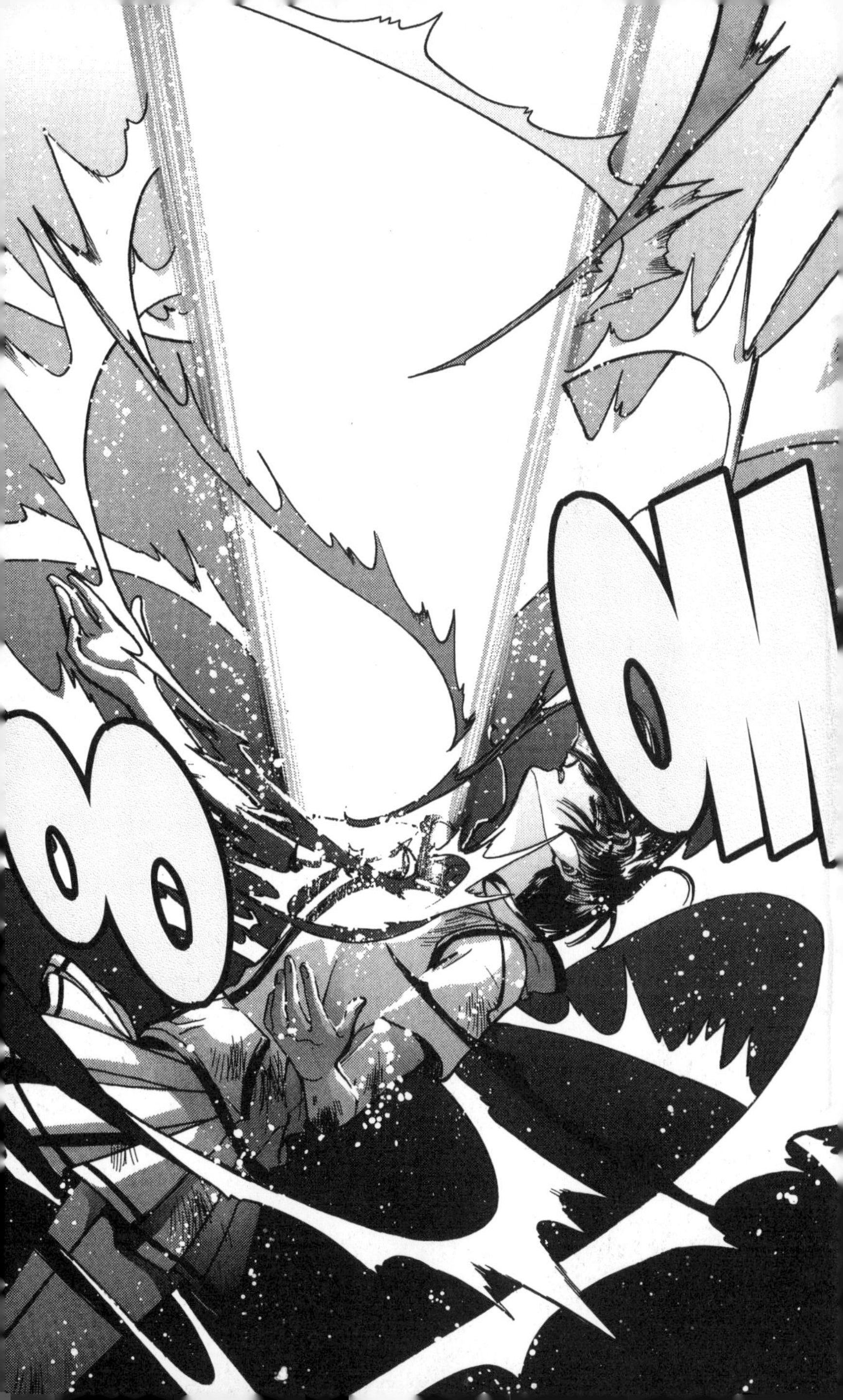
BOOM

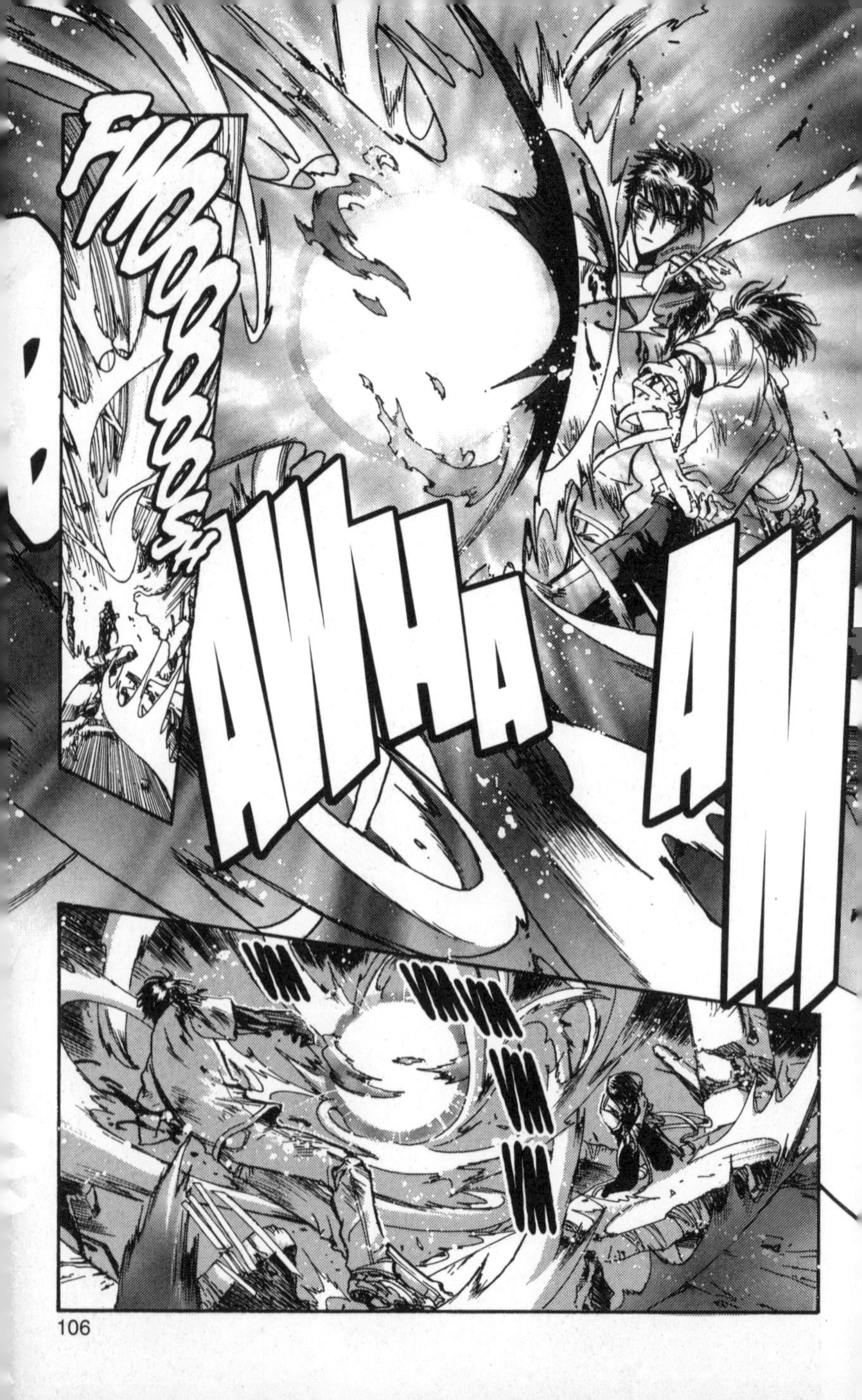
FWOOOOOOOSH
VM
VM VM
VM
VM
VM
VM

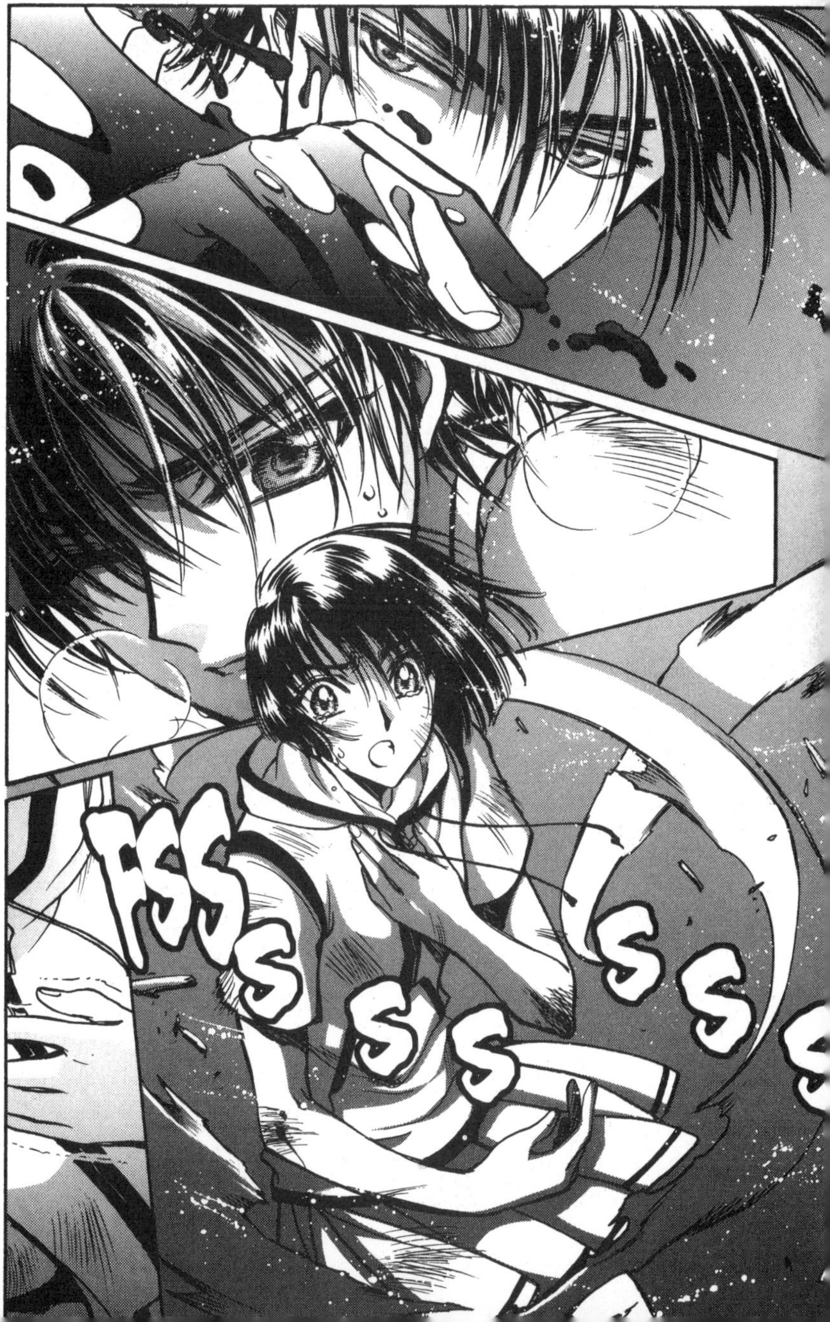
FSSSSSSSSS

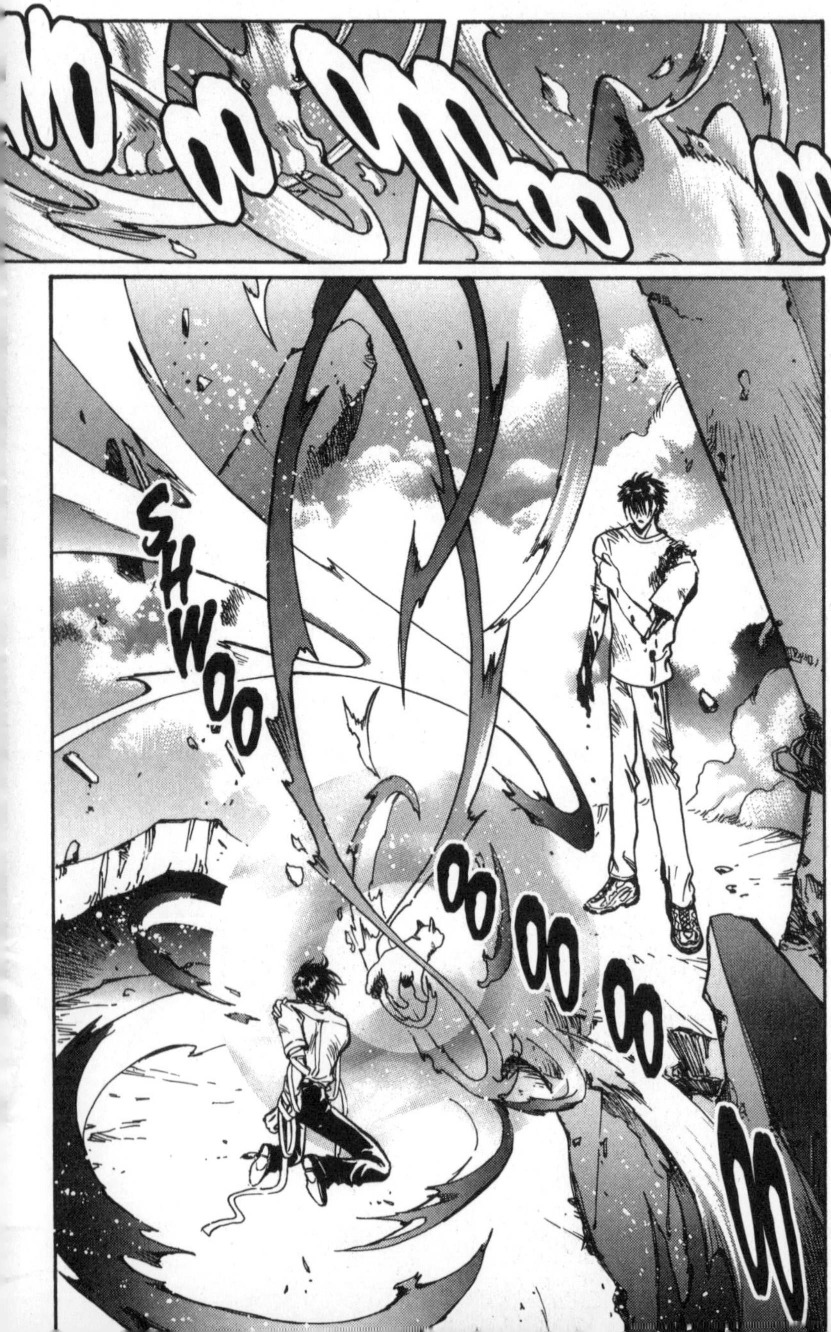
WOOOOOOO
SHWOOOOOOOOOOOO

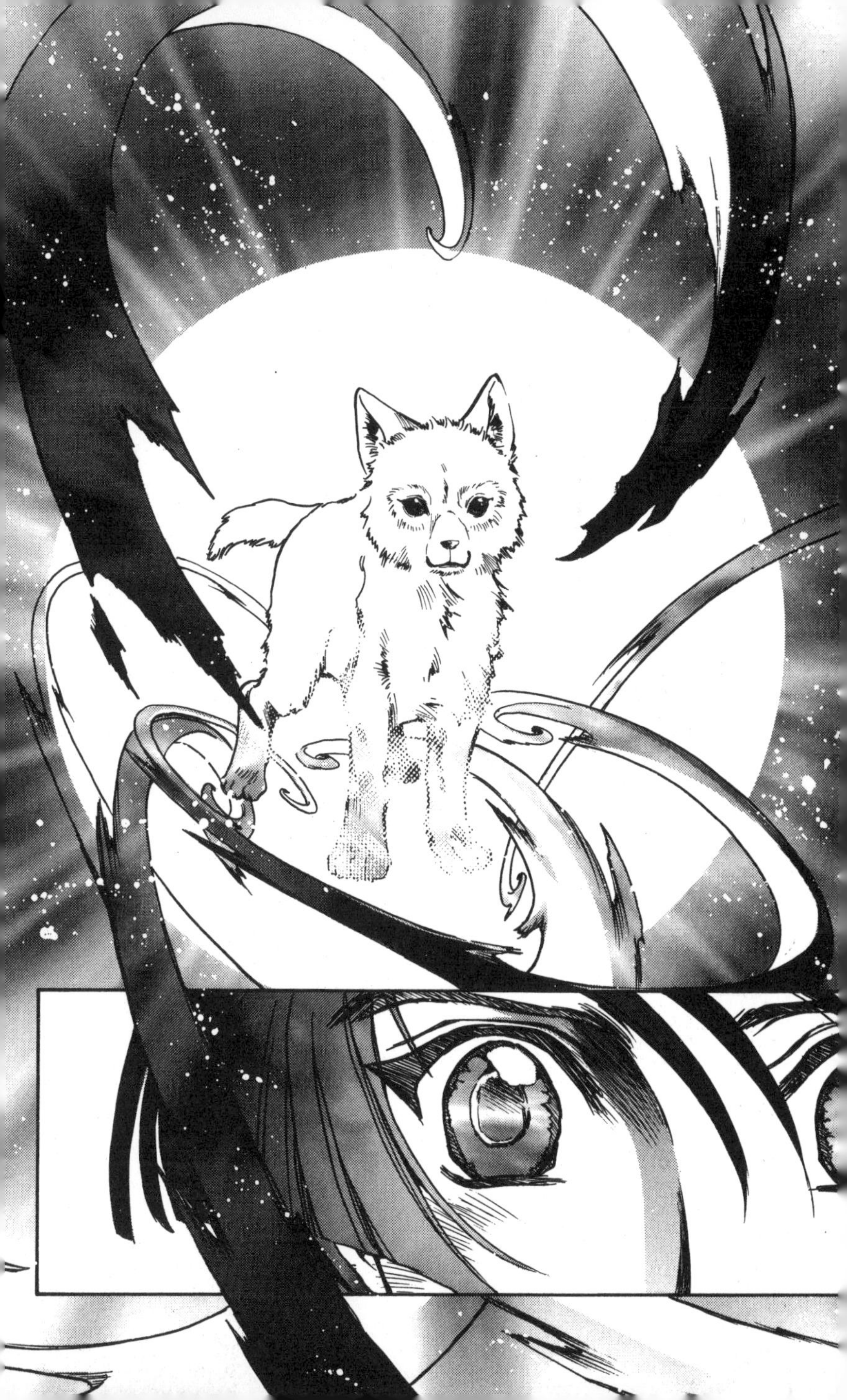

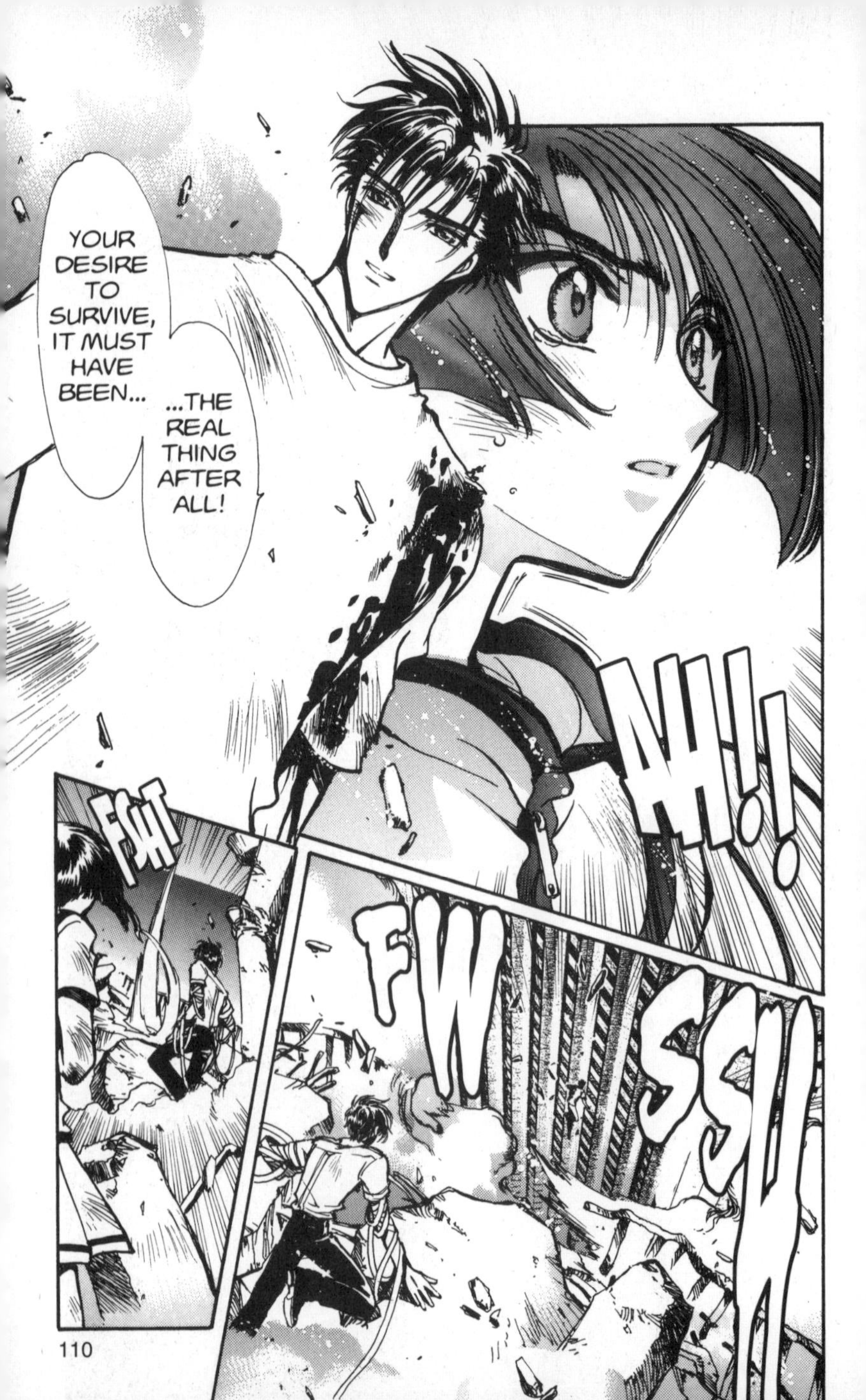
YOUR DESIRE TO SURVIVE, IT MUST HAVE BEEN...
...THE REAL THING AFTER ALL!
AH!!
FWSSH
FSHT

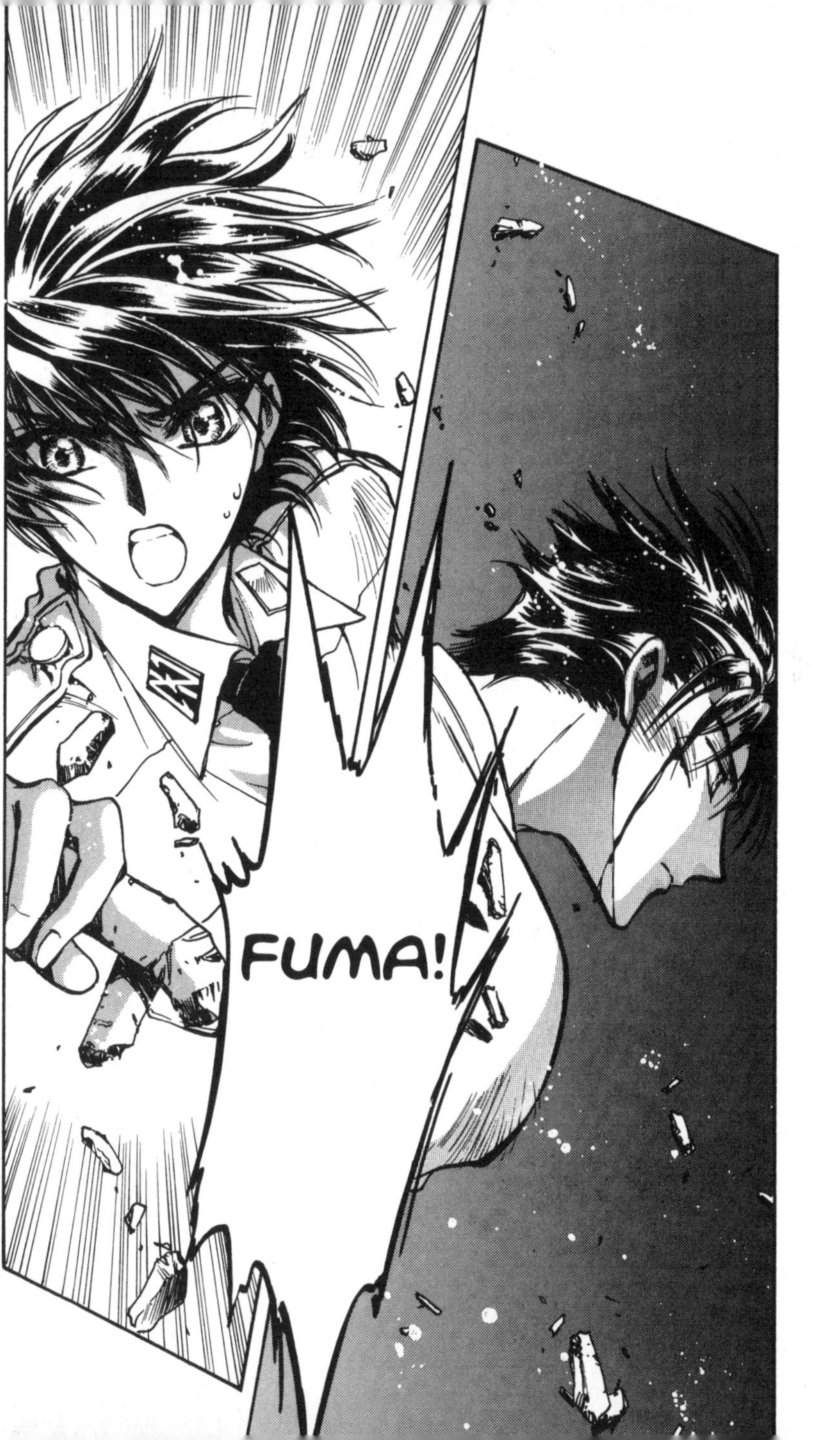
FUMA!

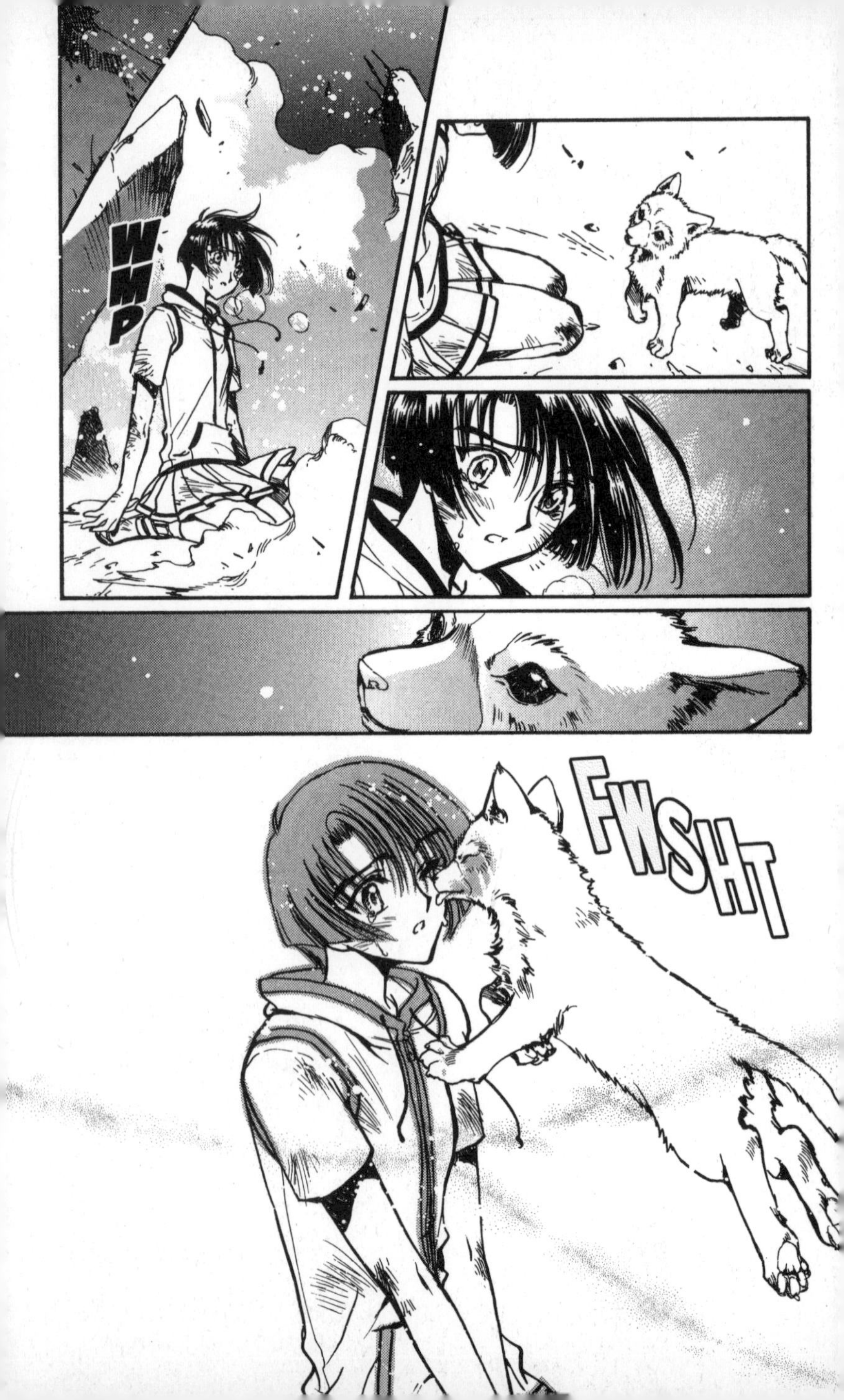
WMP
FWSHT

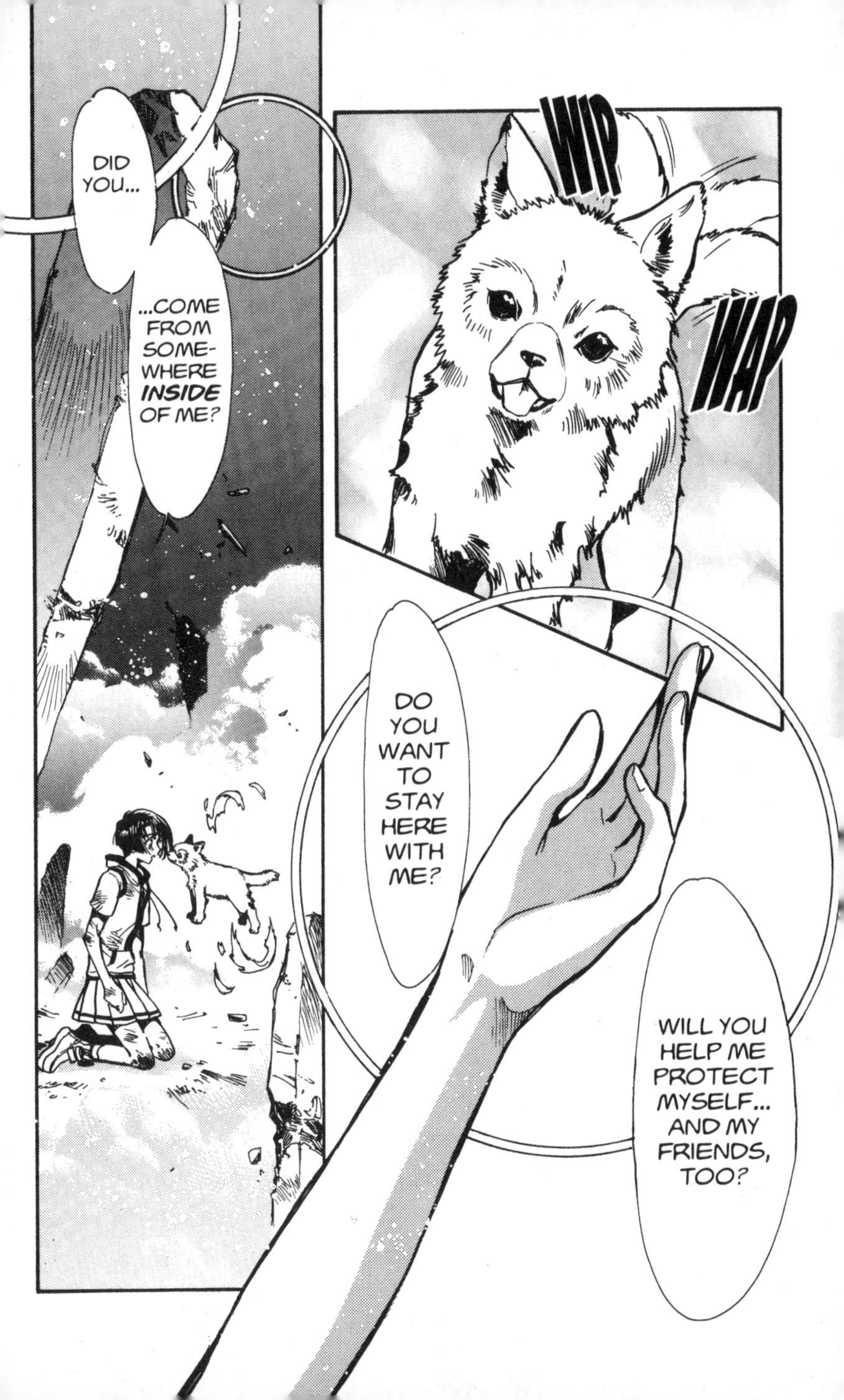
WIP
WAP
DO YOU WANT TO STAY HERE WITH ME?
WILL YOU HELP ME PROTECT MYSELF... AND MY FRIENDS, TOO?
DID YOU...
...COME FROM SOME-WHERE **INSIDE** OF ME?

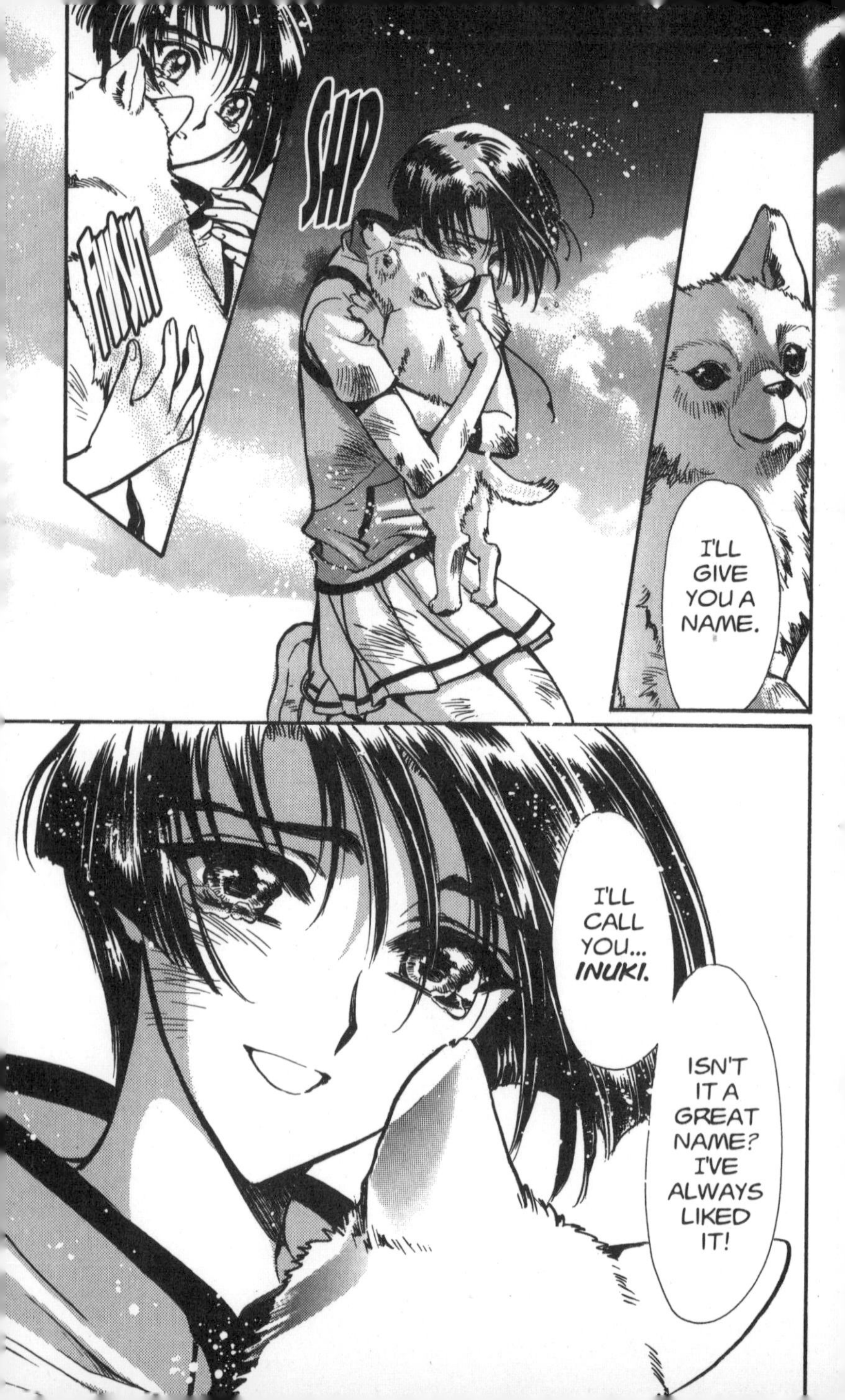
I'LL GIVE YOU A NAME.
SHP
FWISH
I'LL CALL YOU... **INUKI.**
ISN'T IT A GREAT NAME? I'VE ALWAYS LIKED IT!

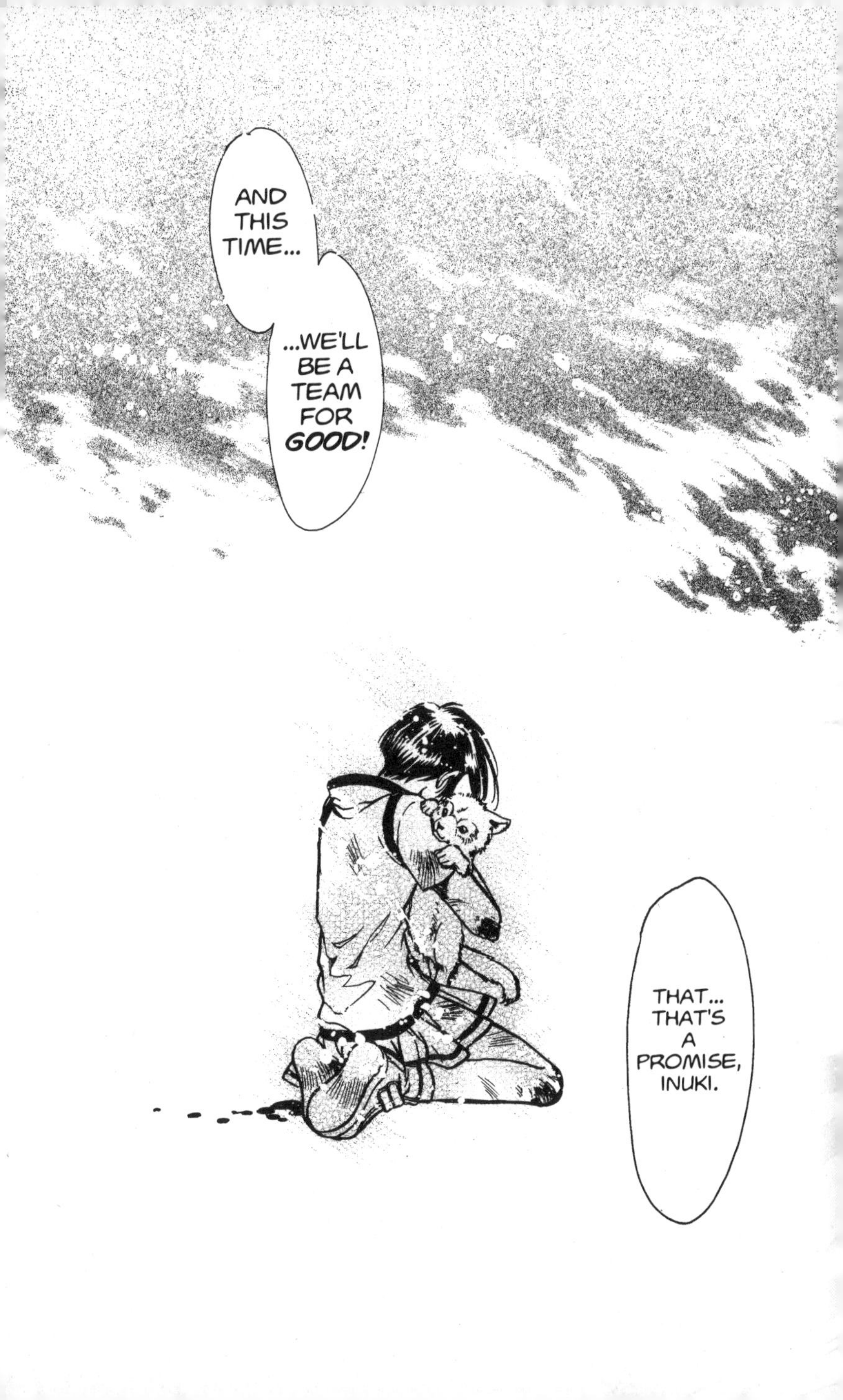
AND THIS TIME...
...WE'LL BE A TEAM FOR **GOOD!**
THAT... THAT'S A PROMISE, INUKI.

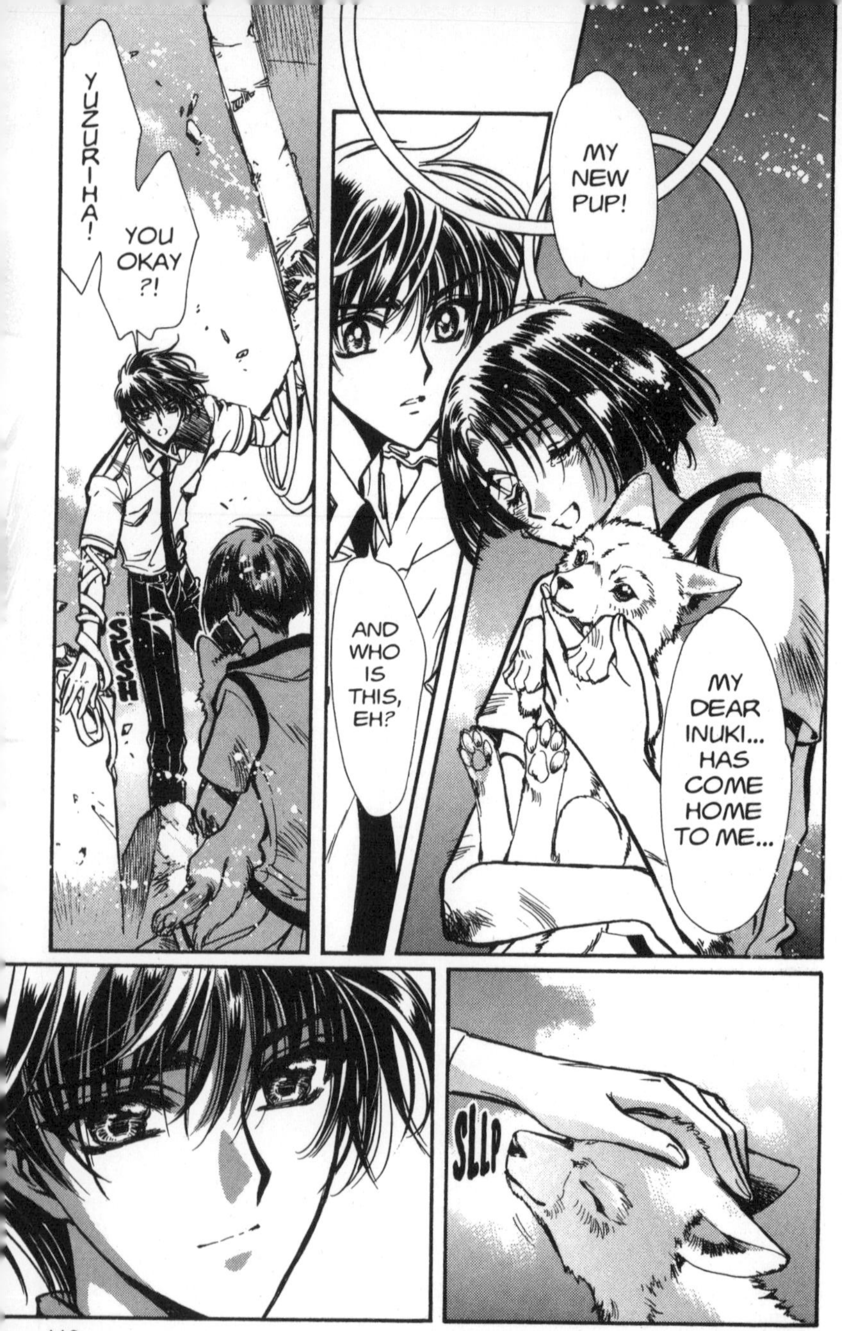
MY NEW PUP!
MY DEAR INUKI... HAS COME HOME TO ME...
AND WHO IS THIS, EH?
YUZURIHA!
YOU OKAY ?!
SKSH
SLLP

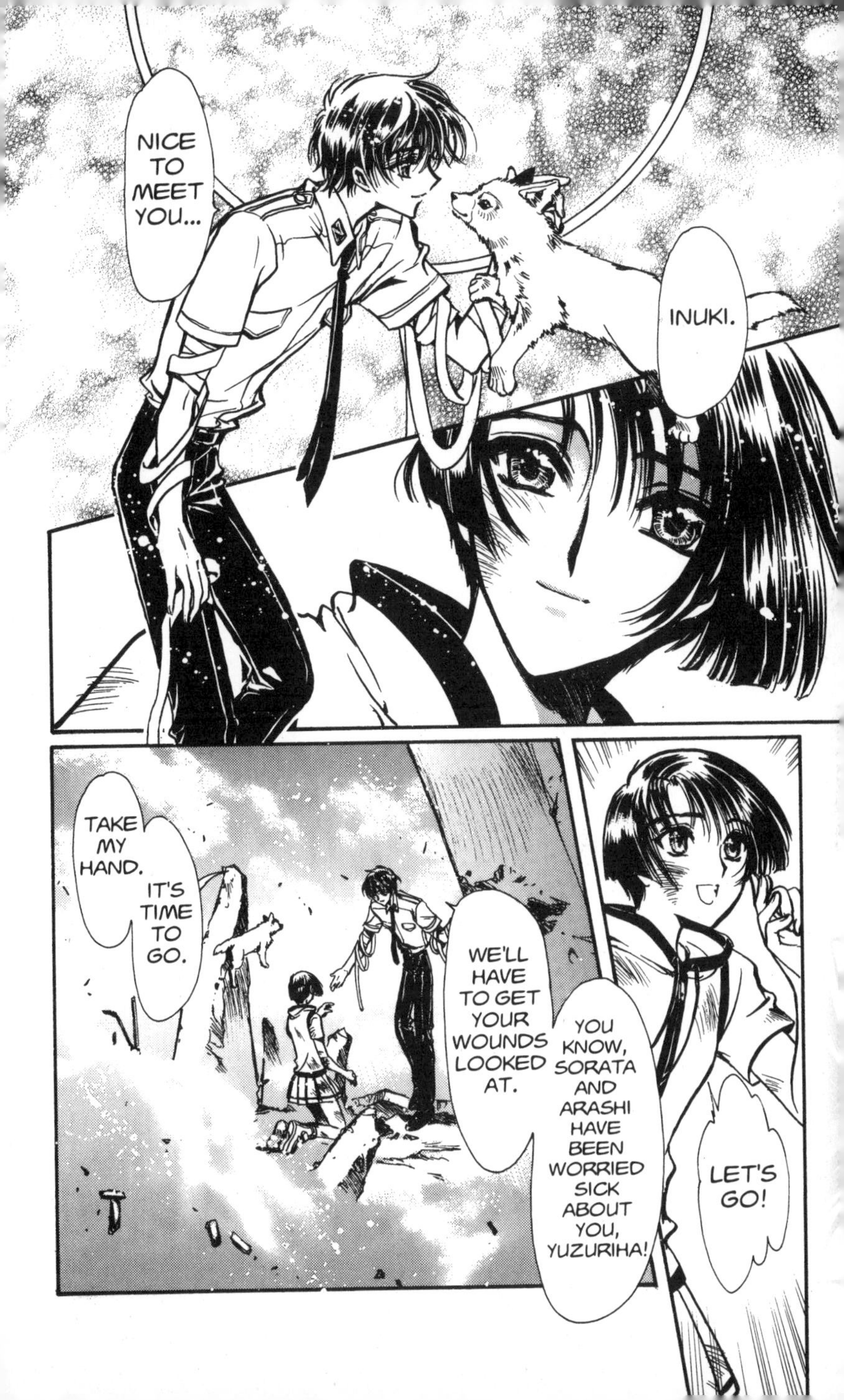
NICE TO MEET YOU...
INUKI.
YOU KNOW, SORATA AND ARASHI HAVE BEEN WORRIED SICK ABOUT YOU, YUZURIHA!
LET'S GO!
TAKE MY HAND.
IT'S TIME TO GO.
WE'LL HAVE TO GET YOUR WOUNDS LOOKED AT.

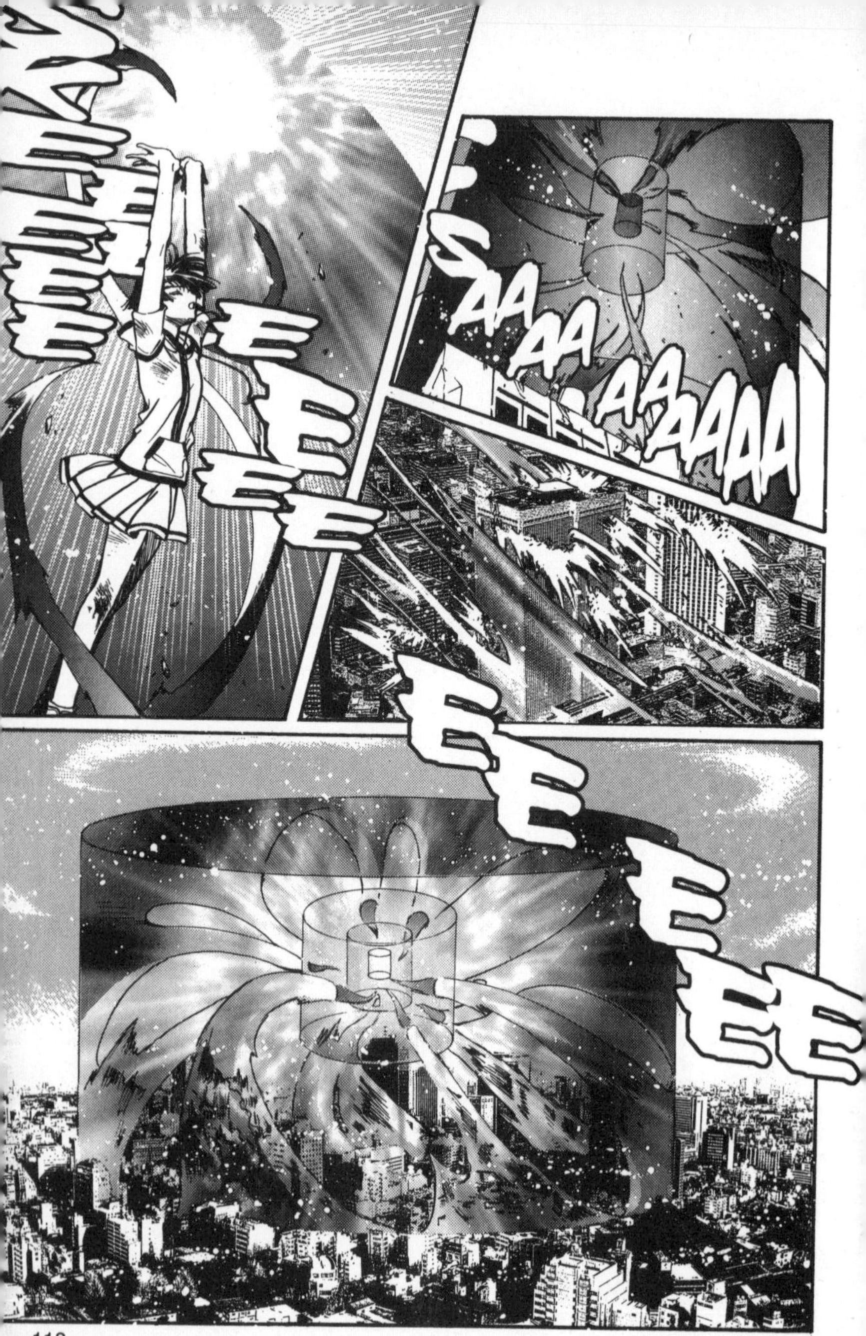
SAAAAAAAAAAAA
EEEEEEEEEEE
EEEEEEE

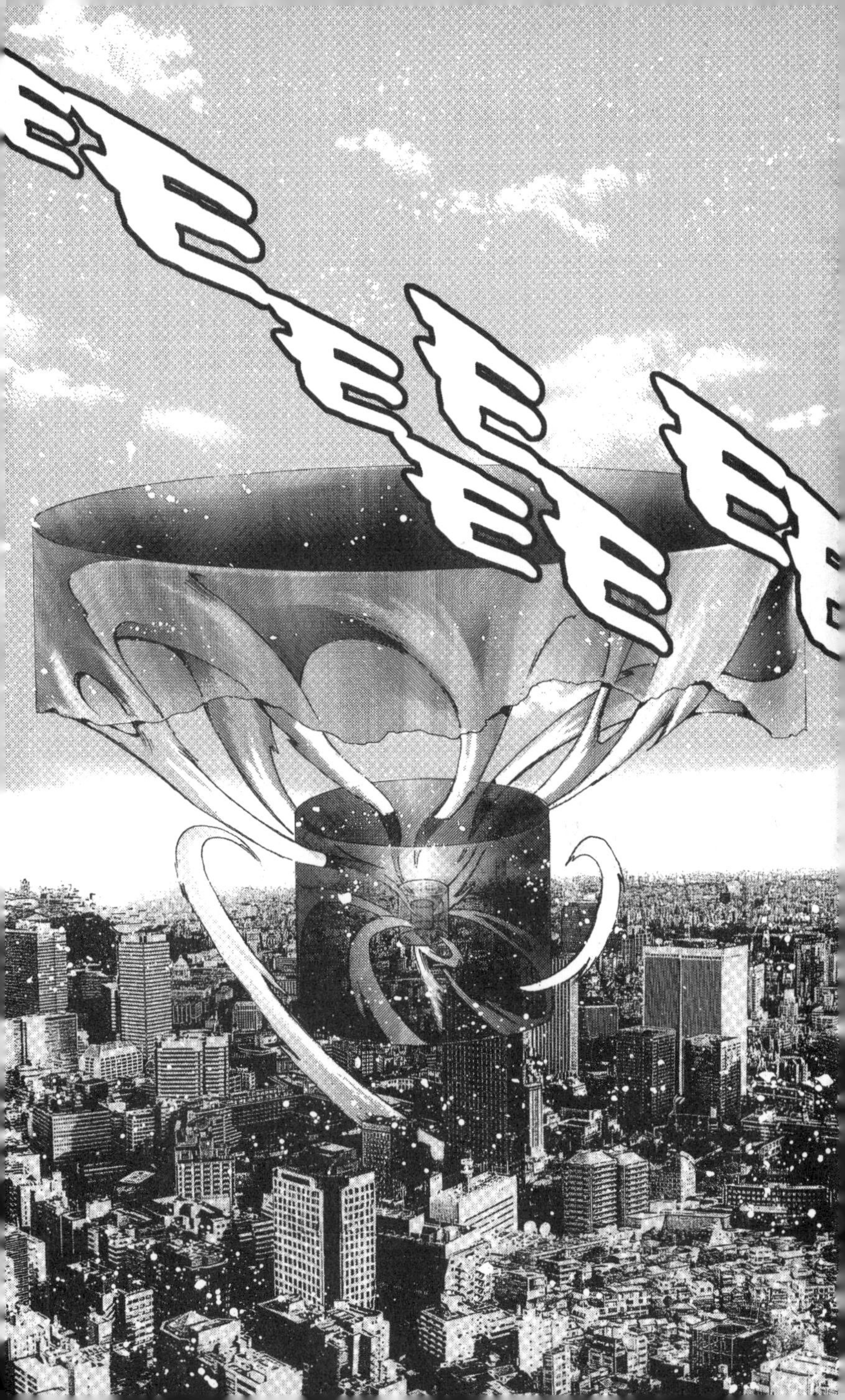

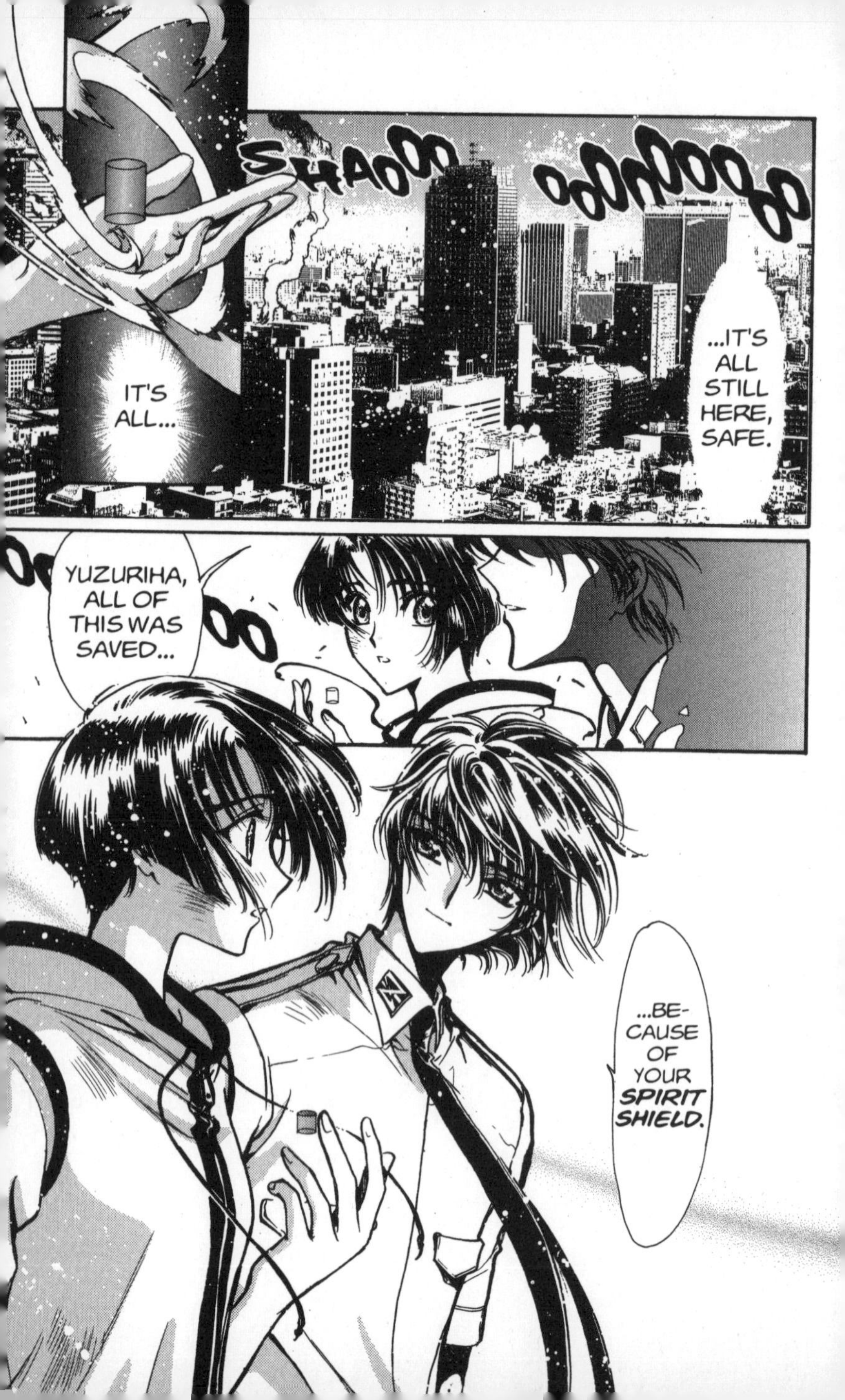
SHAOOO OOOOOOOO
IT'S ALL...
...IT'S ALL STILL HERE, SAFE.
OOOO
YUZURIHA, ALL OF THIS WAS SAVED...
...BE-CAUSE OF YOUR **SPIRIT SHIELD.**

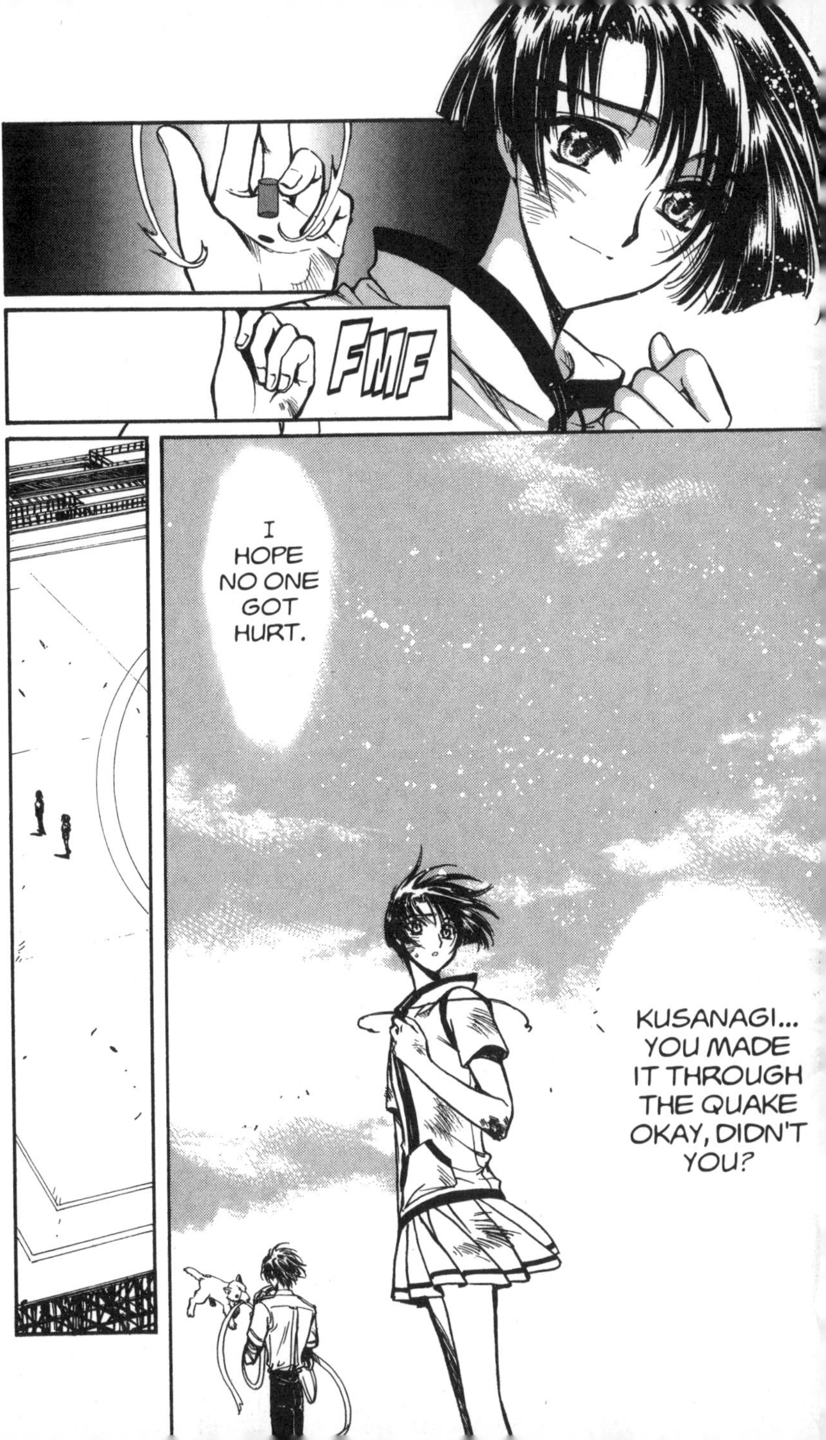
FMF
I HOPE NO ONE GOT HURT.
KUSANAGI... YOU MADE IT THROUGH THE QUAKE OKAY, DIDN'T YOU?

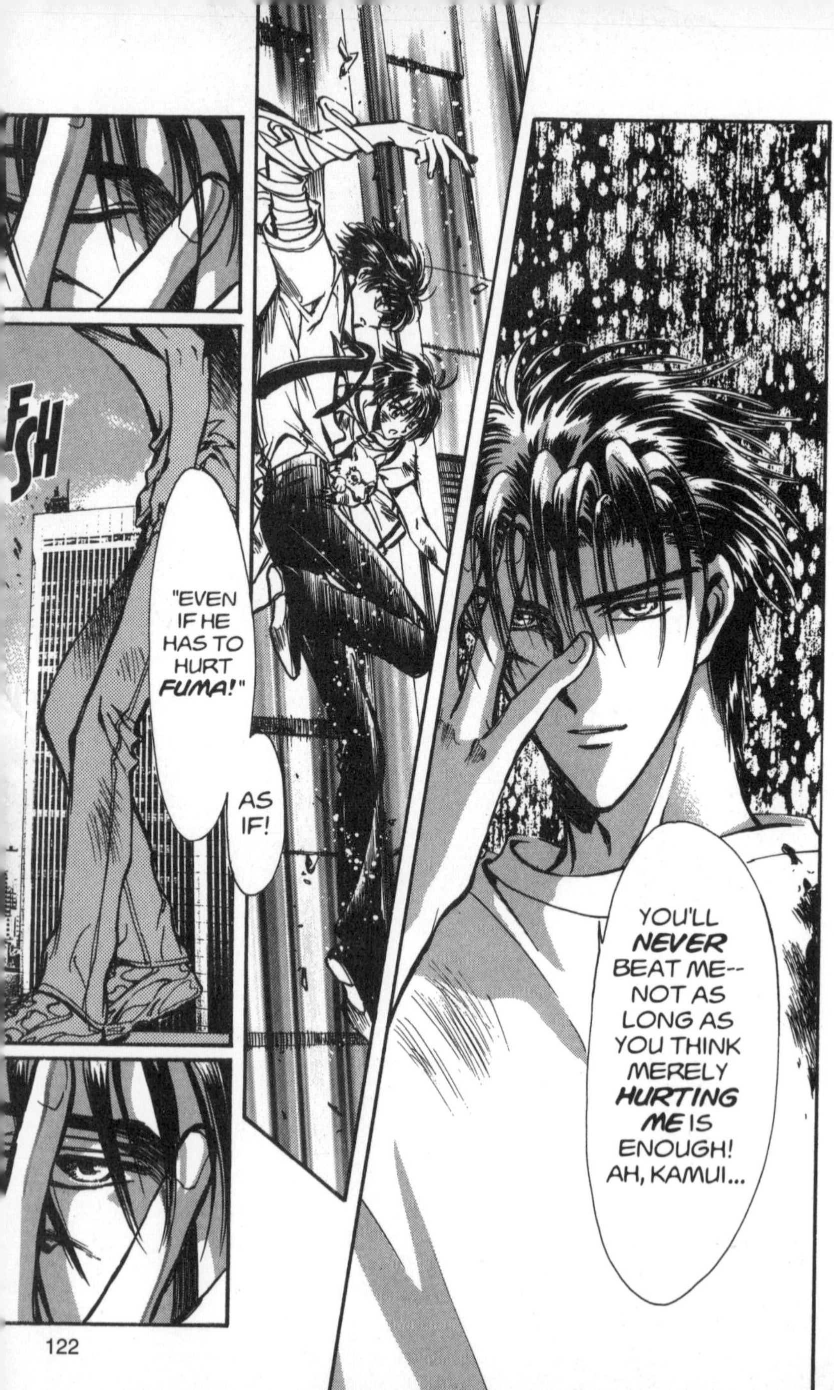
YOU'LL NEVER BEAT ME--NOT AS LONG AS YOU THINK MERELY HURTING ME IS ENOUGH! AH, KAMUI...
"EVEN IF HE HAS TO HURT FUMA!"
AS IF!
FSH

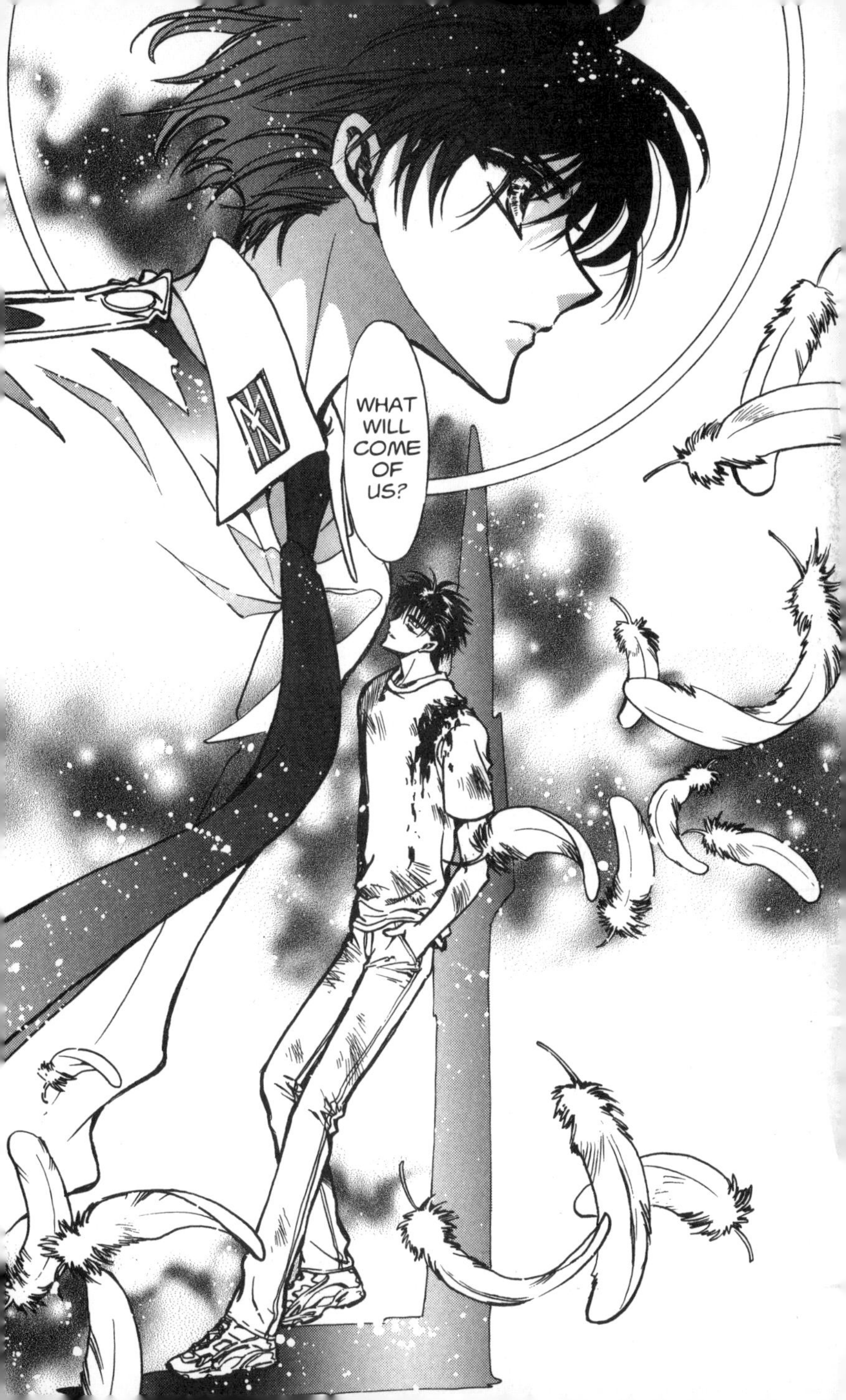
WHAT WILL COME OF US?

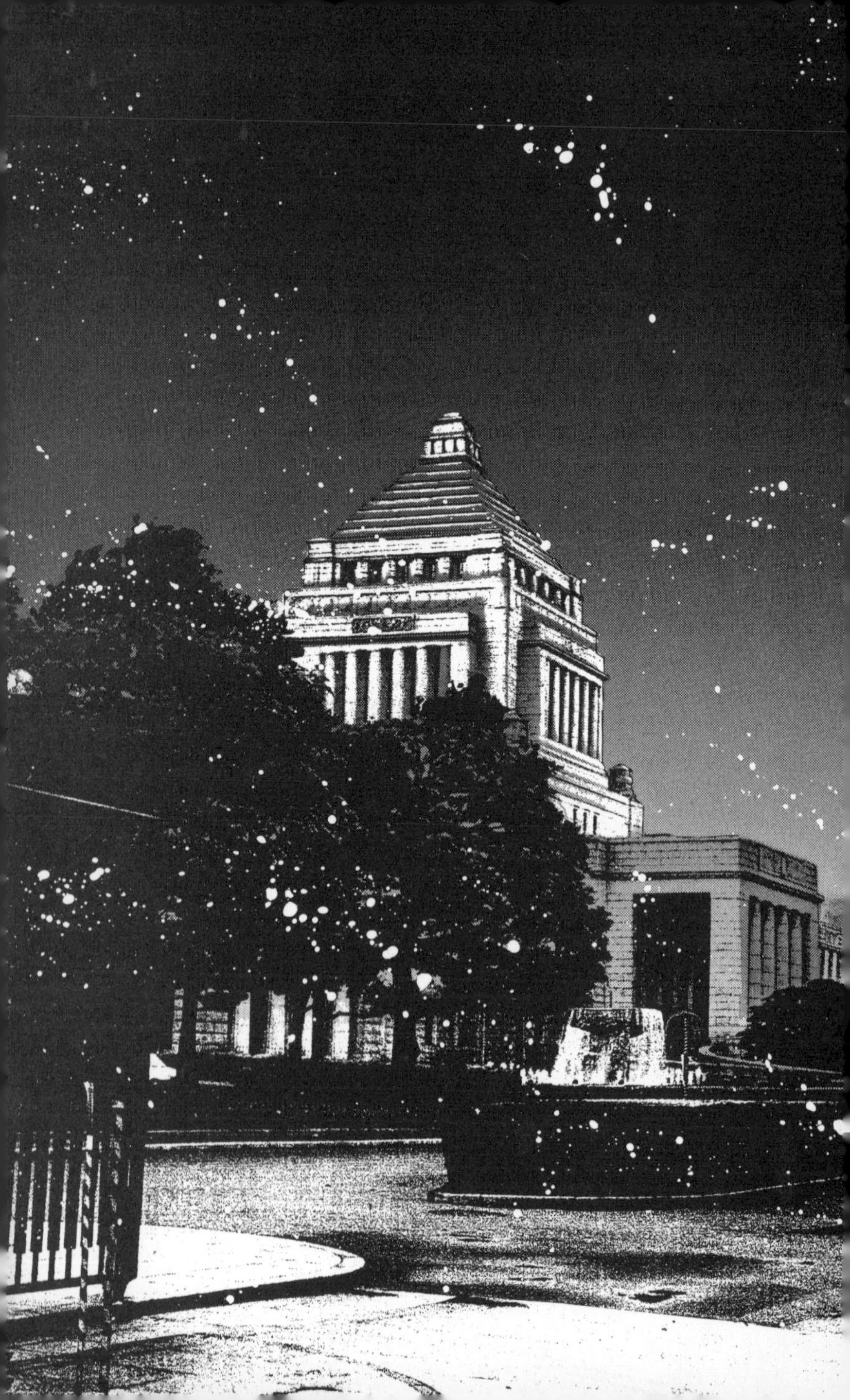

警務部

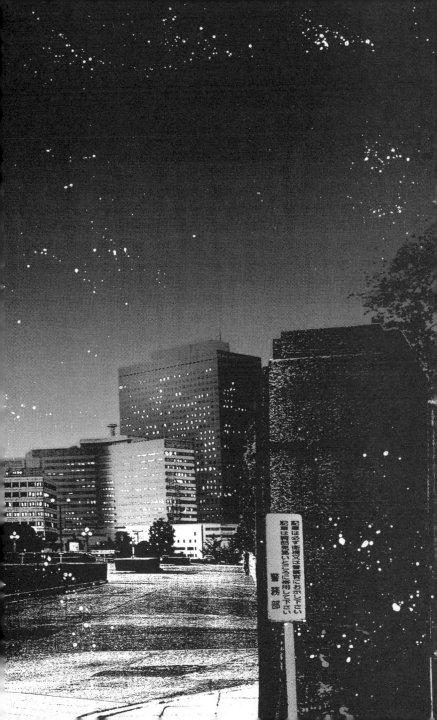

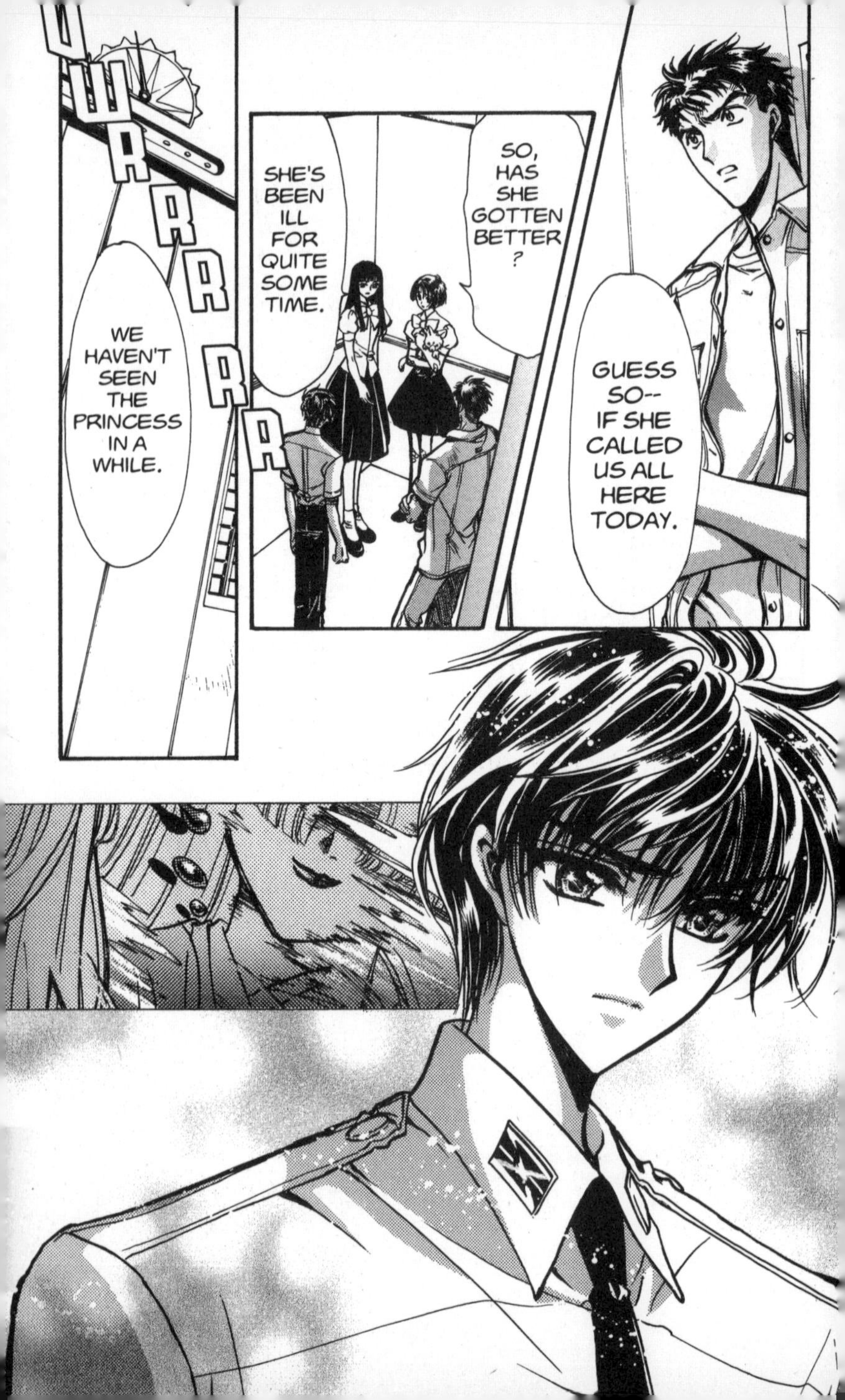
DURRRRR
WE HAVEN'T SEEN THE PRINCESS IN A WHILE.
SHE'S BEEN ILL FOR QUITE SOME TIME.
SO, HAS SHE GOTTEN BETTER?
GUESS SO-- IF SHE CALLED US ALL HERE TODAY.

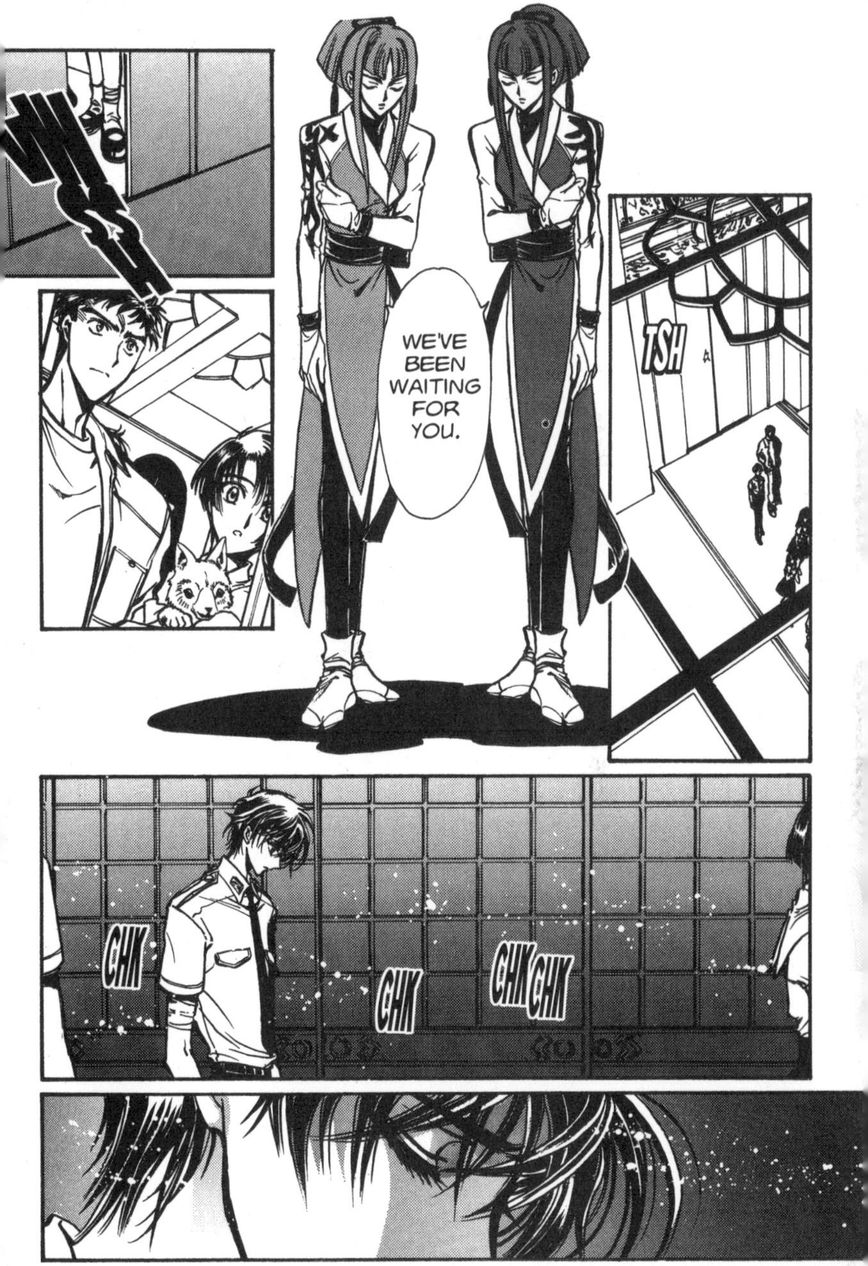
TSH
WE'VE BEEN WAITING FOR YOU.
WSH
CHK
CHK
CHK CHK

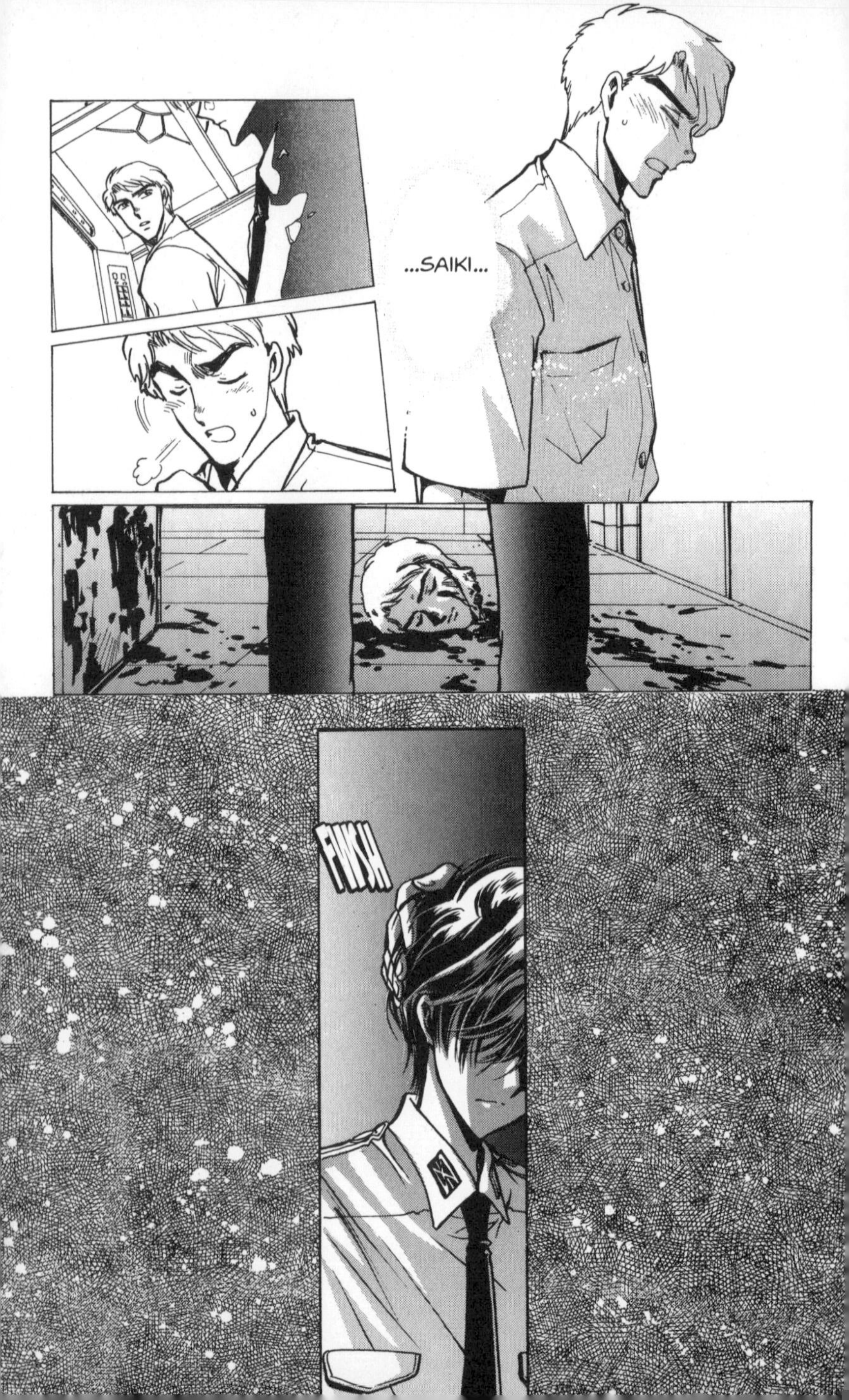
...SAIKI...
FWISH

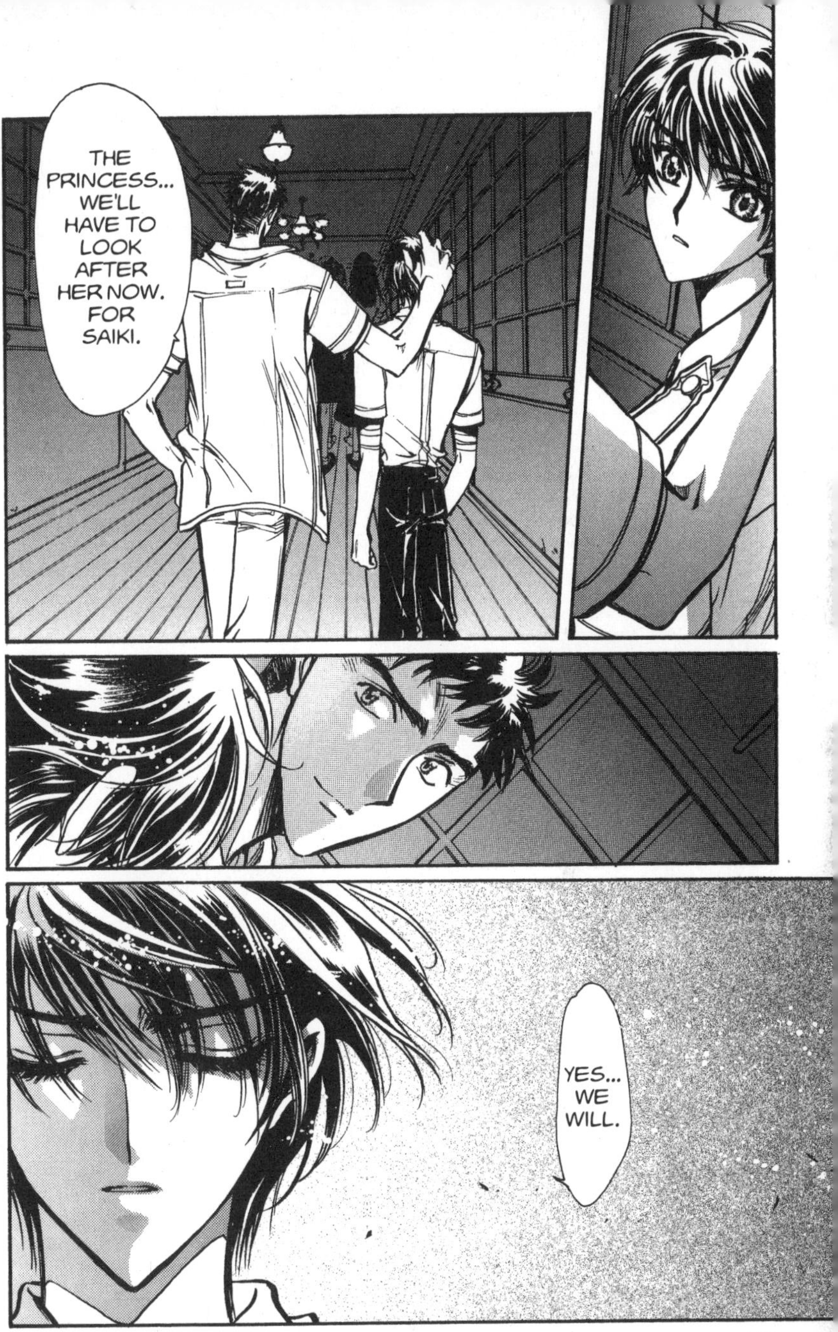
THE PRINCESS... WE'LL HAVE TO LOOK AFTER HER NOW. FOR SAIKI.
YES... WE WILL.

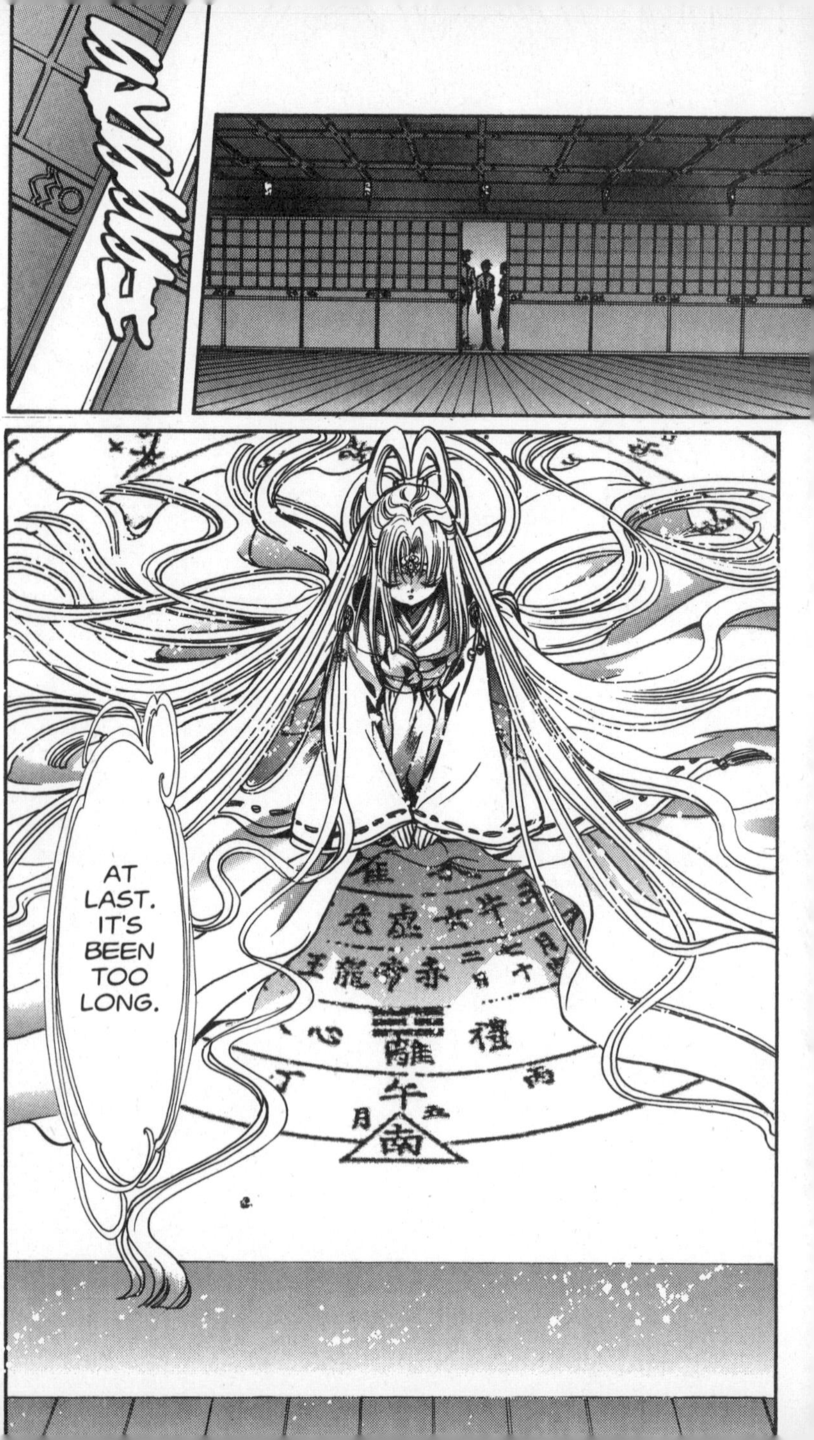
AT LAST. IT'S BEEN TOO LONG.

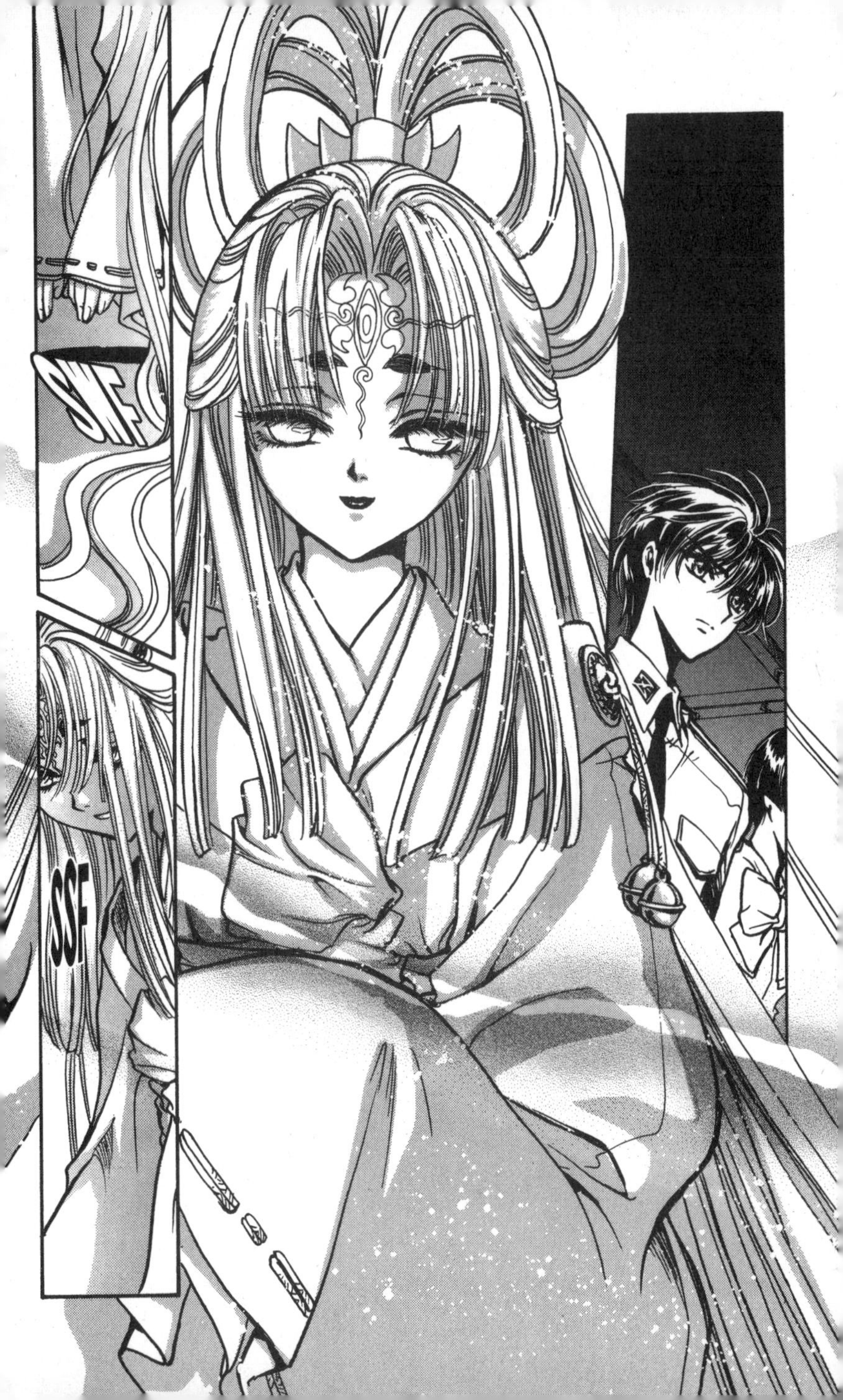
SSF

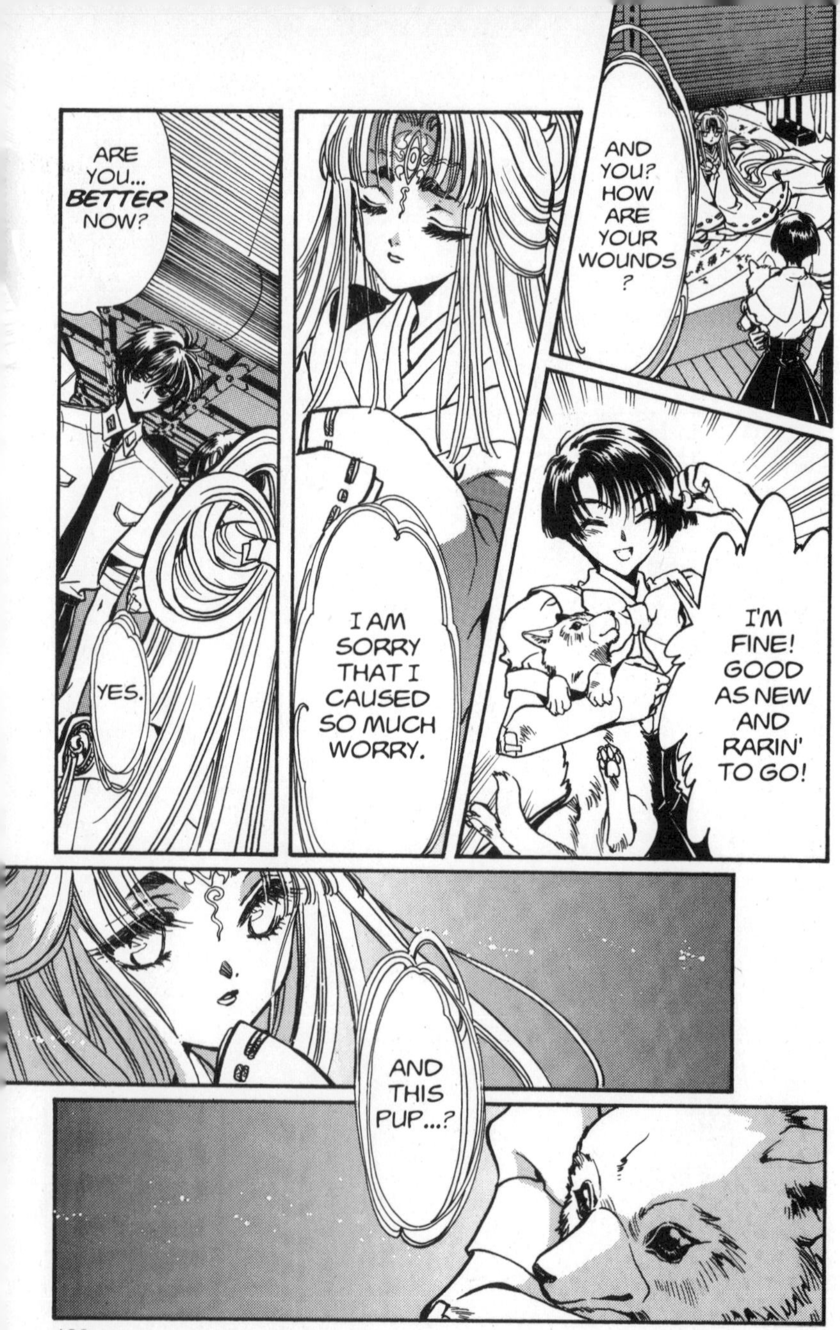
AND YOU? HOW ARE YOUR WOUNDS?
I'M FINE! GOOD AS NEW AND RARIN' TO GO!
I AM SORRY THAT I CAUSED SO MUCH WORRY.
ARE YOU... *BETTER* NOW?
YES.
AND THIS PUP...?

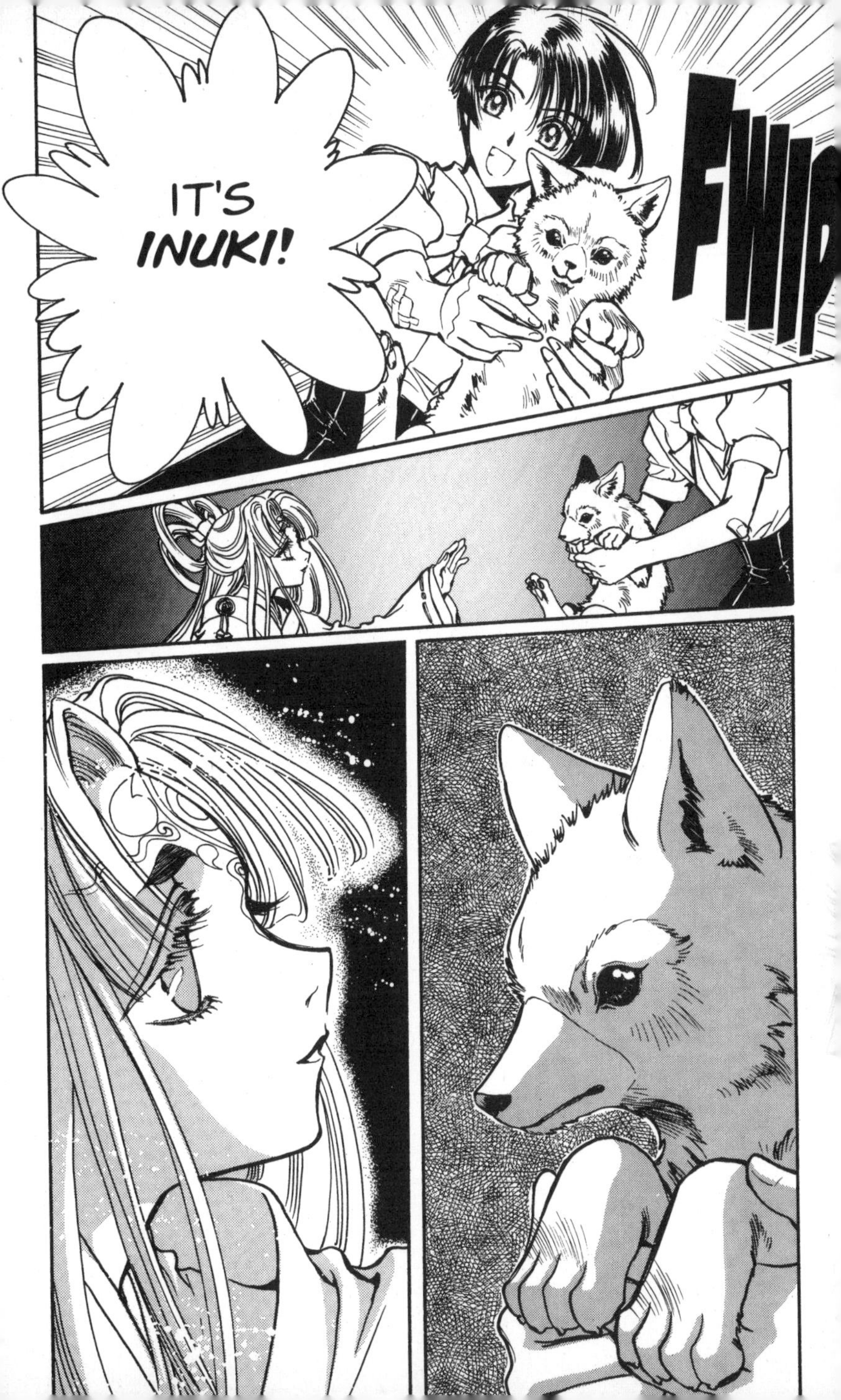
FWIP
IT'S INUKI!

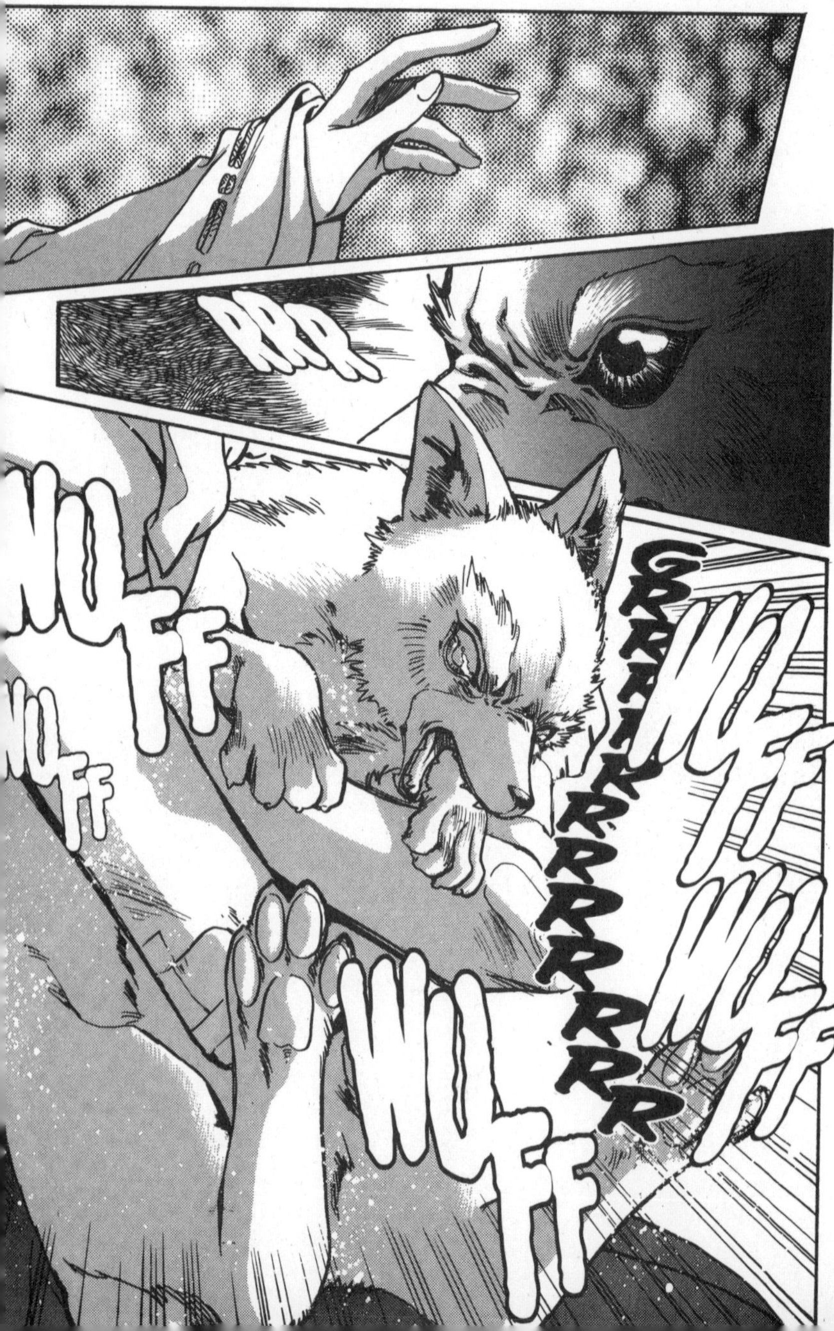
PAP
GRRRRRRRRRR
WUFF
WUFF
WUFF
WUFF
WUFF

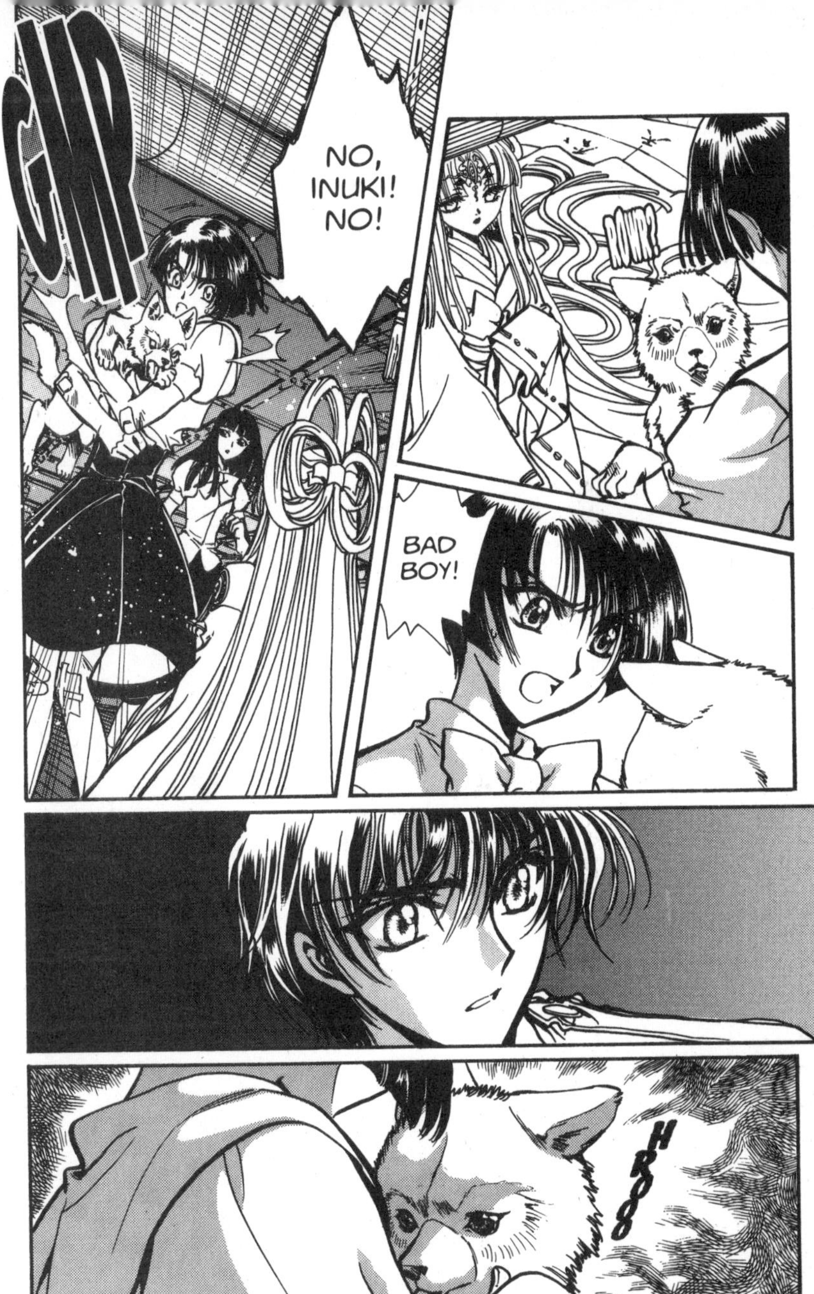
ROWR?
BAD BOY!
GNP
NO, INUKI! NO!
HROOO

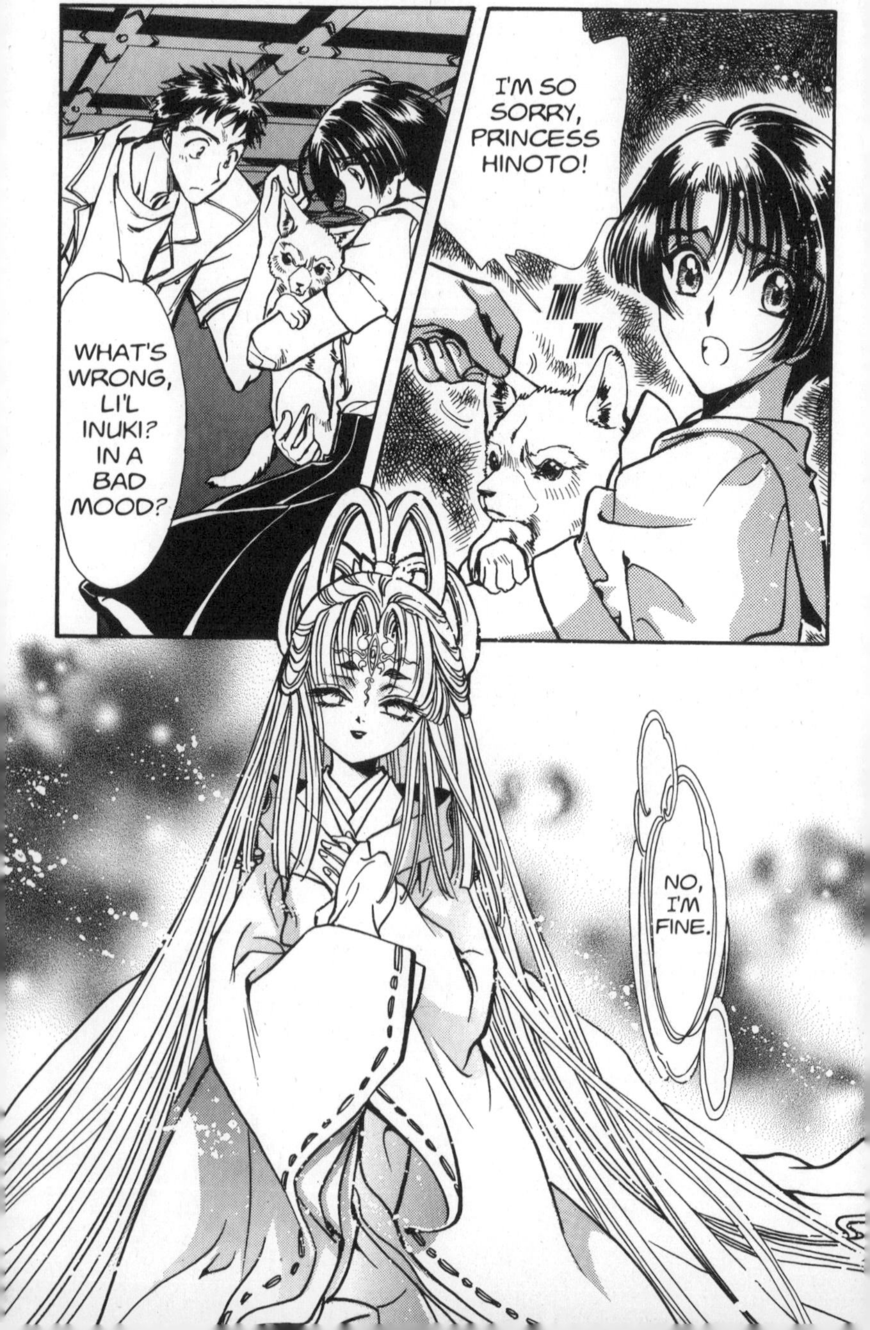
I'M SO SORRY, PRINCESS HINOTO!
WHAT'S WRONG, LI'L INUKI? IN A BAD MOOD?
NO, I'M FINE.

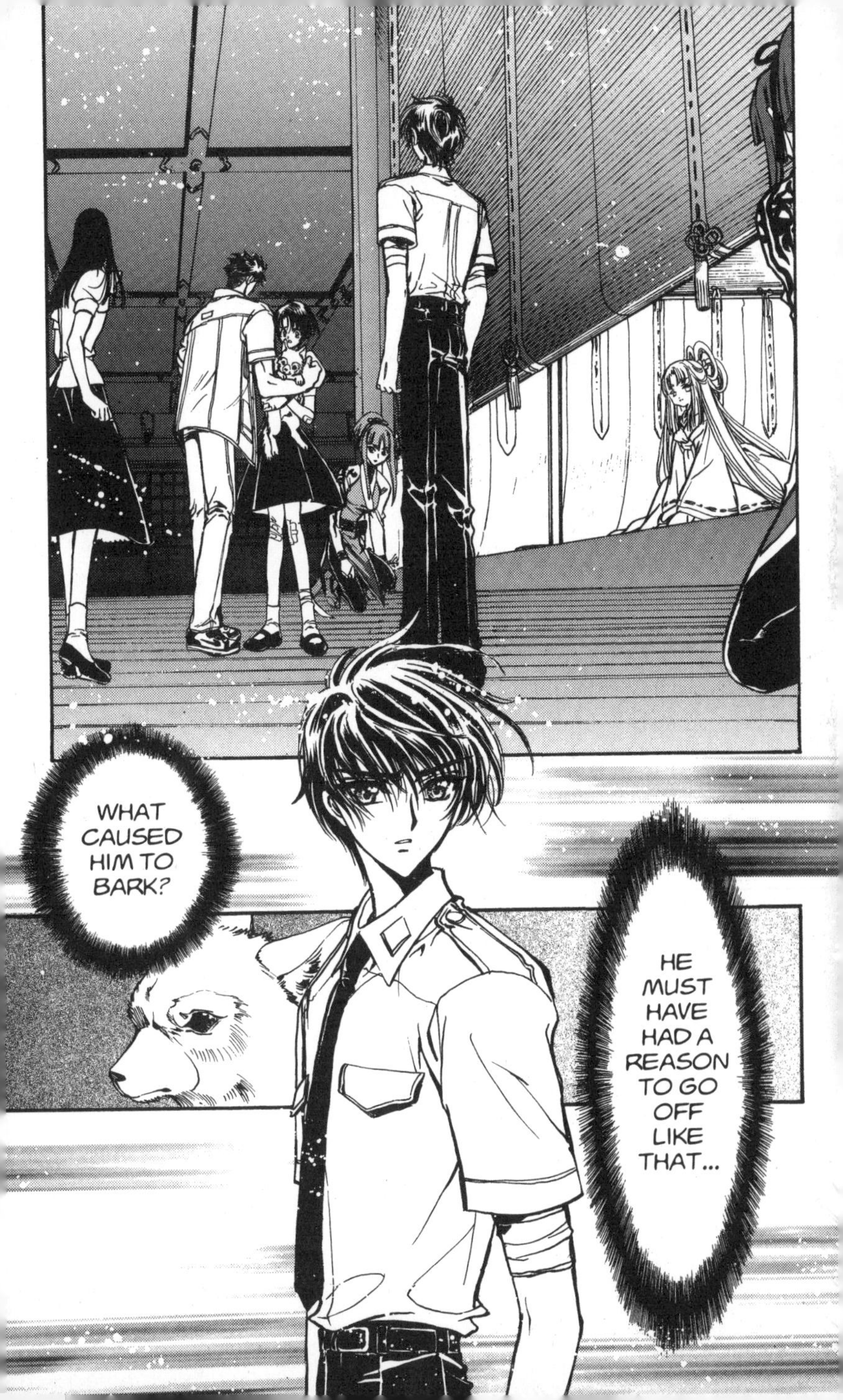
HE MUST HAVE HAD A REASON TO GO OFF LIKE THAT...
WHAT CAUSED HIM TO BARK?

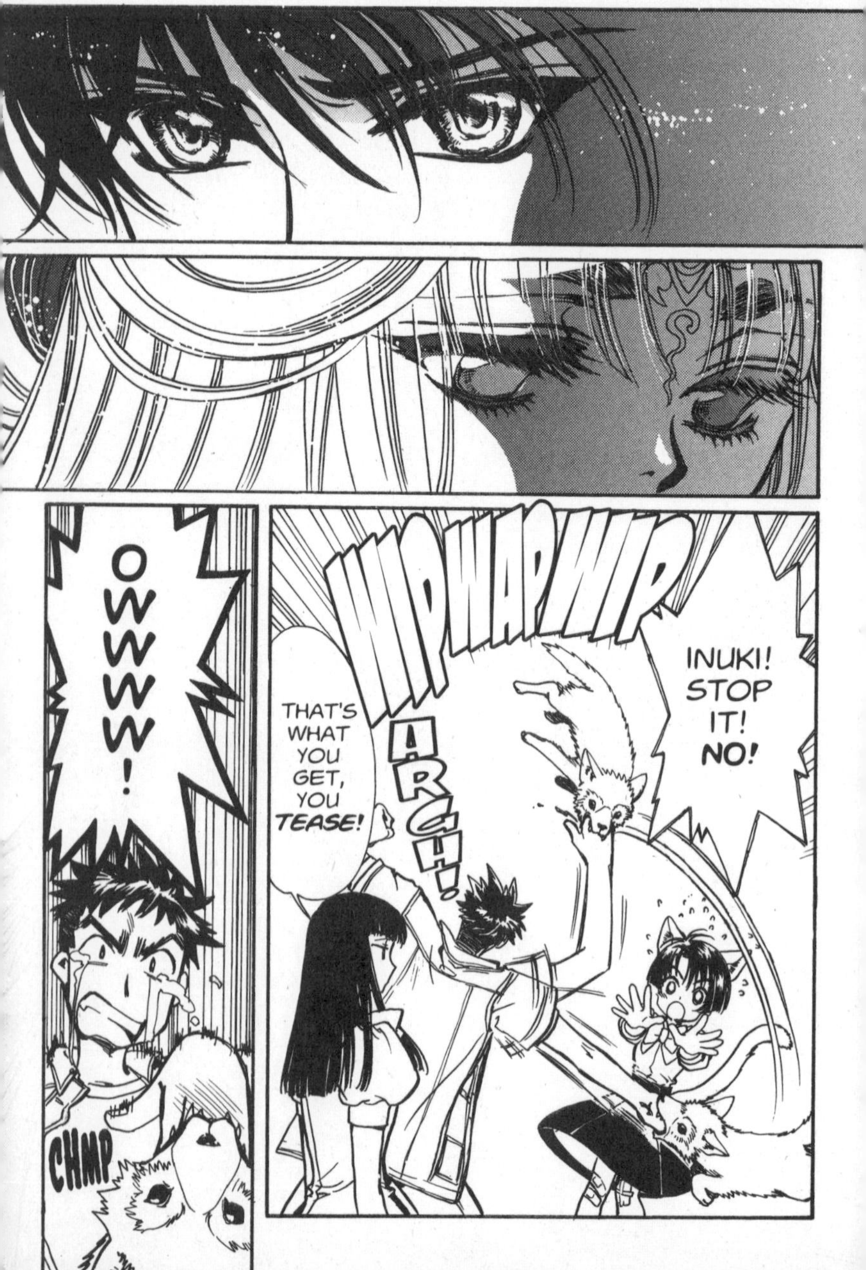
WHIPWAPWIP
INUKI! STOP IT! NO!
THAT'S WHAT YOU GET, YOU *TEASE!*
ARGH!
OWWWW!
CHMP

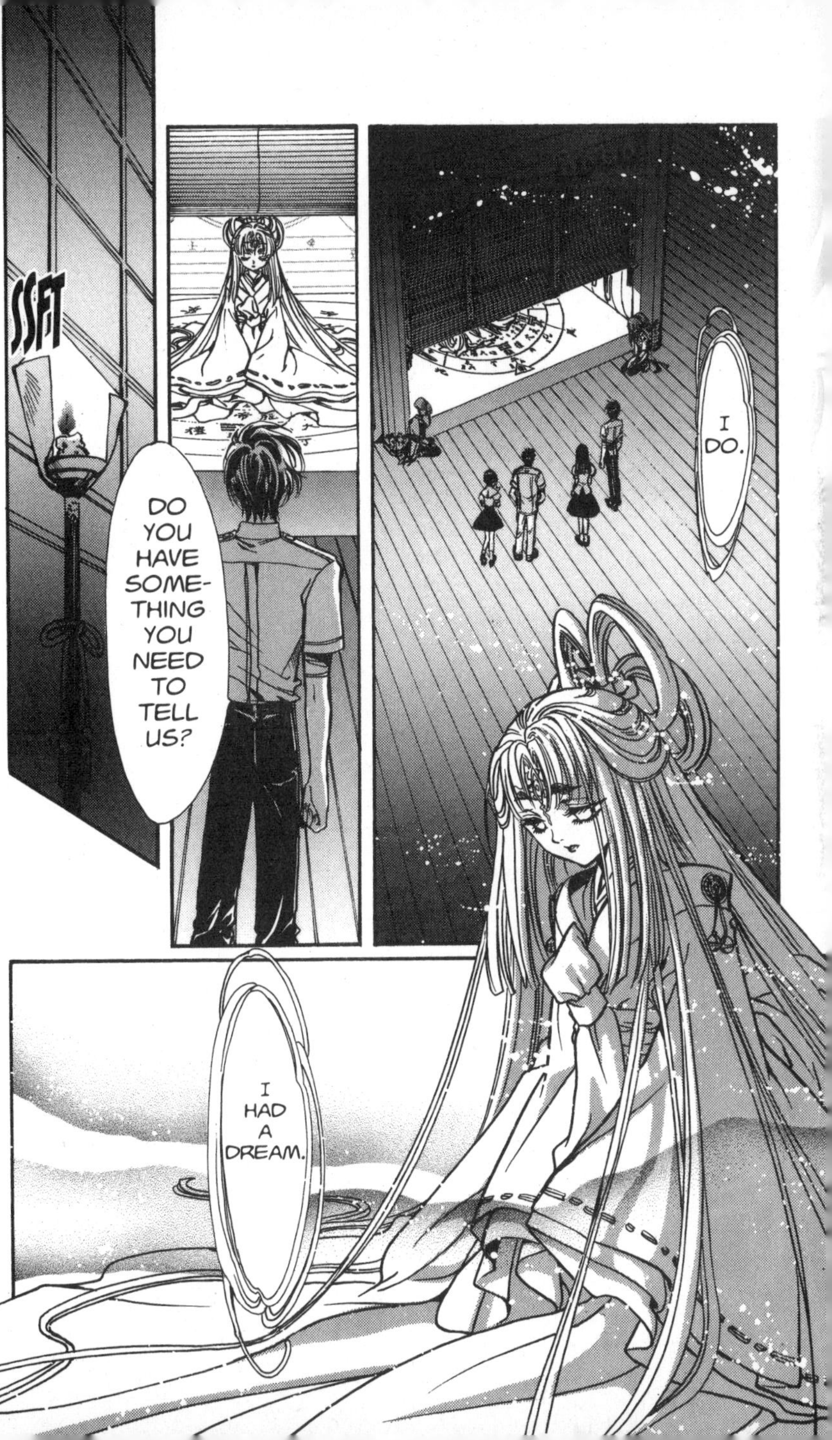
DO YOU HAVE SOMETHING YOU NEED TO TELL US?
SSFT
I DO.
I HAD A DREAM.

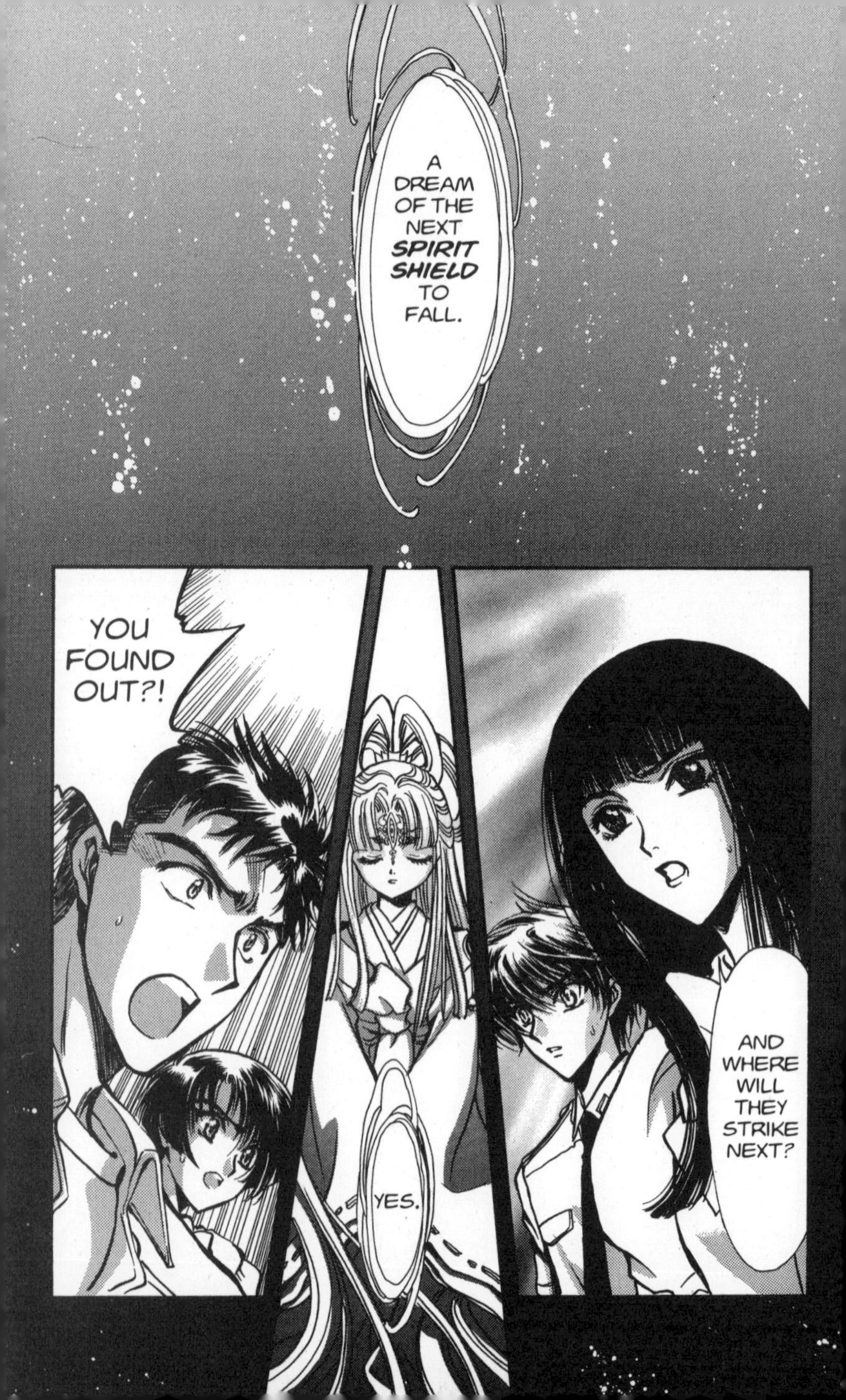
A DREAM OF THE NEXT ***SPIRIT SHIELD*** TO FALL.
YOU FOUND OUT?!
YES.
AND WHERE WILL THEY STRIKE NEXT?

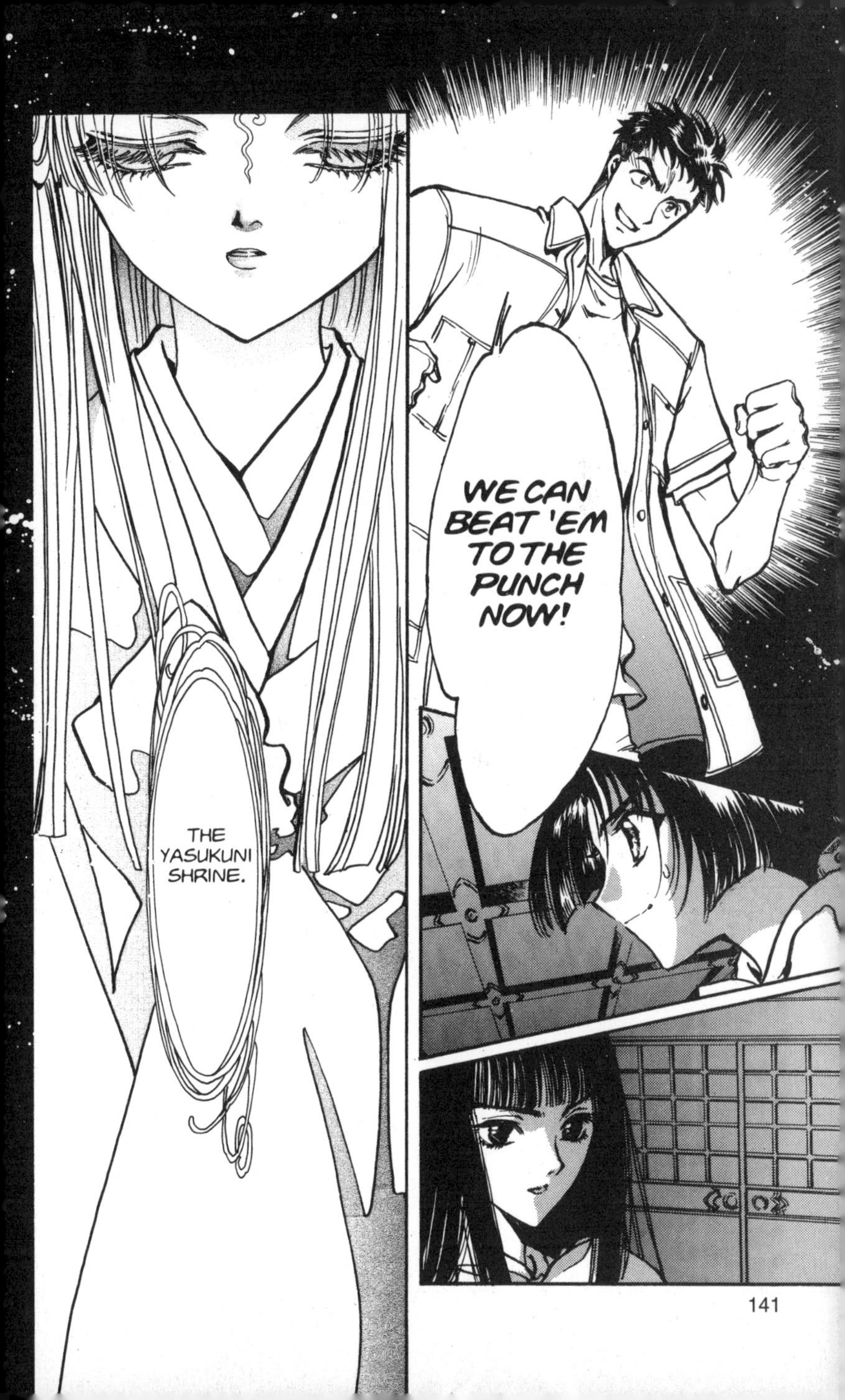
WE CAN BEAT 'EM TO THE PUNCH NOW!
THE YASUKUNI SHRINE.

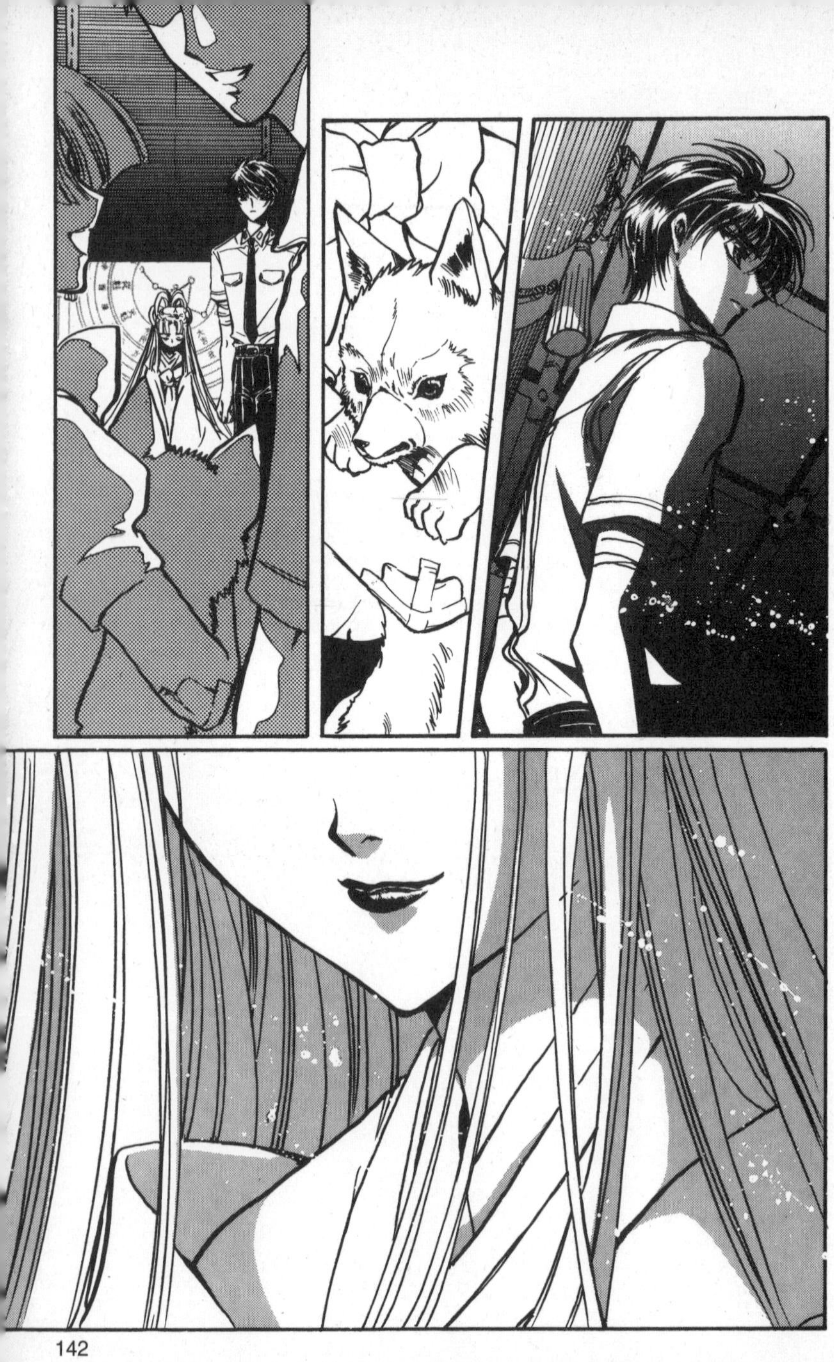

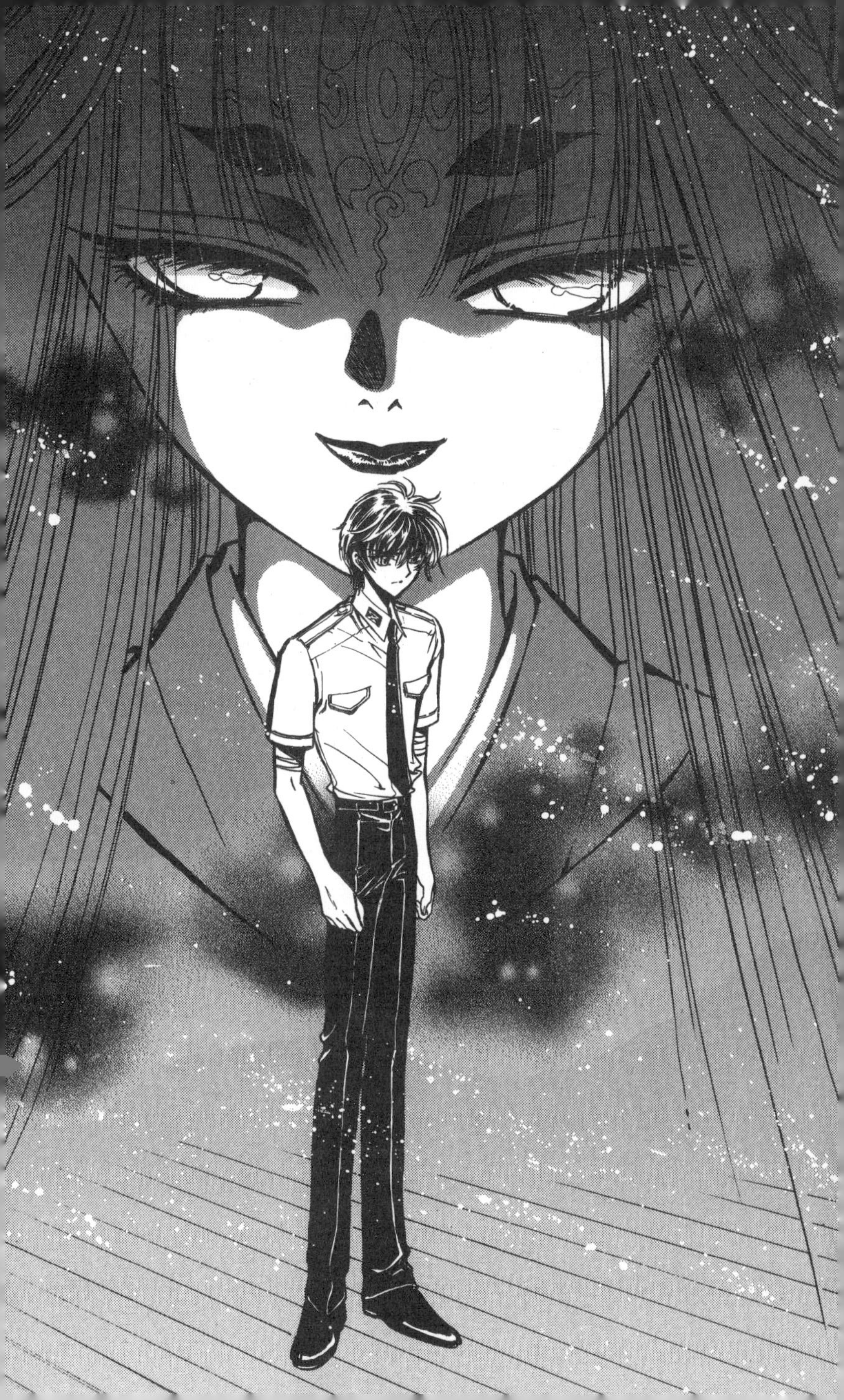

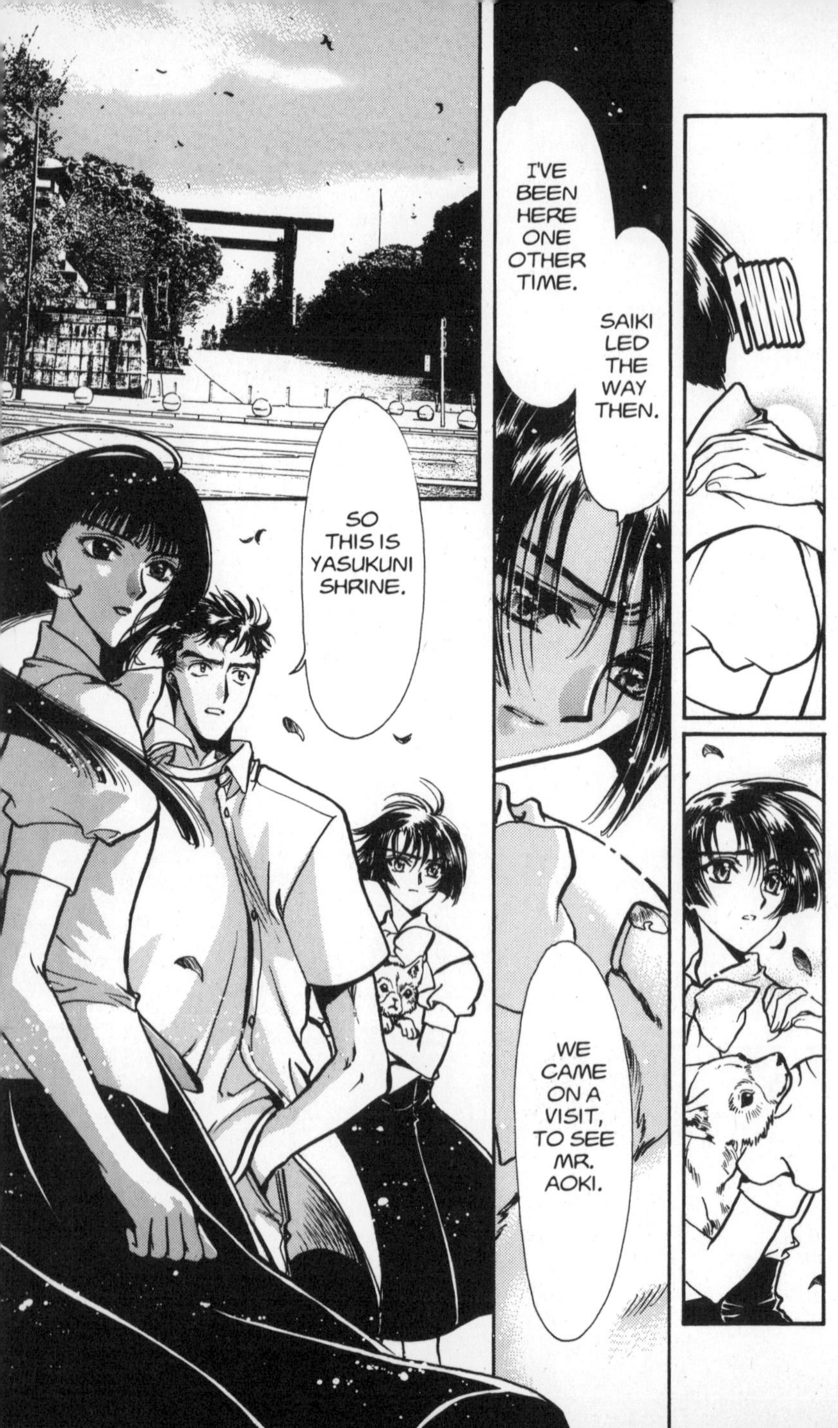
FWMP
I'VE BEEN HERE ONE OTHER TIME.
SAIKI LED THE WAY THEN.
WE CAME ON A VISIT, TO SEE MR. AOKI.
SO THIS IS YASUKUNI SHRINE.

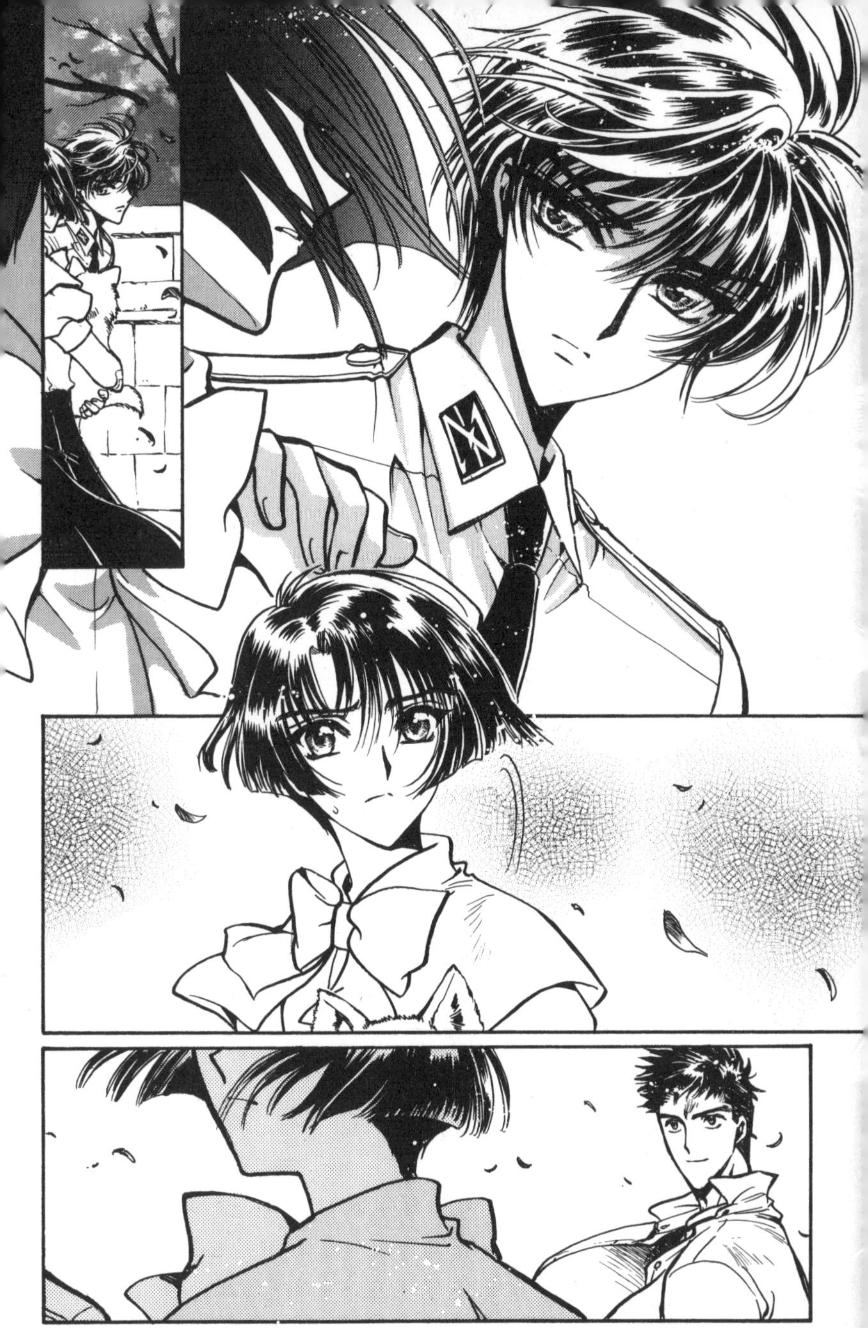

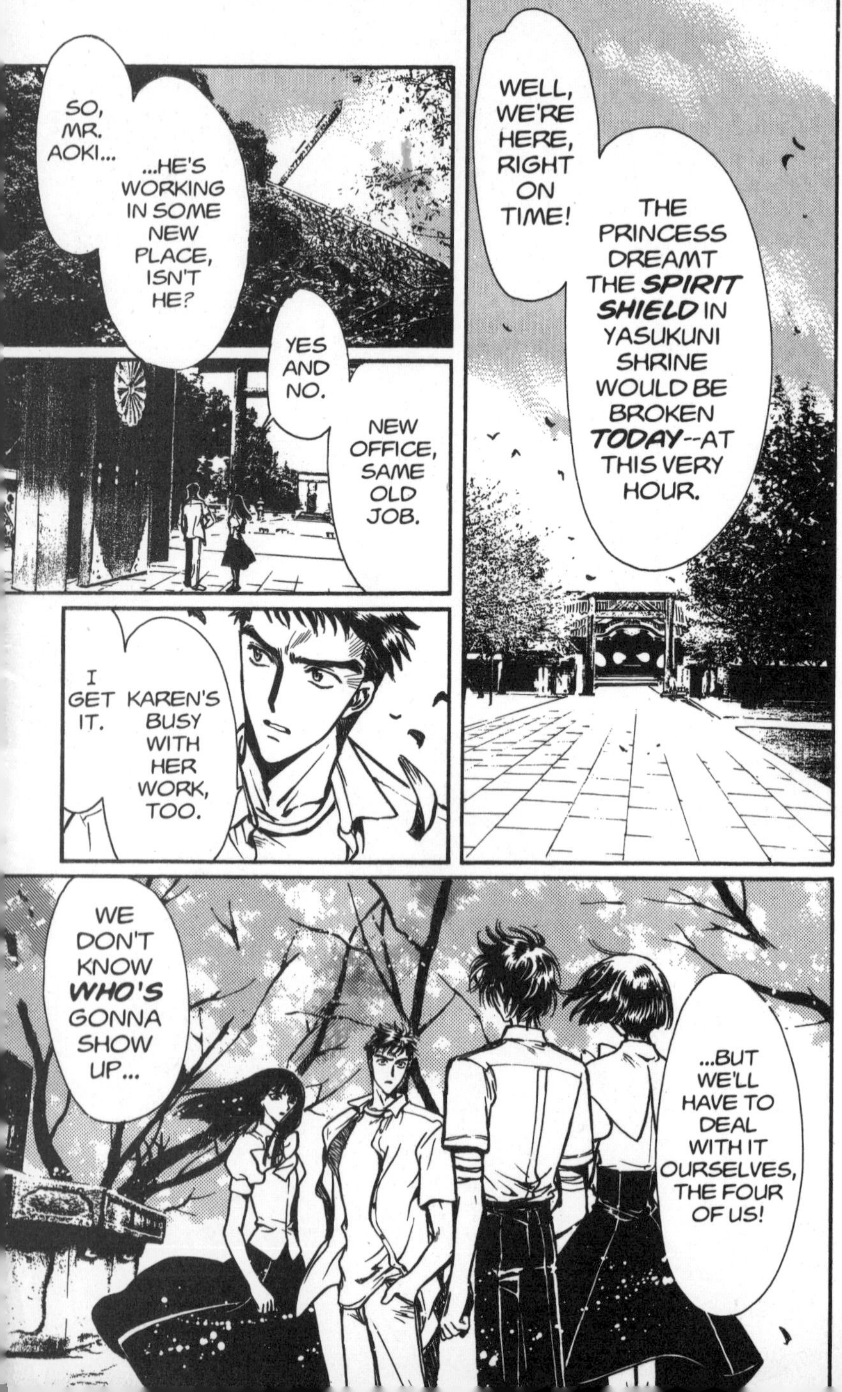
WELL, WE'RE HERE, RIGHT ON TIME!
THE PRINCESS DREAMT THE **SPIRIT SHIELD** IN YASUKUNI SHRINE WOULD BE BROKEN **TODAY**--AT THIS VERY HOUR.
SO, MR. AOKI...
...HE'S WORKING IN SOME NEW PLACE, ISN'T HE?
YES AND NO.
NEW OFFICE, SAME OLD JOB.
KAREN'S BUSY WITH HER WORK, TOO.
I GET IT.
WE DON'T KNOW **WHO'S** GONNA SHOW UP...
...BUT WE'LL HAVE TO DEAL WITH IT OURSELVES, THE FOUR OF US!

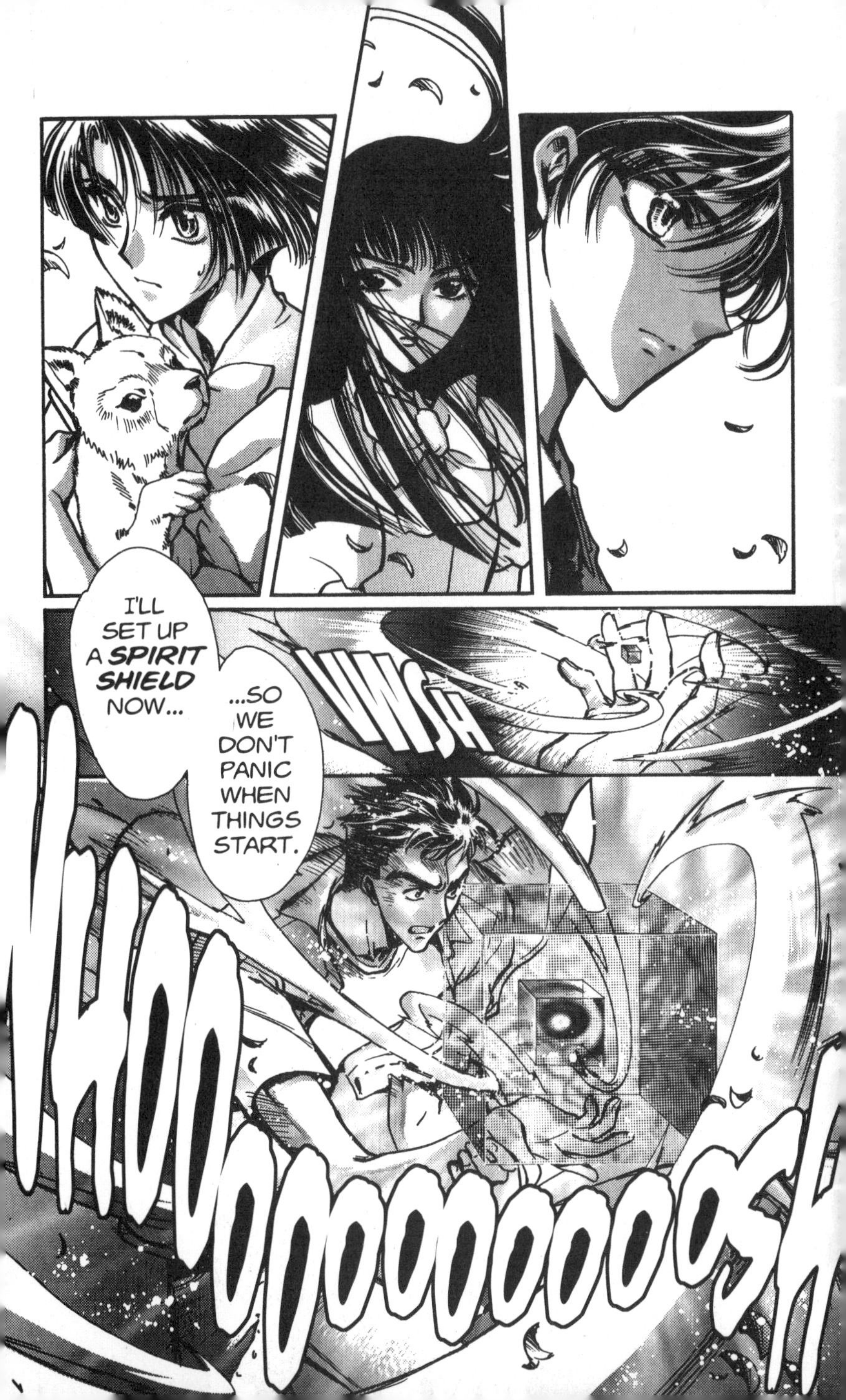
I'LL SET UP A **SPIRIT SHIELD** NOW...
WNSH
...SO WE DON'T PANIC WHEN THINGS START.
WHOOOOOOOOOOOSH

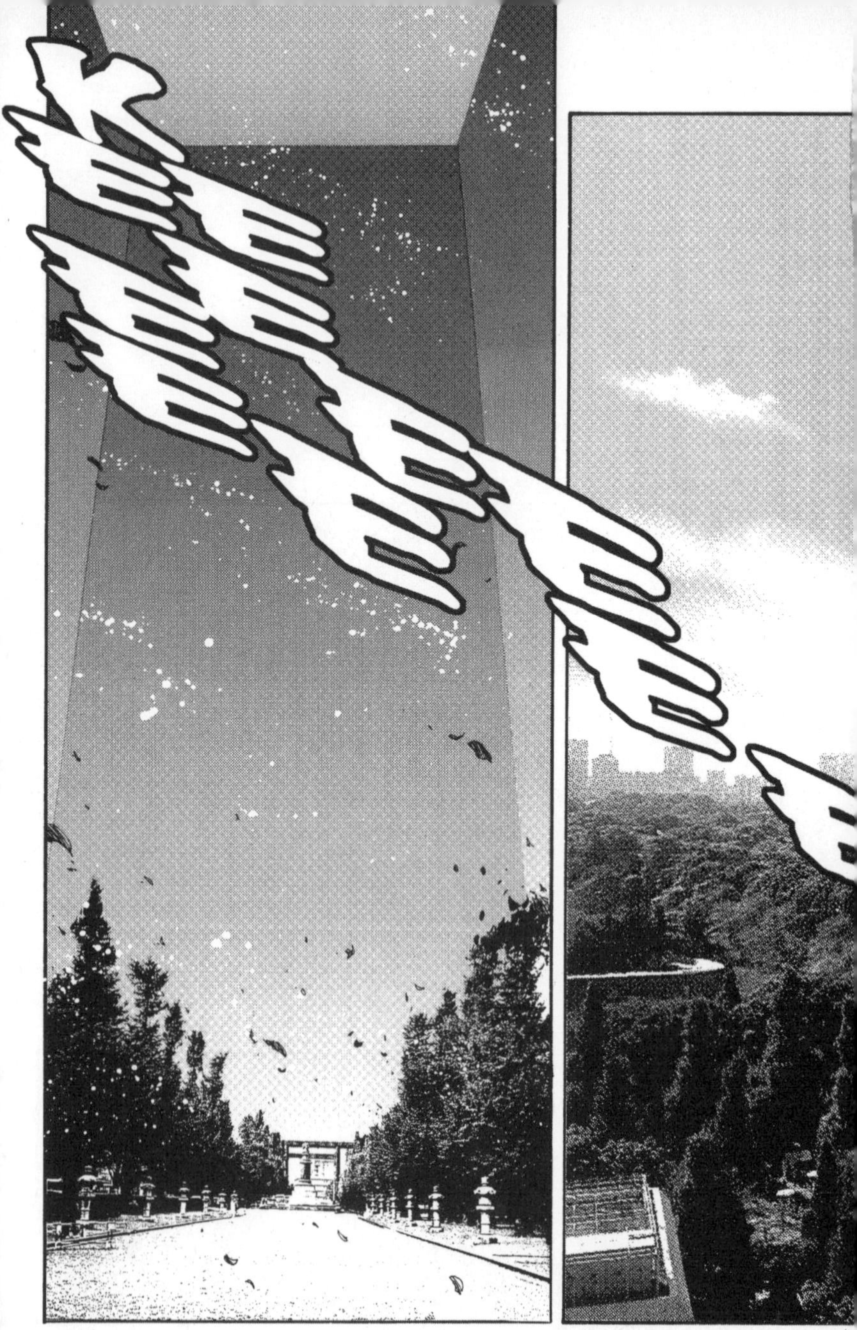
KEEEEEEEEEE

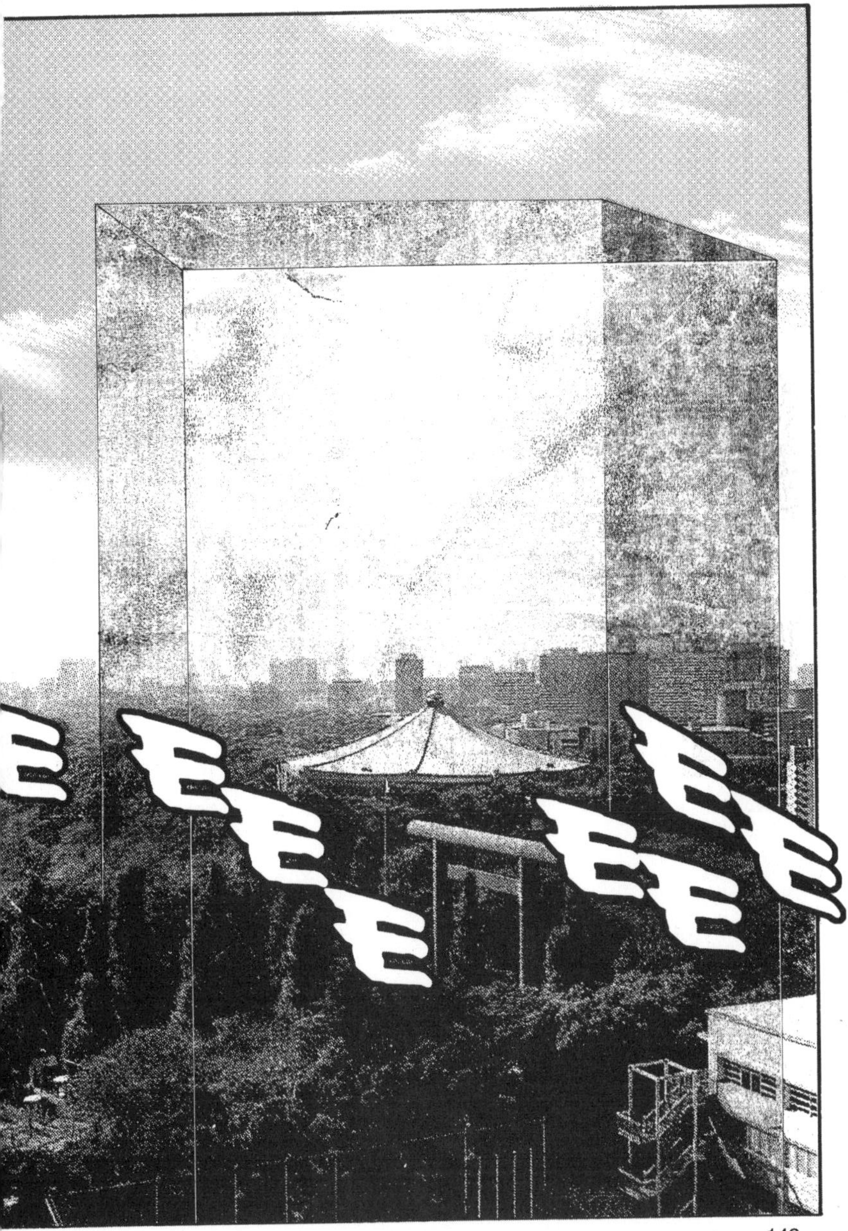
E
EEEE
EEEEE

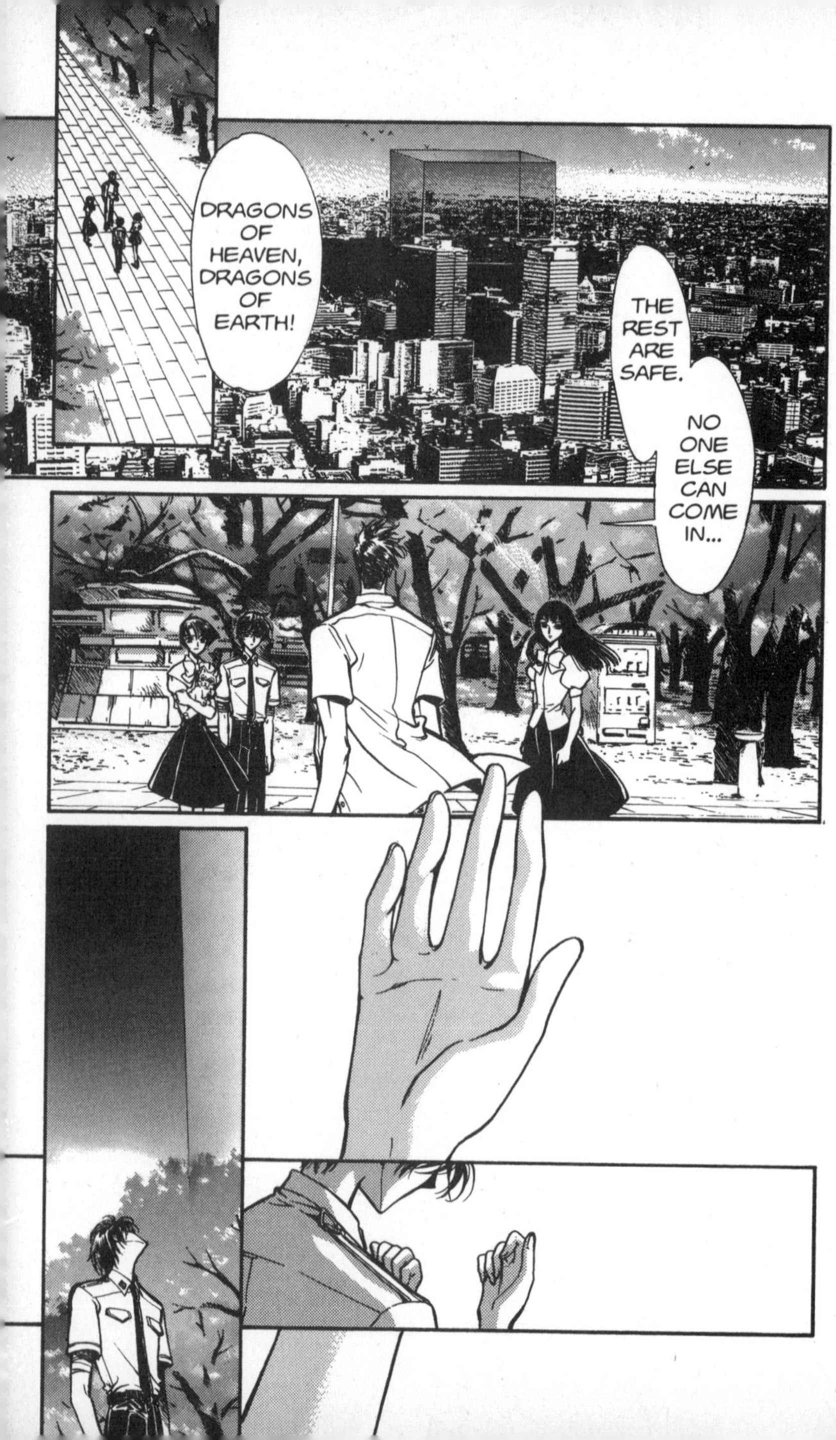
THE REST ARE SAFE.
NO ONE ELSE CAN COME IN...
DRAGONS OF HEAVEN, DRAGONS OF EARTH!

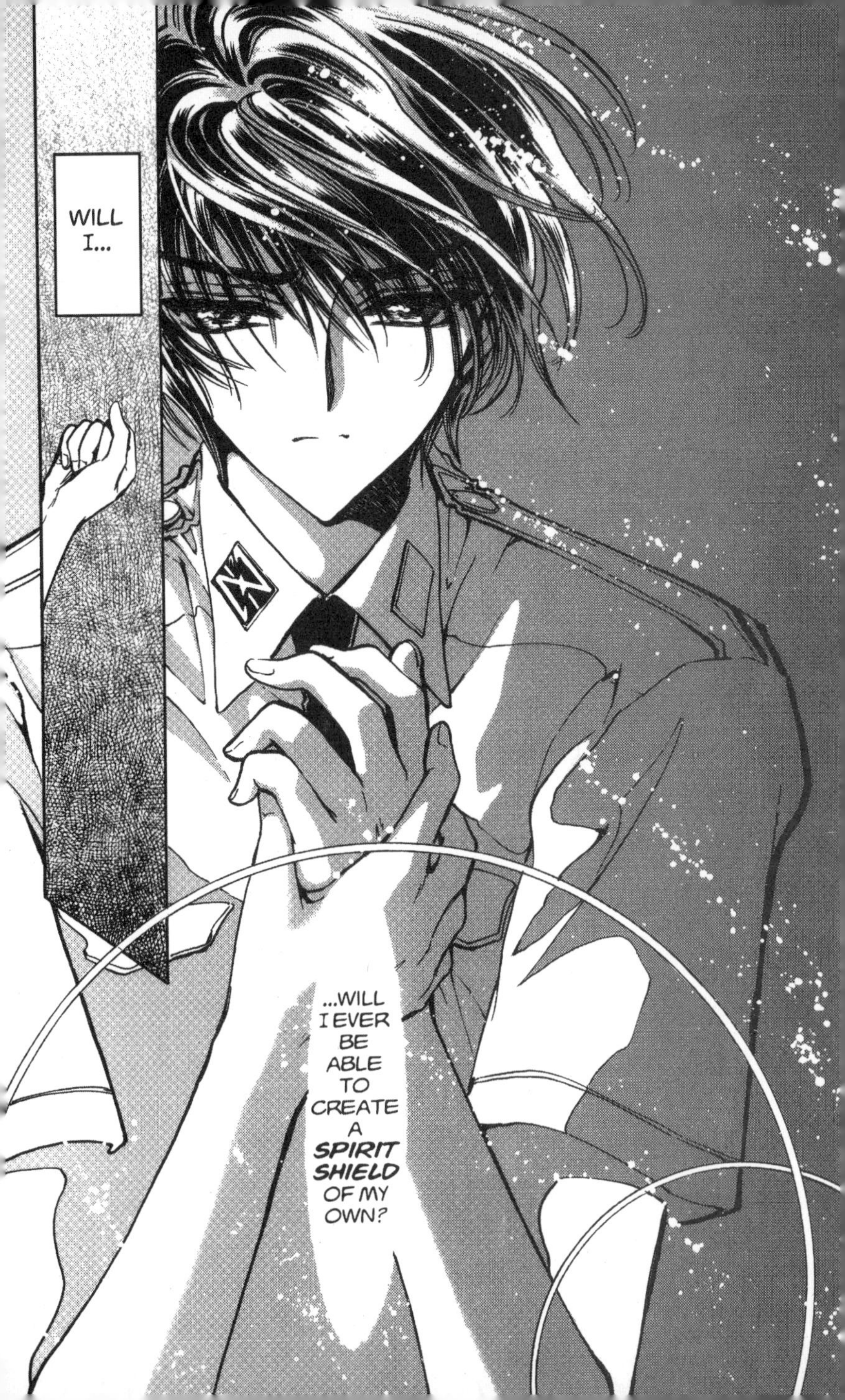
WILL I...
...WILL I EVER BE ABLE TO CREATE A ***SPIRIT SHIELD*** OF MY OWN?

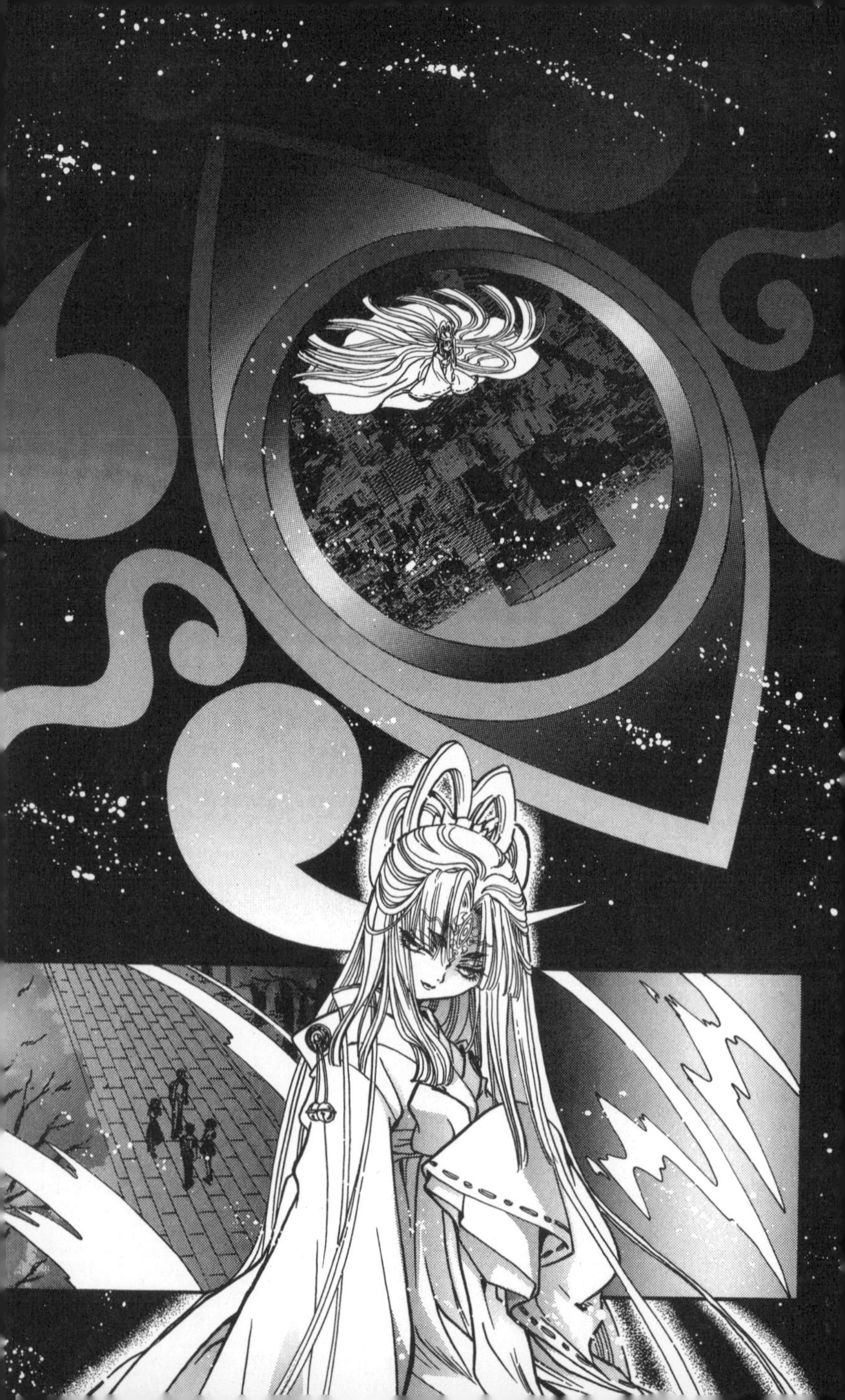

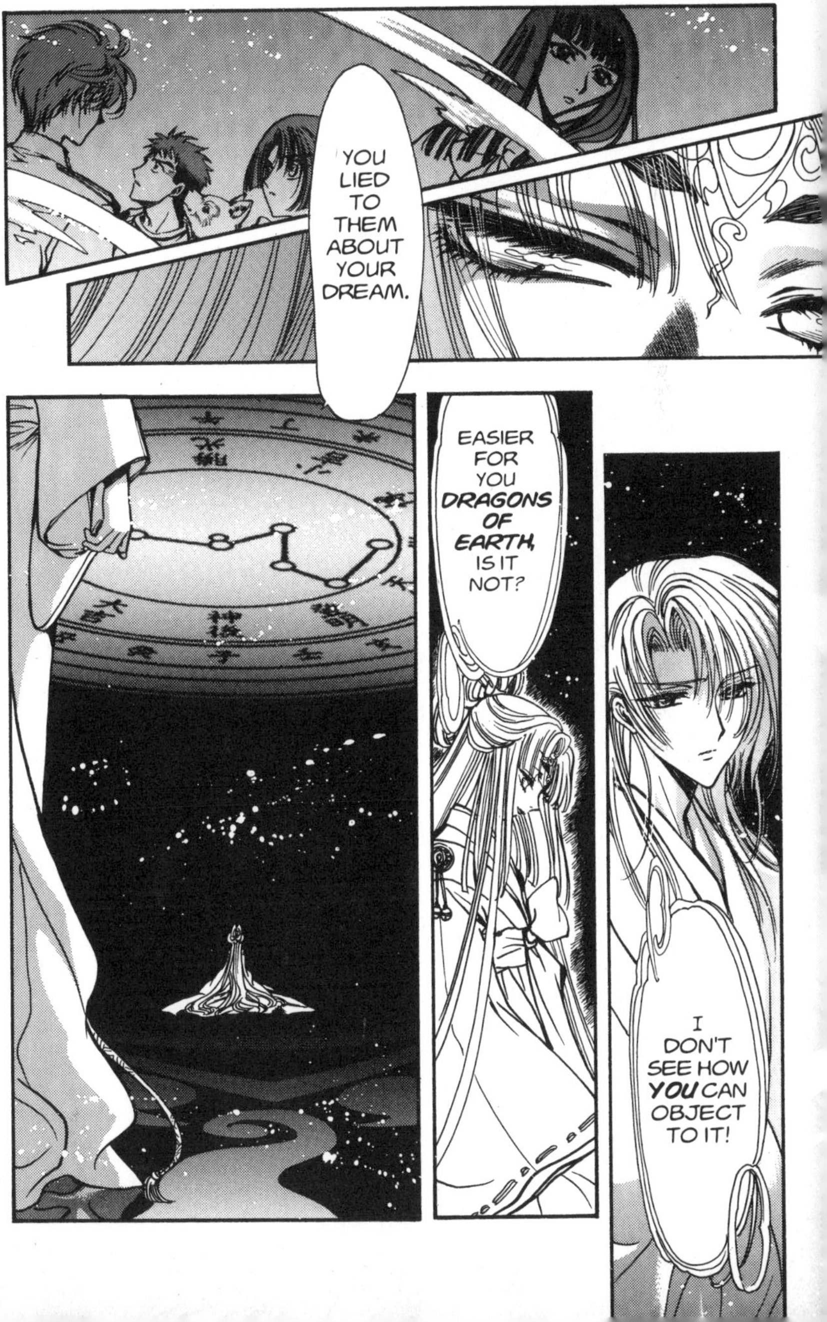
YOU LIED TO THEM ABOUT YOUR DREAM.
EASIER FOR YOU **DRAGONS OF EARTH,** IS IT NOT?
I DON'T SEE HOW **YOU** CAN OBJECT TO IT!

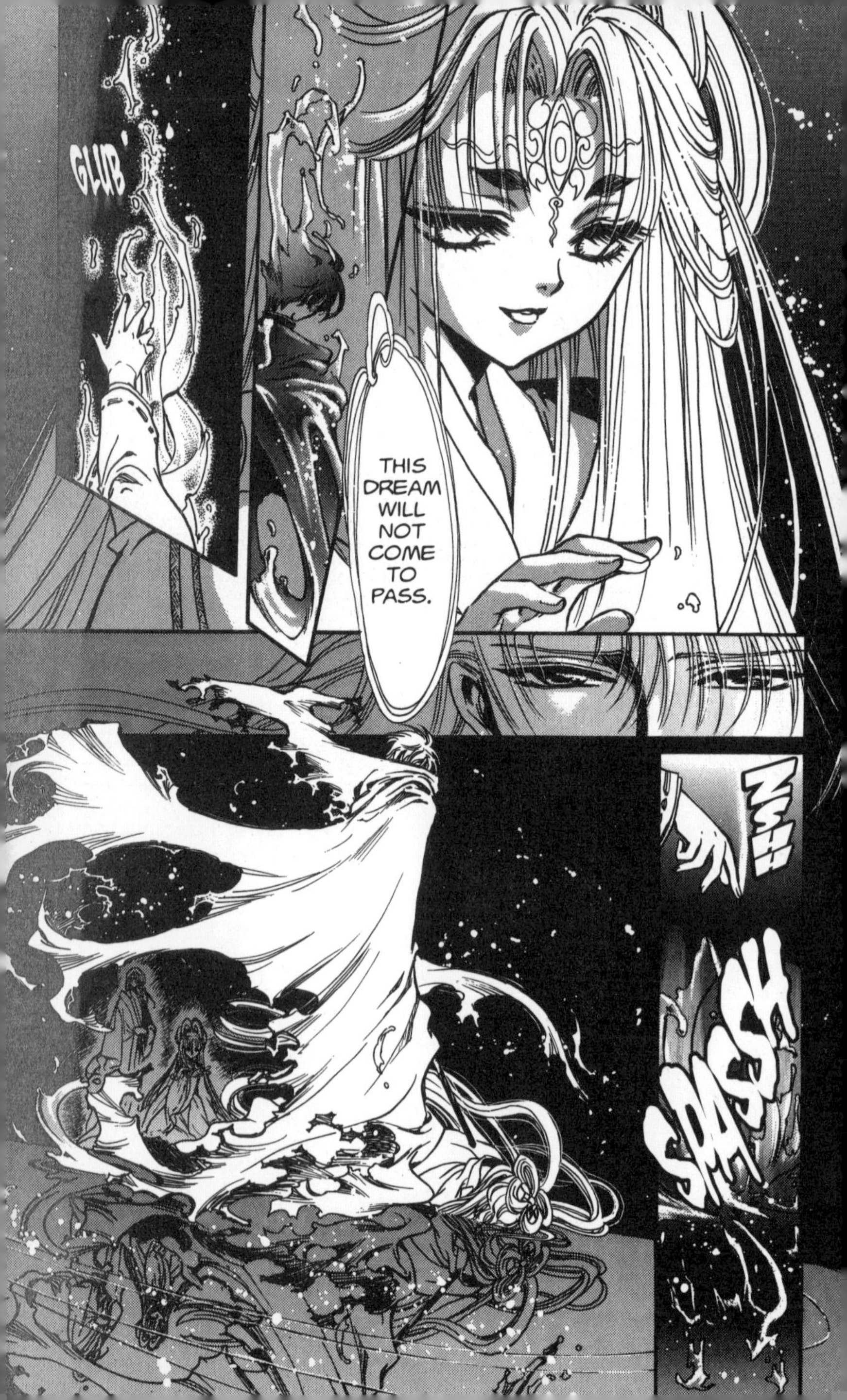
THIS DREAM WILL NOT COME TO PASS.
GLUB
SPLASH

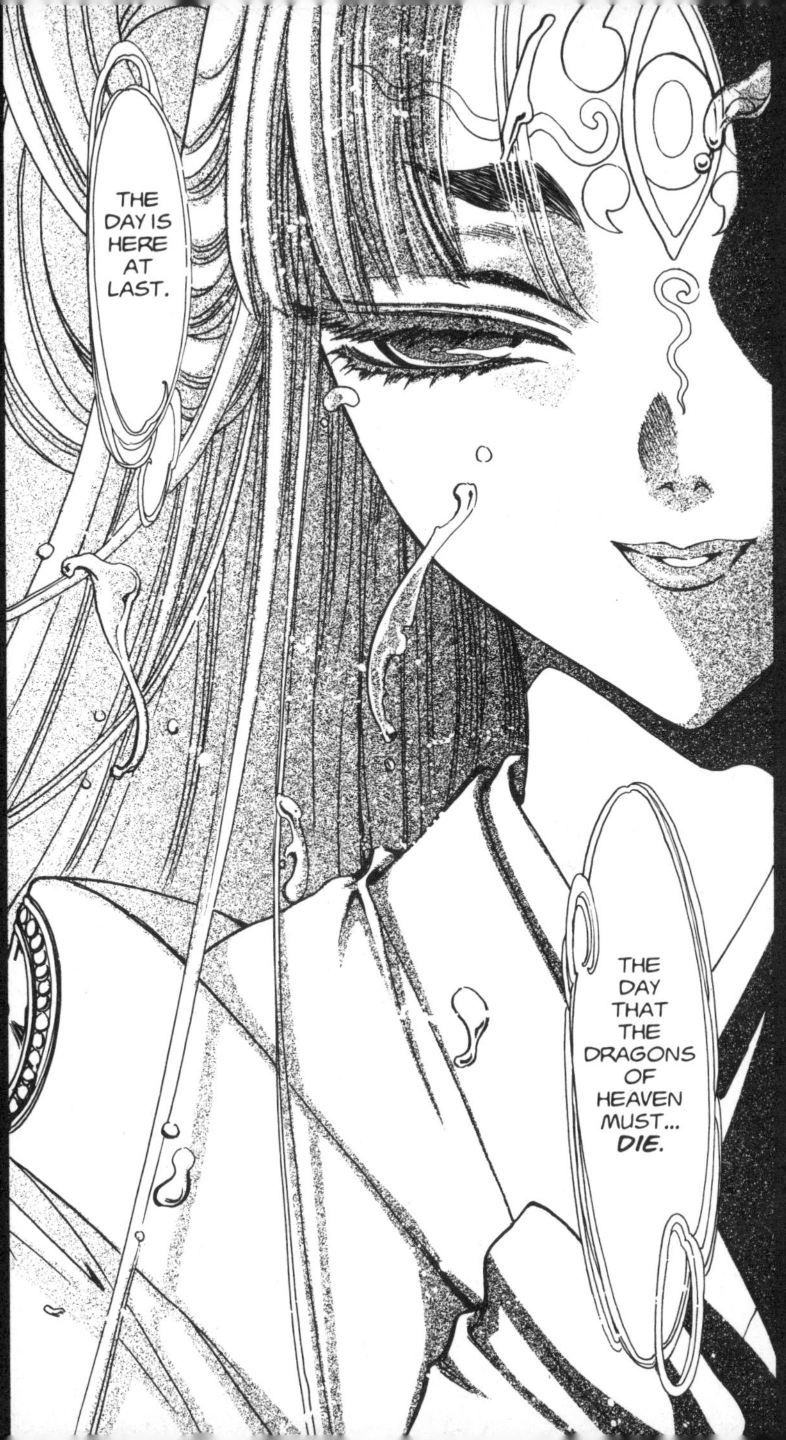
THE DAY IS HERE AT LAST.
THE DAY THAT THE DRAGONS OF HEAVEN MUST... *DIE*.

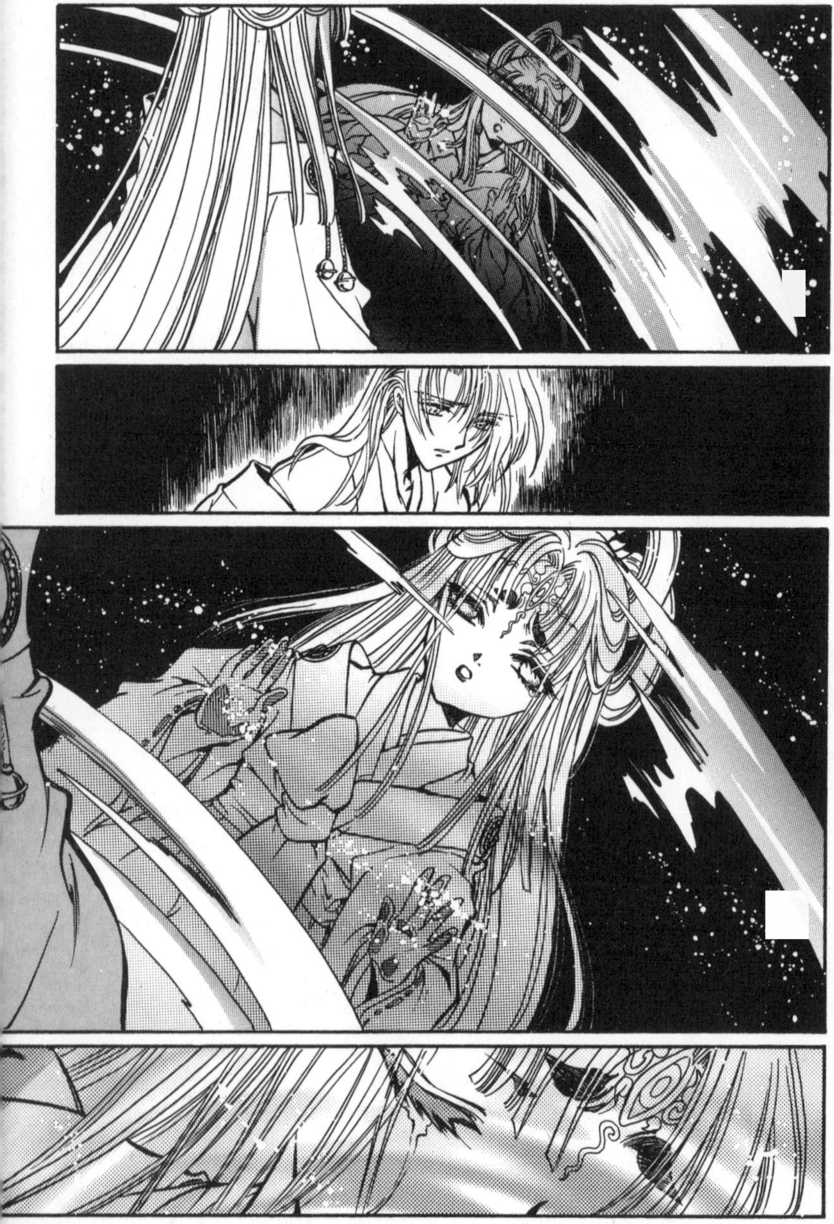

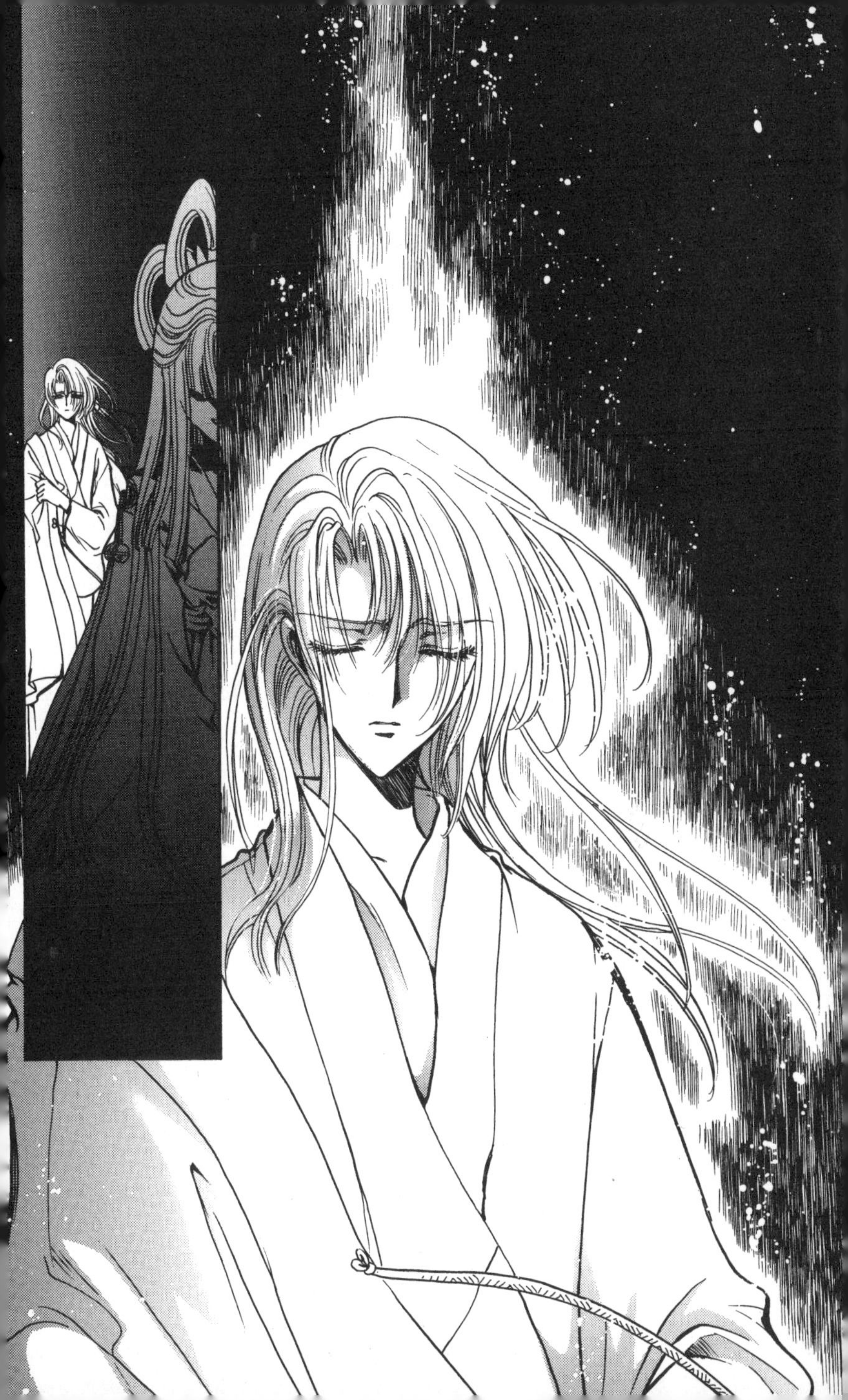

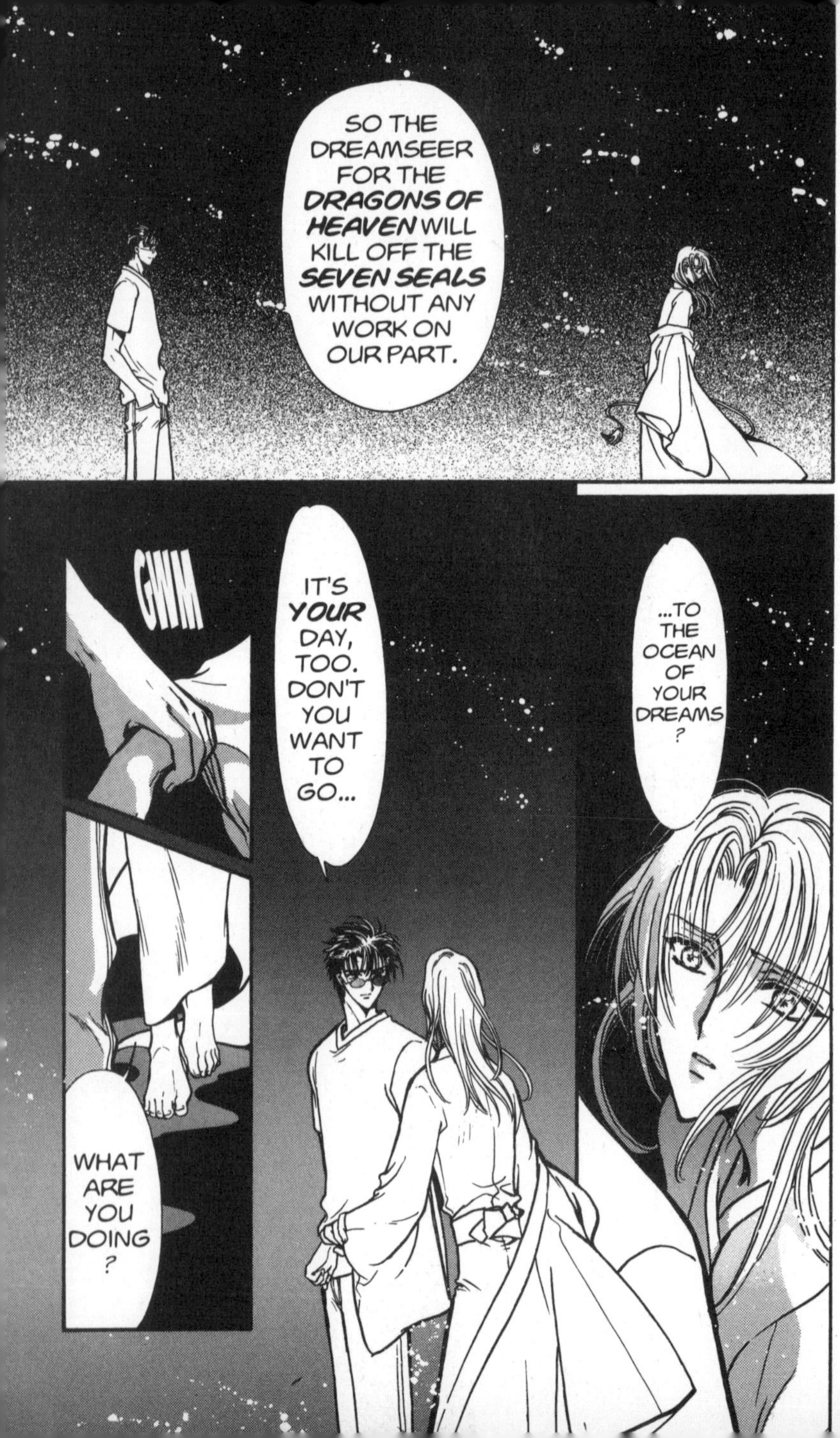
SO THE DREAMSEER FOR THE **DRAGONS OF HEAVEN** WILL KILL OFF THE **SEVEN SEALS** WITHOUT ANY WORK ON OUR PART.
IT'S **YOUR** DAY, TOO. DON'T YOU WANT TO GO...
...TO THE OCEAN OF YOUR DREAMS?
GWM
WHAT ARE YOU DOING?

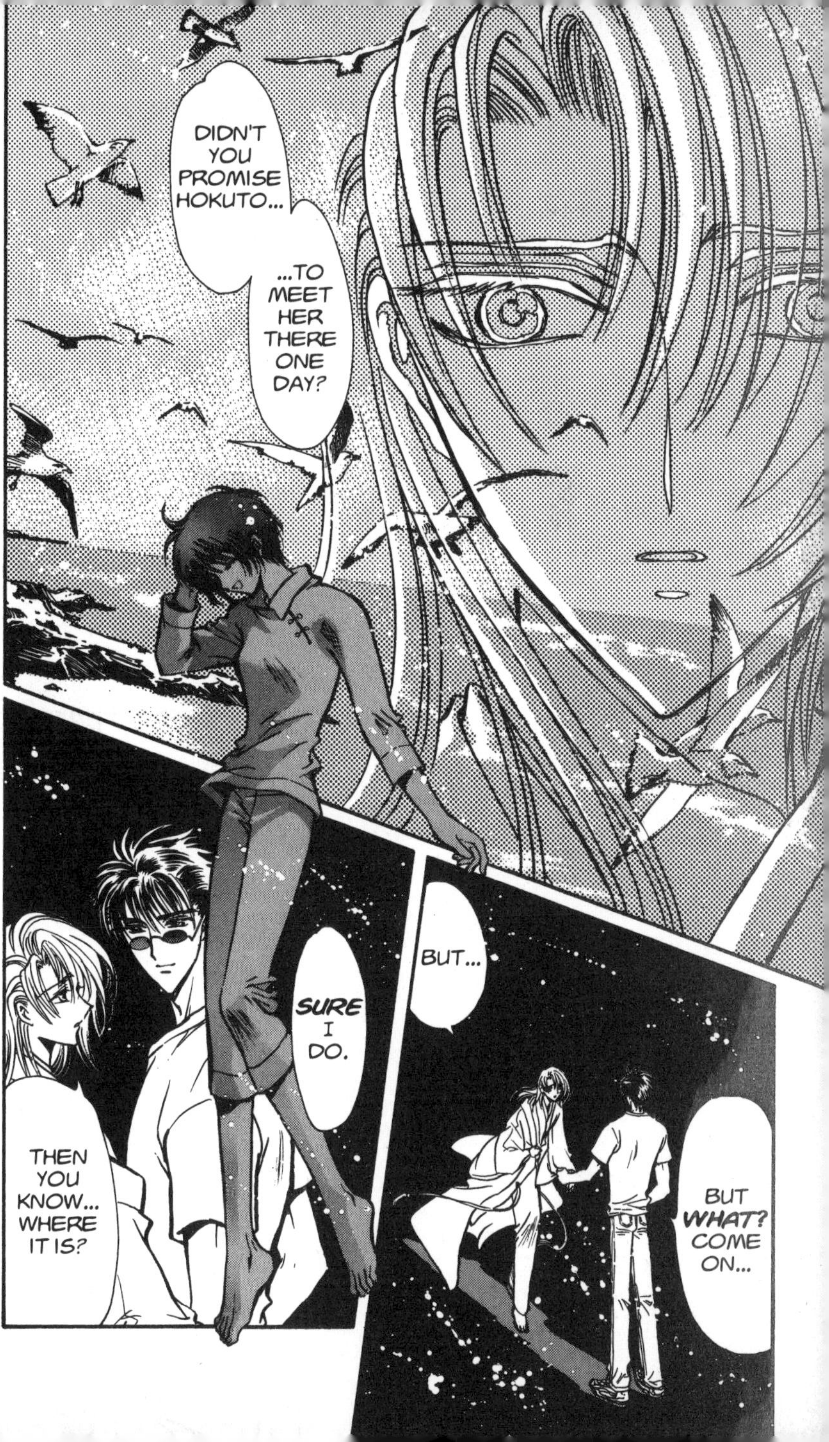
DIDN'T YOU PROMISE HOKUTO...
...TO MEET HER THERE ONE DAY?
SURE I DO.
THEN YOU KNOW... WHERE IT IS?
BUT...
BUT WHAT? COME ON...

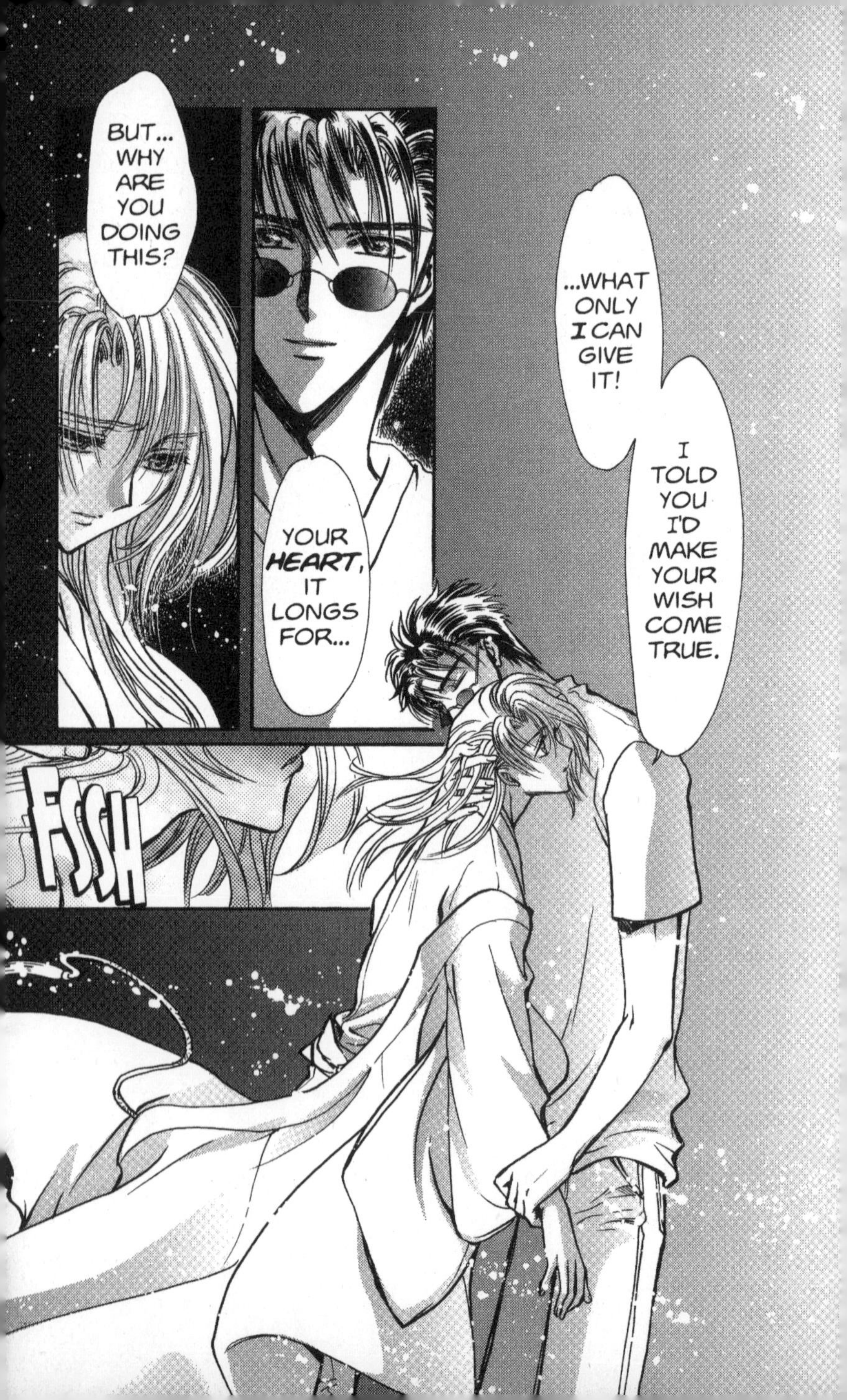
BUT... WHY ARE YOU DOING THIS?
YOUR HEART, IT LONGS FOR...
...WHAT ONLY I CAN GIVE IT!
I TOLD YOU I'D MAKE YOUR WISH COME TRUE.
FSSH

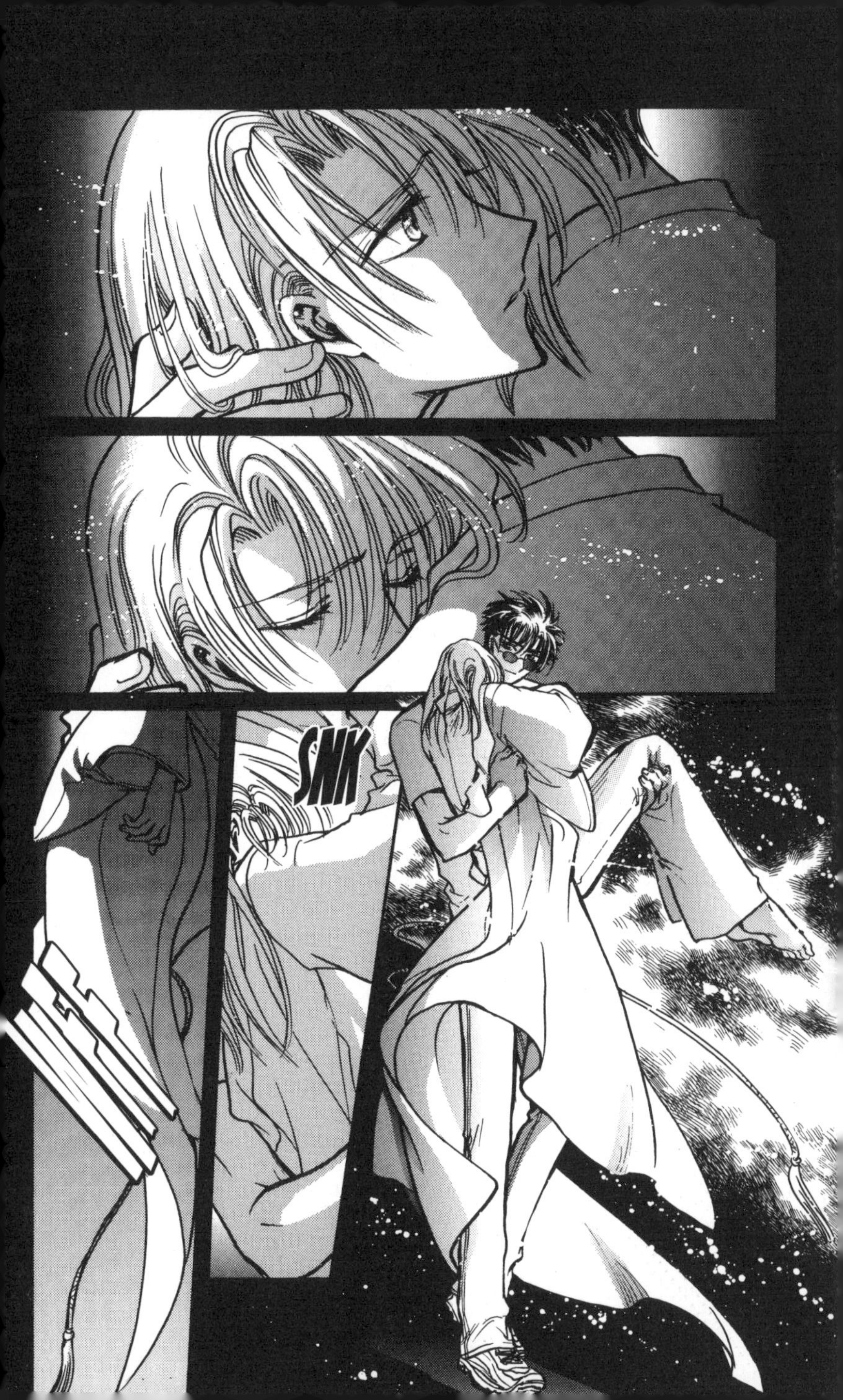
SNK

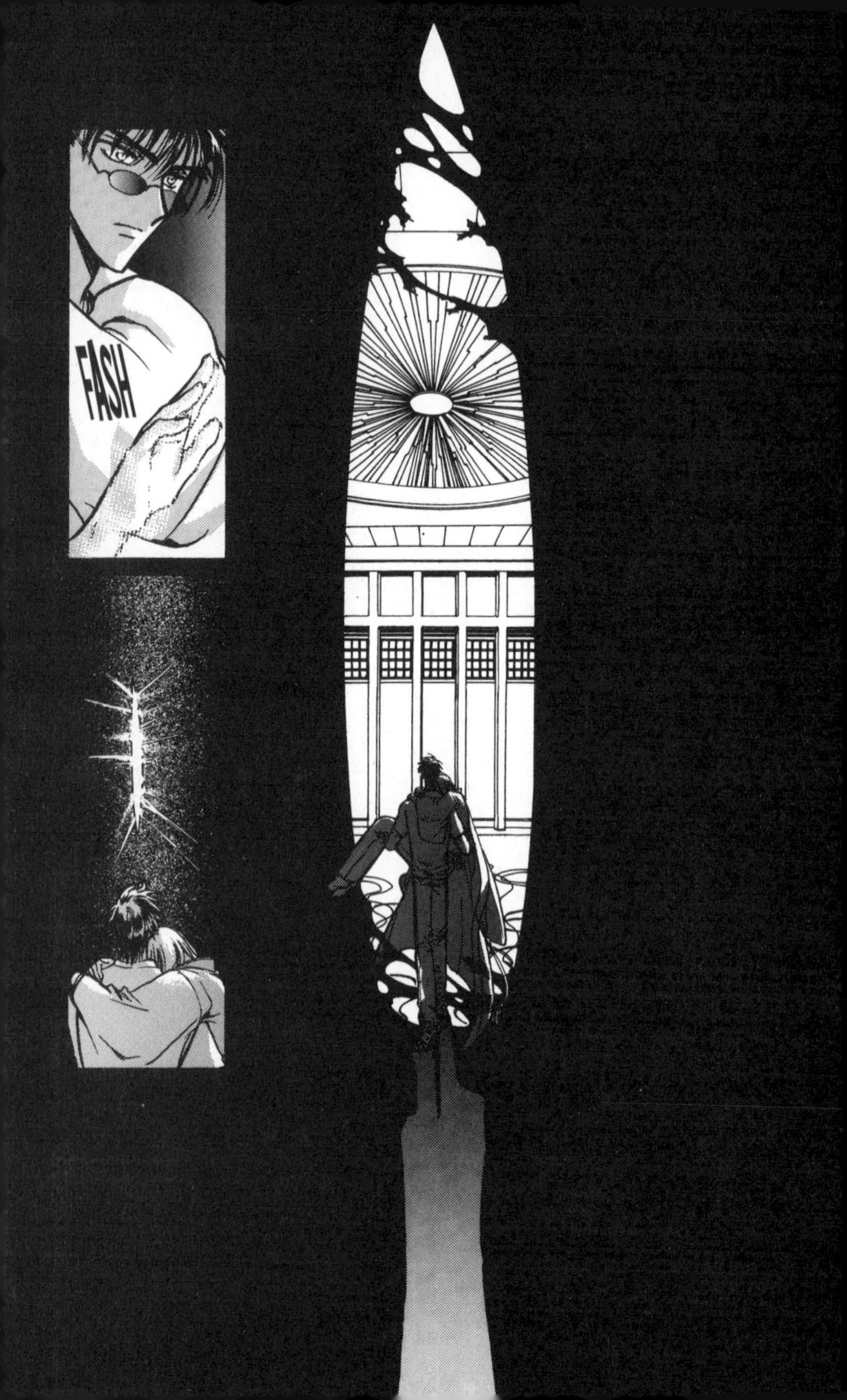
FASH

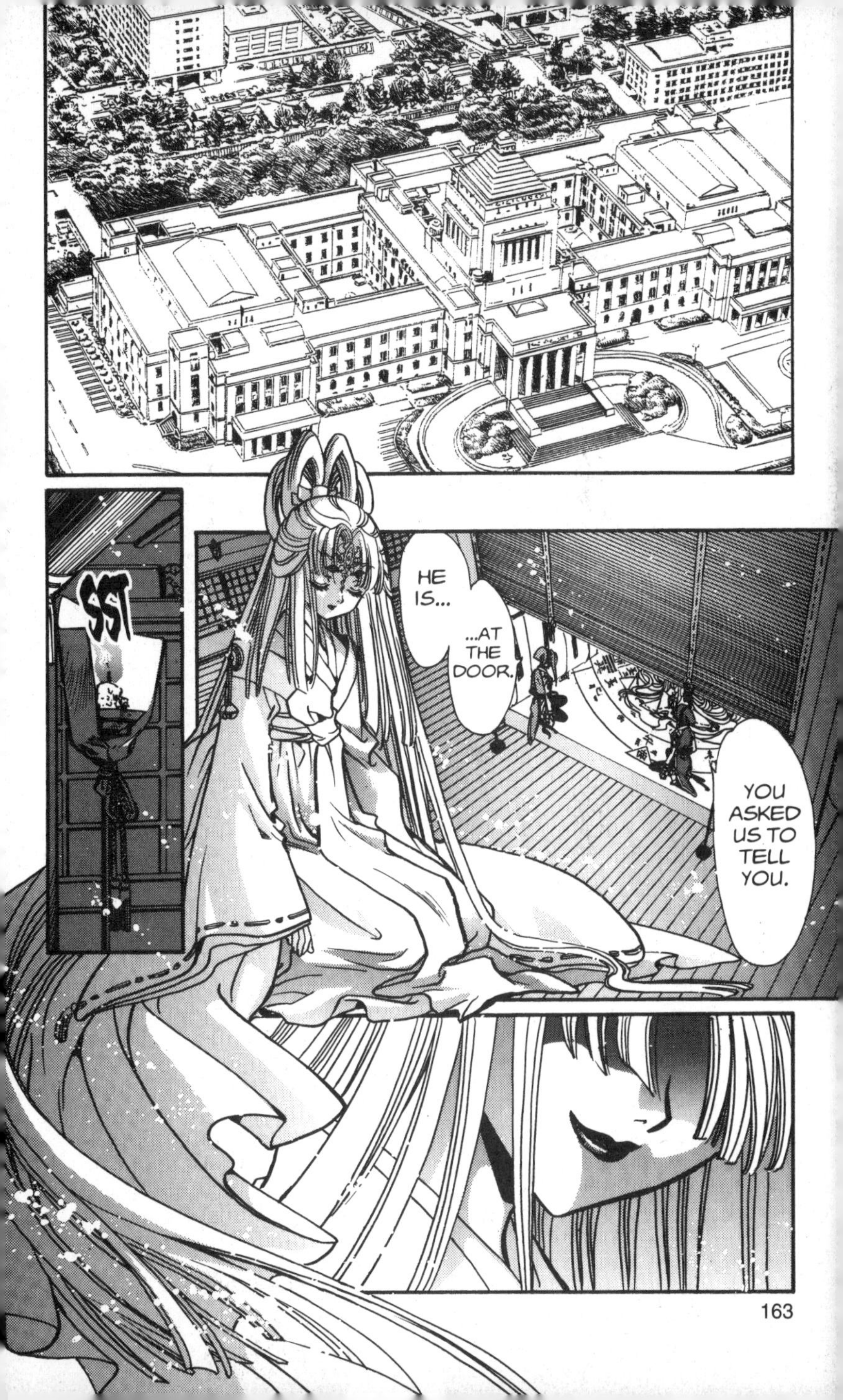
HE IS...
...AT THE DOOR.
YOU ASKED US TO TELL YOU.

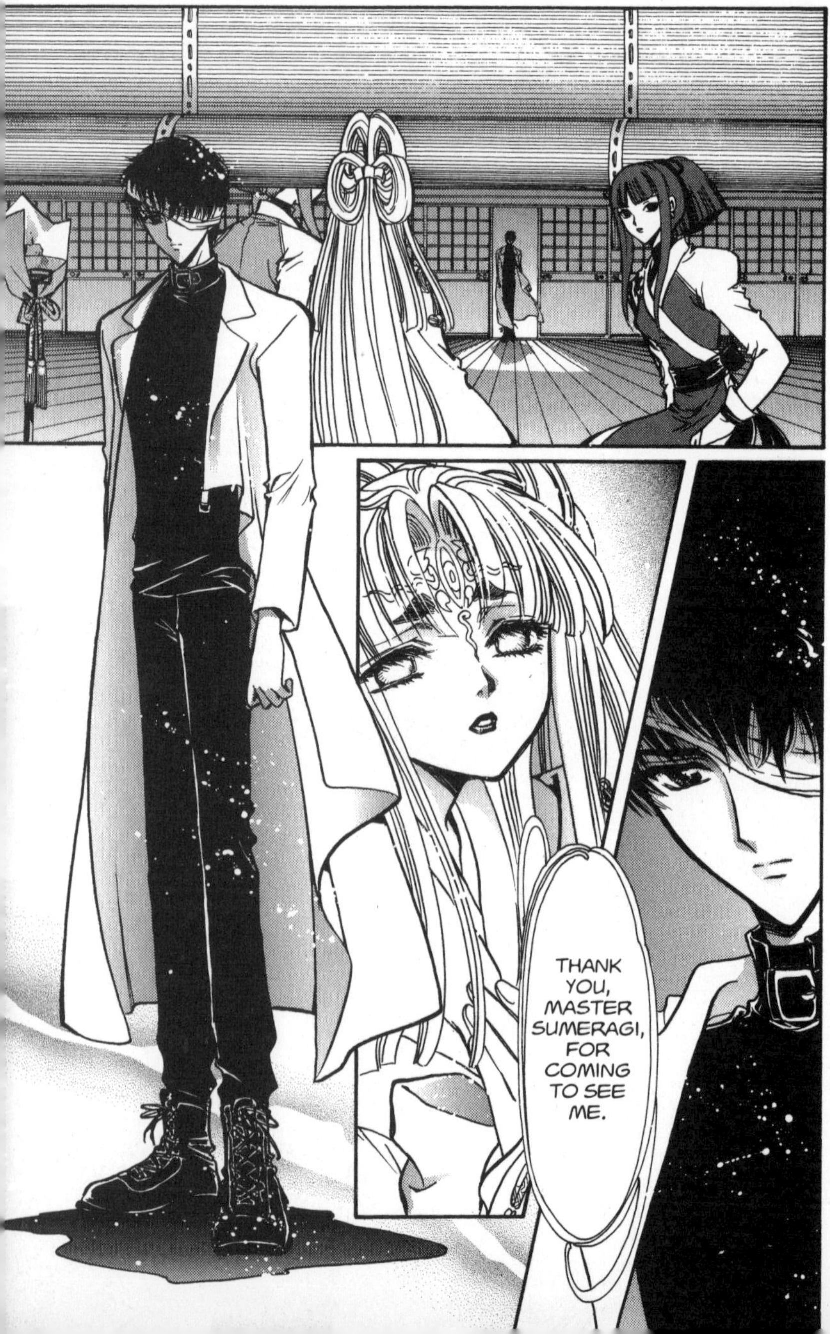
THANK YOU, MASTER SUMERAGI, FOR COMING TO SEE ME.

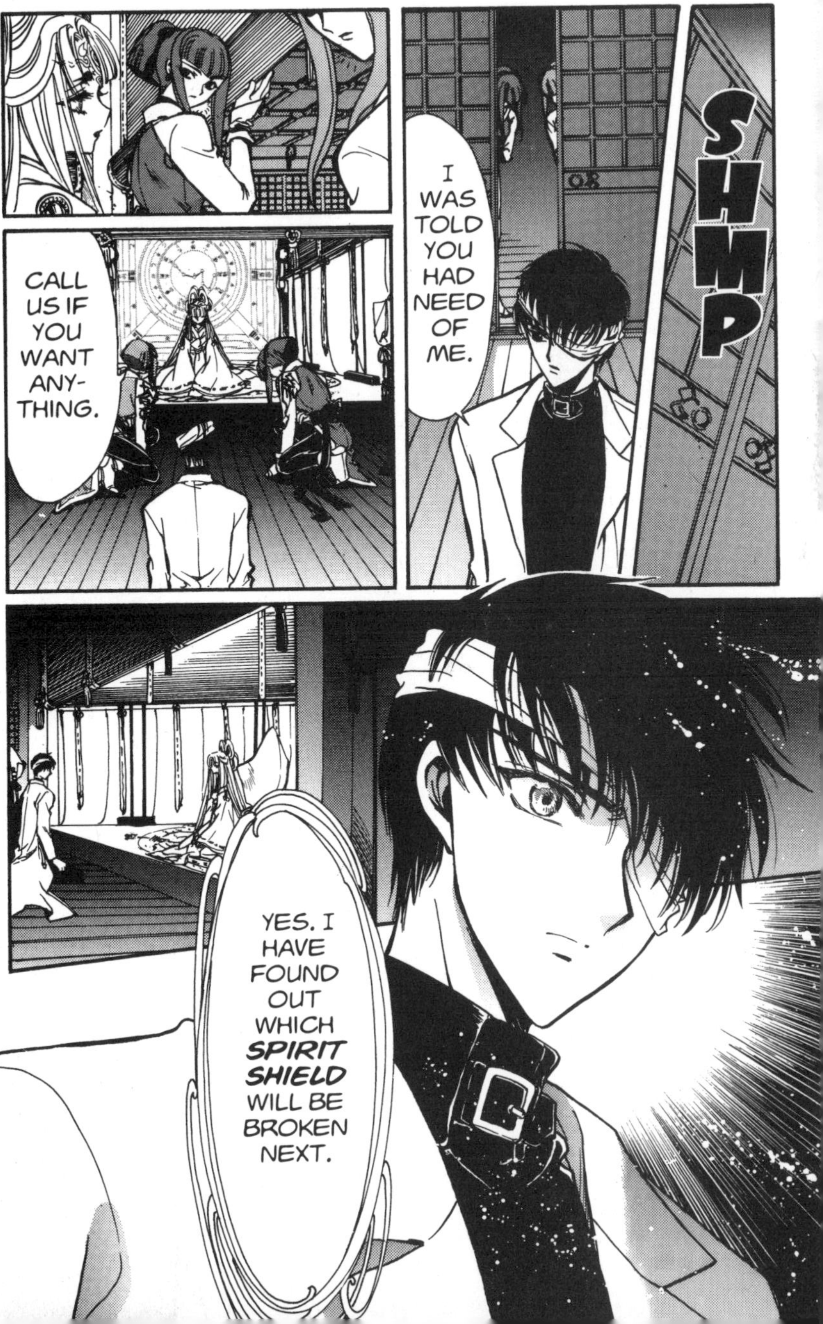
SHMP
I WAS TOLD YOU HAD NEED OF ME.
CALL US IF YOU WANT ANY-THING.
YES. I HAVE FOUND OUT WHICH SPIRIT SHIELD WILL BE BROKEN NEXT.

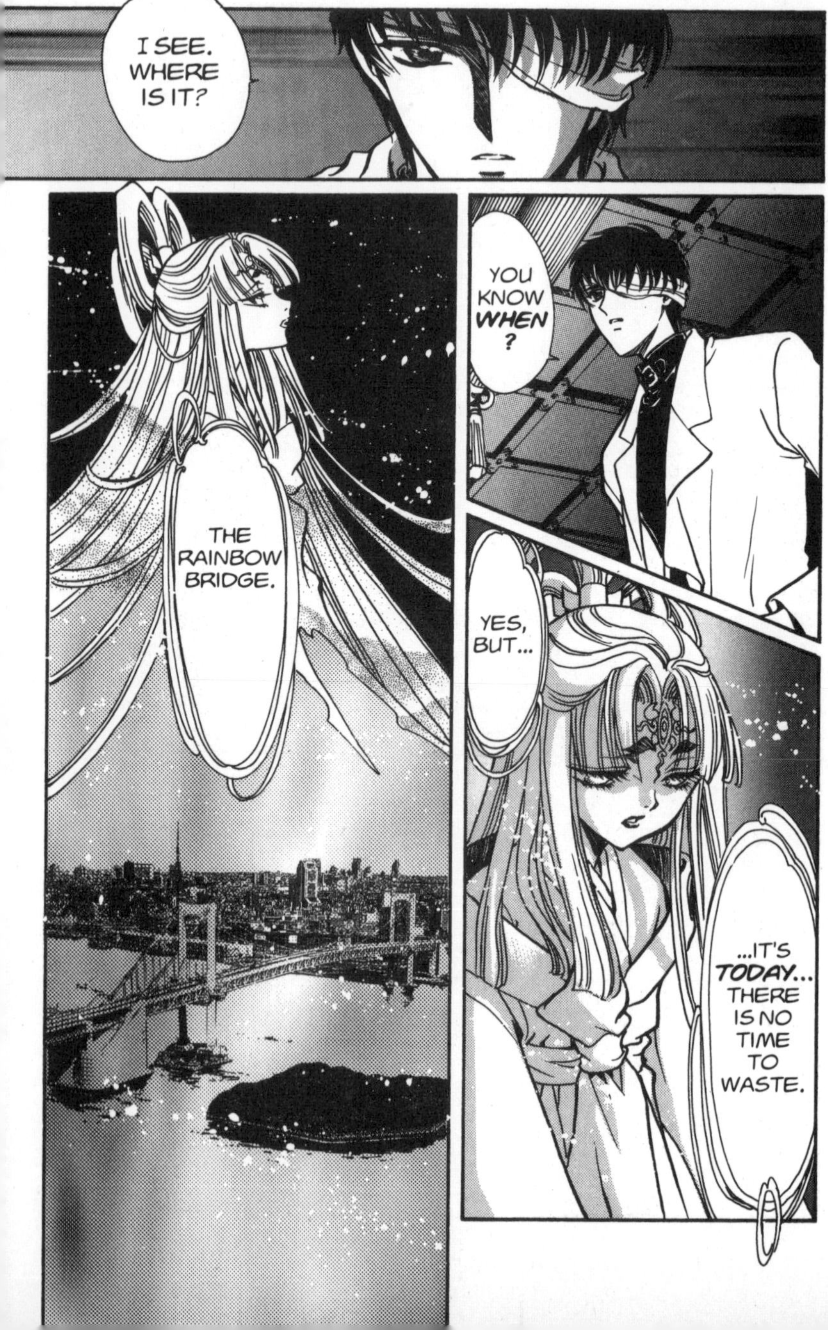
I SEE. WHERE IS IT?
THE RAINBOW BRIDGE.
YOU KNOW **WHEN**?
YES, BUT...
...IT'S **TODAY**... THERE IS NO TIME TO WASTE.

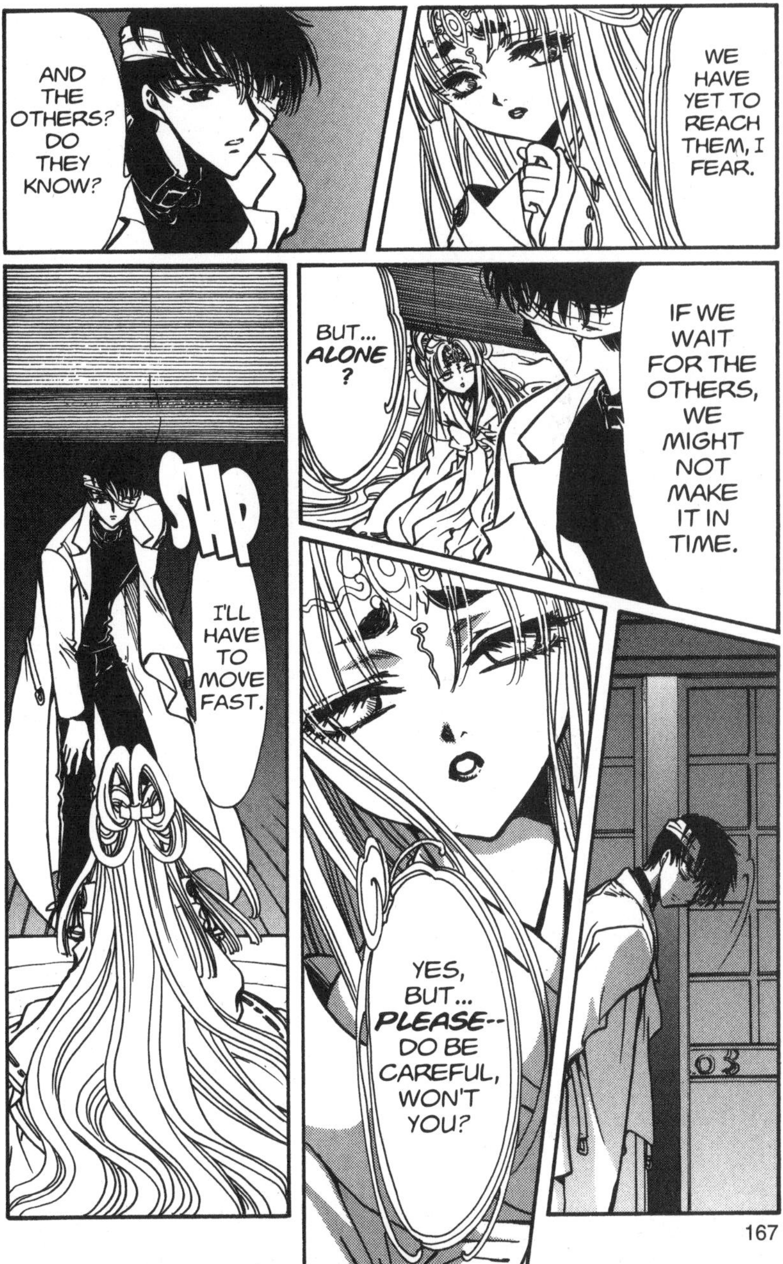
AND THE OTHERS? DO THEY KNOW?
WE HAVE YET TO REACH THEM, I FEAR.
SHP
I'LL HAVE TO MOVE FAST.
BUT... ALONE?
IF WE WAIT FOR THE OTHERS, WE MIGHT NOT MAKE IT IN TIME.
YES, BUT... PLEASE-- DO BE CAREFUL, WON'T YOU?

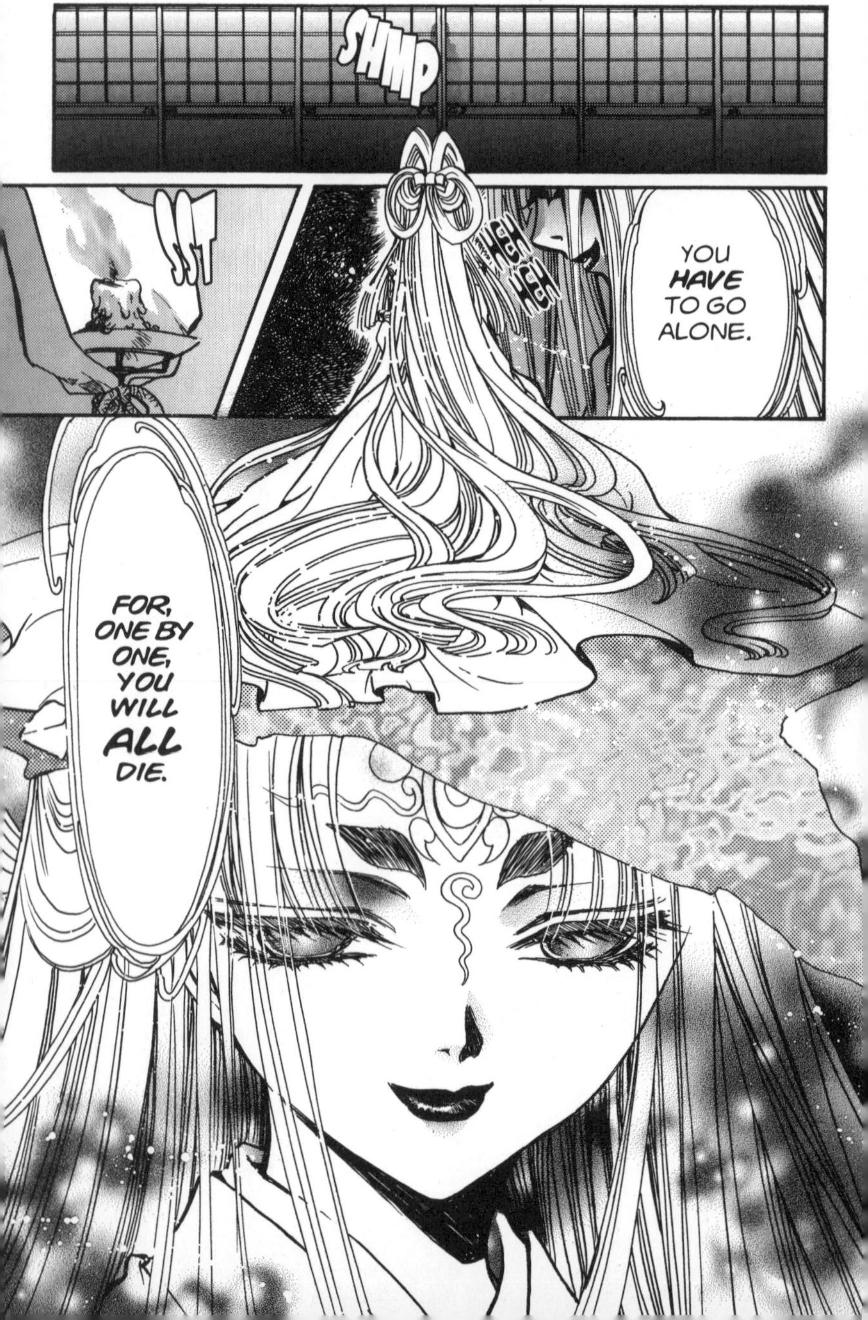
SHMP
HEH HEH
YOU HAVE TO GO ALONE.
SST
FOR, ONE BY ONE, YOU WILL ALL DIE.

X 15 END

X

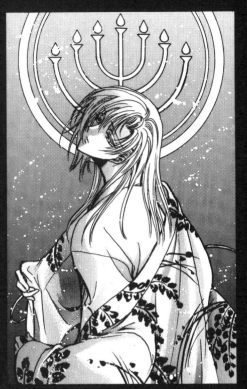

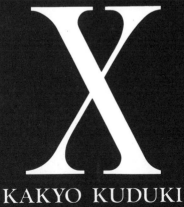

KAKYO KUDUKI

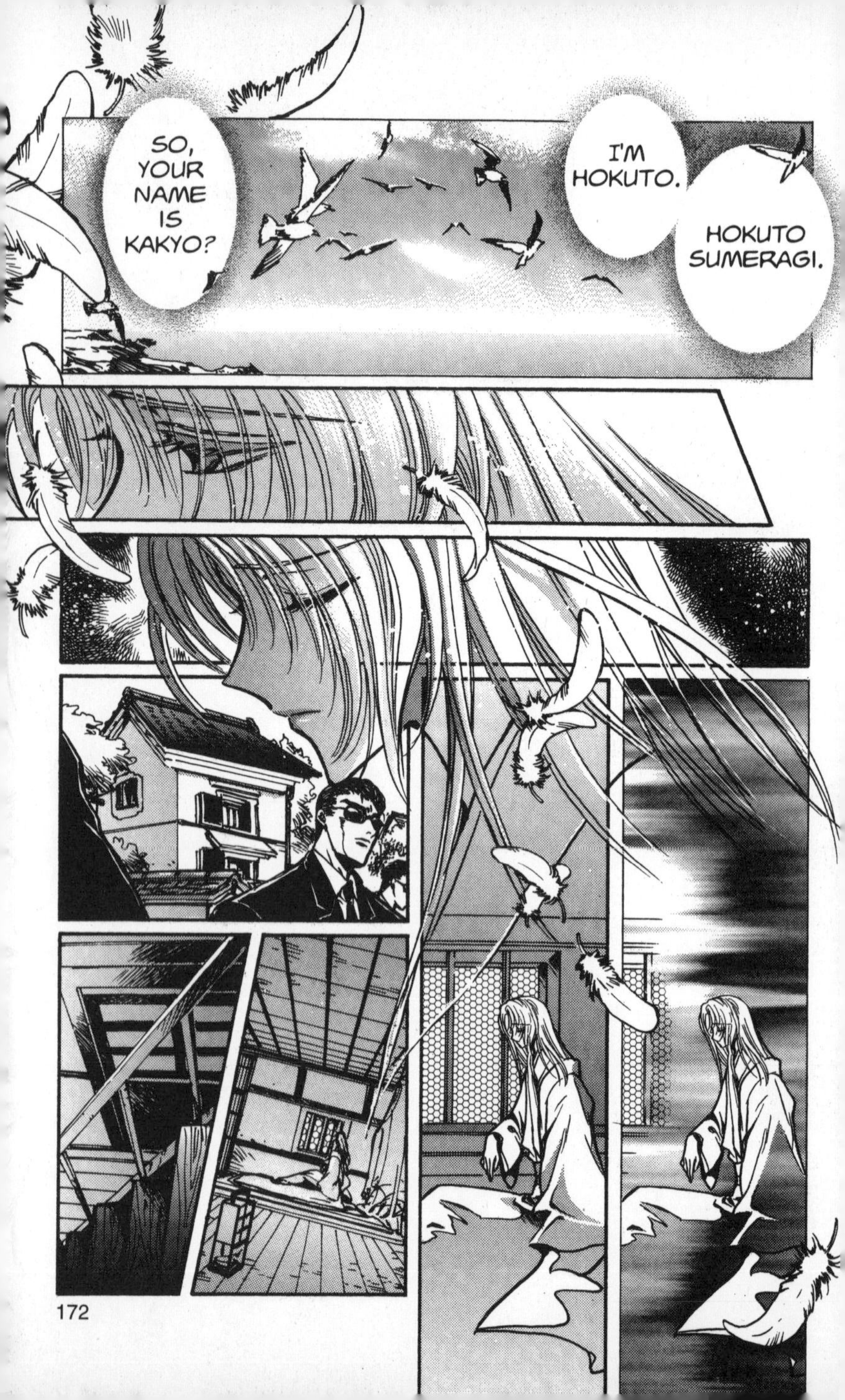

I'M HOKUTO.
HOKUTO SUMERAGI.
SO, YOUR NAME IS KAKYO?

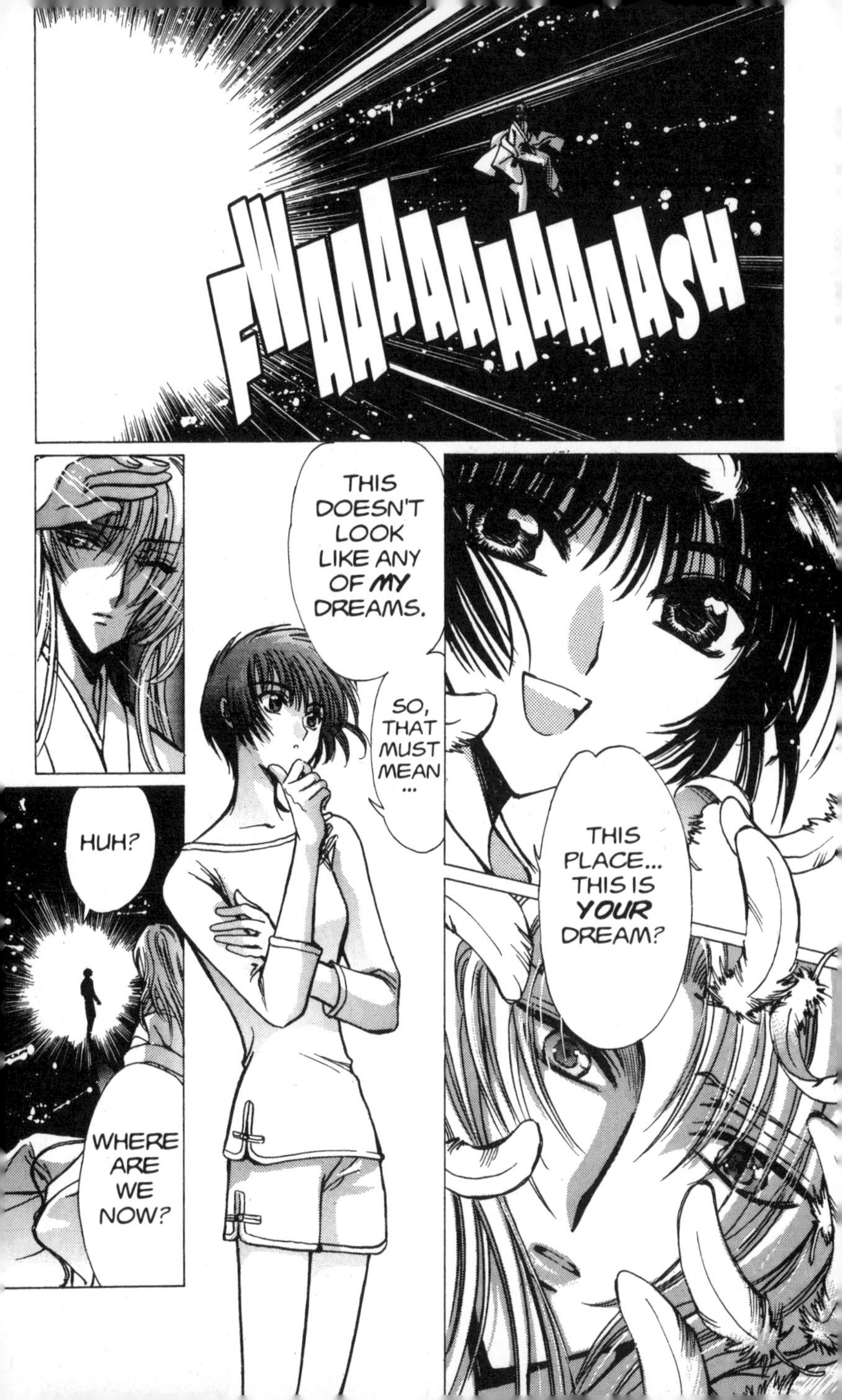

FWAAAAAAAAAAASH
THIS PLACE... THIS IS YOUR DREAM?
THIS DOESN'T LOOK LIKE ANY OF *MY* DREAMS.
SO, THAT MUST MEAN...
HUH?
WHERE ARE WE NOW?

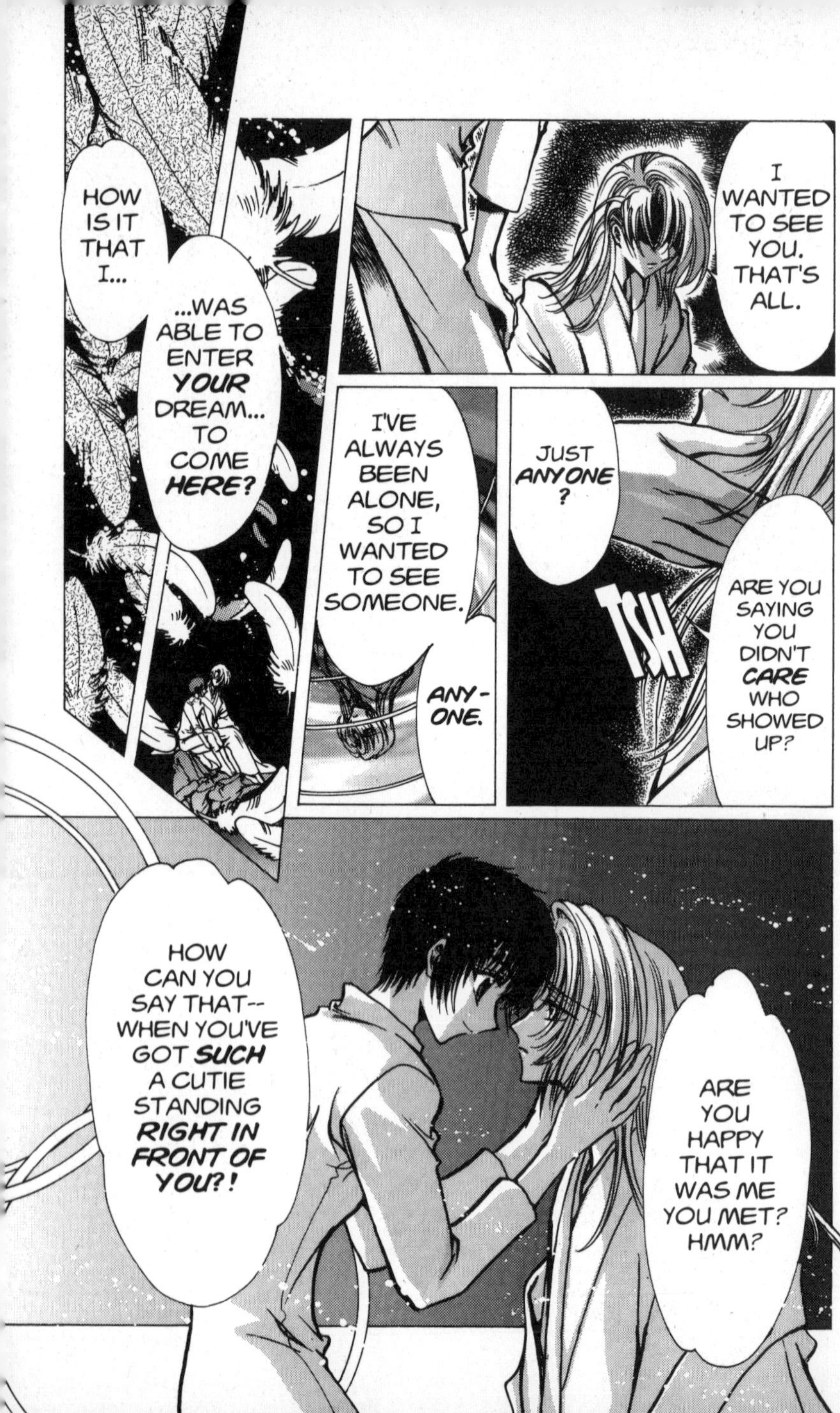
HOW IS IT THAT I...
...WAS ABLE TO ENTER YOUR DREAM... TO COME HERE?
I WANTED TO SEE YOU. THAT'S ALL.
I'VE ALWAYS BEEN ALONE, SO I WANTED TO SEE SOMEONE.
ANY-ONE.
JUST ANYONE?
TSH
ARE YOU SAYING YOU DIDN'T CARE WHO SHOWED UP?
HOW CAN YOU SAY THAT-- WHEN YOU'VE GOT SUCH A CUTIE STANDING RIGHT IN FRONT OF YOU?!
ARE YOU HAPPY THAT IT WAS ME YOU MET? HMM?

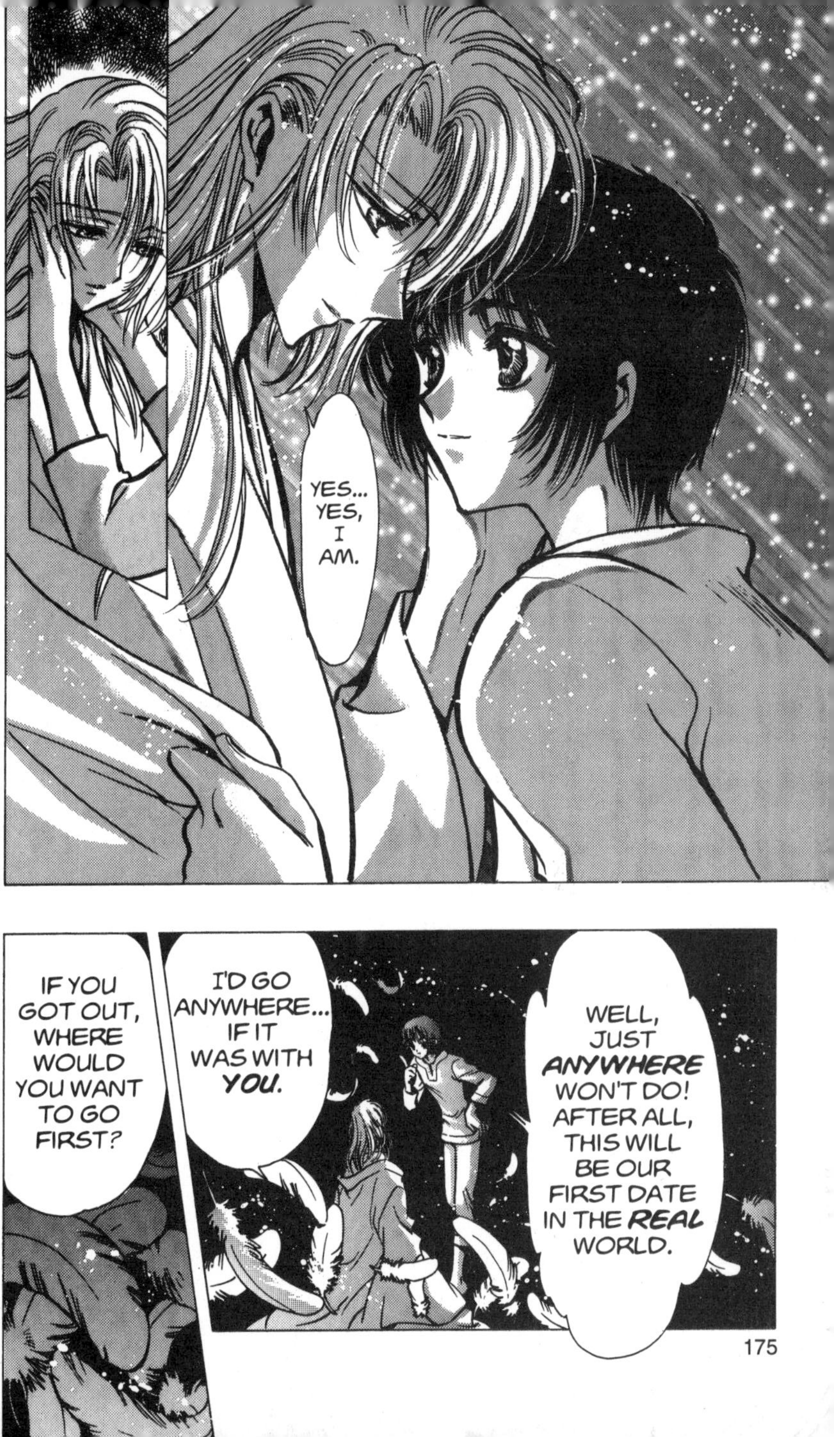
YES... YES, I AM.
IF YOU GOT OUT, WHERE WOULD YOU WANT TO GO FIRST?
I'D GO ANYWHERE... IF IT WAS WITH YOU.
WELL, JUST ANYWHERE WON'T DO! AFTER ALL, THIS WILL BE OUR FIRST DATE IN THE REAL WORLD.

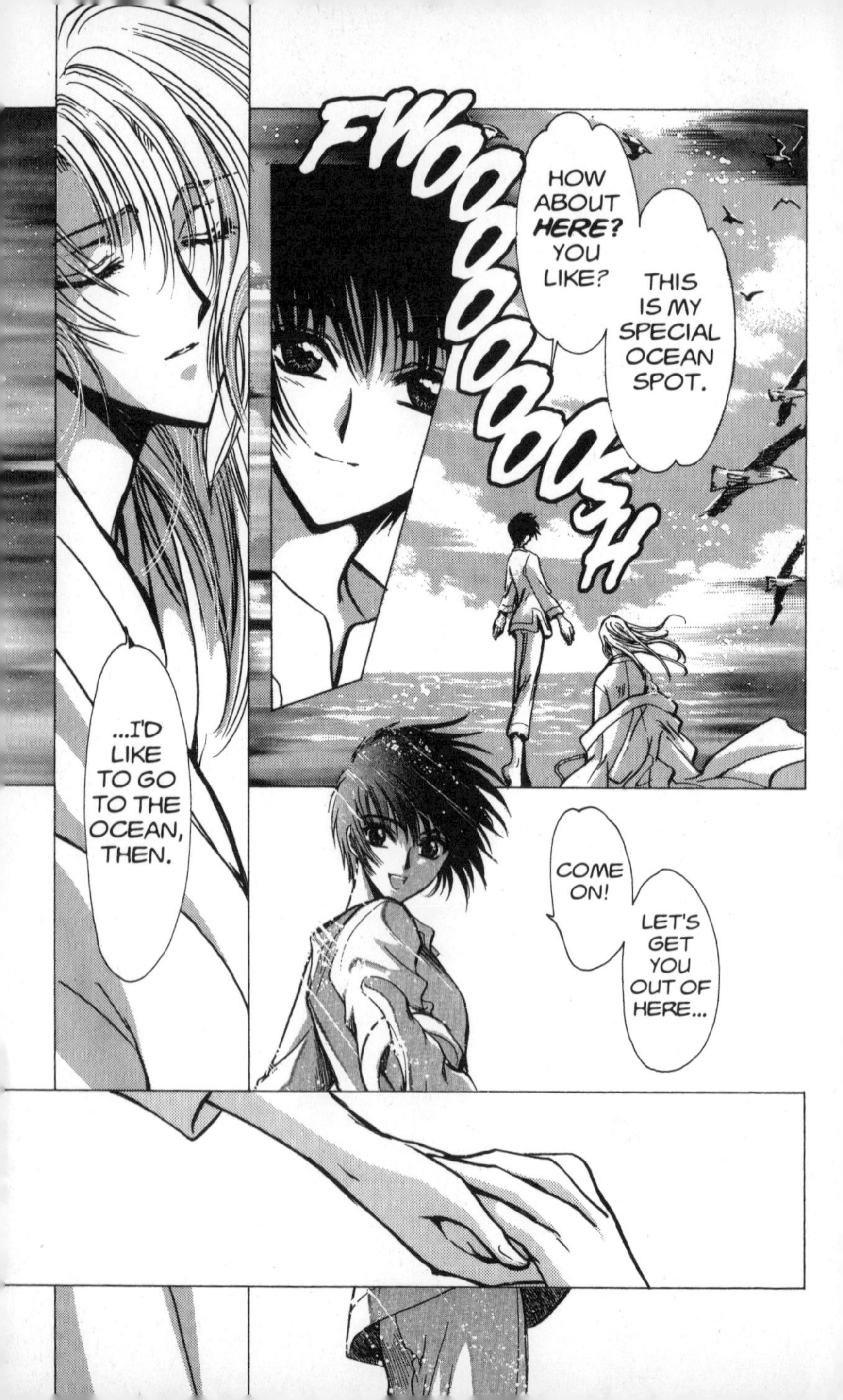
FWOOOOOOOOSH
HOW ABOUT *HERE?* YOU LIKE?
THIS IS MY SPECIAL OCEAN SPOT.
COME ON!
LET'S GET YOU OUT OF HERE...
...I'D LIKE TO GO TO THE OCEAN, THEN.

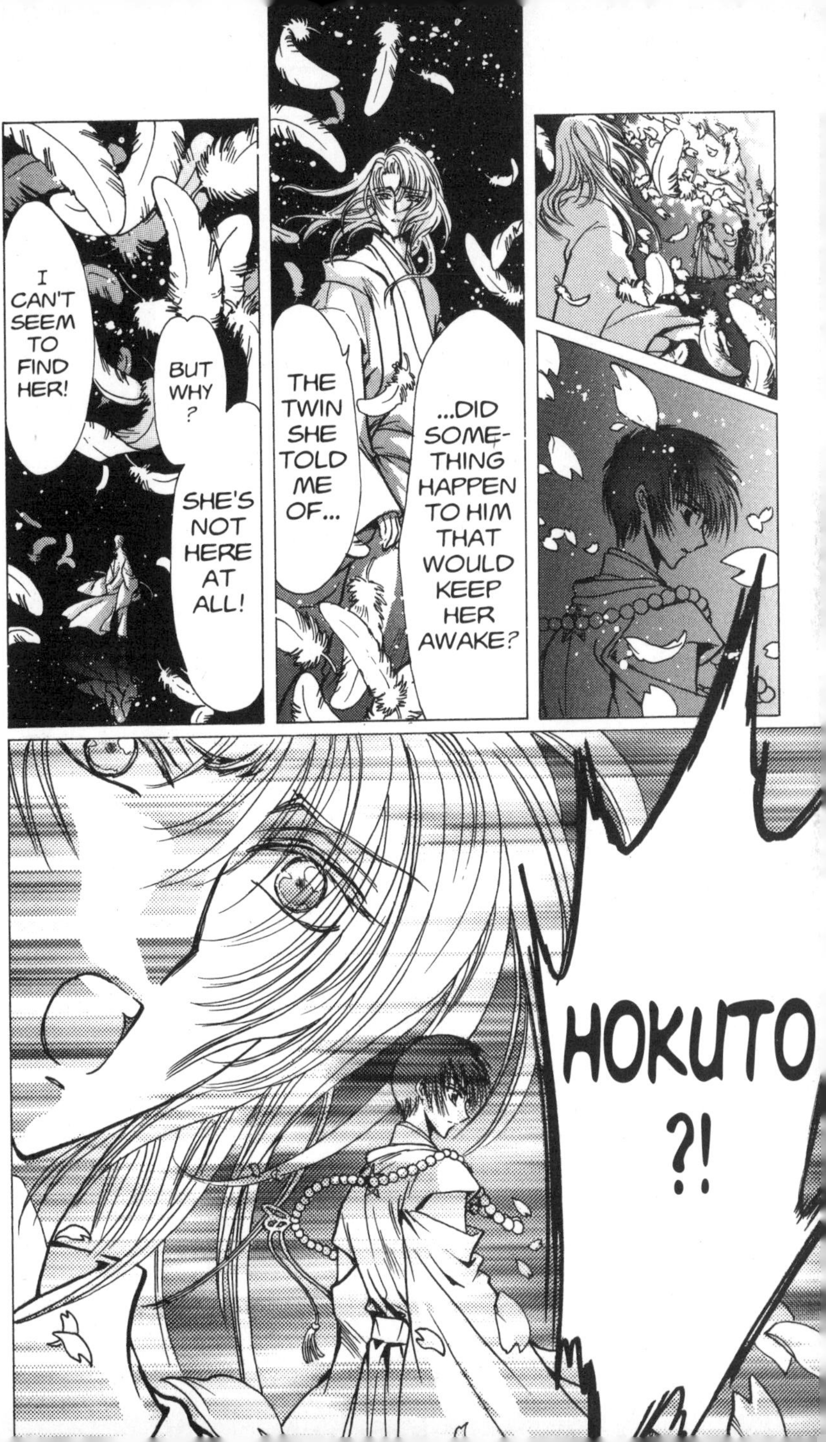
THE TWIN SHE TOLD ME OF...
...DID SOMETHING HAPPEN TO HIM THAT WOULD KEEP HER AWAKE?
BUT WHY? SHE'S NOT HERE AT ALL!
I CAN'T SEEM TO FIND HER!
HOKUTO ?!

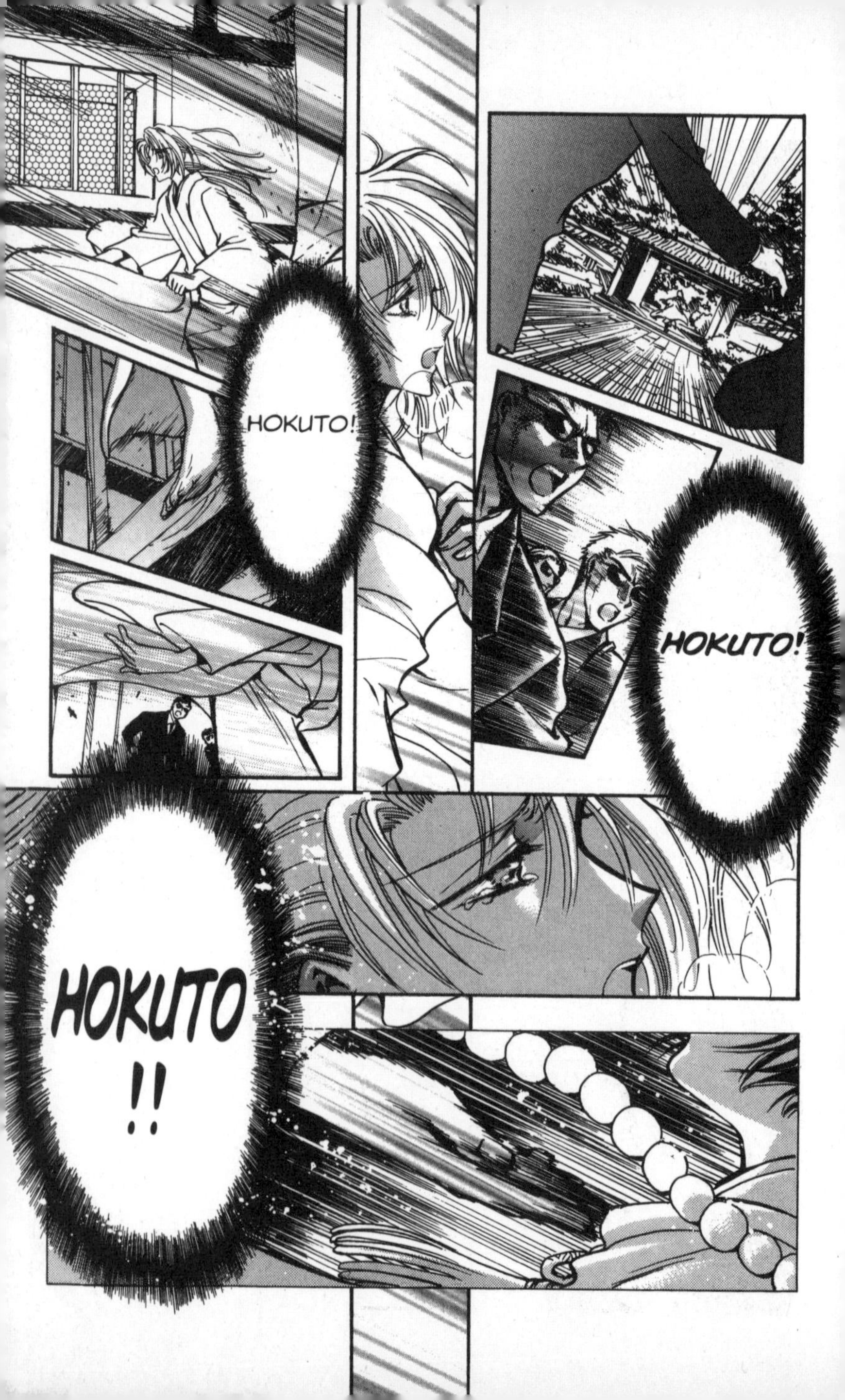
HOKUTO!
HOKUTO!
HOKUTO !!

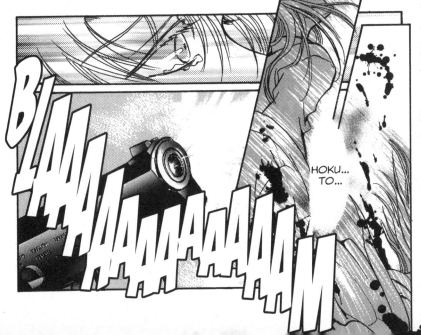

BLAAAAAAAAAAAAAAAAM

HOKU...
TO...

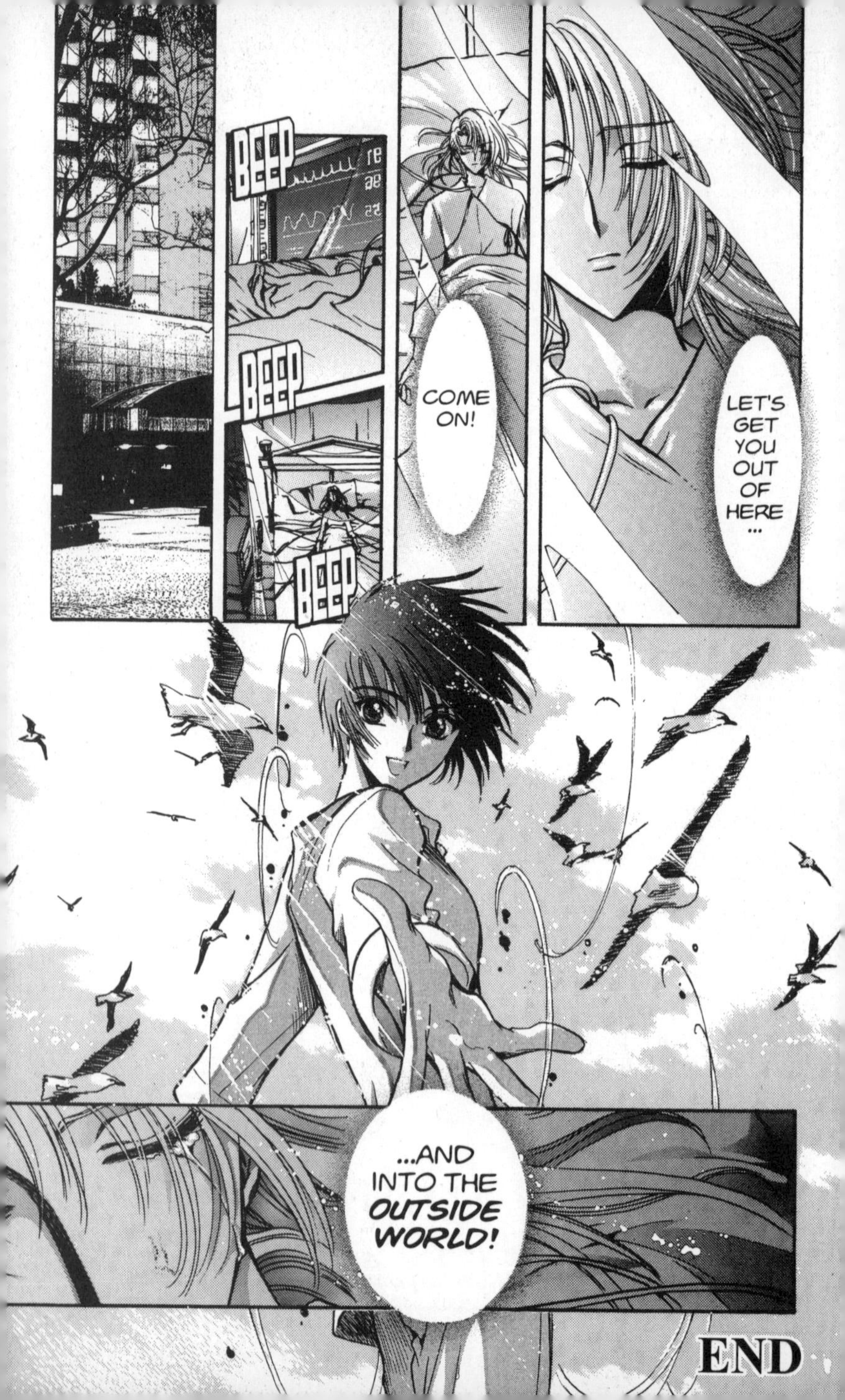
LET'S GET YOU OUT OF HERE...
COME ON!
BEEP
BEEP
BEEP
...AND INTO THE OUTSIDE WORLD!
END

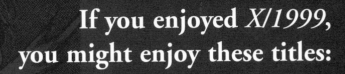

COMPLETE OUR SURVEY AND LET US KNOW WHAT YOU THINK!

☐ Please do NOT send me information about VIZ products, news and events, special offers, or other information.

☐ Please do NOT send me information from VIZ's trusted business partners.

Name: _____

Address: _____

City: _____ **State:** _____ **Zip:** _____

E-mail: _____

☐ **Male** ☐ **Female** **Date of Birth** (mm/dd/yyyy): ___/___/_____ (Under 13? Parental consent required)

What race/ethnicity do you consider yourself? (please check one)

☐ Asian/Pacific Islander ☐ Black/African American ☐ Hispanic/Latino

☐ Native American/Alaskan Native ☐ White/Caucasian ☐ Other: _____

What VIZ product did you purchase? (check all that apply and indicate title purchased)

☐ DVD/VHS _____

☐ Graphic Novel _____

☐ Magazines _____

☐ Merchandise _____

Reason for purchase: (check all that apply)

☐ Special offer ☐ Favorite title ☐ Gift

☐ Recommendation ☐ Other _____

Where did you make your purchase? (please check one)

☐ Comic store ☐ Bookstore ☐ Mass/Grocery Store

☐ Newsstand ☐ Video/Video Game Store ☐ Other: _____

☐ Online (site: _____)

What other VIZ properties have you purchased/own? _____

_____

How many anime and/or manga titles have you purchased in the last year? How many were VIZ titles? **(please check one from each column)**

ANIME	MANGA	VIZ
☐ None	☐ None	☐ None
☐ 1-4	☐ 1-4	☐ 1-4
☐ 5-10	☐ 5-10	☐ 5-10
☐ 11+	☐ 11+	☐ 11+

I find the pricing of VIZ products to be: **(please check one)**

☐ Cheap ☐ Reasonable ☐ Expensive

What genre of manga and anime would you like to see from VIZ? **(please check two)**

☐ Adventure ☐ Comic Strip ☐ Science Fiction ☐ Fighting

☐ Horror ☐ Romance ☐ Fantasy ☐ Sports

What do you think of VIZ's new look?

☐ Love It ☐ It's OK ☐ Hate It ☐ Didn't Notice ☐ No Opinion

Which do you prefer? **(please check one)**

☐ Reading right-to-left

☐ Reading left-to-right

Which do you prefer? **(please check one)**

☐ Sound effects in English

☐ Sound effects in Japanese with English captions

☐ Sound effects in Japanese only with a glossary at the back

THANK YOU! Please send the completed form to:

NJW Research
42 Catharine St.
Poughkeepsie, NY 12601

All information provided will be used for internal purposes only. We promise not to sell or otherwise divulge your information.